BUILDING XML APPLICATIONS

SIMON ST. LAURENT
ETHAN CERAMI

McGraw-Hill

New York San Francisco Washington, D.C.
Auckland Bogotá Caracas Lisbon London
Madrid Mexico City Milan Montreal New Delhi
San Juan Singapore Sydney Tokyo Toronto

McGraw-Hill

A Division of The McGraw·Hill Companies

2 3 4 5 6 7 8 9 0   DOC/DOC   9 0 4 3 2 1 0 9

P/N 0-07-134115-3
Part of ISBN 0-07-134116-1

The sponsoring editor for this book was Michael Sprague and the production supervisor
was Clare Stanley. It was set in Galliard by Patricia Wallenburg.

Printed and bound by R. R. Donnelley & Sons Company.

 This book is printed on recycled, acid-free paper containing
a minimum of 50% recycled, de-inked fiber.

EC: To Amy, who taught me to dance, and helped me to dream.

SSL: To Tracey, always.

ACKNOWLEDGMENTS

First off, we would like to thank all the folks at McGraw-Hill for making this book a reality. Once again, Michael Sprague led us from initial brainstorming to final galleys, and did so with great patience.

Second, we would like to thank three stellar members of the XML community who agreed to review portions of the text. David Megginson, editor of the SAX API, reviewed Chapter 15, and provided us with invaluable feed-back regarding error handling, processing instructions, and other fine points regarding the SAX API. Matt Timmermans of Microstar Software, Ltd. is currently maintaining the Ælfred XML Parser, and reviewed our coverage of Ælfred in Chapter 13. Finally, Chris Lovett of Microsoft carefully reviewed our coverage of MS-XML in Chapter 14. This book is invaluably better due to the feedback we received from these three individuals.

EC:

Once again, there are too many people to thank. First off, special thanks go to Simon. I blame Simon for getting me involved in writing computer books in the first place. He has a rare gift for prose and a contagious enthusiasm for XML, and I enjoyed every day of our collaboration together.

Special thanks also go to my entire family for their constant support: Mom, Dad, Nelli, Daryl, and Carla.

Special thanks also go to all my friends, who once again helped me through a busy summer of writing, and kept me in high spirits (of course, many of my friends were extremely disappointed to have only their first names mentioned in my last book, and hotly demanded that I include their full names this time!) Hence, special thanks to: Dooley Adcroft, Elizabeth Broussard, David Hernandez, and of course the entire CPAC gang: Jon Anderson, Sue Ciprut, and Evan Korth. Also special thanks to two friends at NYU: Dan Barrish, for all his help in preparing for the Fall semester, and enabling me to concentrate on the book, and Professor Arthur Goldberg, who has steadfastly kept me focussed on finishing graduate school. And, lastly, special thanks to Amy Orsenigo for constant support, friendship, and unending enthusiasm for all my crazy ideas.

SSL:

Thanks to Ethan for sorting out the mysteries of parsers in an intelligible way, and for making certain that my sections of the text made sense. The XML community's ongoing discussions of XML and its implications have deepened my understanding of the issues involved in XML development tremendously. In particular, I'd like to thank Paul Prescod, David Megginson (again), Rick Jelliffe, John Simpson, John Cowan, and Peter Murray-Rust, with special thanks to Ron Bourret for helping out tremendously with XSchema when I couldn't find enough time for that project and this one.

Most important, many thanks to my kind, loving, and delightful new wife Tracey Cranston, whose patient love kept me going during the writing of this book.

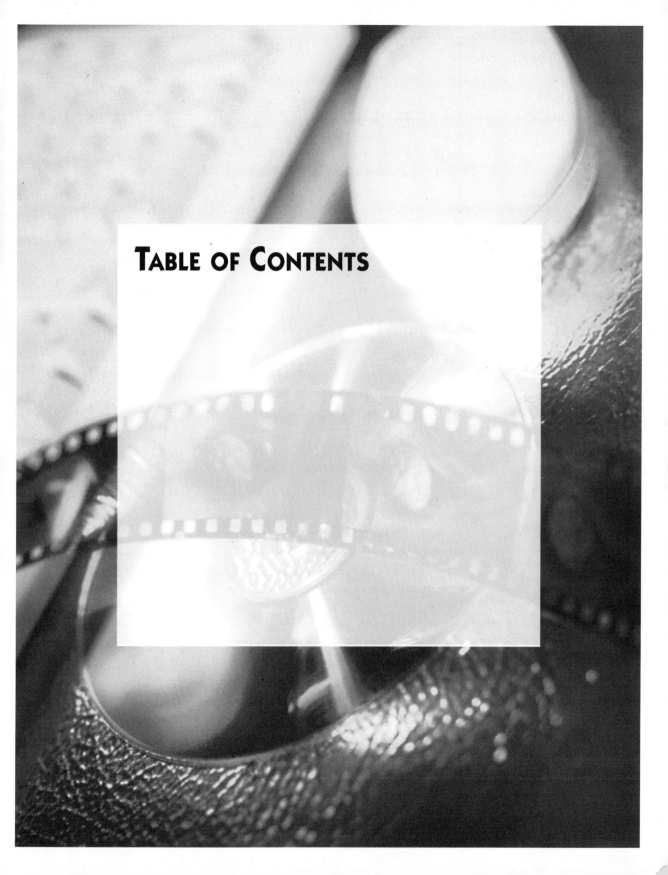

TABLE OF CONTENTS

Introduction:
Building Applications,
Not Hype

XML may be the most-hyped technology since Java, and, at present, seems to be on about the same development curve. Only a small core of developers has a very clear understanding of what XML is and what to do with it, while the standards for XML, and its supporting standards continue to grow rapidly, never quite stable enough to be pinned down. The trade press keeps murmuring that XML is the next revolution, promising dramatic improvements in interoperability, processing convenience, and standards development. For the most part, however, XML is mostly a line in many different marketing brochures. Web developers and programmers alike are trying to figure out what this strange new form of markup is, what it can do, and for what tasks it will be useful.

This book will give you the tools to determine how (and whether) XML will fit into your Java application development strategies. After an introduction to XML's history, capabilities, and its place in the developer's toolkit, this book will present the syntax of XML and its supporting standards in chunks that will get you started quickly while preparing you to use the entire XML toolkit if necessary. Once you've learned how to create XML documents, we'll explore how to transform documents into structures you can use and manipulate in your own applications, exploring the wide world of XML parsers. After we've learned how to build the structures, the next six applications will present a variety of applications that use those structures for useful applications. Finally, the book will conclude with a set of quick reference guides to some of the major parsers in use.

All of the program code presented in this book uses Java, and focuses on the use of the SAX API. For many reasons, explained more fully in Chapter 1, XML and Java fit extremely well together, both supporting hierarchical structures and a common foundation of Unicode for text. Developers working in other languages will still find much in this book that is of use, including the majority of material in Chapters 1 through 11. Python developers may be able to take the SAX development examples and port them to Python without enormous difficulty, as an implementation of SAX is available for Python. Perl programmers may find much of this information interesting, but true Unicode and XML support for Perl is still under (rapid) development.

We hope that you find this book useful, and join the rapidly growing community of developers using XML. Its potential is enormous, and its learning curve is quite reasonable. If XML becomes ubiquitous, as we hope it will, both the Web and the more traditional world of application development stand to gain flexibility and power previously unknown.

EXAMINING XML's POTENTIAL

We begin by taking a close look at the hype surrounding XML, its background, and its potential applications. Chapter 1 examines in detail the problems XML was developed to solve, how XML fits into the World Wide Web, and why the World Wide Web Consortium (W3C) is putting so much energy into this new markup language and its supporting tools. Chapter 2 explores the history surrounding XML and its relationships with HTML and SGML, as well as how it differs from those two key standards. Chapter 3 visits the wide world of XML applications, exploring the implications of XML for document authors, programmers, network architects, and database designers, and concludes with a brief list of some of the diverse applications that employ XML today.

SOLVING PROBLEMS

Extensible Markup Language (XML) and Java both promise to resolve a number of key issues that have kept computers from achieving much of their potential. XML provides a sophisticated format that is easily read and manipulated (in many languages) by both humans and computers, while Java provides an elegant development environment for manipulating and presenting all kinds of information. In combination, the two give developers an enormously powerful tool set, capable of handling information in a variety of structures from a variety of sources and keeping it all interchangeable. XML not only provides a standard syntax for representing information, it includes a set of tools that allow developers and organizations to create their own standards for how that information should be structured. XML is easily transferred over the Web, and readily learned by developers who have worked with HTML, giving it a head start in Web development, where Java also has a strong foothold.

WHY XML?

In many ways, XML is just another file format, yet another way to store information. XML as a file format is just the beginning however—XML promises finally to liberate information from the tyranny of proprietary file formats and make it possible for information to move among multiple programs on different types of computers without facing the battery of conversion programs and lost information that is currently necessary. XML promises dramatically to increase both the efficiency and the flexibility of the ways in which we handle computerized information. In doing so, XML will have an impact on the way in which we use our computers that no other file format has done—changing the way we look at programs, at file systems, at formatting, and at networks. XML has the potential to infiltrate and modify nearly every aspect of at least the software half of computing.

Fundamentally, XML makes it easy to store information in hierarchical formats, providing a consistent, easy to parse syntax and a set of tools for building rules describing the structures used to contain information. This may not sound like much, but this solid foundation provides a much firmer base on which to build standards and programs. Previous interchange file formats tended toward either extreme simplicity (ASCII files with fixed-length fields or delimiters) or extreme complexity (like Rich Text Format [RTF]). Most previous formats were fixed, providing only a limited vocabulary to describe their content. Battles over the HTML vocabulary caused tremendous problems for Web developers as incompatible terms came into regular use. XML provides a format that can represent both simple and extremely complex information, and allows developers to create their own vocabularies for describing that information. XML documents can describe both themselves and their content.

These self-describing documents can provide far more information about their content than do their formatting-oriented HTML counterparts. Instead of marking prices as bold (<B>), for instance, they can mark prices as prices (<PRICE>). As standards for marking up documents with content-based descriptions spread, customized search engines (and agents as well) will be able search the Web for documents of particular types containing information that follows certain structures relevant to the information being searched. With any luck (and a lot of development and XML evangelism), search engines will soon be able to find much more relevant information by filtering out false matches using the document structures. Meta tags filled with endless lists of (often) irrelevant information won't be able to get through, and the high costs of full-text searching can be limited to only certain applications.

XML is not the first tool to promise this; its predecessor, Standard Generalized Markup Language (SGML), promised many of the same things. SGML unfortunately developed a reputation for intense complexity brought on by its enormous levels of flexibility and customizability. XML is more tightly focused, with far fewer options, and much simpler to learn. HTML developers and programmers alike can usually grasp the basics of XML (see Chapter 4 for more details) within an hour, and even XML's most complex features can be teased out in a reasonably brief period of time. The XML specification itself is difficult to read (though short), because it defines a syntax precisely for parser developers, but the concepts inside it are simple and quite approachable.

XML is similarly easy to process. During the XML development process, the Working Group was constantly reminded that XML documents should be easily processed on small devices, like Personal Digital Assistants (PDAs), cell phones, and other appliances. As a result, the XML recommendation focuses sharply on creating an unambiguous syntax that leaves as little as possible for the parser to figure out on its own. XML's strict and extremely consistent syntax is very helpful in this regard. Authors are required to make certain their documents will parse by the brutal punishment—completely failed parsing—meted out to documents that do not work. (This is an enormous change from HTML, in which the browsers attempted to compensate for any and all user mistakes, producing all kinds of difficult-to-reproduce results.) Also, unlike SGML, XML's core document syntax has no options. Missing end tags or abbreviated tags are forbidden. Parsers are assured that they will have consistent material to manage and can be built much more tightly since they have fewer contingencies to battle.

XML also gives parsers two options for complexity. Validating parsers are much larger, but implement the entire XML specification, including testing the document structure against a document type definition (DTD). Non-validating parsers check the syntax of the document instance, but do not have to test the document structure against the DTD or even load external resources referenced by a document. This makes it easy to divide the labor, making servers, for instance, check document structures while allowing small clients just to parse the document and take it on trust that the parts that are supposed to be there actually are present.

Because DTDs provide an unambiguous and reasonably easily understood structure for documents, XML makes it easy to create and share standards. Validating parsers provide a significant level of conformance testing for documents, simplifying the process of checking that standards are actually being implemented. DTD development is happening on many levels, from individual developers designing documents for a single application to huge international consortia hammering out complex standards that will then need to be implemented on a large number of systems and different kinds of systems, all of which need to interoperate smoothly.

XML's hierarchical structures are a good match for both documents and objects. XML documents have a single ("root") element, which may contain other elements, which may in turn contain other elements, which may in turn... Documents sometimes look like Russian dolls, though more typically they look like tree structures, with branches growing out from the center and finally terminating at some point with content (the "leaf elements"). Elements are often described as having parent and child relationships, in which the parent contains the child element. Most documents, from memos to books, will fit in this structure very easily. (Some document issues, like annotations, do not fit well, but are supported by other standards described below.) Other types of information, from relational database tables to objects, will also fit easily into this structure. Properties of an object can be represented as sub-elements or attributes of an element in XML; class structures can be described as DTDs. The logic portion of an object is much harder to describe in XML, but XML provides an excellent container, representation, serialization format, and interchange format for object-based information.

All these developers can take advantage of the same core sets of XML tools. XML makes it easy to use the same basic tools—parsers—for tasks involving any standard created using XML. Parsers are available, even free, from a large number of vendors and individuals, including IBM, Microsoft, Microstar, DataChannel, and others. Better still, the XML community is developing standards that will let applications choose the parser they need on the basis of its size, cost, and licensing, not its API. Both SAX (the Simple API for XML), developed on the XML-Dev mailing list, and the DOM (Document Object Model), under development by the World Wide Web Consortium (W3C), allow developers to communicate with parsers with methods that are standardized across different implementations. Applications can layer themselves on top of these standards, telling a parser to handle the details of working with XML documents and just manipulating the results. The same application can run using different parsers, making it easy to move applications from one parser to another should situations change. (Licensing or pricing changes make developers switch parsers, for instance, or perhaps the parser needs to deal with much larger documents than were originally anticipated.)

XML parsing standards are extremely open, and so are XML documents. While it is possible to build proprietary formats with XML, any XML parser should at least be able to read the information, and a wise developer can probably transfer that information to a friendlier format. XML documents are text documents, and the information contained in that text stream must follow all the rules to be considered XML. If it does not, it isn't XML. While there may be some ways to get around this (encrypting text, for instance), once users become accustomed to having freely convertible documents, they should become much less tolerant of documents that cannot be as easily moved between formats.

This openness makes XML an excellent candidate for applications that require interchange between different programs or computers. XML can be transmitted by any system capable of transferring and storing text, from the classic modem protocols to the more recent HTTP. XML can move over the same systems that transferred delimited text files, for instance, provided that the computers on both ends of the connection have the infrastructure needed to parse and use the XML information. XML document interchange may also ease the challenge of fitting information built in one program into the different environment of another program, allowing the new program either to process the XML itself or to call on a module of the originating program to process the XML. Different circumstances will call for different strategies, but the relative ease with which XML documents can be parsed and their content identified should make this process much simpler. Transformation tools, like architectural forms (an SGML technology) can make this process even simpler.

XML's openness is founded on its being a recommendation of the W3C, built by a team that included representatives from the feuding parties in the browser wars. The complete specification for XML is available for all to see (at **http://www.w3.org/XML**); there are no hidden pieces, no proprietary features, and no undocumented techniques. (Companies implementing XML may try to add their own, but it is to be hoped that non-standard XML implementations will fail amidst an ocean of genuinely compliant implementations.) While the W3C's process is not entirely open (it is, after all, a consortium that collects dues from its members), the results of that process are completely public.

XML is easily extensible with other standards. XML documents are self-describing, but do not necessarily provide the kind of information that is useful for display, for instance. The XML standard itself pays very little attention to how information will be displayed, preferring instead to focus on how it will be structured. The rules for displaying XML come from other specifications, including Cascading Style Sheets (CSS) and Extensible Style Language (XSL), two developments from the W3C, which tell applications how to display the structures contained in XML documents. (Both of these standards are explored in Chapter 8.) Because XML's structures are so clearly defined, it is easy to build supporting standards that specify what should be done with particular structures and sub-structures. Formatting is only one of the many areas in which XML is being extended. The DOM, mentioned above, provides applications with a consistent way to reach and modify the content of XML structures. XPointer (described in Chapter 10) provides a means for identifying substructures within a document, using the names and positions of elements and attributes as well as the content for consistent identification of fragments of information. XLink (described in Chapter 11), gives developers and authors a consistent and powerful (much more powerful than HTML) way to link documents for navigation, reference, embedding, and annotation. All of these supporting standards attach to the foundation of the XML standard, providing extra features and functionality in consistent and highly standardized ways.

The W3C is best known for its role as the keeper of the HTML standards, and XML originated as a complement or a successor to HTML, returning to HTML's roots in SGML. XML behaves much like SGML (technically, it is a subset) and looks very much like HTML. Thus, XML can build on the knowledge of the existing SGML and HTML markup communities. The concept of documents composed of elements and attributes that are indicated with tags has spread far and wide thanks to the ubiquity of the Web, providing a large community of developers who can learn XML quickly. The SGML community provides a core of experts in both markup technology and information modeling, as well as a large set of tools for creating and managing SGML documents that can be (relatively) easily converted for XML use. The SGML community hopes to expand its size to something closer to that of the HTML community, while the HTML community can gain the extra power that XML provides.

XML has another advantage for reaching out to the broadest possible community. It was built with internationalization in mind, using the Unicode character set and providing language identifiers in elements. The Unicode character set provides 65,536 possible characters (not all of which are yet in use) to document creators. Most European text encodings use 8-bit encodings to represent text; Unicode's canonical form, UCS-2, (which all parsers are required to support) uses 16-bit encodings. This much larger space allows the inclusion of characters from all over the world, including a large number of Chinese characters (though not the complete set). Another transformation that must be supported by all XML parsers, UTF-8, uses 8-bit encodings for certain characters, primarily the ASCII set of English characters, while using 16- and 24-bit encodings for other characters. Parsers are not limited to these two sets, but they must support them. Users will need operating system support for these encodings in order to view them—most computers do not come with fonts for hundreds of languages—but the files are entirely interchangeable. On top of its Unicode support, XML provides a language identification attribute (xml:lang) that can identify which language and which country's usage a portion of text is written in.

Plenty of free software is available for initial development. Parsers, tools that layer on top of parsers but under the application, toolkits for serializing objects in XML, and a considerable amount of other code are available for developers to sample, improve, and use. Commercial SGML software is also available, though still fairly expensive. The major browser vendors (Netscape and Microsoft) have also committed to some form of XML support, though exactly what form is not yet clear.

XML's History

This promising standard is the product of years of markup development, culminating in the formation of a W3C working group that built XML. XML's roots go back to 1969, when a team of IBM researchers, led by Dr. Charles Goldfarb, began designing a markup language called Generalized Markup Language (GML). Support for GML grew throughout the 1970s, especially in the publishing community, and a standards committee chaired by Dr.Goldfarb began work in 1978 and issued its first draft for Standard Generalized Markup Language (SGML) in 1980. The final draft appeared from the International Organization for Standardization (ISO) in 1986, as ISO 8879: 1986. The last twelve years have seen steady development in SGML products and implementations, focused primarily on large-scale document management.

SGML has done well, but one of its children has outpaced it dramatically. Hypertext Markup Language (HTML), developed by Tim Berners-Lee in 1991, has become a common tool for millions of readers and hundreds of thousands of document authors. HTML, though it looked a lot like SGML and borrowed some components from popular SGML document type definitions, was generally handled quite differently from SGML. It used a fixed set of tags to mark up documents, and those tags were primarily employed to indicate formatting. HTML and its companion standard, the Hypertext Transfer Protocol (HTTP) spread from their origins at CERN, the European Center for Nuclear Research, becoming more and more popular as their ease of use and hypertext linking made it possible for large numbers of people to create Web sites. This rapid spread, which took off further when the Mosaic browser added images to the documents, created the World Wide Web. Today, Tim Berners-Lee is Director of the W3C, overseeing the future of the system he created.

HTML's rapid growth created a number of problems and the nature of the standard made fixing them difficult. HTML's fixed set of elements grew rapidly once commercial browser developers, especially Netscape Communications and Microsoft, entered the field, and document creation was made much more difficult by the differences between the tags they supported. As HTML became a popular medium for corporate information dissemination (i.e. advertising, annual reports, and other features of corporate Web sites), designers demanded more control over the final appearance of documents. HTML's development focused for a number of years on enhancements to its formatting capabilities. As the formatting capacities developed, the irritations of developing for multiple browsers increased, the readability of the code behind documents decreased (for both humans and computers), and HTML's capacities still did not address the needs of everyone using it. The W3C turned to style sheets, separating the formatting information from the content, as one possible answer. At the same time, search engines were becoming less and less reliable as the volume of information on the Web grew; bad matches and lists of hundreds of thousands of hits became more and more common. With no way to identify document content, search engines were (and are) drowning in a sea of undifferentiated information.

In 1996, the W3C chartered an SGML Editorial Review Board to develop a markup language that provided the power and manageability of SGML but was easily usable on the World Wide Web. The first draft of XML, their creation, was issued in November 1996 at the SGML '96 Conference. Over the next year and a half, the SGML ERB turned into the XML Working Group, and the XML 1.0 specification reached maturity on February 10, 1998, becoming a Final Recommendation of the W3C. Boldly, the XML Working Group prefaced their specification with the goals to which they held themselves:

The design goals for XML are:

1. XML shall be straightforwardly usable over the Internet.
2. XML shall support a wide variety of applications.
3. XML shall be compatible with SGML.
4. It shall be easy to write programs which process XML documents.
5. The number of optional features in XML is to be kept to the absolute minimum, ideally zero.
6. XML documents should be human-legible and reasonably clear.
7. The XML design should be prepared quickly.
8. The design of XML shall be formal and concise.
9. XML documents shall be easy to create.

10. Terseness in XML markup is of minimal importance.

For the most part, people seem to think they succeeded. Since the release of the initial specification, the Working Group has turned to XML's supporting standards (notably XSL, XLink, XPointers, and Namespaces) and developers have begun the construction of tool sets around the XML 1.0 specification.

XML's Future

Despite the high level of hype XML has received, it remains likely to succeed. XML has proven popular with programmers and database developers as well as the document managers who were the primary audience for SGML, and is being integrated into a large number of products and projects, both on and off the Web. The original goal of "SGML on the Web" has been somewhat sidetracked as the browser vendors sort out exactly how they want to support XML, but a number of key signs point to a strong future for XML.

XML is at the core of most new proposals submitted to the W3C, used to provide a set of rules for creating new markup standards. The W3C is moving to an XML-based model for HTML (see **http://www.w3.org/MarkUp/Activity** for details), using XML to define modules for HTML. The Synchronized Multimedia Integration Language (SMIL, pronounced "smile"), which allows developers to create much more sophisticated multimedia presentations for delivery over the Web uses XML as its foundation, as does the new MathML standard for presenting mathematical equations. The W3C is moving wholeheartedly to XML as the basic architecture for future development.

Many hope that ML's impact will be felt well outside of the W3C. It will probably take a few years of development, but XML may transform the file system as we know it, replacing the current large chunks of data stored as files with files composed of readily accessible smaller chunks—of XML, of course! If support for "generic" XML authoring and display become widespread (which depends in considerable part on Microsoft and Netscape, though other vendors are stepping up), the entire model of word processing as we know it today may become a quaint memory, an archaic and inefficient way of processing information. Making XML work in environments that feel familiar to users of the old systems is going to be a key part of this transition, avoiding the shock users and developers may feel moving from stream-based systems that replicate paper documents to hierarchical systems that can provide paper output, but are internally more akin to objects and databases. Application developers, already used to objects and databases, can move in immediately.

WHY JAVA FOR XML?

Java has proven a rich environment for XML programming and development, and more XML-specific resources are available in Java that in any other programming language. Jon Bosak, Chairman of the XML Working Group, declared in his essay "XML, Java, and the Future of the Web" (available at **http://sunsite.unc.edu/ pub/sun-info/standards/xml/why/xmlapps.961117.htm**) that "XML gives Java something to do." There are a number of reasons for this, some simply technical; others reflect a set of common structures that have spread through both the programming and document management worlds.

Java's primary technical advantage is its intrinsic support for Unicode. While older languages like C, C++, and Perl were built around one-byte character encodings, Java was developed after it became clear that the two-byte Unicode character encoding scheme is both useful and necessary. While some developers complained of the extra performance burdens this innovation placed on string processing routines, it certainly makes developing XML applications much easier. Developers using other languages are forced into workarounds and methods that lack much of the one-byte encoding's support from a variety of tools. (In the case of Perl, a massive project is under way to provide full Unicode support to Perl's enormous string-handling library and build an XML parser into the Perl environment.) Because everything in Java is natively Unicode, the complete set of tools is available for handling strings, without the need for complex transformations or odd system calls.

Philosophically, Java meets XML on two levels. The first is their shared reliance on the Internet (and particularly the World Wide Web). XML was designed to be "straightforwardly usable on the Internet", while Java was designed to be used over the Internet, originally with applets running in browsers and now also on the server side, with servlets providing access to all of Java's power. Java is extremely network-enabled, providing access to HTTP routines as well as the TCP/IP infrastructure underlying them. Java works well in a distributed environment, allowing users and programs to share information easily, while XML provides a tool for distributing and storing that information. Java provides the programming environment, while XML provides data formats. (Programming and data can blur as well, as may be the case when XML is used to serialize Java objects.)

The other level on which Java and XML meet is their shared use of hierarchical structures. Java's object-orientation and XML's fundamental use of nested hierarchies are a very natural match. Programmers can easily develop tree structures with Java that match the structures of an XML document, making it easy to convert XML files into instantly usable data in a Java application or applet. As we shall see later in the book, parsers provide these services through a number of interfaces, which may then be harnessed by a Java application. The modular architecture of Java lends itself well to the layering of parsers and protocols in the XML world; whether this is because of the needs of XML or because the early development has largely been in Java is a difficult question to answer. In either case, the intersection is proving fruitful.

The rest of this book will explore that intersection in much greater detail. The next two chapters will discuss the basic technologies involved and their implications for applications development; there will then be a detailed examination of XML and its supporting standards. The rest of the book will be devoted to making XML work with Java, addressing first the transformation of XML files to Java objects and then the useful manipulation and display of those objects.

SGML, HTML, XML, AND THE WEB

HTML, which now seems like a fundamental part of the computing tool kit, was once as alien as XML may seem today. Markup's gradual shift from revolutionary to ordinary has taken nearly 30 years, and markup is still far from perfectly understood. Examining the structures of HTML and XML, and to some extent those of their common parent SGML, can shed some critical light on this important set of tools and the many ways it fits into application developers' tool kits.

NOTE Despite its recent ubiquity, and frequent usefulness, markup itself remains somewhat controversial. For an excellent perspective on the subject, see the essay "Embedded Markup Considered Harmful," by Theodor Holm Nelson, in "XML: Principles, Tools, and Techniques." (This is the Winter 1997 edition of the "World Wide Web Journal," published by O'Reilly and Associates in conjunction with the W3C. See **http://www.w3j.com** for more details.)

BASIC MARKUP

SGML, HTML, and XML are all markup languages, in which document structures are indicated in the same stream as the text. Basically, this means that all of these languages contain content which is periodically interrupted by markers that divide the text up into certain structures. For all three of these languages, the markers divide documents into elements and attributes, using markers like < and > and particular syntax within those markers to provide additional information. Elements are containers that can hold additional content and even more elements inside them, while attributes provide additional information about a particular element and are incapable of holding other elements or attributes inside of them. Elements and attributes are indicated using tags, enclosed in < and >, marking them off from the rest of the text. All three markup languages use start and end tags to indicate the beginning and end of element, using the basic syntax below:

Start Tag:**`<elementName attributeName="attributeValue">`**
End Tag:**`</elementName>`**

End tags are not always required; applications are allowed to "guess" where an element ends in some environments (like many SGML and HTML implementations.) Elements may have one attribute, many attributes, or no attributes. The example below shows a simple element with two attributes.

```
<PARAGRAPH IMPORTANCE="NONE" PURPOSE="DISTRACTION">This is a
very silly paragraph. It's fun, but not at all important.</PARAGRAPH>
```

This PARAGRAPH element has two attributes: IMPORTANCE and PURPOSE. The value of the IMPORTANCE attribute is NONE; the value of the PURPOSE attribute is DISTRACTION. The PARAGRAPH element itself contains the content "This is a very silly paragraph. It's fun, but not at all important." An application can read these values and decide accordingly what to do with the element. A reader who is tired of nuisance text might have told the application to hide all elements with an IMPORTANCE value of "LOW" or "NONE", for instance, and positively to prohibit all elements with a PURPOSE value of "DISTRACTION". Someone more light-hearted might just have the element rendered in light green. It is entirely up to the application.

An element can also contain other elements. Should this paragraph require emphasis on silly and fun, for instance, the fragment might read:

```
<PARAGRAPH IMPORTANCE="NONE" PURPOSE="DISTRACTION">This is a
very <EM>silly</EM> paragraph. It's <EM>fun</EM>, but not at all impor-
tant.</PARAGRAPH>
```

Now the contents of the PARAGRAPH element are more complex. It now contains, in sequence, the text "This is a very ", an EM element (itself containing the text "silly"), the text " paragraph. It's ", and EM element (containing the text "fun"), and the text ", but not at all important." This is more typically displayed with a tree diagram, as shown in Figure 2.1.

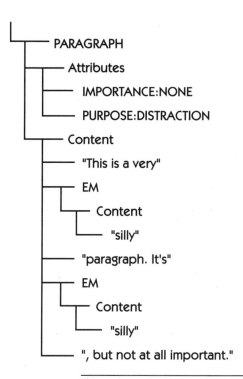

Figure 2.1 Diagramming the PARAGRAPH element

Elements are not required to have any content (or even attributes, though an element with no content and no attributes is a fairly rare thing.) Empty elements may be represented in several different ways, and here the markup languages diverge a bit in practice. The most obvious way to create an element with no content is to put the end tag immediately after the start tag, as in <TAG></TAG>. This works in SGML and XML, but causes problems in many HTML browsers, which sometimes interpret the closing tag as a second instance of the first tag. For example, the BR element (for forcing line breaks) is normally written with a simple <BR> in HTML. Using
</BR> may generate an extra, unwanted line break. Empty tags in HTML are typically written with a start tag that is simply missing its end tag, as in:

```
<P>Here's my picture! <BR> <IMG SRC="mypic.gif"></P>
```

This practice is also acceptable in SGML, but XML forbids the practice, requiring empty elements to end with a /> instead of > or use the full end tag immediately after the start tag.

Entities are also an important aspect of all three markup languages. In HTML, the usage of the term has shrunk to the references used to represent text that is difficult to enter directly into files (like < for the < character to avoid misunderstanding of what is markup and what is content.) SGML and XML use them more expansively, to refer to entire files, chunks of text that can be included in files, and even non-SGML/XML information that needs to be referenced by applications reading an SGML or XML document (or, more formally, entity).

Elements, attributes, and entities are the foundation of all these markup languages, and, despite differences in the way they indicate them (and sometimes process them), all three systems use the same basic parts. The details (and their importance to developers) receive more attention below.

NOTE   Another word which has a somewhat unusual meaning in the markup world is "application." In the title of this book and throughout, we use "application" in its conventional sense, as a program that can operate on a set of data. In SGML, and to some extent in XML, an "application" is a particular document structure specified through the use of tools like document type definitions (DTDs). HTML, for instance, is (at least in its standards) an application of SGML, while XML is a subset of SGML. Documents themselves are often referred to as "instances" or "document instances", especially when they conform to a DTD.

SGML Markup and Hyperlinking Before (and After) the Web

SGML is the founding technology for markup. As the parent of both HTML and XML, echoes of SGML can be heard throughout both its child technologies. SGML underwent a fairly long development process, as noted in the last chapter, and continues to grow today. While a detailed understanding of SGML is not necessary to begin working with HTML or XML, a brief examination of SGML's nature and the purposes to which it has been used may illuminate some key issues that have generated controversy and complexity for both HTML and XML.

The factors that most clearly separate SGML from its children are its scope and its size (and, as a result, the cost of its implementations.) SGML is defined in ISO 8879, itself a lengthy document. The fuller explanations and interpretations of that specification needed to detail how to implement SGML occupy a $95.00 662-page book (which includes the full text of the standard), Charles Goldfarb's *The SGML Handbook*. (Oxford University Press, 1990.) SGML includes far more than the simple element and attribute structures described above. It includes a complete set of tools for minimizing and modifying markup, including non-textual information, referencing both SGML and non-SGML data from within SGML entities, linking processing tools to specific elements, declaring character set usage, describing processing models, and determining conformance to the standard (on many levels). It also provides some example document structures (one of which, in Annex, provided some key elements for HTML) and tutorials.

SGML is an extraordinarily general-purpose tool for structuring information, and has always been focused on documents. The initial project that spurred the creation of GML was a law-office automation project, in which document management was a central concern. At the same time, the Graphics Communication Association (GCA) was developing a "generic coding" project for manuscripts. The two projects came together in SGML. According to Clause 0 (Introduction) of ISO 8879, the SGML standard:

> This International Standard specifies a language for document representation referred to as the "Standard Generalized Markup Language" (SGML). SGML can be used for publishing in its broadest definition, ranging from single medium conventional publishing to multi-media data base publishing. SGML can also be used in office document processing where the benefits of human readability and interchange with publishing systems are required.

SGML itself does not specify which elements and attributes must be used for these applications (though it provides some examples). Rather, SGML allows developers (and standards bodies) to create applications of SGML that provide these details. Different applications can use their own tag sets, but all of the applications can share basic syntax and tools built on the SGML standard.

This vision succeeded fantastically for a number of applications. IBM and the United States Government Printing Office, two of the largest document publishers, both use SGML for an enormous part of their work. The United States Internal Revenue Service, the United States Department of Defense (and military organizations around the world), defense contractors, airlines, publishers, some academic sectors, and many other large organizations have turned to SGML to simplify and standardize their document management tasks. The SGML standard provides them with a set of formal tools for defining document structures and syntax, making it much easier to define standards for particular applications.

NOTE

For a much more detailed set of case studies describing how organizations have applied SGML successfully, see Chet Ensign's "$GML: The Billion-Dollar Secret" (Prentice-Hall, 1997).

SGML's enormous power and flexibility, however, came at very steep price. Implementing a complete, generic implementation of SGML that could parse any SGML document proved extremely difficult, and the tools for working with SGML documents similarly proved expensive. (There are of course, some exceptions—James Clark's SP parser is available free from **http://www.jclark.com**, and Corel's Word-Perfect 8 can work with SGML.) An "SGML solution in a box" was more of a dream than a purchasable product, and most implementations of SGML document management systems remained custom-built, carefully designed by architects who could combine document modeling with systems integration to build large-scale systems.

SGML continues to dominate some sectors of the document management field, its structured approach to documents providing significant benefits (and reduced costs) to many happy users. SGML has continued to develop, with notable initiatives including HyTime (the Hypermedia/Time-based Structuring Language) and DSSSL (the Document Style Semantics and Specification Language) providing sophisticated linking and styling capabilities to SGML documents. Much of the SGML community clearly hopes that broad acceptance of XML will lead to a spurt of growth in full SGML implementations, as some organizations find that they need the many power tools available in SGML but removed from XML's more concise feature set.

HTML AND HTTP: BUILDING THE WEB

The World Wide Web is built on two standards, HTML and HTTP, that combine to bring users the seamless, friendly, and (reasonably) quick hypertexts that have become a common part of business and entertainment. HTTP has nothing at all to do with markup, and will be explored more thoroughly in the next chapter, but provides the transport mechanisms that bring HTML-encoded information (and other supporting material, like graphics) to users. HTML is what most Web designers see most directly, specifying the format and content of documents so that they can be presented to users through browsers.

When Tim Berners-Lee first set about building the Web in 1991 and 1992, he did not expect anyone to have to manipulate the document markup directly. HTML provided a foundation upon which his browser/editor could operate, but all the document structuring and management was to be done through the browser application, not by direct editing. HTML's abbreviated tag names reflect this intent (and the sample DTD in Annex E of ISO 8879), simpler for machines to process, but not especially human-friendly. HTML's connection with SGML was informal. Though HTML clearly applied SGML's basic syntax and many of its structures, HTML was not formally an SGML application until the much later publication of a DTD for HTML 2.0.

NOTE   Despite all of HTML's differences from SGML, there are enough similarities between the two that a number of SGML-focused firms were able to produce successful HTML-based products. HTML developers may be familiar with Soft-Quad, makers of HotMetal, and Inso, which sells the DynaBase family of site management tools.

HTML's rapid spread beyond the original confines of its development environment added to its informality. The developers of Mosaic, the first graphical browser, added the IMG tag, making it possible to combine images with the text that had been HTML's original focus, and the commercial Web became possible. Unlike the original CERN browsers, Mosaic was focused on display, not editing, leading a generation of HTML developers into the basic text files used for HTML and the syntax itself. As Mosaic's popularity grew, and especially when its developers moved on to Netscape, HTML become a more and more common authoring environment. Even today, when many graphical tools are available for HTML development, many developers (including both of the authors of this book) prefer to hand-code their HTML, working directly among the tags.

This move into the document itself produced (somewhat understandably) an enormous amount of variation in the precise syntax used to create HTML documents. To accommodate the largest number of developers, HTML browsers became extraordinarily forgiving of syntactical difficulties like missing end tags, misplaced and unquoted attributes, malformed structures, and oddly-used white space. Because designers and users focused on the document appearance, not the document structure, created by the markup, browser vendors found themselves having to support each other's mistakes when designers took advantage of program oddities to create the precise look they wanted.

At the same time that HTML syntax conformance was declining, the number of elements and attributes began to explode as vendors (especially Netscape and Microsoft) began creating extra "features" for HTML, luring designers with their promise of a more powerful set of tools for document layout. The W3C, to some extent, regulated this process, though the W3C standards lagged the browser implementations badly until HTML 4.0. Even now, many of the tools provided by Microsoft and Netscape are outside of the W3C specs, producing headaches for designers and problems for users caught using the "wrong" browser.

NOTE   If standards conformance is a significant issue for you, be sure to investigate the Web Standards Project (WSP) at **http://www.webstandards.org**.

The combination of messy syntax and a growing number of presentation-oriented tags created a number of problems for designers and users. HTML documents were turning into enormous and unpredictable conglomerations of markup, difficult both for designers to edit and browsers to parse. Because the browsers used proprietary systems for guessing which elements ended where, and because software tools for editing HTML might modify code fed them and output code marked up in a similarly proprietary way, editing and managing HTML was rapidly exploding into an enormous and thankless task. At the same time, it was becoming more and more difficult to extract information from HTML, at a time when more and more organizations were beginning to use HTML as a front-end to datacentric applications. As new demands for "dynamic" documents arose, it became clear that browsers needed to manipulate documents with clearer structures.

The W3C began several initiatives to address these problems. One of them developed into its Styles area, which has developed Cascading Style Sheets and is developing Extensible Style Language, while another evolved into the XML Working Group.

MARKUP AND STYLE SHEETS

Although it remains a far cry from the demands of some commentators for total separation of document content and formatting, the W3C's initiatives to separate the many details of formatting from the document content presented in HTML have borne significant fruit. By moving the fine-grained controls demanded by designers (used to having explicit and precise control over every aspect of a printed page, they wanted similar control over Web documents) to separate style sheets, the W3C took an enormous step forward in cleaning up the Web. At the same time, style sheets gave programmers a key set of tools they needed to manipulate HTML content after it had been rendered, making the evolving "dynamic HTML" much more powerful.

The concepts behind style sheets are fairly simple. (The details will be explored at much greater length in Chapter 8.) Style sheets provide browsers with a set of formatting rules to be applied to particular elements. When a browser encounters an element for which a style has been provided, it renders that element according to the instructions in the style sheet rather than using the default rendering behavior of the browser. Style sheets remove formatting specific elements (like the now-deprecated FONT tag) from the element tree of a document, simplifying the document structure. In an extreme case, perfectly acceptable HTML documents can be built using only DIV and SPAN elements inside the BODY element. (This will only work, of course, with recent browsers that support DIV, SPAN, and style sheets.) DIV provides a block element, separated from surrounding elements by line breaks, while SPAN is an in-line element, with no such separation. Formatting for these plain-vanilla elements can be provided through rules that attach to class and ID attributes of these elements, allowing all formatting to be specified outside of the document structure. More typically, the rules of a style are attached to previously existing HTML elements, declaring, for instance, that H1 elements should be rendered left-justified, in cornflower blue 18-point sans serif type with 3 points of padding above and below the element. This approach is much safer than the more extreme use of DIV and SPAN, since older browsers will still at least render an H1 element even if they do not understand the style sheet. Style sheets can even specify locations for elements, and how overlapping elements should behave, effectively providing the layout control designers have been demanding for years.

Another significant feature that style sheets bring to HTML markup is reusability. A single style sheet may serve for hundreds or thousands of documents, beginning the move toward sets of documents that share common resources. For designers, this means that changes may be implemented across an entire set of documents by making changes in a very small number of files. (This kind of centralization of information is a key concept for XML, as we shall see in the next chapter.) This reusability may be further enhanced through the use of script files that manipulate the style information in conjunction with the simplified document structures to create customized interactive applications built on top of documents. The separation of formatting from content and the appropriate use of fairly simple scripting can create documents that have far more depth than the traditional Web page, blurring the lines between documents and applications.

XML AND THE WEB

Though style sheets have great potential for cleaning up HTML and making it more scriptable, the HTML approach is still limited by its restricted vocabulary and the extremely tolerant approach HTML browsers have taken to processing documents. XML promises to solve these problems, enabling a much more powerful generation of Web-based applications, while avoiding the extreme complexity and high cost of SGML. More flexible than HTML, less complex than SGML, and deliberately kept extremely small, XML promises to let markup live up to its potential.

XML fits into the Web in two key areas. The area in which it has seen the most activity so far is standards-building. The next generation of standards for the Web (including HTML) is going to arrive specified in XML, and will require that documents live within XML's strict syntactical rules. Microsoft's Channel Definition Format (CDF), which provides Web site information and "Push" channels, was one of the first proprietary standards to appear, and SMIL was the first XML-based standard to arrive from the W3C. Both of these standards provide formats for information that programs then present through their own interfaces. Viewing documents built using these standards requires a viewer built to interpret that particular standard. XML provides a foundation for these standards, but users work with those standards and not XML directly.

The other area in which XML fits the Web is as "generic" XML, more in keeping with XML's SGML heritage as an open document standard. While users and organizations will of course need to define their own tag sets, they will be able to use tools built openly enough to support documents written in any DTD, combined perhaps with a style sheet (the style sheets developed for HTML will work, thank to common structures) for presentation. Instead of needing to build custom applications for each document type, users will be able to apply generic, off-the-shelf tools to editing and viewing. This model works best with documents that are primarily text, but may be extended (as style sheets and linking tools mature) to documents that contain a mixture of text and other components. This approach allows developers to expand the limited vocabulary of HTML to support industry-specific and content-based (like <PRICE>) markup without having to build new applications for every new vocabulary. The spread of such "generic" tools would dramatically lower the cost of XML development and authoring, making XML a ubiquitous and useful document format. At the same time, the spread of distinct but widespread XML vocabularies would make it far easier for search engines to index the Web's content intelligently, limiting searches to appropriate vocabularies and reducing the problems incurred by false hits.

Ideally, both of these paths could cooperate, making it possible to create use browsers as the foundations of extensible applications that can both display generic XML and route information that needs more processing to applets or applications that can provide more sophisticated support. It may take a number of years to reach that nirvana of browser as extensible application platform, however. As of September 1998, Microsoft appears to be taking the first of these routes, and Netscape appears to be moving along the second. The next chapter will explore the implications of these two paths in the context of client-server and distributed application technologies, and consider the potential for both paths.

 NOTE The example applications in this book all take the first approach, building custom applications to handle specific sets of elements and attributes. Whether or not generic XML becomes ubiquitous, this approach is guaranteed to be useful to a wide variety of development situations.

XML AND OTHER DISTRIBUTED APPLICATION TECHNOLOGIES

XML is, at its heart, a mere file format. Making XML perform up to its promise will require applying a lot of other technologies, building on work that has been done for the Web, for databases, for networking, and for distributed application development. XML can help these technologies interoperate, providing convenient interchange (typically supported by middleware services) of information, and can also help these technologies communicate with their end-users on the client. By providing a structured format for transmitting information, XML makes it much easier to transfer information from centralized data stores to distributed clients and back again, providing an infrastructure on which many different applications can be built.

XML DOCUMENTS AND HTTP

One of the simplest models for using XML in distributed applications puts XML to use in much the same way that HTML is used now: to send information from a server to the client in a format the browser can display. XML can (with the assistance of style sheets, described in Chapter 8) be used as a display format. In this model, the HTTP is used to send information from a Web server to the client, as shown in Figure 3.1.

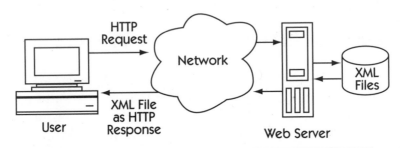

Figure 3.1   Using HTTP to serve XML documents from a Web server

This model makes XML a replacement for HTML, using the document structure and a set of corresponding style sheets to create a new presentation format. In fact, until browsers learn to display XML with style sheets, the XML used may simply be cleaned-up HTML. (See **http://www.simonstl.com/** for a site that is adopting this strategy.)

The first result of this model is simply convenience for designers and document editors. Freed of the HTML vocabulary, designers can develop style sheets that reflect their formatting needs, not the needs that someone at Netscape, Microsoft, or even the W3C thought was appropriate for a given formatting tag. DIV and SPAN, the "blank" elements discussed in Chapter 2, make it possible to do similar things in HTML, but require the use of Class attributes to create different types of elements and do not provide the extra power (document validation and tighter syntax) available in XML. Designers building a memo document can specify the document structures involved, like a logo, spaces for To, From, Re, and the memo's content, and build a single style sheet that implements the look of the memo the way they want it. Users can build simpler documents, filling in the appropriate spaces without needing to consider where the logo belongs on the page, whether or not to boldface headings, and where on the page the memo belongs. Templates will be far simpler and can, in fact, be constructed from the same document type definition, described in Chapter 6, which is used to validate the document. Tag-filled HTML files with comments indicating where information needs to be placed can be banished, and small document-specific applications built to replace the text editors and generic WYSIWYG formatting tools that have been used in the past to build these documents.

The impact of this model may prove to be much larger than a simple change in design and authoring, however. Serving up XML, especially XML that uses a content-based vocabulary, makes possible an enormous number of new client applications. In addition to helping out designers and authors, it enables applications to find the information they need, consistently and easily. Instead of stripping out tags in document content, as they currently do, search engines will be able to use the tags as an additional tool for determining the meaning of the content. By allowing users to limit searches to particular tag vocabularies, search engines will be able to serve up much more useful results, giving users smaller and more focused lists of possible matches. If document structure designers focus on search capability as an aspect of their document design, documents and search engines will both receive a huge usability boost.

NOTE Adding explicit metadata, information about information, is a key part of this process. Metadata development (beyond the level provided in typical XML element names) goes well beyond the scope of this book, but a number of resources are available. The World Wide Web Consortium (**http://www.w3.org**) maintains a metadata activity, which is producing the Resource Definition Framework (RDF). The Dublin Core initiative, primarily the product of a group of librarians, has also described key metadata resources in its informational RFC 2413, "Dublin Core Metadata for Resource Discovery" (**ftp://ftp.isi.edu/in-notes/rfc2413.txt**).

Centralized search engines will not be the only tools to benefit from the extra information provided by XML element structures. Agents, which enjoyed a brief spurt of popularity when the Web was getting started and collapsed when the Web became too complex and large for them to navigate, now have another chance. Instead of having to search through enormous volumes of formatting information to try to find the key information a user actually wanted, they can restrict their searches to appropriate document types and elements within those documents. The amount of processing power and bandwidth required to conduct effective searches can be dramatically reduced, because XML's information is presented in a manner that can reflect its content more accurately than the formatting information used in HTML documents. (The ease with which XML syntax can be parsed also contributes to agent development, making it possible for agents to use a much lighter-weight parsing engine than they would otherwise require.)

Another scenario that XML may make easier is connections between agents and search engines. XML could provide a foundation on which interchange standards for communications between agents and search engines could be conducted. The enormous centralized sets of information stored in a search engine could be shared with an agent (perhaps for a fee), which would then perform more detailed searching of the indexed information for the material the user actually needs. By dividing the duties between the centralized search engine, which performs broad indexing, and the user's own agent, which conducts more focused searches, it may be possible to develop efficient (and effective, the true holy grail) search technologies.

Using XML as the transfer medium between servers and browsers creates additional potential for extending the browser. XML is extensible, so an extensible browser seems like a good way to support its many capabilities. By combining an engine for displaying styled information with a registry listing tools for handling specific elements (not just MIME types, but actual elements), a browser could combine its typical text-and-graphics display with a set of small programs that can do something with the XML data in a document. A table, for instance, could be rendered as a graph, even in different formats. Sets of elements that are intended for display with a style may also be useful in the context of a spreadsheet, where the user can perform more sophisticated analysis. Instead of the current messy cut-and-paste, applications that can interpret XML vocabularies can import shared information without losing context, making it possible to exchange information seamlessly. Best of all, this transfer can be achieved through reference to common and public standards, reducing the reliance on proprietary file formats and opening up information to a much wider set of application tools and vendors.

A halfway approach to this, which appears to be the direction Microsoft is taking in Internet Explorer, embeds XML data inside of HTML documents. The W3C has considered this approach to some extent (see **http://www.w3.org/TR/1998/ NOTE-xh-19980511.html**), but no standard for such embedding yet exists. (It is also notable that the W3C discussion refers to "real-world HTML" as "crud".) Rather than processing XML documents, this approach processes XML fragments embedded in HTML documents, allowing access to the XML only through programs—scripts, ActiveX controls, etc. This approach may work for the application-specific encodings Microsoft appears to have in mind for its work (like Chrome, their new multimedia package, or their likely Office 2000 formats), but it severely restricts the possibilities outlined in the paragraphs above. HTML documents that contain XML but do not directly display it remain only weakly searchable, and there is little incentive for document authors to duplicate the information presented in the HTML document in the XML fragment.

NOTE   This book will not cover XML-in-the-browser applications in any depth, though Chapter 8 will cover the style sheets needed to make this happen. Because of the varying levels of support for XML in the different browsers, their uncertain development paths, and their extremely uncertain development timelines, it seems wiser to stick with building dedicated Java applets and applications that we know can handle the XML we send. The Web framework remains an important part of the tool kit, but the browsers are not yet a reliable part of that framework for XML applications.

Another approach, which seems likely in the short term, is use of transformations from XML to HTML for the final journey to the browser, as shown in Figure 3.2.

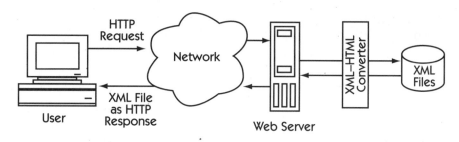

Figure 3.2 Using XML on the server but sending HTML to the browser

This approach provides some of the advantages of XML to authors and designers, but uses a transformation to send HTML information to the client. The client loses much of the structure provided by XML documents, though perhaps the original XML element names may be provided in attributes after the transformation. The possibilities for agents and search engines are blunted here, unless Web site developers take the extra steps (and time, money, and storage space) to provide XML versions of the files as well as HTML versions. This may also incur additional processing power demands, especially if the XML files being converted are generated dynamically. Some version of this approach will be necessary for many browser applications in the short term, however, as the installed base of non-XML aware (and even non-style sheet-aware) browsers is not going to disappear overnight.

NOTE

The E-Commerce example presented in Chapter 21 uses a simple version of this transformation. Extensible Style Language, discussed in Chapter 8, also provides some tools that may be used for this type of transformation.

PROCESSING XML ON THE SERVER

Transformations like the ones described above may be performed in a number of different ways. The simplest method requires authors to save their work in multiple formats, providing both an XML and an HTML version that the server may access as needed. This puts minimal burdens on the server, and could, if the authoring application was cooperative, be a fairly transparent process. Somewhat more likely, however, is the use of additional processing of XML files by the server, either on an as-needed basis or in batches. Building server-side XML applications, though not always involved in a transformation per se, requires the development of appropriate architectures for moving information into and out of XML.

In a Web context, this will typically involve tools like Common Gateway Interface (CGI) applications, or, in a Java context, servlets. The original HTML model of files stored on a server for distribution over the Web is still appropriate in some situations, especially those where the document is completely prepared for the client's browser and where information changes only infrequently or not at all. Because many of the applications XML is used for will either involve "live" data or require a transformation, many XML documents will come to users after significant processing on the server.

When the server receives the request from the user, it routes the request to a servlet that provides a transformation facility, converting the XML (and possibly associated style sheets) to HTML for use in the browser. A smart version of this transformation might also provide caching of transformed documents (to reduce the amount of processing needed for multiple identical requests) and an option (possibly based on the browser information provided in the HTTP request) for delivering the original XML files to the client rather than the HTML transformation.

Even if the client can support XML directly, a very similar application model may be appropriate to convert information in other formats (like that stored in databases) to XML. This model is much like that currently used by many HTML applications, providing a front end to the information stored in an unfriendly application or one that needs a layer of protection between it and the public. A model for an application connecting a database to a Web server is shown in Figure 3.3.

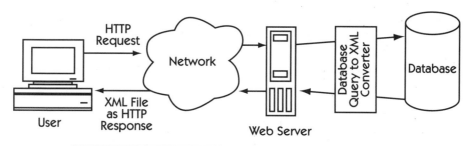

Figure 3.3   Converting stored information to XML using a servlet

When the server receives a request, it passes it to the servlet. The servlet queries the database through JDBC, and converts the recordset returned by the database into an XML document. The client may then display the XML document or process it further.

NOTE

A transformation from XML to HTML could also be performed to the XML generated by this kind of application, creating a multilayer application. Caching services in the HTML transformation might even be able to reduce the load on the XML generator, improving overall efficiency.

XML AND RELATIONAL DATABASES

XML's hierarchical structures may not seem like a perfect match for the more tightly structured tables of relational databases, but XML has a bright future here as well. XML can describe both the contents of the tables and the relationships between tables, making possible the exchange of information between databases, even database of different types from different vendors. At the same time, XML presents a new opportunity to send information from the database to clients in a form that clients can interpret and process locally, enabling a new generation of client-server application development.

Expressing table structures in markup is actually quite simple. Instead of the many-layered hierarchies common to documents, a simpler structure that reflects rows and columns is more appropriate. A small example may suffice. The following table contains information about products and their prices.

Product	Price
Red crayon	$0.49
Blue crayon	$0.39
Green crayon	$0.69
Yellow crayon	$0.29
White crayon	$0.19
Brown crayon	$0.49

Delimited text files have been a common tool for moving tables like this to another database. Encoding this table in typical syntax produces a file like this:

```
"Product", "Price"
"Red crayon", .49
"Blue crayon", .39
"Green crayon", .69
"Yellow crayon", .29
"White crayon", .19
"Brown crayon",.49
```

For many simple applications, this lightweight (and concise) format works very well. Unfortunately, it doesn't actually contain all the information needed to transfer the table successfully to all possible parties. It is fairly obvious (because of the encoding convention) that the information in quotes is strings, and the information without quotes is some form of numeric information. It is not clear, however, what format that numeric information is in. It could be cents (these are some cheap crayons), pounds (expensive crayons), Euros (crayons of the future), or Won (incredibly cheap crayons). Encoding this table in XML makes it possibly to state all assumptions explicitly. There are several different possible formats, of course. Two of the more reasonable ones are shown below.

```
<TABLE NAME="CrayonPrices">
<COLUMN NAME="PRODUCT" TYPE="STRING">
<COLUMN NAME="PRICE" TYPE="DOLLARS">
<ROW>
<PRODUCT>Red crayon</PRODUCT><PRICE>.49</PRICE>
</ROW>
```

```
<ROW>
<PRODUCT>Blue crayon</PRODUCT><PRICE>.39</PRICE>
</ROW>
...</TABLE>
```

or

```
<TABLE NAME="CrayonPrices">
<PRODUCT>
<NAME>Red crayon</NAME>
<PRICE CURRENCY="DOLLARS">.49</PRICE>
</PRODUCT>
<PRODUCT>
<NAME>Blue crayon</NAME>
<PRICE CURRENCY="DOLLARS">.39</PRICE>
</PRODUCT>
...</TABLE>
```

The first version more closely resembles typical database design practice, where the columns are all assigned formats and the contents of the rows correspond to the column formats. The second version would require more processing, but presents a more flexible model that would allow, for instance, prices to be represented in multiple formats. A relational database accepting this information would need a program to interpret it, choose the pieces that fit into its table structures, and add (or modify) records to the database as appropriate. Though the format is much more verbose, it is capable of handling far more complex information than its delimited text predecessors. The needs of the application will determine how much verbosity is appropriate. (To some extent, verbosity can be reduced through the default values for attributes assigned in document type definitions and discussed in Chapter 6.)

The same information can be transferred to a browser or other client application. Because the information comes with its data structures (and possibly a description of its data types) intact, the information can be easily transferred to other applications for processing. With support from style sheets, it may be possible (depending on browser support) to display the XML information directly on the user's screen, giving applications a clear window into databases. By combining traditional SQL queries (which will need to built into a client interface) with XML presentation of the results, users can explore databases and perform local processing of their contents. They can add it to their own local databases for convenient filing, reuse the information in documents, or request new data sets based on the results of their queries.

NOTE

Relational database developers have begun a number of projects aimed at standardizing XML-formatted interchange and querying. Though this field may take a little while to develop, there is definitely activity among the vendors.

XML AND OBJECT DATABASES

While XML can be a good medium for transferring information between relational databases for interchange and for transferring information between the database and the client, relational databases are not a very good place to hold more complex XML documents. Other database structures, notably object databases (and a related type of relational database, the object-relational database), are more capable of storing XML documents because the structures they support bear more similarity to the hierarchical nature of XML documents.

Object databases appeared during the rise of object-oriented programming languages. Developers working on certain kinds of projects found themselves spending enormous amounts of time converting stored information to objects and back again. Relational databases proved to be a bottleneck in this process, often requiring multiple queries to reassemble object structures. As a result, object-oriented databases (also known as object databases or object stores) were developed to provide a convenient storage system for large quantities of object data that needed to remain persistent between sessions. Object databases have filled a large number of roles in object-oriented development, allowing programmers to store to disk information that might not be needed immediately while processing large data sets, store large highly structured sets of information for long periods of time, query information stored hierarchically, and move information from one object-oriented development system to another. Object databases have found use in Computer-Aided Design (CAD), geographic and geological applications, multimedia, software development, expert databases, artificial intelligence, and office automation.

XML is easily parsed into object structures, which are easily stored in object databases. Using an object database to store XML documents, or sets of information which need to be converted rapidly into XML documents, provides a useful shortcut in a number of applications. In effect, an object database allows applications to stored a parsed version of a document, making it easy to access elements and attributes rapidly without requiring the loading and parsing of a sequential file. If an application needs to rapidly access or modify the last three paragraphs of a long file, the savings can be quite significant. Converting the information stored in an object database to a file for transmission over the Web will require some processing, but complex documents can be put together much more rapidly (and easily) from an object database than from a relational database. For many applications, especially those making heavy use of centralized data storage, an object database can make managing XML documents much simpler.

Object databases are still fairly new technologies, and have not achieved nearly the market penetration of relational database systems. The adoption process for relational databases was quite long, however, with a learning curve of a difficulty comparable to that for object databases. Incompatible query methods for object databases have also hindered their spread, though standards are being adopted and implemented. Developers building applications that rely heavily on these tools have built a number of applications on top of them, but object databases typically remain much more of an integration project than their better-known competitors in the relational market.

Document management systems have been extensive users of object databases, and a considerable number of SGML implementations have used them. Some object database software is available with SGML and XML interface support. POET Software (**http://www.poet.com**) offers an SGML/XML system for the POET database system, for instance, as well as an interface for Java programs. While the tools involved are somewhat complex (at present, you'll need to learn a whole new API or at least a query language to reach information in the object database), the performance and management benefits involved make this a potentially valuable storage system for large-scale and high-performance document management.

XML AND THE DOCUMENT OBJECT MODEL

A natural extension of the similarity between XML document structures and object structures allows programmers to treat documents as objects. The Document Object Model (DOM), one the W3C's latest projects, provides a standardized way to access and modify the content of elements within a parsed document. The DOM will initially find use as an API for accessing information in browsers and parsers, but may find use as a general-purpose API for accessing markup information from a variety of media.

NOTE

As of this writing, the DOM Level 1 is a Proposed Recommendation of the W3C. The DOM may be rejected by the director or modified from the version (**http://www.w3.org/TR/PR-DOM-Level-1/**) discussed here. Because of this, and because of its widespread availability and suitability to small applications, most of the example applications in this book use SAX, the Simple API for XML, rather than the DOM to access document content. See Chapter 20 for a DOM example which reads and writes document trees.

The DOM's origins lie in Round 4 of the browser wars, when both Microsoft and Netscape implemented "dynamic HTML" in their browsers. Developers could create scripts that modified elements of their documents after the document had loaded, using an object-based interface to style sheets and other element properties. The two versions, of course, were brutally incompatible, making it difficult to create Web sites that worked in both browsers. The W3C stepped up to the challenge, establishing the Document Object Model activity and including representatives from the feuding browser companies and many other firms in the Working Group. The Abstract of the Proposed Recommendation describes the DOM:

> This specification defines the Document Object Model Level 1, a platform- and language-neutral interface that allows programs and scripts to dynamically access and update the content, structure, and style of documents. the Document Object Model provides a standard set of objects for representing HTML and XML documents, a standard model of how these objects can be combined, and a standard interface for accessing and manipulating them. Vendors can support the DOM as an interface to their proprietary data structures and APIs, and content authors can write to the standard DOM interfaces rather than product-specific APIs, thus increasing interoperability on the Web.

The DOM provides a core specification with optional extended XML interfaces, as well as an HTML specification that supplements the core specification. The specification is defined using the Object Model Group Interface Definition Language, which is a part of the CORBA 2.2 specification, to keep everything platform- and language-neutral. Despite this neutrality, the specification provides a more explicit set of bindings for Java and ECMAScript (more commonly known as JavaScript).

The DOM provides a complete set of tools for "walking the tree" of a parsed XML or HTML document. As a tree-based API, it requires the parser to build a complete tree representation of the document that can then be explored. (SAX, used for our examples, is an event-based API. See Chapters 12 and 15 for further discussion of the differences.) In effect, a parser or other application that exposes information through the DOM must have a complete representation of the document available, either in memory or in readily-available storage, and provide hooks that other applications can use to navigate this tree and retrieve or modify the information they need.

"Accessing and manipulating" gives the DOM an enormous amount of power. While accessing XML document information is important, being able to manipulate that information opens up a great number of possibilities. In its most trivial form, it allows scripts in a browser to change the styles or visibility of some text in a document, allowing the creation of more interactive interfaces or just plain "eye candy". In a more sophisticated implementation, connected to a system where the tree can be written back to storage, it makes possible a separation between an interface for editing a document and the tools used for data storage. The interface could use the DOM API to access the information in a document, and transmit user changes back to the parser or other system that holds the information. A user who wants to make changes permanent, can choose to save the information and write information back to a storage medium, as a file or as a collection of database records as appropriate.

The DOM will definitely be the API of choice for applications that want to access a tree of information but do not want to build it themselves. By abstracting the tree, the DOM will allow applications to use multiple types of data storage and retrieval, and make it easier for interfaces to modify the local tree without modifying the permanent, original tree. It does require a significant amount of resources, primarily in memory but possibly also in storage. The DOM is probably more appropriate for large applications than small ones, though applets may be able to use the DOM interface of the browser in which they appear. Whether the DOM will replace proprietary parser APIs completely is uncertain. While being able to interchange parsers is a convenience to application developers, it may not prove so popular with parser developers and others with an interest in locking in customers. Parsers will most likely come with support for the DOM and for their own "convenience" implementations, designed to provide quicker performance or handier implementations.

NOTE

As of this writing, few of the parsers currently available provide a native implementation of the DOM. Sun's ProjectX parser and the IBM Java parser supports the DOM. However, an SDK that can provide a DOM interface to SAX-compati-

ble parsers is available. For more information on the Docuverse DOM SDK, see
http://www.docuverse. com/domsdk/index.html.

XML AND MIDDLEWARE

The first commercial area in which XML seems to be taking off (if announcements
are an indicator) is middleware. XML makes a superb halfway-house for all kinds of
textual and numeric data, no matter what the source or the structure. Relational
databases, documents, objects, and an enormous range of other data types can be
expressed in a common vocabulary and processed with a common set of tools.
While XML may not be the most efficient way to store relational database information (even with the file system possibilities discussed above, a dedicated relational
database will be more efficient for information that can be easily normalized to its
table structures), it offers the promise of a new way to distribute that information,
making it accessible to more applications and more users. XML's easily processed
and highly flexible structures promise to make far easier the interchange between
systems, even those using very different data structures.

XML has a role to play in many different middleware operations. Client-server
applications have developed tier after tier of tools to keep data sets in sync with
each other and to translate information sent between clients and servers. At its
simplest, middleware may take the information returned from a query and covert
it into a format that a user can view in a browser; at its most complex, middleware
can coordinate large numbers of queries on multiple systems, prune and transform the results, and format them to meet a user's needs, possibly even building
pictures and graphs to send users. Middleware can also accept data going the
other direction, from client to server, or information moving between servers.
XML can simplify these movements, combinations, and transformations by providing a common format. Converting the information coming in and out to a
common XML format (even ones using different structures) is a key first step to
making the information portable. An XML front end for databases is one
approach; another approach, which many database vendors are taking, is to build
XML interfaces into the database itself, thereby reducing the number of layers (or
at least the number of visible layers) needed to get information from the database
to the middleware tool.

Middleware tools can take XML documents (even of different types, provided
the middleware understands the format) and combine their information, using

common parse trees as a foundation for processing. Because accessing and modifying information in a parse tree is reasonably simple, and because that parse tree can be shared with a number of different applications, the process of building middleware can be simplified substantially. Developers can focus on the data transformation, not the data format, avoiding the hassles of parsing information presented in different formats.

NOTE   There are still a considerable number of missing pieces in the middleware picture. Tools for querying XML documents are under development. Several proposals have been submitted to the W3C as notes, but none is yet under official consideration. Another key piece of the puzzle, data typing, is also still under development. See Chapter 6 for more information on the schemas and data typing scheme that promise to increase considerably the viability of XML for data-processing applications.

XML AND FILE SYSTEMS

Object databases and the DOM make possible new ways of storing and addressing XML documents in a way that addresses their naturally hierarchical form. If XML becomes ubiquitous, this natural hierarchy promises another potential improvement in computing environments. Because XML documents, no matter what kind of data they contain, all have the same structure, it is possible for a file system to provide more support to XML files than is currently possible with the enormous numbers of varied, proprietary, and unstructured binary file formats currently used to store most information.

File systems have always been a place to store chunks of information. Generally, a file system provides a structured view of the information it stores, whether as a list or a group of nested lists, which then link to files that are treated as large blocks of undifferentiated information. The file system has no idea, for instance, what kind of information is stored in a Microsoft Word file on a PC. All it knows is that it has a name, a location in the directory structure, some time stamp information, possibly some security information, and an associated group of bytes. By convention, the end of the file name (usually .doc) identifies the file so that the operating system can open an appropriate application for viewing and modifying the file. The file "belongs" to that application; while it may be imported to other formats or viewed through a simpler program, the format of the file and the official interpreter of its contents is the application. This has made possible some significant gains in efficiency, but at the cost of compartmentalizing information in formats that cannot be easily interchanged.

XML files present no such obstacles to file systems or applications. While specific applications will definitely be needed to interpret or modify these documents' content, any program with a parser can determine their underlying structures. Unlike binary files, the structures of XML documents are completely open, available for manipulation by file systems as well as applications, making possible an entirely new level of collaboration between operating systems, file systems, and applications. Addressing this new structure through standardized interfaces—built, for instance, on the DOM or the W3C's upcoming XPointer specification, described in Chapter 10—frees applications from having to make calls to platform-specific APIs to get and modify file information.

Building the structures on which this new collaboration can rest will require a thorough reconsideration of file system structures, making it possible for the new "file system" to store and manage structures within files as well as the binary chunks of the past. By moving the parser out of the application and into the file system, it becomes possible for applications to display and modify fragments of information without needing to parse and rebuild large sequential files. A considerable amount of effort in binary file structures has gone into making save times as short as possible and files as small as possible, driving developers to create "fast save" options that tack changes on to the end of files, requiring more work when the file is loaded and more hassle if the file structure ever becomes corrupted. Creating a new system in which applications can modify and save fragments and sets of fragments removes this problem, making it much easier to work with large sets of information efficiently. A file system, built carefully to specifications one time, can avoid the need for applications developers to create their own specifications over and over. (In practice, this is likely to be an object database with a front end built to make it look more like a traditional file system.)

An example of a field in which this fragmentation can be useful is log files. Log files have long been the bane of system administrators whose backup strategies are frustrated by files that are always "open". In many applications, the log file is kept open for 24 hours (the time may vary, of course), after which a new log file is opened and the old log is closed. The old logs can be backed up or deleted as necessary, but the new log is always in use. Processing the logs (typically done for Web server logs to determine usage) is complicated by the need to open a large set of files and combine their contents. Some applications have avoided the file issue by logging directly to a relational database, which provides more flexibility as far as storing information on a per-record rather than a per-day basis, but locks the log into a very fixed format with no room for multiple layers of information in a single entry.

Putting the logs in XML (see the XLF project at **http://www.docuverse.com/ xlf/index.html** for one approach) allows the logs to have a more complex structure and also makes the logs easier to manipulate, but still leaves them as huge open files. Storing them in a granular file system like the one above, however, provides the logging system with the structural flexibility of text files, the clear syntax of XML, and the record-by-record benefits of the database. Log management can focus on records and sets of records without having to import an enormous set of log files, because the records have already been "imported". The same log format and file system structure may also be used for multiple applications, making it easier for administrators to track interactions between applications for integration and troubleshooting. This kind of sharing information on a very granular level is what XML is best at.

Building file systems that store a parsed representation of XML documents rather than flat text files provides a few other advantages to users making regular use of XML documents. A set of inherited attributes, in which attributes declared for a parent element apply to its child elements as well, has crept into the XML specification. The **xml:lang** and **xml:space** attributes, described in Chapter 5, and the namespaces facilities all exhibit this behavior. By parsing a document in advance (actually, as it is created and saved), the file system can establish flags for these inherited attributes, making it possible quickly to retrieve a particular element from a document with this information intact but without needing to parse the document backwards to find the parent element that set the attribute values. Fragment processing in XML promises to be an important and exciting field, making it possible to describe, link to, and retrieve portions of documents instead of the entire document. The W3C's XPointer specification (in development, but see Chapter 10 for a preview) promises a reasonably easy and standardized vocabulary for describing document fragments. Fragment processing is a task that has been nearly impossible in the past for most documents because of the lack of standards, and it will probably be a few years before this task is commonly understood and standards are implemented. By that time a file system that can support them efficiently should have arrived.

NOTE

This file system of the future remains very much in the future. Document management systems that provide this level of functionality remain very expensive and typically custom-built solutions for large-scale implementations. Security is a significant issue with this kind of system. If XML becomes a ubiquitous document format, however, someone (maybe an object database vendor) will probably find a way to make a tidy profit from such a system.

XML AND SERIALIZED OBJECTS

XML's structural match with objects makes it a useful tool for representing persistent objects. Objects can save their data content to an XML file periodically, and combine (a parsed representation of) that data with their programming code to recreate the object, as it had been at the time it was saved. Persistent object storage was one of the key tasks for which object-oriented databases were created, and their match with XML's structures is a potentially exciting coincidence. Just as object databases can be useful for storing large quantities of XML documents efficiently, XML documents, stored as simple files, can store small quantities of object information efficiently.

One of the first tools for creating serialized Java objects with XML is Coins, a toolkit available at **http://www.jxml.com/coins/**. Building on the SAX API (described in Chapter 15), the W3C Document Object Model, and the Docuverse DOM SDK, Coins provides a complete set of tools for saving object data as XML documents and for reconstructing objects from XML files (or DOM trees of whatever kind). Though Coins uses JavaBeans in part, it is effectively a replacement for JavaBeans. Instead of relying on Java serialization and the java.io.Serializable interface, which produces opaque files that can only be opened by deserializing them, Coins relies on XML files. The simple readability of XML files provides a number of significant advantages. Debugging is much simpler when you can open the file directly. Other applications, which may not be in Java and which may not have any direct understanding of the Coins model, can open the documents and conceivably retrieve information for their own use. In an extreme case, this could even provide a way for an object written in a different object-oriented language to construct itself using the information found in the Coins file, allowing interchange among languages as well as platforms.

When a Java object that implements Coins needs to save its information, it writes it out to an XML file using the Coins services. When it needs to be reinstantiated with the saved values, it opens the XML file through the Coins services and is rebuilt, as shown in Figure 3.4.

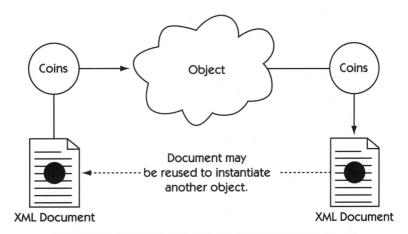

Figure 3.4   From object to XML and back again with Coins

Another key advantage of XML as a serialization format is hyperlinking. The XLink tools (described in Chapter 11) provide a vocabulary that can be used to link Coins to each other in ways that reflect the relationships between different objects in a program. Unlike serialized Java components, which contain a serialized form of everything referenced by that component (and which can therefore grow enormous), Coins allows components to be partitioned, creating multiple hyperlinked XML files rather than a single large file that may contain information from multiple objects. As the Coins site puts it, this allows "a set of coins to be converted back to an XML document without including anything more that a reference to external components." Coins provides for coin application documents, which contain the actual object contents, and coin meta documents, which contain information describing the contents of application documents.

Coins is the starting pistol in a technology shift that may change the way programs store persistent data, and may lead to other changes as well. Coins can be used to feed XML document information into objects, even when that information didn't originate inside a Java object. In effect, developers can create XML descriptions of initialization states for Java objects with Coins, and can use this to provide functionality from preference files to sophisticated document display. By making object properties and the content of an XML file correspond neatly, Coins opens the way to a new set of programming paradigms.

XML as a Foundation for Standards

All these examples so far have considered XML in a fairly generic sense, exploring possibilities that apply to any and all XML documents. While the features common to all XML documents provide a critical foundation on which XML-handling tools can build, XML is receiving much attention as a tool for creating other standards. XML's easily processed syntax and tools for describing document structures make it an ideal language for creating other specifications. These other specifications may, in turn, take advantage of any of the XML infrastructures described above. The sections below describe a number of established and emerging standards that are built on XML, presenting a (still fuzzy, early) picture of the many tasks to which XML is suitable.

NOTE

The following brief descriptions do not by any means constitute endorsement, and undoubtedly many worthy projects have been omitted or are newer than this list). Some of these standards developments are the work of individuals or small groups, and XML standards development is only getting under way. Explore the sites describing these standards before building any plans that use them to get a clear picture of their stability and their level of support.

Chemical Markup Language (CML)

Creators/Backers: Open Molecule Foundation, Peter Murray-Rust

For more information: **http://xml-cml.org**

Chemical Markup Language provides chemists with a sophisticated set of tools for exchanging information, both at the document level, where CML can be used to format papers, and at the molecule level where CML can be used to describe molecular structures, sequences, and spectra, and present them in a variety of different ways. CML began as an SGML application, and has developed into one of the most robust XML applications, complete with its own browser, which is under constant development, and which may be used to work with XML documents from a wide variety of sources.

Chemical Markup Language documents may be viewed and edited with the Jumbo browser, a Java application which shows the structure of documents and allows readers and editors to examine and manipulate that information. Jumbo provides a number of views for molecules and other structures, as shown below in Figure 3.5.

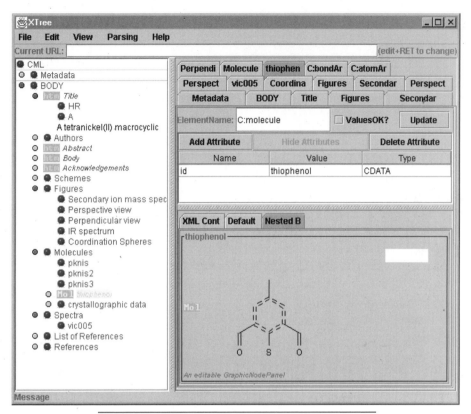

Figure 3.5 Viewing a molecule structure in Jumbo 2.0

http://www.vsms.nottingham.ac.uk/vsms/java/jumbo/

Encoded Archival Description (EAD)

Creators/Backers: US Library of Congress and several research level institutions
For more information: **http://www.loc.gov/ead/**

The Encoded Archival Description language is intended to be a:

> nonproprietary encoding standard for machine-readable find-
> ing aids such as inventories, registers, indexes, and other doc-
> uments created by archives, libraries, museums, and manu-
> script repositories to support the use of their holdings.

The EAD project began in 1993 as a project at the University of California, Berke-
ley, and became a larger project in 1995 with the development of design principles

and the commencement of work on an SGML-based system. In the final iteration between the beta standard and version 1.0, the system was made XML-compatible as well. EAD sites may currently be searched with Interleaf's (formerly SoftQuad's) Panorama viewer or transformed to HTML documents for easy viewing.

EXTENSIBLE LOG FORMAT (XLF)

Creators/Backers: XLF mailing list (**http://www.jxml.com/archive/xlf/**), XML-Dev mailing list (**http://www.lists.ic.ac.uk/hypermail/xml-dev/**)

For more information: **http://www.docuverse.com/xlf/**

The Extensible Log Format initiative is an open project aimed at creating a document structure and processing model for XML log files. By putting log files into an XML format, the XLF project hopes to simplify the administrative tasks involved in handling and processing log files. Web server files have been identified as the first target. The XLF initiative uses an open mailing list-based process to collect and codify ideas for the format.

GEDML

Creator/Backer: Michael H. Kay

For more information: **http://home.iclweb.com/icl2/mhkay/gedml.html**

GedML is a new format for genealogical information based on the GEDCOM format. Like GEDCOM, it is capable of representing individuals, families, and sources, but GedML takes advantage of XML's structures and its flexibility to open up new possibilities for extensions to the GEDCOM model—like "the introduction of a separate model for geographical places, or a modular approach to culturally-dependent events (e.g. the ceremonies of Judaism or of the LDS church)"—as well as take advantage of XML's internationalized text handling and easier processing with standardized tools.

MATHML

Creators/Backers:W3C

For more information: **http://www.w3.org/Math/**

MathML is an XML application that finally provides reliable markup of equations, both for interchange between applications and within HTML documents. As Elliotte Rusty Harold describes the problem in his excellent *XML: Extensible Markup Language* (IDG Books, 1998):

> Legend claims that Tim Berners-Lee invented the World Wide Web and HTML at CERN so high-energy physicists could exchange papers and preprints. Personally, I've never believed that story. I grew up in physics; while I've wandered back and forth between physics, applied math, astronomy, and computer science over the years, papers in all these disciplines contained lots of equations. Until now, seven years after the Web was invented, there hasn't been any good way to include equations in Web pages.

Earlier attempts at including mathematical notation in HTML had been rebuffed, so the W3C set up a separate Math Activity. MathML opted to use XML syntax toward the end of its development, becoming the first W3C recommendation to actually implement an XML syntax. MathML support is starting to arrive in tools like Maple and Mathematica, and a subset of MathML is currently supported by the W3C's testbed browser, Amaya (**http://www.w3.org/Amaya**), as shown in Figure 3.6.

NEWSPAPER ASSOCIATION OF AMERICA—CLASSIFIED ADS FORMAT

Creators/Backers: Newspaper Association of America
For more information: **http://www.naa.org/**

Several of the most common types of classified ads may soon get a new standard format that will allow newspapers to instantly and easily exchange several of the most common types of classified ads for both print and online formats, including:

- automotive
- real estate
- recruitment.

The NAA hopes to finish the project by the end of 1998.

OPEN FINANCIAL EXCHANGE (OFX)

Creators/Backers: Microsoft, Intuit, and CheckFree
For more information: **http://www.ofx.net**

"Open Financial Exchange is a unified specification for the exchange of electronic financial data over the Internet." OFX provides a set of tools for implementing electronic banking services, allowing banking customers (both consumer and business) to access their account information, credit card information, and transactions and balances, and pay bills, present bills, and make and manage investments. OFX is a set of services built around a core XML DTD, though the document syntax used is not completely XML compatible. While the XML format gives OFX extra interoperability, building OFX into existing installations is a large-scale integration task.

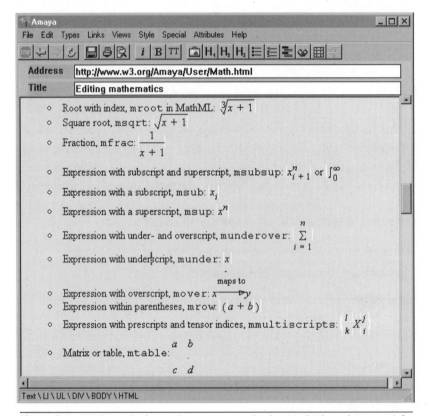

Figure 3.6 Mathematical notations presented using MathML and Amaya 1.3a

Open Trading Protocol

Creators/Backers: The Open Trading Protocol Consortium (members include many financial institutions and technology firms)

For more information: **http://www.otp.org/**

The Open Trading Protocol is a project aimed at creating a set of standards for use in retail transactions. Among the types of information being encoded in XML are:

- offers for sale
- agreements to purchase
- payment (by using existing payment products, such as SET, Mondex, Cyber-Cash, GeldKarte, etc.)
- the transfer of goods and services;
- delivery
- receipts for purchases
- multiple methods of payment
- support for problem resolution
- payment brand and protocol selection.

The OTP also hopes that this information may be used for record keeping, giving businesses and consumers an easily analyzed set of records. The OTP has submitted one version of its work to the Internet Engineering Task Force.

REAL ESTATE LISTING MARKUP LANGUAGE (RELML)

Creators/Backers: OpenMLS Software

For more information: **http://www.openmls.com/**;

http://www.4thworldtele.com/public/design/

Real Estate Listing Markup Language is a conversion of the MLS standard used by the real-estate industry to describe structures and other properties to XML. RELML presents MLS-based information in an XML format, making it much easier to present real estate information through Web browsers and other interfaces, as well as to combine it with information from other sources. (The sample site currently requires Internet Explorer 4.01.)

P3P

Creators/Backers: W3C

For more information: **http://www.w3.org/P3P/**

The W3C's Platform for Privacy Preferences Activity is developing a standard, based on XML and RDF (see below), that allows users to submit personal information to sites on the Web while clearly prescribing the use that may be made of that information. Currently, users who want to keep their personal information private have to seek out company privacy policy statements, compare those with their feelings about the privacy of their personal information, and decide whether this usage is acceptable before entering their information into a custom-built form. P3P will provide a "privacy assistant" that automates this process. Sites that need personal information can specify what information they need, along with an explicit description of their privacy policy, which is then compared to a policy set by the user. If the policy matches, (and possibly if the user consents), the "privacy assistant" may then transmit the information, avoiding the need to type everything in every time. Policies and user information are both described using XML.

PRECISION GRAPHICS MARKUP LANGUAGE (PGML)

Creators/Backers: Adobe, IBM, Netscape, and Sun Microsystems

For more information: **http://www.w3.org/TR/1998/NOTE-PGML-19980410.html** and

http://www.w3.org/Submission/1998/06/

The Precision Graphic Markup Language specifies markup language that can be used to render vector graphics. It uses the imaging model of Adobe PostScript and Adobe Portable Description Format (PDF), but is designed to meet Web needs. The W3C has only begun work in this area, and will probably consider this proposal in conjunction with the Vector Markup Language described below.

NOTE

Chapter 18 implements an applet capable of displaying a subset of PGML's functionality.

RESOURCE DESCRIPTION FRAMEWORK (RDF)

Creators/Backers: W3C

For more information: **http://www.w3.org/Metadata/**

The Resource Definition Framework is a product of the W3C's metadata activity. Intended to provide a standard format to describe documents and other information, RDF actually predates XML and has only adopted XML syntax recently. (In some ways, RDF's node and property structures may be seen as competitors to XML's element and attribute-based structures.) While RDF itself rests on XML, other standards in turn rest on RDF, notably the Dublin Core Initiative, " a 15-element metadata element set intended to facilitate discovery of electronic resources."

For more on the Dublin Core Initiative, see its home page at **http://purl.oclc.org/metadata/dublin_core/**, and RFC 2413, **ftp://ftp.isi.edu/ in-notes/rfc2413.txt**, which describes the elements used to describe documents.

The development of RDF has been a slow process, and its specifications are fairly complex, but RDF may well be one of the first XML applications to receive extensive use on the Web, even in HTML documents. RDF promises dramatic easing of the cataloging and searching issues that make the Web difficult to use.

Synchronized Multimedia Integration Language (SMIL)

Creators/Backers: W3C

For more information: **http://www.w3.org/AudioVideo/**

SMIL allows developers to create multimedia presentations through declarative markup rather than programming. It supports the use of audio, video, text, and graphics, and allows designers to specify timelines (both absolute and relative), positioning, alternate representations for low-bandwidth situations, and facilities for captioning multimedia. SMIL uses XML syntax for all of its markup, and is formally specified in a W3C Recommendation (**http://www.w3.org/TR/REC-smil/**).

SMIL's future has been cast in some doubt by the refusal of Microsoft and Macromedia to implement SMIL in their products. These two companies, with Compaq, have submitted HTML+TIME, a proposal for integrating SMIL's features with HTML, to the W3C. (HTML+TIME is available at **http://www.w3.org/TR/ NOTE-HTMLplusTIME**).

Vector Markup Language (VML)

Creators/Backers: Autodesk, Hewlett-Packard, Microsoft, Visio

For more information: http://www.w3.org/TR/1998/NOTE-VML-19980513

Like PGML, Vector Markup Language uses XML to describe graphic vectors that may be combined to create a picture. VML combines its own markup with that of cascading style sheets to build descriptions that can be combined easily with HTML. VML is designed to fit easily into the existing Web framework of HTML browsers, cascading style sheets, and scripting.

VIRTUAL HYPERGLOSSARY (VHG)

Creators/Backers: Peter Murray-Rust and Lesley West

For more information: **http://www.vhg.org.uk/**

The Virtual Hyperglossary (VHG) is an ambitious project for creating structures and applications that support the building of large technical glossaries. The VHG relies heavily on the ISO FDIS 12620 standard for terminology categorization, and uses categorization and a key tool for structuring its information. Glossaries use a very simple DTD to indicate glossary components, like terms, cross-references, and synonyms. Though simple, the VHG is capable of expressing an enormous amount of glossary information, and glossaries can be readily processed and connected to other glossaries, simplifying the task of creating cross-disciplinary connections. Like Chemical Markup Language (described above), the VHG can be read and edited with the Jumbo browser. (See **http://www.vhg.org.uk/software.html** for details.)

WEATHER OBSERVATION MARKUP FORMAT

Creators/Backers: United States Navy

For more information: **http://zowie.metnet.navy.mil/~spawar/JMV-TNG/XML/OMF.html**

The Weather Observation Markup Format seeks to improve upon a number of pre-existing formats for transmitting weather observations. The current formats are limited in the information they can contain and often unsuited for archival storage (missing, for instance, the month and year). OMF provides a more verbose format capable of carrying more detailed meteorological information, as well as calculated information. Using XML as the foundation promises to make processing and storing the information easier, as well as providing structures that can be easily extended in the future.

XML/EDI

Creators/Backers: XML/EDI Group

For more information: **http://www.xmledi.net**

The XML/EDI group is developing "Guidelines for Using XML for Electronic Data Interchange," a set of guidelines for applying XML to business-to-business communication. Current Electronic Data Interchange (EDI) systems use a set of standards for transmitting information (EDIFACT and others) that is less flexible than XML and less applicable to complex transaction situations with multiple layers. XML/EDI seeks to build an environment in which XML is used to allow the creation of more complex transaction systems, shared by large numbers of organizations, in which the rules for transactions are not dependent on the particular participants. XML/EDI is one of a number of organizations retrofitting XML to older business communications standards.

XML AND DISTRIBUTED APPLICATIONS

XML offers a revolutionary opportunity: to tear down the old structures in which information in a particular format was stuck in that format. Information is frequently good for multiple applications, and the limitations that have been placed on document interchange by existing formats have meant that enormous numbers of people have wasted many hours performing tedious translations. Making the transition to XML may not be a simple process, but once that transition has been made, the cost of future transitions should decline dramatically. The implications of this for networked applications, in which large numbers of people need to share and work on the same information, are enormous.

XML promises to open up distributed applications so that any XML-enabled application will be able to connect to a document repository, retrieve the information it needs, perform processing with or without a user, and store information in the repository. The repository could be a hard drive, or it could be an object database. The application could be a tool for processing "generic" XML documents, or it could be a specialized tool built to handle a particular type of document. The transmission and storage facilities may be shared for any number of XML documents and document types, and specialized search and cataloging tools may also supplement the storage. By putting information into a single universalizable format, XML makes it possible to create new architectures that provide enormous new shared capabilities to a variety of applications.

INTRODUCTION TO XML SYNTAX

XML is defined in a series of recommendations from the W3C, only one of which, defining the core syntax, is a final recommendation. Other aspects of XML, like namespaces and linking, are still under development. Styles, critical links that provide programs with guidelines for displaying XML, are also in flux. Cascading Style Sheets (CSS) has reached a second version, while a new contender, Extensible Style Language (XSL) is under development.

The first four chapters of this section are devoted to explaining the XML specification in reasonably digestible chunks. The XML recommendation divides XML documents into two categories: well-formed documents, and the more complex valid documents. The relationship between these two kinds of documents is fairly complex, and often intimidating. While it is easy to say what a valid document looks like and how a validating parser works, it's more difficult to say what will work in a well-formed document or a non-validating parser, because well-formed documents are more than a simple subset of valid documents, making description difficult. Even on the best of days, well-formed documents contain a considerable number of options that make XML seem more complex than it really should be. The four chapters explaining XML start with the simplest possible markup (Chapter 4), move through other markup that should be useful in lightweight applications (Chapter 5), cover validation (Chapter 6), and then explain the remaining tools that might work in a non-validating environment but really need validation to be useful (Chapter 7).

After that detailed tour of the core specification, Chapter 8 will address styles in their many forms. The applications in this book build their own dedicated viewers for XML, but a more generic approach will hopefully become popular as XML becomes more ubiquitous. Chapter 9 will examine namespaces, one of the stickiest issues in XML and one which comes with considerable controversy. Finally, Chapters 10 and 11 will look at XPointer, which lets you specify subsections of documents, and XLink, which lets you connect documents and subsections in much more sophisticated ways than were possible with HTML.

CREATING SIMPLE XML DOCUMENTS

Simple XML documents are well-formed documents, and will run through any XML parser. This simplified XML is completely adequate for many applications, and provides a foundation for the additional features covered in the next three chapters. Some developers will never need to go beyond the capabilities addressed in this chapter, while others will need to continue for the next three chapters into the more complex but more powerful tools available in XML.

"Simple" XML documents are not referred to in the XML specification, but are rather a subset of the capabilities of well-formed documents and will work with any XML parser. Rather than exploring the full capabilities of well-formed documents, it makes sense to start small and build up.

DATA AND MARKUP

XML documents contain character data and markup. The character data is often referred to simply as content, while the markup provides structures for that content. The distinction between data and markup is drawn more sharply and more visibly in XML than it is in many other systems.

In a simple word processor, for instance, tabs, spaces, and paragraphs breaks provide much of the "natural" structure of a document. While these characters are, to a certain extent, markup, they are stored as ordinary characters, just like letters and numbers. Other information about the document—the codes that turn bold on and off, for instance—is stored in the file, but hidden away (though WordPerfect users may remember how to see them). XML does to some extent allow the use of white-space characters, including tabs, spaces, and line breaks, for formatting, but XML's strength comes from its use of markup that is readable by both humans and computers.

HTML ignored most white space—multiple spaces and line breaks disappeared. XML parsers will pass all white space to the application, but the application may choose to recognize it or ignore it depending on its needs. Another technique for handling white space is described in the next chapter.

Markup is distinguished from text with the less than (<) and greater than (>) symbols. (Ampersands [&] and semicolons [;] are also used to indicate text substitutions.) Information in the space between a < and a > is not character data, but markup, instructions that tell the parser how to structure the document and possibly tell the application what to do with it. XML's markup syntax and the strict rules that govern its use are the keys to XML's great promise. By separating markup from content in a much more structured way than other systems, and by making that markup easily extensible, XML makes possible the easy transfer of data structured for enormously different applications. The same tools can be used to create a data format for relational database tables and the works of Shakespeare; XML also makes it easy to represent complex chemical molecules using the same basic tools. HTML barely begins to tap the immense power of markup, while XML brings it to all kinds of different applications.

NOTE   There are a few odd situations in XML where the distinction between markup and character data is less clear. The CDATA section, a primary culprit in this blurring, is covered in the next chapter.

DOCUMENT FOUNDATIONS

XML documents consist of preliminary declarations, followed by the content of the document. Declarations should always come before the content, and the XML declaration should always be the first of these declarations. Comments may appear both in declarations and in the content, but should never appear before the XML declaration. This structure allows a parser to determine what it has to process before reaching the content.

A few general rules apply throughout all XML documents, and should be noted before examining the parts. First, XML is case-sensitive. All declarations and markup must match in case. <MYXML> is not the same as <myXML>. This applies throughout XML processing. Second, the name XML is reserved. Never start an element or attribute name, for instance, with XML. Only the XML specification may specify declarations that begin with the letter sequence XML, xml, or any combination of upper- and lowercase versions of XML. Breaking this rule may lead to difficult incompatibilities as the XML specification grows.

THE XML DECLARATION

All XML documents should begin with a prologue containing the XML declaration. The XML declaration looks like a processing instruction, but technically it isn't. Processing instructions ("PI") are used by documents to pass instructions to applications, and will receive further coverage in the next chapter. The XML declaration is a closely-specified instruction to the parser with only a few options. A minimalist XML declaration could look like:

```
<?xml?>
```

The XML declaration can also include three other declarations: the Version Information, the Encoding declaration and the Standalone Document declaration. All except the Version Information are optional, but they must appear in order.

NOTE

The XML declaration is technically optional, to maintain compatibility with HTML and SGML documents. If the XML declaration is missing, parsers and applications have no way to know what version of XML is in use. The specification provides that "Processors may signal an error if they receive documents labeled with versions they do not support", but it is not clear what parsers should or can do with documents that have no XML declaration whatsoever. In general, always use an XML declaration to assure compatibility.

Version Information

Because the XML standard may someday be improved (or at least developed further), the XML 1.0 specification provides a mechanism for indicating which version of the specification applies to a particular document. Version information must be provided in the XML declaration as shown below.

```
<?xml version='1.0'?>
```

This tells a parser that it is processing an XML document that uses version 1.0 of the syntax. (The quotes around the version number may be single or double quotes; either is acceptable.) Use of the version option is strongly recommended. If the specification changes after a set of documents is complete, a smart parser might be able to handle old versions appropriately, without the need for painful conversions, as long as the version is properly declared.

NOTE

XML does not set a default version number for documents. Always include a version number in any documents that might have a significant life span.

The Encoding Declaration

The Encoding declaration is used to specify how characters are represented in the document. XML requires that all parsers provide Unicode support. Unicode is a character encoding that uses 16 bits per character to represent 65,000 glyphs. Its most commonly used predecessor, ASCII, could only support 128 characters consistently. While ASCII worked well for the English language, it did not support accented characters or special characters for European languages, much less the characters used for other script systems. Unicode creates a single enormous character space that supports Latin, Cyrillic, Arabic, Hebrew, Japanese, Korean, Chinese,

Thai, Vietnamese, and *many* other character sets. Few applications are capable of displaying the entire Unicode set (it requires many fonts, and a cooperative operating system), but more and more systems, including Windows NT and Solaris, are providing support. Java uses Unicode as its native format for string handling, making it a prime contender for XML processing.

The most commonly used Unicode encoding in the English language world is UTF-8, an eight-bit Unicode transformation. Conveniently for English-speakers, the first 128 characters of UTF-8 correspond exactly to the ASCII character set. Another encoding, UCS-2, the canonical Unicode character set, uses the full 16-bit space for each character. Other commonly used encodings include ISO-8859-1 (which contains most Western European characters and is often called Latin-1), ISO-8859-5 (which includes Latin and Cyrillic characters), and EUC-JP and Shift_JIS (which encode Japanese.)

NOTE

If you want to know more about Unicode, the main resource currently available is the Unicode Consortium's "The Unicode Standard, Version 2.0" (Addison-Wesley, 1996). Most of the book is a detailed listing of the characters available, though the front portion provides information for implementors. The Unicode Consortium also maintains a Web site at **http://www.unicode.org**. For the most part, developers need not worry; Java will handle the details.

All the examples in this book will use the UTF-8 encoding, though most parsers support many more. Section 4.3.3 of the XML 1.0 specification provides complete detail on the kinds of notations that can be used to represent encodings. UTF-8 and UCS-2 should always be available, but check the documentation that comes with each parser for further details. All the examples in this book will use a declaration that looks like:

```
<?xml version='1.0' encoding='UTF-8'?>
```

THE STANDALONE DECLARATION

The Standalone declaration tells a parser whether it needs to retrieve external resources to validate the document. Effectively, it indicates whether the parser will have to make multiple requests in order to test that the document is in fact well-formed. For the simple XML documents discussed in this chapter, standalone will always be "no". (If standalone is not declared, it is assumed to be "no".) The XML declaration for simple documents could be:

```
<?xml version='1.0' standalone='no'?>
```

The next three chapters will discuss the standalone declaration's relation to entity processing and validation. For the simple XML documents in this chapter, it could be set to either value and not have any effect. In general, leaving it set to 'no' (or just not declaring it) is a good idea unless for some reason you need to test whether your documents access external resources.

COMMENTS

Comments in XML look like comments in HTML, and behave almost identically. Comments begin with a less-than sign (<), followed by an exclamation point (!) and two dashes (--). Comments end with two dashes (--) and a greater-than sign (>). A typical comment would look like:

```
<!-- This is a comment. Processors will ignore me. --->
```

XML parsers may pass comments on to an application, but are not required to. In general, use comments to make documents more readable for humans, but never use them to pass instructions to an application—that is what processing instructions are for.

XML has a few key rules to remember about the use of comments. Comments may **not** appear inside of markup. The following usage is **illegal**:

```
<CommentedElement <!--this is a comment -->/>
```

Throughout the next two chapters, other places where comments are illegal will be noted. The easiest way to stay out of trouble is to keep comments out of markup that needs to be interpreted by the parser.

WARNING

For compatibility with SGML, the XML specification also recommends that users avoid using two dashes within a comment. For instance, <!-- This -- no, this --> could cause problems. Even if you do not plan to use SGML for anything ever, it is hard to predict how systems and documents will be changed in the future. Avoid using two consecutive dashes within comments.

DOCUMENT CONTENT

After the initial declarations have been made, the actual content of the document appears. The document content must be contained in a single element, and all elements must nest properly. Elements, described below, are markup containers that hold character data and/or other elements. An XML document, at its most fundamental, is simply a collection of elements and their content.

ELEMENTS

Elements are marked with "tags". All tags must begin with a < and end with a >. Element names must begin with a letter and may only contain letters digits, hyphens, underscores, or "full stops"—in English, at least, a period. (Colons may be used in element names but are reserved for use with namespaces, which are discussed in Chapter 9.)

NOTE   Because XML uses the Unicode set of characters, a wide variety of letters, digits, and full stops exists outside the range that is normal for English. See "The Unicode Standard: Version 2.0" for details. Appendix B of the XML 1.0 specification also lists ranges of characters and their type.

There are three kinds of tags allowed in XML: start tags, end tags, and empty-element tags. A start tag marks the beginning of an element, and contains the element name within the < and >. For instance, to mark the opening of a PRICE element, the following tag might appear:

```
<PRICE>
```

The closing tag for the same element begins with </, contains the element name, and ends with >. The closing tag for a PRICE element might look like:

```
</PRICE>
```

A complete PRICE element, with a start-tag, an end-tag, and some content, might look like:

```
<PRICE>$1.95</PRICE>
```

NOTE

Remember that XML is case-sensitive. The start and end tags must use the exact same case for the element name or the parser will report an error.

Empty-element tags provide a shortcut. Not all elements contain information, or even other elements. Some only contain attributes (covered in the next section), or serve as completely empty placeholders. Empty-element tags begin with < and end with />. For instance, an empty element named EMPTY might be represented by an empty-element tag as:

    <EMPTY/>

The use of empty-element tags is not mandatory. The same element could also be represented by:

    <EMPTY></EMPTY>

Empty elements are commonly used to indicate non-textual content (think of the IMG element in HTML) or to store more information than might easily fit in an attribute.

All of these kinds of elements must nest cleanly. Most HTML browsers allowed the following code to work:

    <I><B>This is italic bold</I> and this is plain old bold.</B>

Note how the I (italic) element closes before the B element closes. Because the B element starts after the I element, these tags are overlapping and therefore will cause an error. Fixing this code is not very difficult, requiring only the switching of the opening <B> and <I> tags:

    <B><I>This is italic bold</I> and this is plain old bold.</B>

Now the tags nest—the B element now complete contains the I element, without any overlap. All XML elements must behave this way. Each element may have one (and only one) parent element containing it, though it may have multiple child elements contained within it. The root element, the first element in the document, will not have a parent element, but this is acceptable.

WARNING

Unlike HTML browsers, XML parsers will report loud errors if tags do not nest properly. Although this may seem like an annoyance, it is in fact one of XML's best features. Requiring XML documents to parse correctly simplifies parser and application development considerably, and avoids the difficulty of creating parsers that can accept broken documents that were passed by a different application.

XML elements may contain character data, other elements, or a mix of both. The following XML fragment shows some acceptable combinations of regular and empty elements. The empty elements will need to be interpreted by an application that is looking for them; they won't show up on a display normally.

```
<MEMO>
<TO>Joe and Jim</TO>
<FROM>Your boss</FROM>
<PARAGRAPH>I've been looking for a good reason to fire the two of you for the
last six months, and I can't find anything <EMPHASIS>reasonable</EMPHASIS>.
I was feeling extraordinarily depressed about it until this morning, when the
two of you announced your intentions to start your new <SNORT/>fire-hydrant
cleansing company<GIGGLE/>. I wish you the best in your new venture, if only
so you can get off our health-insurance plan. It might help your business if
you started wearing something other than togas.</PARAGRAPH>
</MEMO>
```

The MEMO element contains a TO element, a FROM element, and a PARA-GRAPH element. The TO and FROM elements contain only character data, while the PARAGRAPH element contains a mixture of character data and elements. The EMPHASIS element contains additional character content, while the SNORT and GIGGLE elements are empty.

NOTE

Confused about SNORT and GIGGLE? As empty elements, they most likely will not show up in a browser. They could, however, be interpreted by a browser which can provide sound effects. This XML document could even be read aloud by an application, which would accent the EMPHASIS and play appropriate effects for SNORT and GIGGLE. As with much of XML, the interpretation is really up to the processing application.

ATTRIBUTES

Attributes provide the application with a bit of extra information about an element. In HTML, attributes were used to more closely specify the type of formatting for many elements. To change the height of a horizontal rule, for instance, a designer could specify a height in pixels with the SIZE attribute. To create a horizontal rule 4 pixels high, a designer might use:

```
<HR SIZE="4">
```

XML allows developers to create attributes as well as elements. Attributes and their values must appear in the start tag. The names of attributes must begin with a letter and may otherwise be composed of letters, digits, hyphens, underscores, and full stop characters just as they are for elements. (And, as with elements, colons may be used in attribute names but are reserved for use with namespaces, which are discussed in Chapter 9.)

Attribute values must be demarcated by quotes, which may be either single or double. In a well-formed document, attributes may contain character data. The < and & characters are not permitted in attributes, and may be represented with the entities described in the next section. (Quotes may also cause disruption, and may also be represented with entities when necessary.)

NOTE

In valid documents, described in Chapter 6, the type of information in an attribute may be limited to certain values.

Attribute values are typically much shorter than element content, and are often used as flags to identify a particular element or define its behavior. For instance, a PRICE element might carry a flag indicating whether or not the price is discounted:

```
<PRICE DISCOUNT="0">$9,999.00</PRICE>
```

or:

```
<PRICE DISCOUNT="50">$1.49</PRICE>
```

In the first (expensive) case, there is no discount. In the second, the price might represent a 50% discount. (The application would still have to understand what the

"50" referred to in order to make sense of the discount. It could think this was dollars rather than percent, for instance.)

Creating and using attributes is simple, but choosing when to use them can be difficult. Misused attributes can lead to enormous start tags that are difficult to read. Choosing between attributes and subelements is sometimes difficult. For instance, the discounted PRICE example above could have been written:

```
<PRICE><DISCOUNT>50</DISCOUNT>$1.49</PRICE>
```

The application would receive the discount information through a subelement rather than an attribute, but (provided the application knew which to look for) the information contained in the two examples is identical. Attributes are often a little less verbose, and can be somewhat less obtrusive. Still, there are several good reasons to consider using subelements instead of attributes:

- Subelements are more easily displayed to users without the use of complex style sheets.
- Attributes cannot nest. An attribute can only hold character data, while an element can hold subelements as well as data. For complex information, elements are almost always more appropriate.
- Subelement markup is often easier to read than markup where the start tags are incredibly long lists of attribute values.

The element-attribute controversy goes on and on, sometimes taking on the appearance of a religious war. Technically, elements can provide all the functionality of attributes, but attributes are more concise and more easily hidden. Choosing between the two forms of data representation is often a personal decision that can be difficult to justify conclusively.

BUILT-IN AND CHARACTER ENTITIES

Because XML uses <, >, &, ', and " as markup indicators, creating documents that use these characters for data can cause enormous parsing problems. In order to get around this potential nightmare, XML provides three built-in entities available to the authors of any XML document. These entities can be used in character data and can also be used in attribute values when necessary. Table 4.1 lists the built-in entities with examples of each.

Table 4.1 Entities Built into XML

Entity	Value	Example	Parsed Result
<	less than (<)	3 < 5	3<5
>	greater than (>)	12 > 8	12 > 8
&	ampersand (&)	AT&T	AT&T
'	apostrophe (')	ain't	ain't
"	quote (")	&quotwhy?&quot	"why?"

NOTE

The ' and " entities are only needed in attributes. ' and " can be used in element content without causing any problems.

Entity notation can also be used to reference characters outside the range of a particular keyboard. To reference a British pound sign (£), an author could use the entity:

£

or

£

Use of the #x combination indicates that the reference will be made in hexadecimal notation, while use of just the # character indicates that the character value will be decimal.

This is only a tiny start into the world of entities. In addition to these fairly simple "character entities", XML provides full facilities for defining more complex entities, which will be explained in the next two chapters.

BUILDING XML DOCUMENTS

Creating simple XML documents is a matter of combining these structures to create data containers that reflect the structure of your data. The set of containers presented above is much like a set of LEGO™ blocks, which can connect to each other in predefined ways. While it is easy to connect the blocks in a random way, mixing colors and building unstable structures, connecting the blocks to create attractive buildings and other structures is more difficult. Data modeling is a complex task all its own, and this book will provide mostly pointers and examples rather than a full-blown course in data modeling.

NOTE

Beginners approaching XML may want to explore "XML: A Primer," by Simon St. Laurent (MIS: Press, 1998). While it does not go into as much detail about XML syntax as this and the next two chapters, it provides a much larger set of examples built to handle many different kinds of document and data situations.

Fortunately, simple XML documents that only apply to a single situation are not very difficult to create. Some documents come with a clear structure already built into them, the result of many years of use, while others are not nearly as clear. Figuring how to turn those documents into useful XML documents can be difficult.

Information that already has a structure, like relational database information, can be transformed into XML extremely easily. The following table might appear as part of a database (the numbers are a bit optimistic):

FirstName	Position	Salary
George	Author	5,000,000
Fluffy	Collector	10,000,000
Joan	Author	5,000,000

An XML document containing this table could look like:

```
<?xml version='1.0' encoding='UTF-8'?>
<SALARYTABLE>
<EMPLOYEE>
<FIRSTNAME>George</FIRSTNAME><POSITION>Author</POSITION>
        <SALARY>5000000</SALARY>
</EMPLOYEE>
<EMPLOYEE>
<FIRSTNAME>Fluffy</FIRSTNAME><POSITION>Collector</POSITION>
        <SALARY>10000000</SALARY>
</EMPLOYEE>
<EMPLOYEE>
```

```
<FIRSTNAME>Joan</FIRSTNAME><POSITION>Author</POSITION>
          <SALARY>5000000</SALARY>
</EMPLOYEE>
</SALARYTABLE>
```

Relational database developers may be wondering if this is worth all the hype surrounding XML. After all, the text below provides a much less verbose and nearly as readable way to encode the same data.

```
FirstName, Position, Salary
George, Author, 5000000
Fluffy, Collector, 10000000
Joan, Author, 5000000
```

XML provides a few advantages that delimited text cannot provide. The most important in this context is that XML can be understood by any application with a parser, and mixed with other data easily. An e-mail message written in XML could include this information as part of its body text, and a smart e-mail application could extract the information and add it to the local data store, whether in a relational database or in another structure. XML is a much more flexible interchange format than delimited text.

The XML version can also carry information that is difficult to include in the delimited version, transferring information about the data as well as the data itself. For instance, the following addition of an attribute declaration to the SALARY element would have a dramatic impact on the paychecks issued to these people:

```
<SALARY UNIT="CENTS">
```

While this could be represented with the addition of an extra column in the table, it might have other impacts on the display of the data. XML's supporting display technologies (especially XSL, the most powerful XML-focused style technology) can interpret attribute information and modify the display of information based on the attribute values. Another advantage that XML has over normalized database tables is that it uses nesting to represent relationships. While such structures can be created with relational structures, XML uses nesting as its basic data model. This makes it a good tool for modeling hierarchical data, from organizational structures to objects and properties in object-oriented programming structures.

NOTE   Relational database developers will probably use XML as an interchange format, not as a core data format. XML's verbose nature makes it very useful for interchange, but gets in the way of the high performance that relational databases provide. XML also uses a fundamentally different data model, as was discussed in Chapter 3.

Relational database interchange is useful, but hardly exciting. XML is most exciting and at its best when it can be used to highlight content and create useful structures for organizing that content. XML can convert documents into databases, making text that previously required careful scanning and indexing into easily located and cross-referenced information. The following XML document contains information about birds in a format that makes indexing, searching, and cross-referencing much easier.

```
<?xml version='1.0' encoding='UTF-8'?>
<Bird>
<Name>
<CommonName>American Robin</CommonName>
<LatinName>Turdus migratorius</LatinName>
</Name>
<Size Unit="inches"><SizeMin>9</SizeMin> to
<SizeMax>11</SizeMax><SizeNote>Robins are known to be of different sizes
in different climates. They tend to be smaller in hot, humid climates, and larg-
er in cold, dry climates</SizeNote></Size>
<Color>Grayish brown on top, orange-red on breast. Young Robins have spotted
breasts.</Color>
<Habitat>Forests and gardens</Habitat>
<Range>Most of North America. Winters as far north as British Columbia and
Newfoundland, though tends to migrate south in winter. Summers north into
Alaska and northern Canada.</Range>
<Description>One of the most widely recognized American birds, the Robin is
often associated with the arrival of spring. Robins are also known for their
bright blue eggs.</Description>
</Bird>
```

This description could fit into a bird book or appear on a web page almost directly. Its parts could be stored in a database with all kinds of information about birds. In fact, this XML could be generated from the information stored in a database, and customized to meet the needs of its recipient, from backyard enthusiast to serious bird watcher to ornithologist. The markup is intermingled with the text, allowing certain key sections to be indexed or extracted for easy use in a different format.

Many of the examples in this book will use simple XML documents, though some may use the document definitions discussed in Chapter 6. For many XML developers, simple documents provide all the tools they need. These simple documents are also useful for planning more complex strategies using the tools in the next two chapters. Keep in mind that working with simple documents is, to a certain extent, working without a net. It is very easy to start creating attributes and elements that an application developer has never seen. Simple documents will get you started, but in the long term they can be dangerous. Fortunately, the Document Type Definitions discussed in the next few chapters will provide a framework for documents, making them far more predictable and easier to manage.

5

COMPLEX WELL-FORMED DOCUMENTS: PROCESSING INSTRUCTION, CDATA, AND GENERAL ENTITIES

While the simple tools presented in the previous chapter are enough to get many projects rolling, they are only a small subset of the tool set that can be used for well-formed documents. Developers may find these tools useful, and some of them will likely be required to use XML with browsers and other applications. The XML recommendation provides additional tools for passing information to applications, for keeping sections of documents from being parsed, and for substituting and including information from other files. This chapter explores tools that can be used safely and meaningfully in a non-validating environment.

WELL-FORMED AND VALID DOCUMENTS

The XML specification refers to well-formed documents and non-validating processors. In effect, non-validating processors (also known as non-validating parsers) check documents for well-formedness and report their results (if an error occurred) or present the document's content to the application. The meanings of these terms are fairly complicated because the spec defines well-formed and valid documents at the same time, exempting non-validating processors from having to perform certain functions. The division is less than clear because some of these functions become optional, and because some of the tools that a non-validating processor may need to understand only make sense in the context of a valid document.

Choosing which tools to use when you do not have complete control over every stage of document processing can be quite a challenge. The tools in this chapter should all be "safe" for use in both validating and non-validating processors, though some exceptions (handling of external entities) are noted. The tools in Chapters 6 and 7 may or may not work in non-validating environments, especially if some of valid XML's nicer features, like default values for attributes, are used. Each chapter and section will provide warnings about potential landslides, as well as detours that can bypass the problems.

PROCESSING INSTRUCTIONS: TALKING TO THE APPLICATION

The XML declaration described in the previous chapter is only one of many processing applications that may typically appear in XML documents, and developers are welcome to create more. The general syntax of processing instructions is extremely simple:

```
<?instruction?>
```

The *instruction* must start with a name construction (letters, numbers, periods, dashes, underscores, or colons, but starting with a letter, underscore, or colon) that does not begin with the character sequence XML (in any combination of upper and lower case—XML, xML, xml, etc. are all illegal). Processing instructions that begin with XML are reserved for use by the W3C. The instruction will be passed to the processing application by the parser. Parsers may interpret some processing instructions (PIs), but generally PIs are instructions for applications, not for parsers.

Most developers create a standard style for their processing instructions, typically identifying the PI and then providing additional details, much like identifying an element and then providing attributes. (PIs cannot be used like elements, however - they have no closing tags.) A typical PI might look like:

```
<?Alert content="vapid" meaning="nil"?>
```

This alert could be taken by an application as a trigger to warn users of the vapid and meaningless content to follow. The scope of the processing instruction is hard to determine; it could be that the parent element is vapid and empty, or that the content following the alert is vapid and empty, at least until another alert appears. Developers need to make sure that applications handle PIs (at least the ones they understand) consistently, allowing authors to have expectations of how they will behave.

NOTE

Processing instructions can identify the application that should process them by starting with a notation identifier, which are described in the Notations section of Chapter 7. This usage is suggested by the standard, but is not required, and developers cannot assume that it will work in all situations. It may still be useful for some applications.

This does not mean that the content of PIs must necessarily be limited. It is possible, though unlikely, that an application could understand how to handle the following:

```
<?Use red acrylic paint for the following three elements?>
```

An application would have to do a lot of processing to make sense of that PI, but it is conceivable that a PI could be used that way.

Processing instructions are something of a contentious subject in XML (and in SGML as well). Processing instructions provide developers with a tool for sending an application instructions that go outside the basic element and attribute hierarchies. This is necessary in many instances, but can cause all kinds of problems if abused. The example below is a typical example of what many word processing applications do with text; it creates hassles for structured data.

```
<PARA>Once upon a time, <?STARTBOLD?> <CHARACTER>Prince
<?ENDBOLD?> Charming</CHARACTER> was walking along a
stream...</PARA>
```

This would work well in a stream-based application where formatting is turned on and off as necessary, and where the complete contents of the stream are available at any time. In XML, where applications typically produce tree-based structures for storing and manipulating data, this approach can cause many headaches. The STARTBOLD instruction is in the PARA element, while the ENDBOLD is in the CHARACTER element. This is legal XML—a parser will pass it faithfully to the application—but it makes it hard to write efficient applications. There are better ways to achieve similar results.

Processing instructions do, however, play an important role in XML, linking documents to resources applications will need to process them completely. Some uses of processing instructions are considered acceptable, or at least on their way to acceptable, by the W3C. For instance:

```
<?xml:stylesheet href="stylesheet.css" type="text/css"  ?>
```

This processing instruction is from a W3C Note (**http://www.w3.org/TR/ NOTE-xml-stylesheet**), which describes how to use a processing instruction to associate style sheets with XML documents; the note will be described in Chapter 8.

CDATA SECTIONS: HIDING FROM THE PARSER

HTML developers will already be familiar with the problems involved in using <, >, and & in a document. (Anyone who ever wrote an HTML tutorial in HTML will certainly be familiar with the difficulties it involved.) The entities described in the previous chapter are a partial solution to this, but some situations call for an alternative. Developers creating scripts will frequently need to use syntax of the form:

```
if a<b
```

 In HTML, this was allowed; the DTD for HTML declared the SCRIPT element to be of type CDATA, allowing the symbols <, >, and & to appear in its content without the use of entities. XML removed this type for elements (which causes considerable problems for parser developers and SGML compatibility), so developers who want to use scripts or need to insert chunks of text content that contains forbidden characters have to use CDATA marked sections. These tell the parser to pass all of the characters within the section to the application verbatim, without checking for elements or entities within that section. The syntax for CDATA sections is certainly distinctive:

```
<![CDATA[ content ]]>
```

CDATA sections make it easy to encode content, like JavaScript code, that uses markup characters for other meanings. It is also handy for dropping sample markup into a document without having to use the built-in entities, like:

```
XML uses tags, which look like <![CDATA[<OPENINGTAG>, <ENDTAG>, and
</EMPTYTAG>]]> to mark up document content.
```

The only content which may not appear in the CDATA content is the closing string]]>. For most types of content, this will not be a problem. It appears fairly frequently in JavaScript, however, where arrays are indicated using square brackets. The example below will cause parser errors because of a mistaken ending to the CDATA section.

```
<SCRIPT><![CDATA[
if array1[array2[someNumber]]>smallNumber {
...}
]]></SCRIPT>
```

The simplest way to avoid this calamity is to place a space between the]] and the >. Another alternative is to begin a new CDATA section right after the accidental break; this may be appropriate for situations where adding the space would actually change the meaning of the content.

USING THE DOCUMENT TYPE DECLARATION

Entity information (which provides handy "shortcut" references to information) is typically combined with the document structure declarations described in the next chapter to create a complete document type definition, or DTD. All entities apart from the built-in entities need to be defined in a declaration at the beginning of the document or documents that used them. For now, we will explore document type declarations and document type definitions only so far as they are processed by non-validating parsers.

NOTE

All document type declarations must be made at the beginning of a document, after the XML declaration but before the start tag of the root element.

The document type declaration, or DOCTYPE declaration, may contain further declarations or provide a link to an outside file that contains declarations. The contents of DOCTYPE declarations that contain declarations directly comprise the internal DTD subset, while the declarations in external files referenced by DOCTYPE declarations comprise the external DTD subset. Document type declarations that include all declarations internally use the syntax:

```
<!DOCTYPE rootElementName [ ...declarations... ]>
```

NOTE   Documents where the standalone document declaration of the XML declaration has been set to "yes" may only have an internal DTD subset. Use the above syntax for all documents where standalone='yes' and do not use any document type declarations that refer to external resources.

Document type declarations that reference external declaration sets may use two different types of syntax. The first is simpler and will likely be more common among Web developers, while the second reflects SGML usage more closely. The first form only includes a system literal—a Uniform Resource Identifier. (URLs are a subset of URIs.) The URI points the parser to the location where the external declarations may be found:

```
<!DOCTYPE rootElement SYSTEM "URIforExternalSubset">
```

For example:

```
<!DOCTYPE SPEC SYSTEM "http://www.simonstl.com/spec.dtd">
```

This tells the parser to retrieve the file `spec.dtd` from the Web server at **www.simonstl.com** and treat its contents as part of the external subset. The root element of the document must be SPEC.

The second form uses a public identifier followed by an optional system literal to identify the needed declarations. SGML uses a system of Formal Public Identifiers (FPIs). FPIs are somewhat like MIME types, except that they use a different syntax identifying the origins of the identifier and its content. Most developers will not need to use FPIs, at least until such time as a standard catalog of FPIs is developed that applications can use to resolve FPIs to real locations. A typical DOCTYPE declaration that used an FPI might look like:

```
<!DOCTYPE SPEC PUBLIC "-//SIMONSTL//DTD SPEC//EN">
```

If the parser had a catalog of FPIs, it might be able to look up the FPI and track down the DTD. At this point, that goes above and beyond what most parsers are capable of, so developers should include a system location where the file can be found in addition to the FPI, as shown below.

```
<!DOCTYPE SPEC PUBLIC "-//SIMONSTL//DTD SPEC//EN"
          "http://www.simonstl.com/spec.dtd"">
```

Providing both allows developers to use FPIs, while maintaining compatibility with the non-FPI systems that currently predominate.

The last case for DOCTYPE declarations provides for both an internal and an external subset.

```
<!DOCTYPE rootElement SYSTEM "URIforExternalSubset"
[ internalSubset
]>
```
or
```
<!DOCTYPE rootElement PUBLIC "PublicIdentifier" "URIforExternalSubset"
[ internalSubset
]>
```

NOTE

When using a public identifier, the URI is always optional in theory but worth including in practice.

This is the most flexible option, allowing developers to use a standard DTD but also enhance it with entities or declarations appropriate only to this particular document instance. The rules for the two subsets are different, as will be seen below, but the most basic issue involved for non-validating parsers is that reading the external declarations is *optional*. The implications of this receive an entire section below. Even if the external declarations are read, the internal subset is always assumed to come before the external subset. As declarations that come first always win when there are duplicate declarations for attributes and entities, this allows developers to override some declarations from the external subset.

GENERAL ENTITIES: TOOLS FOR CONTENT INCLUSION

Entities provide a number of functions in XML, all of which have something to do with including referenced content and defining those references. The previous chapter explored the use of the built-in entities <, >, & ' and ", which are frequently necessary for the proper representation of markup characters in content. These built-in entities make use of a more general mechanism for including content, which is available to authors and developers as well.

XML includes several different methods of including content with different kinds of entities. The first division is between general entities, which are for use in documents, and parameter entities, which are for use in the declarations used in document type definitions, described in the next chapter. Within general entities, there are two further divisions: internal and external entities, and parsed and unparsed entities. Unparsed entities must be external, reducing the number of types of general entities to a more reasonable three.

NOTE   External unparsed entities and both internal and external parameter entities will be covered in Chapter 7. While they may be used in some situations involving well-formed documents, they make sense primarily in the context of valid documents and validating parsers.

INTERNAL PARSED ENTITIES

Internal parsed entities may be declared in either the internal or the external DTD subset. Both use the same declaration syntax:

```
<!ENTITY entityName "entityContent">
```

The entity name must begin with a letter, underscore, or colon, and be composed of those characters plus digits, periods, and dashes. The entity content must itself be well-formed. Entities that contain elements must include matching start and end tags for all of the elements contained and follow the proper syntax for all the constructions it contains. Entities will also be evaluated to see if they contain other entities, expanding all the possible entities.

After they have been declared, parsed entities may then be referenced in the content of the document (both in element content and, for internal parsed entities, in attribute content) using the syntax:

&entityName;

The document below contains two entities that the parser will need to expand:

```
<?xml version="1.0" encoding="UTF-8"?>
<!DOCTYPE NOTE [
<!ENTITY JimFlavor "jelly">
<!ENTITY JoeFlavor "glazed">
]>
<NOTE>Jim's favorite type of donut is &JimFlavor;. Joe's favorite is &JoeFla-
vor;. If anyone invented a &JoeFlavor; &JimFlavor; donut, they'd have these
two as customers for life.</NOTE>
```

After a parser had finished with this, the content of the NOTE element would read:

> Jim's favorite type of donut is jelly. Joe's favorite is glazed. If anyone invented a glazed jelly donut, they'd have these two as customers for life.

Similar results could have been achieved if these entities had been kept in a separate file, connected to the main document through the document type declaration: entity.dtd:

```
<!ENTITY JimFlavor "jelly">
<!ENTITY JoeFlavor "glazed">
```

donuts.xml:

```
<?xml version="1.0" encoding="UTF-8"?>
<!DOCTYPE NOTE SYSTEM "entity.dtd">
<NOTE>Jim's favorite type of donut is &JimFlavor;. Joe's favorite is
&JoeFlavor;. If anyone invented a &JoeFlavor; &JimFlavor; donut, they'd have
these two as customers for life.</NOTE>
```

Note that the entity.dtd file only contains the entity declarations; no other supporting information is necessary. Using this form makes it easy for authors and developers to create libraries of entities stored separately from a group of documents, but used by all of them. This library management permits changes to be made to multiple documents simultaneously. If, for example, a manual for the XJ-2000 Lawn Mower used an entity declared this way to reference the product name, changing the name of the mower to the 2000XJ would require a change only one place in one file. This kind of entity management can save developers tremendous headaches.

There is one considerable drawback to managing entities through the use of an external DTD subset: processors that check only for well-formedness are not required to load entity references stored in the external DTD subset. This was done to improve the performance of XML parsers handling information delivered over the Web. While it certainly means that users may see information faster, they will be receiving an incomplete version of that information, possibly littered with unexpanded entity references. How this will play out in implementations, especially browser implementations, is not yet clear.

EXTERNAL PARSED ENTITIES

External parsed entities allow developers to use an entity to include the contents of an entire external file, not just the contents of a small string. External parsed entities are useful for managing tasks like boilerplate in legal documents and other situations where large quantities of text are shared by multiple documents. Changes made to the file referenced by the entity will be immediately reflected in documents that use the entity, making it easy to update large numbers of files.

WARNING

This easy-update feature can cause enormous problems with files kept for historical reasons. Contracts, for instance, should not be changed after all parties have signed. Making changes to a boilerplate entry can make changes to older files that then have legal or other inconvenient ramifications. If files need to be kept for historical reasons, it may make much more sense to keep a file copy that has been normalized—all entity references have been expanded - rather than relying on the entity content to remain stable. See the section on well-formedness and entities below for more information on normalization.

External parsed entities are declared and used much like internal parsed entities, and are subject to the same requirements for their content. The primary difference occurs in the declaration; instead of a string defining the contents of the entity, the SYSTEM keyword appears, followed by a URI in quotes that tells the parser where it can find the contents of the entity.

```
<!ENTITY entityName SYSTEM "entityContentURI">
```

External entities may also be declared with public identifiers, in which case the syntax is:

```
<!ENTITY entityName PUBLIC "PublicIdentifier" "entityContentURI">
```

For example, suppose the following Latin text is stored at **http://www.simonstl. com/latin/BG1.txt**:

> Gallia est omnis divisa in partes tres, quarum unam incolunt Belgae, aliam Aquitani, tertiam qui ipsorum lingua Celtae, nostra Galli appellantur. Hi omnes lingua, institutis, legibus inter se differunt. Gallos ab Aquitanis Garumna flumen, a Belgis Matrona et Sequana dividit.

A document that then referred to the text could do so with the declaration:

```
<!ENTITY BelloOpening SYSTEM "http://www.simonstl.com/latin/BG1.txt">
```

After this declaration, all appearances of &BelloOpening; appearing in the text would be replaced by the Latin text in the file.

NOTE

Unlike internal parsed entities, external parsed entities may not be used in attribute values. <DESCRIPTION TEXT=" &BelloOpening; "/> is illegal.

Like internal parsed entities, external parsed entities may be declared in either the internal or the external subset. The declaration above could appear directly in a DOCTYPE declaration or in a separate file referenced by a DOCTYPE declaration.

WELL-FORMEDNESS CHECKING AND ENTITIES

As was discussed at the beginning of this chapter, using entities in a document that will be processed by non-validating parsers creates a significant number of risks: that external entities and entities in the external DTD subset will be ignored, and that processors will not be able to identify attribute references for unparsed entities. Developers planning to use these features need to have a very clear understanding of the environments in which their documents will be processed, especially if the documents will be used in applications over which the developer has very little control (i.e., browsers).

The standalone declaration regulates this process to some extent, but mostly by telling the parser to report or not report errors related to declarations made in the internal subset. If standalone is set to 'yes', the parser is required to report errors caused by missing declarations (and errors caused by external declarations.) If standalone is set to 'no', and the parser encounters entities for which it has no declaration (probably because it didn't access external resources), the parser can just leave those references in the text, notify the application that it didn't process the entity, and continue parsing.

NOTE

A document may include external parsed entity declarations in the internal subset and still have the standalone value of 'yes'. As the XML recommendation puts it (in Section 2.9): "Note that the standalone document declaration only denotes the presence of external declarations; the presence, in a document, of references to external entities, when those entities are internally declared, does not change its standalone status." Non-validating parsers that opt to ignore external parsed entities will generate plenty of errors with this rule. In practice, avoid using external parsed entities with XML documents where standalone might be set to 'yes', or just do not set standalone to 'yes'.

Developers having trouble with general parsed entity processing can normalize their documents. Normalization is the expansion of all inclusions, creating a document that contains all of its text directly, without the use of entity references. Normalized documents can be useful for a number of reasons. First, as discussed above, normalized documents are much more stable. A change in an entity reference will not have any effect on a previously normalized version of that document (though authors will undoubtedly want to keep an un-normalized copy of the document around in case they need to make those changes.) Second, normalized documents often require much less processing by the client. Although they are often longer, parsers can focus strictly on elements and attributes and never need to expand entities or do lookups of entities over an often slow and sometimes unreliable network. Finally, as mentioned above, normalized documents are safer; authors need not worry about non-validating parsers that ignore external entity declarations.

TIP

If you need to normalize documents, the sgmlnorm utility, included in James Clark's SP SGML package (**http://www.jclark.com/sp/index.htm**) can expand all entities in a document.

LANGUAGE AND WHITE SPACE

XML provides one last set of tools that may be useful for the developers of well-formed documents: attributes that provide applications with information about the content of elements. The xml:lang attribute allows authors to identify the language used for an element's content, while xml:space allows authors to identify whether the application should preserve white space in element content, allowing paragraphs to be separated by carriage returns, for instance.

The xml:space attribute is the simpler of the two by far. It only accepts two values: default and preserve. The value default allows the application to treat the white space within the element however it normally does, while the value preserve orders it to keep all the white space in the element. (Chapter 8 will demonstrate a different way to do this with style sheets.) Using xml:space is easy—it just appears in the element to which it applies. The xml:space attribute value is inherited by sub-elements; it should remain effective for all of its child elements and their child elements unless an element contains another xml:space attribute declaration, which may override the declaration made in the parent. A typical xml:space declaration would look like:

```
<MyElement xml:space="preserve">Hello!  This is line 1.
This is line 2!
This is line 3!</MyElement>
```

The content of MyElement would then be:

```
Hello!  This is line 1.
This is line 2!
This is line 3!
```

instead of:

```
Hello!  This is line 1. This is line 2! This is line 3!
```

The xml:lang attribute behaves like the xml:space attribute in that its value is inherited by sub-elements. It has a much broader range of values, however. The value of the xml:lang software indicates the language (and sometimes the country) of the content of the element. Languages are identified through ISO 639 codes, like en for English, de for German, and fr for French, or through codes registered with the Internet Assigned Numbers Authority (IANA). IANA codes must be prefixed with an "I–" or "i–". Developers can create other codes, but must prefix them with an "X–" or "x–". ISO 639 codes may combined with country codes to more closely identify the language used. For instance, "en-GB" identifies English from the United Kingdom, while "en-US" identifies English from the United States.

NOTE

The contents of the xml:lang attribute are one of the rare places where XML is not case sensitive. 'EN-US' and 'en-us' and 'en-US' are all equivalent. For more details about these codes and their processing, see the Internet Engineering Task Force's RFC 1766, available at **http://www.isi.edu/in-notes/rfc1766.txt**.

The xml:lang attribute will eventually make it easier to create multilingual documents that are styled differently based on language. A document could contain greetings in multiple languages, and the application might display only the language set by the user, ignoring other content. Papers that contain quotes in multiple languages could leave quotes in the original, trusting translation software to help users who do not speak the original language.

Using xml:lang in documents is simple (though implementing it in applications may prove a challenge.) Well-formed documents just need to use it where appropriate, as in the example below:

```
<?xml version='1.0' encoding='UTF-8'?>
<NOTE xml:lang='en-US'>
<PARA>One of my favorite quotes has always been <QUOTE
xml:lang="la">Veni, vidi, vici</QUOTE> - I came, I saw, I conquered.</PARA>
</NOTE>
```

Documents that will encounter validation processing need to declare the xml:lang and xml:space attributes in their DTD, as described in the next chapter.

BUILDING VALID DOCUMENTS

Many applications can get along just fine with the tools presented in the previous two chapters, but a considerable part of XML's power lies in its ability to specify document structures and enforce those structures. Validation provides a certain degree of conformance testing, making it easy for organizations and industries to create their own standards on top of XML. Validation is also an important tool for making sure that documents are suitable for processing by a particular application, taking some of the burden of checking data structures off the application and leaving it with the parser.

WHAT IS THIS CRAZY VALIDATION?

Validation was described briefly in Chapter 1, and is one of the core elements of the XML 1.0 specification. Validation is a process for making certain that documents conform to structures set forth in the Document Type Definition (DTD). Validation only checks document structure and some very basic data types. In effect, it makes sure that all the parts are present and accounted for, but does nothing to make sure that the parts are correct. While validation is an optional tool for XML authors and developers, it can provide a boost in reliability as well as a language for making explicit the often-unstated structures used in processing.

VALIDATION AND DOCUMENTS

The current set of tools for validation is most effective in the area for which they were designed: document management. Documents are typically composed of a number of parts with fairly indeterminate content, though the overall structures (books contain chapters, which contain sections which contain paragraphs and other material, for instance) are fairly standard. Validating the structure of a chapter of a book involves making sure that all the parts are present, not that an author used a particular data type in a certain part of the document. For most document systems, structural validation is perfectly adequate, and the type of validation needed beyond structure (connecting authors to a directory, for instance) can be provided by the application, using other tools to complete the inspection.

VALIDATION AND DATA

Many developers who use XML for data interchange have found the validation tools lacking. While document type declarations can do an excellent job of specifying the containers used for data—elements and attributes—they do very little to specify what kind of content belongs in those containers. As we shall see below, the declarations for elements and attributes provide only a limited amount of control over the type of information held in an element or attribute, leaving further inspection to the application. Database developers and programmers, used to having extreme control over data types, often find the "well, it's all text" approach of XML discomfiting.

Validation can still be an important part of data interchange, even in its current state. Validation provides at the very least the assurance that the document is syntactically complete, helping to prevent processing of half-finished files and other oddities of data transfer. Validation can provide a foundation for further development, allowing specification developers to provide a formal description of the structures used to contain data as a part of their spec. The use of validating processors also ensures that features like default values for attributes can be used reliably, allowing developers to specify default values to minimize transmission costs.

Addressing the limitations of XML validation will probably be a focus of XML development for the next several years. A number of schema proposals have already arrived at the W3C, and working groups should address issues of data typing and validation. In the meantime, the current structures can provide some support for developers, though additional information will need to be provided to applications.

VALIDATION AND APPLICATION ARCHITECTURES

Validating parsers provide applications with a number of useful services. Validating parsers (should) consistently provide a full implementation of the entire XML 1.0 recommendation. There are no optional features in the recommendation for validating parsers. Unlike non-validating parsers, validating parsers must load all of the external components needed to support a document and process them. Error reporting is more brutal, reporting problems with the structure of the document (as specified in the declarations of the DTD) as well as in the syntax. Despite requiring a bit more overhead, validating parsers are useful because they provide much more reliable service.

Choosing when to use a validating parser and when to use a non-validating parser can be difficult. The safest, though not always the most efficient, approach is always to use a validating parser. Every tool in the XML 1.0 recommendation is available, from external resources to default values for attributes, making it much more certain that your documents will arrive in exactly the shape you intended. This is not always appropriate, as validating parsers do require more memory and processing power, to provide functionality that is not always necessary. Combining a validating parser on one end of an application (typically on the server) and a non-validating parser on the other end (typically a lightweight client) may be more appropriate. Documents that use external resources may also need to be normalized before being sent to an application using a non-validating parser; again, this is a task more suited to the server side, in this case because of its greater potential for caching and reuse.

Application developers who use validating parsers are spared the often significant task of locating information and checking to make sure it exists. While using a validating parser, developers only need to check that the data is of an appropriate type, not hunt it down and check to make sure that it exists. Some applications may be able to check the structure of their document more quickly than a validating processor can, using code specifically built to check that document type, but this approach loses the generic power of validation, requiring both more development time initially and significantly greater changes to the program if the document structure ever changes. Validation is often the easy way out (and schemas will make it easier), but for many programmers, using these shared tools can be a significant time saver.

BUILDING DOCUMENT TYPE DEFINITIONS

Creating documents that will pass muster with validating parsers requires specifying the structure of the document with a set (or sets) of declarations. The declarations are connected to the documents they describe through the document type declaration that was covered in Chapter 5. All the rules that applied to that declaration with regard to entity declarations also apply to element, attribute, and notation declarations, although validating parsers can at least be counted on to load the external subset. Validating parsers will load the internal and external subsets to build a complete document type definition, building a model from the declarations in the DTD that is then applied to the document. If the content of the document matches the model presented in the DTD (and passes all the other syntax tests), the parser will pass the document's contents to the application. If validation fails—because of either a syntactical problem or a mismatch with the DTD—the parser will return an error to the application.

NOTE

Before you build a DTD, take a look around to see if anyone else has already done your work for you. There is rarely any point in reinventing standards that someone else has already created, particularly if tools for the other standard are available or it is some form of industry standard. Even if you use other people's standards, however, knowing how to read a DTD can be extremely useful. Checking the sites of industry organizations is a good place to start. Two other sites worth noting are Schema.net (**http://www.schema.net**) and Robin Cover's site (**http://www.oasis-open.org/cover/**), which includes news on many different implementations.

ELEMENT DECLARATIONS

Elements are the fundamental structures on which XML documents are built. Element declarations describe those building blocks, defining which structures are acceptable and which are not. Elements need to be declared before they may be used in a valid document, and those declarations identify which sub-elements or data may appear in a given element as well. Validating parsers take these lists of declarations and compare them to the tree structures of documents, making certain that every element is in a location that corresponds to a position approved by the declarations.

The basic element declaration syntax is simple:

```
<!ELEMENT elementName contentModel>
```

Element names must begin with a letter and may only contain letters digits, hyphens, underscores, or "full stops"—in English, at least, a period. (Colons may be used in element names but are reserved for use with namespaces, which are discussed in Chapter 9.) The use of the character sequence XML (in any case combination) at the beginning of an element name is prohibited.

The content model may be one of four types: EMPTY, ANY, a set of child elements, or a "mixed" declaration that allows elements or text to appear in the element. Each of these models is discussed below.

TIP

If you just want your elements to include text, you need the simplest version of the mixed declaration, described below.

WARNING

You may only declare a given element once. You may not, for instance, try to override an element declaration from the external subset with a new declaration in the internal subset. Multiple declarations should produce errors.

The EMPTY Content Model

The simplest model is EMPTY, which specifies that an element may have no sub-elements and no content. Declaring an EMPTY element is simple:

```
<!ELEMENT SNORT EMPTY>
```

SNORT elements may now appear in the document, but they may not have any sub-elements or contain text. They must always appear as either <SNORT/> or <SNORT></SNORT>, though they may have attributes if an attribute declaration defines attributes for the SNORT element.

The ANY Content Model

The ANY content model is the freest of all the content models. Elements with an ANY content model may contain any elements or text. (The subelements will have their own content models, which will still need to be enforced.) Like EMPTY content models, declaring elements with ANY content models is simple:

```
<!ELEMENT GENERIC ANY>
```

The GENERIC element may now contain any content, from no content (an empty element) to any combination of text and sub-elements.

Use of the ANY content model is typically discouraged. Unlike the other content models, the ANY contact model provides no guarantee of any structure whatsoever, which may be a potentially dangerous situation in applications that count on the parser to determine the presence of necessary elements. ANY is often a useful first step, however, allowing information modelers to experiment with different combinations of elements during document structure development, replacing it with more specific content models when needs become clearer. ANY is also commonly used as a sort of duct tape to fasten together structures that use multiple (and sometimes changing) DTDs. It is always worthwhile to take a close look at ANY content models and ask if they really need to be there; on the other hand, ANY may be extremely useful in many situations.

The Mixed Content Model

The mixed content model allows an element to contain text, possibly interspersed with the elements named in the declaration. (Elements with a mixed content model may also be empty.) Elements that use the mixed content model are typically elements near the bottom of a document tree, storing information directly while other elements (typically defined using the child elements content model described below) provide overall structure for the document. The simplest use of the mixed content model permits an element to hold parsed character data (#PCDATA), which can contain any text or general entities. For example, the declaration for a FIRSTNAME element that contains only text is:

```
<!ELEMENT FIRSTNAME (#PCDATA)>
```

Sometimes an element will need to contain text and elements interspersed. Paragraphs of text often include more than text—links and formatting are common elements. To create a PARAGRAPH element that contains text, citations, emphasis, and links, the declaration below might be appropriate:

```
<!ELEMENT PARAGRAPH (#PCDATA | CITATION | EMPHASIS | LINK)*>
```

The CITATION, EMPHASIS, and LINK elements would need to get their own mixed content declarations as well. Note that vertical bars are used to separate the element names, and that an asterisk must be placed after the closing parenthesis. (This makes mixed content model declarations look much like the child element declarations described below.)

WARNING

> Mixed content models cannot be combined with the child elements content model described below. #PCDATA may **only** appear in a mixed declaration.

Developers who want to identify the kind of content stored in elements will find #PCDATA disappointingly open. All it declares is that an element may contain textual (or numeric—considered as part of text) data. DTDs do not provide tools for declaring that elements must hold dates, or long integers, or hexadecimal information. Everything is text. For a closer look at future tools that might provide more of this kind of power, see the section "Beyond Validation: Schemas" at the end of this chapter.

Child Elements as Content Models

Using child elements in the content model allows DTD creators to specify complex structures that must be followed precisely. Elements can be required to appear as sub-elements once, once or more, or zero or more times, in various combinations with other elements. The syntax for these declarations uses a combination of element names, occurrence indicators, and connectors like commas, vertical bars (|), and parentheses.

The simplest child element content model declares that one element, and one element only, may be the child of the element. (This is rarely done, except occasionally to represent recursion or to use a container element that expresses itself wholly with attributes.) For example, if the SPECIES element contained only a NAME element, its declaration would look like:

```
<!ELEMENT SPECIES (NAME)>
```

The NAME element would require its own declaration, probably the #PCDATA declaration described in the previous section. In practice, the elements that this declared would look like:

```
<SPECIES><NAME>nameElementContent</NAME></SPECIES>
```

More typically, the element would contain multiple sub-elements, which might look like:

```
<!ELEMENT SPECIES (NAME,DESCRIPTION)>
```

Again, NAME and DESCRIPTION would need to be declared elsewhere. In a document instance, this content model declaration would require a structure like:

```
<SPECIES>
<NAME>nameElementContent</NAME>
<DESCRIPTION>descriptionElementContent</DESCRIPTION>
</SPECIES>
```

Separating element names with commas in the content model requires that they appear in sequence. Using the vertical bar instead of the comma allows only one of the elements in the group separated by vertical bars to appear, effectively providing the author a choice. For instance, if a DTD was created to track spies, its keepers might want to force authors to use only the code name or the real name, but never both in the same document, to keep people from figuring out the connections. (No, this isn't a serious example.) The declaration below would make this provision easy to enforce.

```
<!ELEMENT SPYNAME (CODENAME | REALNAME)>
```

Choices may be combined with sequences to create more complex structures, using parentheses to separate the two. The SPYNAME element above could use separate elements for the spy's real first and last names instead of the REALNAME element, using this declaration:

```
<!ELEMENT SPYNAME (CODENAME | (FIRSTNAME,LASTNAME))>
```

This would require that either the CODENAME element appear, or that the FIRSTNAME and LASTNAME elements appear in sequence.

NOTE   SGML users may notice the disappearance of the ampersand as an occurrence indicator. It allowed elements to occur in any sequence, but caused a considerable amount of difficulty for parsers and did not make it into the XML specification.

While these sequences and choices can be used to create some complex structures, many documents include features that are optional or that may appear repeatedly in sequence. Chapters, for example, contain an indeterminate number of paragraphs. A very short chapter might contain only a single paragraph, while a long chapter could contain hundreds or conceivably thousands of paragraphs. To make these optional structures possible, XML provides occurrence indicators, which allow DTD authors to specify how many times an element may appear. The three indicators listed below in Table 6.1 (four, if you count no indicator at all) give DTD authors the flexibility they need to create genuinely usable structures.

Table 6.1   Occurrence Indicators·

Indicator	Meaning
?	The element may appear zero or one times. (In effect, the element is optional.)
+	The element may appear one or more times. (The element has to appear at least once, but multiple occurrences in sequence are possible.)
*	The element may appear zero or more times. (This is the most flexible option. The element may appear as many times as needed, even zero times.)

Occurrence indicators are used in combination with element names or groupings of elements in parentheses. For instance, a chapter might contain a title, an optional introduction, one or more paragraphs of text, and possibly some citations. This could be easily expressed as:

```
<!ELEMENT CHAPTER (TITLE, INTRODUCTION?, PARAGRAPH+, CITATION*)>
```

The TITLE element would have to be the first subelement inside the CHAPTER element. INTRODUCTION could then (optionally) follow, and then one or more PARAGRAPH elements could follow. If there were any citation elements, they could appear after the last of the PARAGRAPH elements, inside the CHAPTER element. After the optional CITATION elements, the closing tag </CHAPTER> would have to appear. If PARAGRAPH and FIGURE elements needed to be interspersed, the declaration could be updated to allow PARAGRAPH and FIGURE elements to appear in the same area, in any order:

```
<!ELEMENT CHAPTER (TITLE, INTRODUCTION?, (PARAGRAPH | FIGURE)+,
        CITATION*)>
```

These basic parts can be combined in any combination, allowing developers to specify complex structures. At some point, it is definitely a good idea to simplify these declarations with container elements. Suppose the CHAPTER element declaration above grew into the much larger declaration below:

```
<!ELEMENT CHAPTER (CHAPTERNUMBER?, TITLE, (SUMMARYTITLE?, SUM-
MARYAUTHOR?, SUMMARYTEXT)?, INTRODUCTION?, (PARAGRAPH | FIGURE
| NOTE)+, CITATION*, BIBLIOGRAPHY*)>
```

This might be more smoothly expressed (and managed) by breaking it up into multiple elements, each containing their own section of the information:

```
<!ELEMENT CHAPTER (CHAPTERHEADER, SUMMARY?, INTRODUCTION?,
        (PARAGRAPH | FIGURE | NOTE)+, ENDMATTER?)>
<!ELEMENT CHAPTERHEADER (CHAPTERNUMBER? TITLE)>
<!ELEMENT SUMMARY (SUMMARYTITLE?, SUMMARYAUTHOR?,
        SUMMARYTEXT)>
<!ELEMENT ENDMATTER (CITATION*, BIBLIOGRAPHY*)>
```

Deciding when to use a container element can be complicated and is often arbitrary. (Remember, though—any information that requires a mixed content model must be expressed as a subelement.) Element declarations with more than two layers of parentheses are generally good targets for this kind of breakup, though sometimes the practice is acceptable. It depends on the needs of your application, the resources you have available for storage and processing, and how you plan to reference elements.

ATTRIBUTE DECLARATIONS

Attribute declarations define the list of acceptable attributes for an element. Attribute declarations are more flexible than element declarations in many ways, though they also provide (somewhat) more detailed information about the content of the attribute than is possible with element content. Attribute declarations may be made anywhere in the document type declaration; there is no requirement that an attribute declaration for a particular element appear after that element has been declared. In fact, attribute declarations may be made for elements that do not exist without causing an error. Attributes may be defined repeatedly, allowing the internal subset to override declarations made in the external subset.

NOTE The ability to add or override attributes can be a key part of the decisionmaking process regarding whether to use a subelement or an attribute for a particular piece of information. This ability makes it possible to change the types of attributes declared for an element or add attributes to an element very easily.

The syntax for an attribute declaration looks much like that for an element declaration:

```
<!ATTLIST elementName
    attributeName attributeType defaultDeclaration
>
```

The attribute declaration first identifies the element to which these attributes apply. Then a list of attribute names, their type, and their (optional) default values may appear. Multiple attributes may be declared for a single element within the same declaration, as will be demonstrated below. The names of attributes must begin with a letter and may otherwise be composed of letters, digits, hyphens, underscores, and full stop characters just as they are for elements. (And, as with elements, colons may be used in attribute names but are reserved for use with namespaces, which are discussed in Chapter 9.)

The attribute type must be one of ten types. Two of them are enumerated types, allowing the DTD author to specify an acceptable set of values, while the other eight types are specified with the short identifiers listed below in Table 6.2.

Table 6.2 Attribute Types in XML 1.0

Identifier	Meaning
CDATA	The attribute value may be any legal string.
ID	The attribute value must begin with a letter and may otherwise be composed of letters, digits, hyphens, underscores, and full stop characters. The attribute value must also be unique within the document. ID attributes may not have fixed default values. Only one attribute per element may be of type ID.
IDREF	The attribute value must match the value of an ID value for an element somewhere in the XML document.

continued on next page

Identifier	Meaning
IDREFS	The attribute value must contain at least one ID value matching that of an element somewhere in the XML document; multiple values may appear, separated by white space, but all must match ID values in the document.
ENTITY	The attribute value must match the name of an external unparsed entity (see the next chapter for details) declared elsewhere in the document.
ENTITIES	Like ENTITY, except that multiple names may appear, separated by white space.
NMTOKEN	The attribute value must contain letters, digits, periods, dashes, underscores, colons, combining characters or extenders. No other characters (including white space) may appear.
NMTOKENS	Like NMTOKEN, except that multiple values may appear, separated by white space.

Enumerated types provide a listing of acceptable values rather than a description of the type of content that must appear. Enumerated attribute types come in two flavors: notation types and enumerations. The declarations for the two are very similar, except that notation types are prefixed with NOTATION and their values must match the names of notations declared with notation declarations (covered in the next section below and further in the section on external unparsed entities in the next chapter.) Values are grouped in parentheses, with values separated by vertical bars. Values do not need quotes around them.

Programmers will most likely look at the system of attribute types and wonder why any of this is of much use to anyone. Enumerated types limit choices to a list, a common enough practice, but the only other option that will typically be useful in a non-document context is CDATA, which is just a string. Keep reading to get the gist of the present standard, and look ahead to the last section of the chapter for information on how this may change.

The default declarations for attributes, which are simpler and more functional, are listed below in Table 6.3.

Table 6.3 Attribute Defaults in XML 1.0

Default	Meaning
#REQUIRED	A value must be provided for the attribute every time the element is used in a document instance.
#IMPLIED	A value for this attribute is optional.
"quotedValue"	A value for this attribute is optional; the **quotedValue** will be used as a default if no value is given.
#FIXED "quotedValue"	The value of this attribute is permanently fixed to **quotedValue** and may not be changed. (Attempting to change it in a document instance will result in an error, though the attribute may be redeclared in the internal subset to get around this limitation.)

Attribute defaults provide a number of handy features. They can demand that users provide values for attributes, provide a default value in case they do not specify one, fix a value for all time, or even do nothing. Defaults provide convenient minimization, allowing developers to specify values in the DTD and not have to write out the attributes in document instances. (In serious cases, this can reduce the size of documents considerably.)

WARNING

Remember, non-validating parsers are under no obligation to read external declarations. This can mean that all the default values for your documents are ignored, presenting an application that uses a non-validating parser with a very different picture of the document than an application that uses a validating parser would have.

A complete attribute declaration identifies the element to which the attribute is attached, and then combines the attribute name, the type of attribute, and a default value. The simple declaration shown below creates an attribute of type CDATA that provides a basic volume control for the SNORT element.

```
<!ATTLIST SNORT
   VOLUME CDATA #IMPLIED>
```

In this case, the VOLUME attribute takes a string for its argument, and does not require any value. (The application will still need to have a default behavior if no

VOLUME is specified.) Alternatively, the declaration could require the document to specify a value for volume, as shown below:

```
<!ATTLIST SNORT
    VOLUME CDATA #REQUIRED>
```

A slightly more sophisticated approach would use a default value, making it easier to process SNORT elements:

```
<!ATTLIST SNORT
    VOLUME CDATA "5">
```

If volume were set from 0 to 9 (or even 0 to F in hexadecimal), the value of 5 might be a reasonable default, not too loud, not too soft. The application would need to know how to handle these values, and it would need to have some idea what to do if the VOLUME attribute had a value that was out of range (i.e., "16022034") or of a completely different type ("What's up, Doc?"). Using an enumerated declaration can avoid this kind of problem, restricting values to a smaller set of acceptable values.

```
<!ATTLIST SNORT
    VOLUME (silent | quiet | normal | loud | loudest) "normal">
```

A validating parser would use normal as the default, and accept any of the other values listed here. If a document contained a value outside the specified set, the parser would halt processing and signal an error.

NOTE   While it might be tempting to use the tools in the next chapter to create an enumerated list of integers from 0 to 255 (for instance), making a parser work with huge enumerated lists will most likely slow down your application more than simple value checking on the results of the parse done inside your application would. Implement value checking in the application, and wait with hope for the next generation of schemas.

If all SNORT sounds were to be at the same volume, a fixed default value might be appropriate:

```
<!ATTLIST SNORT
    VOLUME CDATA #FIXED "5">
```

This might be useful for an application with a master volume control, in which the VOLUME attributes for SNORT and GIGGLE and other elements simply determined their relative volume.

Many XML applications will find it possible to get by with the set of possibilities demonstrated above. There are a few applications, however, that will need to use the other attribute types. Identifying notations can be useful to help applications process information that is referenced from a document but is not XML. Using an enumerated notation attribute provides a list of possible types, and also ensures that the application has received the notation information (from notation declarations, covered in the section below) that it needs to process this referenced information. For example, to create an IMG element that uses an SRC attribute to provide the location of the image and a TYPE element that identifies the format used to store the image, the following declarations might be appropriate:

```
<!ELEMENT IMG EMPTY>
<!ATTLIST IMG
   SRC CDATA #REQUIRED
   TYPE NOTATION (GIF | JPG | PNG) #REQUIRED>
```

IMG elements would be required to provide both an SRC attribute telling the application where to find the content, and a TYPE attribute identifying the file format used for that content. (This might be redundant in the case of an HTTP transfer, which typically identifies the MIME content type, but could be useful in dealing with a local file system.)

ID attributes (often named "id") are another fairly commonly used tool for identifying parts of documents, as we shall see in Chapters 10 and 11. (IDREF and IDREFS could conceivably be useful in an XML application, but are mostly included for compatibility with SGML documents.) Using an ID attribute makes it easy to reference an element quickly. Instead of saying "I want to reference the third SNORT element that is a child of the fourth JOKE element that is a child of the third COMEDYACT element," you can say "I want to reference element 'XYZ42'." Because ID attributes must be unique within a document, the value of an ID attribute can be used as a shortcut to uniquely identify that element. Each element may have only one attribute of type ID, typically "id". For instance, to add an ID-type attribute to the SNORT element, the declaration below would be appropriate:

```
<!ATTLIST SNORT
   id ID #IMPLIED>
```

ID-type attributes must always have a default of #IMPLIED or #REQUIRED; they may not have default values, of type #FIXED or otherwise.

NMTOKEN and NMTOKENS are typically used where an attribute refers to an element by name, as in many of the schema descriptions under development, but are otherwise fairly uncommon. ENTITY and ENTITIES will be explored in the next chapter in conjunction with unparsed external entities.

NOTATION DECLARATIONS

Notations allow documents to identify the types of content they will contain. Notations are only enforceable in valid documents, but can provide information that may be useful to applications processing well-formed documents. Notations are most commonly used with unparsed entity declarations (covered in the next chapter) and as attribute values.

Notation declarations, like external entity declarations, define the name of the notation and a system or public identifier the application may use to find further information about how to process this content type. The syntax for the declaration is:

```
<!NOTATION notationIdentifier SYSTEM "notationType">
```

or:

```
<!NOTATION notationIdentifier PUBLIC "PublicIdentifier" "notationType">
```

Again, the system identifier after the public identifier is optional. Most notations will be identified with a simple MIME content type, as shown in the example below:

```
<!NOTATION gif SYSTEM "image/gif">
```

The use of notations in XML is fairly different from the free-for-all in HTML, where the HTTP transfer, not the surrounding HTML notation, is responsible for identifying content to the browser. Authors can tell what kind of content is going to appear from the file extension on the source URL, but browsers wait for the download to begin before making assumptions about how to render a graphic. Whether the XML style of explicit notations or the HTML/HTTP style of file extensions and MIME identifiers prevails remains to be seen.

BUILDING AND USING DTDs

Building and using DTDs effectively demands more than a basic understanding of the syntax; it requires that developers examine their information closely and decide how best to represent it. Although the structures of DTDs and relational database schemas are quite different, both offer similar pitfalls, allowing developers to get away with poorly designed structures until someone asks a question that the structure cannot handle. On the bright side, relational database architectures were seen until fairly recently as a difficult art, appropriate only for those with a degree in computer science and a thorough understanding of normalization. Today, many relational databases, even highly normalized and extremely useful databases, have been produced by people with a firm understanding of the data they need to work with and a basic grasp of the principles involved in relational database development. XML should follow a similar path, bringing the information modeling that has been the signature of the SGML community to a much wider audience, becoming easier as it becomes more familiar.

Information modeling is a task most programmers have faced before, though more often in the context of solving tightly defined problems through smooth manipulation of variables rather than the larger, murkier, and more variable structures that can be expressed through the hierarchical structure of an XML document. Contingencies that might never have appeared in the context of a simple database program can arrive quite suddenly when programs need to process multiple documents from different sources and all of the information needs to be interchangeable.

DTDs provide a level of structure in the chaos that can result from the exchange of these hierarchical documents. Provided that they use the same DTD, documents from different sources can be processed identically. Different works by different authors stored in different repositories can all be handled by the same set of applications build to handle document instances that use that DTD. Creating a DTD is a first step toward interoperability, laying a foundation around which documents and applications can be built. Whether that DTD is created by an industry consortium or by a single programmer, it identifies the basic rules for a document's structure.

Typically, multiple documents will share a common DTD, stored externally and referenced by all of them. A public identifier or a publicly reachable URL makes it possible for multiple users at different sites to stay in sync, though applications may often keep a private copy locally. A DTD rests at the core of a library of documents, providing a set of rules that make certain they have the same (or at least similar) structures. Those documents may all reside on the same server, or they may be preference files spread across millions of computers on different and unconnected networks. Using a DTD ensures that applications can read the files, even files modified by a different application, provided all the applications produce information conforming to the DTD.

A critical part of debugging applications, especially applications that work on complex DTDs, is that all possible document structures that can be built using a particular DTD will actually work. Testing an application on an insufficient number of possibilities may lead to problems down the line. Using a DTD guarantees documents will conform to the DTD; it does not guarantee that your **application** does.

DTDs provide a key service to XML users and developers, allowing the creation of formalized standards for document structures. Using validating parsers and developing (or using) DTDs will allow you to share in the proper use of these structures, reading and modifying information while keeping it in a form that can be accessed by many different applications and even types of applications.

Two excellent resources providing help in DTD design are "Structuring XML Documents," by David Megginson (Prentice-Hall, 1998) and "The XML & SGML Cookbook," by Rick Jelliffe (Prentice-Hall, 1998). Both books address the more complex issues of DTD design.

Beyond Validation: Schemas

While DTDs provide a description of a document's structures in terms of nested containers, they do very little to define the contents of those containers. Attribute declarations provide much finer-grained control over content than element declarations, but this control is still minimal when compared to that of data typing functions available in most programming languages. (True, there are many languages that treat all data as strings, but some kind of typing is usually available.)   In response to the need for more sophisticated validation, and also to take advantage of XML document syntax for schema declaration, a number of schema proposals have appeared.

As of this writing, the W3C has not taken action on any of these proposals, though it is widely expected that the XML Working Group will move forward on these issues at some point in 1998 or 1999.

Three proposals have driven most of the debate about schemas. The first was XML-Data (**http://www.w3.org/TR/1998/NOTE-XML-data-0105/**), a proposal from Microsoft and ArborText, that a complete replacement for DTDs and a set of rules for using XML to represent data sets. A smaller schema proposal created on the XML-Dev mailing list (and co-edited by one of the authors of this book), XSchema (**http://purl.oclc.org/NET/xschema**), provides a set of tools for defining XML document structures with XML document instances. It does not provide replacements for entities or support for data typing, but provides support for more complete documentation and extensibility than is possible with a DTD. Finally, Document Content Description (DCD; **http:/www.w3.org/TR/NOTE-dcd**), a proposal from Microsoft and IBM, is a smaller successor to XML-Data.

SYNTACTICAL ISSUES AND SCHEMAS

All the schema proposals, apart from XML 1.0's own DTD structures, have departed from the SGML-style declarations explored in this chapter in favor of XML instance syntax. Current DTD syntax produces a list of elements, attributes, notations, and entities, but does so in a format that is difficult to document and impossible to extend. Using XML document instance syntax—declaring elements and attributes using XML elements and attributes—opens up the entire process and makes the declarations extensible.

There is no room for documentation in an XML 1.0 DTD declaration, except in comments inserted between the declarations. Comments may go with the previous declaration or the following declaration or even the entire following section; there is no standardized way to tell what comments describe. By using elements to define data structures, documentation may be nested in the declaration, making clear what is described by the documentation.

There is equally little room for extensibility in an XML DTD. Even if a developer wanted to add stronger data typing to an XML DTD, there is no place to do it, except with comments, which are hardly a useful tool for it. (As we shall see in Chapter 15, SAX, a commonly used API for linking parsers to applications, drops all comments.) Again, using XML instance subelement can make extensibility simple, as long as the schema developers provide for it.

DATA TYPING AND SCHEMAS

Data typing is the hot-button issue for most programmers, though its place in schema specifications is not completely clear. XML-Data and DCD both provide extensive lists of data types that can be used within their frameworks, while XSchema holds off and waits for a separately defined list of data types to emerge from the W3C. Whether data types end up embedded in the schema specification itself or in a separate specification (which would make it easier to reuse or modify data types separately from the schema syntax), more sophisticated data typing is clearly on the wish list of an enormous number of developers. To provide a glimpse into one possible future, the list of data types presented in DCD is provided in Table 6.4.

Table 6.4   Data Types Presented in DCD

id	idref	idrefs
entity	entities	nmtoken
nmtokens	enumeration	notation
string	number	int
fixed or decimal	boolean	dateTime
dateTime.tz	date	time
time.tz	interval	i1, byte (1-byte integer)
i2 (2-byte integer)	i4, int (4-byte integer)	i8 (8-byte integer)
ui1 (unsigned 1-byte integer)	ui2 (unsigned 2-byte integer)	ui4 (unsigned 4-byte integer)
ui8 (unsigned 8-byte integer)	r4 (4-byte real number)	r8 (8-byte real number)
uuid	uri	bin.hex
bin.base64	char	picture

If this list, or a list resembling it, is added to the list of constraints for document validation, programmers may get the full level of conformance testing they need to remove document inspection from the application and keep it in the validation process.

THE EVENTUAL PLACE OF SCHEMAS

Schemas may prove to be a replacement for DTDs, or a supplement used in an extra layer of processing. The current DTD system's weaknesses are becoming more apparent as XML moves out from its document management and SGML origins into the broader field of data interchange. Although the W3C has been slow to move on a tool that could obsolete much of XML 1.0, schemas seem likely to become an important piece of the XML toolbox.

7

DTD POWER TOOLS

This chapter provides an overview of several tools that simplify DTD construction, allowing developers to create more concise and more flexible DTDs that can be reused easily in a number of situations. It also covers one of the more difficult tools in the XML toolbox (at least for those used to HTML), the external unparsed entity, which uses entity declarations to identify external (and non-XML) content that needs to be handled by the application.

Technically, these tools **should** be usable in a non-validating environment. However, you'll find them much more powerful and considerably more useful in a validating environment, where their tools have more material on which to work.

PARAMETER ENTITIES: TOOLS FOR DECLARATION INCLUSION

Parameter entities operate much like general entities, but their use is limited to the DTD. Parameter entities (or PEs as they are often abbreviated) allow authors to use references to describe declaration content much like general entities allow references to describe document content. Although constructions similar to parameter entities may appear in document content, they will not be expanded, unlike general entities. (Similarly, general entities included in DTD content will not be expanded.) Like general entities, parameter entities may be internal or external, and may appear in the internal or external DTD subset. If the same entity is declared in both the internal and the external subsets, the internal declaration will always override the external.

The declarations for parameter entities look much like those for general entities, with the addition of a percent sign (%). All declarations for internal parameter entities follow the syntax:

```
<!ENTITY % entityName "entityContent">
```

External parameter entities may use either the SYSTEM or PUBLIC keywords to identify their content:

```
<!ENTITY % entityName SYSTEM "entityContentURI">
```

or:

```
<!ENTITY % entityName PUBLIC "PublicIdentifier" "entityContentURI">
```

As always, the URI is optional after a public identifier, but is typically needed in practice. As with other external entities, non-validating parsers are not required to process external parameter entities. For valid documents, however, external parameter entities are a useful and flexible way to reference prebuilt DTD sections, allowing developers to assemble new DTDs out of DTDs that have already been built.

Parameter entities are used much like general entities, except that they appear only in DTDs. Instead of being prefixed with the ampersand (&), they are prefixed with a percent sign (%).

%entityName;

The content of the parameter entity must prove syntactically correct in the context in which it is used. A "broken" parameter entity (for instance, one with mismatched parentheses) will generate an error when the parser tries to include it and cannot process the resulting declarations.

NOTE

Parameter entities must be declared before their first use. This limitation does not apply to general entities.

Parameter entities used in the internal subset face another limitation: their contents must be complete declarations, not portions of declarations. For example, the parameter entity usage below is illegal in the internal subset, but perfectly acceptable in the external subset:

```
<!ENTITY % externalLocation "SYSTEM
'http://www.simonstl.com/Latin/bg1.txt'">
<!ENTITY BelloOpening %externalLocation;>
```

A legal declaration for both subsets would have been:

```
<!ENTITY % Bello "<!ENTITY BelloOpening SYSTEM
'http://www.simonstl.com/Latin/bg1.txt'>">
%Bello;
```

The entity reference %Bello; would be expanded to the full "<!Entity BelloOpening SYSTEM 'http://www.simonstl.com/Latin/bg1.txt'>" which the parser would then have processed as an ordinary external parsed general entity declaration.

NOTE

The internal subset may define parameter entities that are not complete declarations; it just cannot use and expand any of those parameter entities. These partial declarations will be useful with INCLUDE and IGNORE, covered below.

Parameter entities are responsible for most of the high-end magic that experienced SGML developers have come up with to make document structure management easier. By allowing developers to group chunks of repeated declarations, parameter entities encourage modularity. Modules can be nested beyond the simple internal and external subset provided by the DOCTYPE declaration, as modules can reference other modules. (Circular references, however, produce an error.) These modules can be reused or modified as necessary, put together in new combinations and used to switch features on and off.

The best way to demonstrate parameter entities is with a fairly extensive example that illustrates the amount of savings that can be had. John Cowan's Itsy Bitsy Teeny Weeny Simple Hypertext (IBTWSH) uses parameter entities as a basic tool in its recreation of much of HTML's document formatting markup.

NOTE   IBTWSH is a very convenient halfway step between XML and HTML, and a taste of the direction in which the W3C plans to develop HTML in the future. By providing a subset of functionality, IBTWSH makes it possible to use the familiar HTML markup for tasks like documentation and rendering.

IBTWSH uses a considerable number of parameter entities, both internal and external, to organize its declarations and bring in external resources. The organizational parameter entities are declared at the top of the DTD, and the external resource entities (which bring in lists of general entities) are declared at the end. Attribute groups and content models are defined for the entire set of elements with a small set of parameter entities at the beginning, though some attribute sets appear with the section to which they are appropriate. Listing 7.1 presents the IBTWSH DTD.

```
<!--

        ibtwsh.dtd
This is the Itsy Bitsy Teeny Weeny Simple Hypertext DTD.
Its public identifier is -//XML-DEV List//DTD IBTWSH 1.0//EN
The contents are dedicated to the public domain by
the author, John Cowan <cowan@ccil.org>, except that
John Cowan retains the moral right to be known as the author.
This is draft 4.0.2

-->

<!--

================================================================
This is an XML DTD which describes a subset of HTML 4.0 for embedded use
within other XML DTDs. It is by intention equivalent (within its scope) to
-//W3C//DTD HTML 4.0 Transitional//EN, but is not a derived work in the
copyright sense. (Brief excerpts from HTML 4.0 Transitional appear here
and there.)
```

It is often convenient for XML documents to have a bit of documentation somewhere in them. In the absence of a DTD like this one, that documentation winds up being #PCDATA only, which is a pity, because rich text adds measurably to the readability of documents. By incorporating this DTD by reference (as an external parameter entity) into another DTD, that DTD inherits the capabilities of this one. Using HTML-compatible elements and attributes allows the documentation to be passed straight through to HTML renderers.

Current HTML renderers can cope with most XML tags, but empty tags require special treatment. Inserting a space before the terminating "/>" usually makes the "/" (which is not HTML) invisible. Using "<TAG></TAG>" is not as effective, as the latter is often misinterpreted as a second "<TAG>".

Note that since the elements of this DTD are intended to be used within domain-specific elements of the surrounding DTD, there is no "root element" corresponding to the HTML element in HTML. Recommended content models for elements containing documentation are "%horiz.model;" for simple text fragments, and "%struct.model;" for documents in extenso.

You can use the XML element to embed arbitrary XML content into elements declared in this DTD. If you'd rather use some other element instead, define it (or a group of alternatives) as the value of the parameter entity "ibtwsh.include".

Note on draft 4.0: This draft removes the ugly FONT element in favor of BIG and SMALL, and no longer provides ways to set color, the support for which is broken in many browsers anyhow.
==
-->

<!-- ========== Common attributes ========== -->

<!-- All elements have these attributes -->
<!ENTITY % all   "id ID #IMPLIED
                       class CDATA #IMPLIED
                       style CDATA #IMPLIED">

```
<!-- All non-empty elements have these attributes -->
<!ENTITY % i18n                "lang CDATA #IMPLIED
                      dir (ltr|rtl) 'ltr'">

<!ENTITY % basic      "%all; %i18n;">

<!-- =========== Models =========== -->

<!ENTITY % local "CITE | CODE | DFN | EM | BIG | SMALL
              | KBD | SAMP | STRONG | VAR
              | ABBR | ACRONYM">

<!-- default definition of "ibtwsh.include" is "XML" -->
<!ENTITY % ibtwsh.include "XML">

<!ENTITY % horiz "#PCDATA | %local; | A | BR | SPAN | %ibtwsh.include;">

<!ENTITY % lists "DL | UL | OL | DIR">

<!ENTITY % blocks "BLOCKQUOTE | DIV | HR | P | PRE">

<!ENTITY % vert "%horiz; | %blocks; | %lists;">

<!ENTITY % headers "H1 | H2 | H3">

<!ENTITY % struct "%vert; | %headers; | ADDRESS">

<!ENTITY % horiz.model "(%horiz;)*">

<!ENTITY % vert.model "(%vert;)*">

<!ENTITY % struct.model "(%struct;)*">

<!-- =========== Horizontal formatting elements =========== -->

<!-- Citation (italics) -->
<!ELEMENT CITE %horiz.model;>
```

```
<!ATTLIST CITE
        %basic;>

<!-- Source code (monowidth) -->
<!ELEMENT CODE %horiz.model;>
<!ATTLIST CODE
        %basic;>

<!--Terms being defined (normal) -->
<!ELEMENT DFN %horiz.model;>
<!ATTLIST DFN
        %basic;>

<!--Emphasis (italics) -->
<!ELEMENT EM %horiz.model;>
<!ATTLIST EM
        %basic;>

<!--Keyboard input -->
<!ELEMENT KBD %horiz.model;>
<!ATTLIST KBD
        %basic;>

<!-- Sample output text (monowidth) -->
<!ELEMENT SAMP %horiz.model;>
<!ATTLIST SAMP
        %basic;>

<!-- Strong emphasis (boldface) -->
<!ELEMENT STRONG %horiz.model;>
<!ATTLIST STRONG
        %basic;>

<!-- Variable names (italics) -->
<!ELEMENT VAR %horiz.model;>
<!ATTLIST VAR
        %basic;>
```

```
<!-- Abbreviations (normal) -->
<!ELEMENT ABBR %horiz.model;>
<!ATTLIST ABBR
        %basic;>


<!-- Acronyms (normal) -->
<!ELEMENT ACRONYM %horiz.model;>
<!ATTLIST ACRONYM
        %basic;>


<!-- Text importance (change of size) -->
<!ELEMENT BIG %horiz.model;>
<!ATTLIST BIG
        %basic;>


<!ELEMENT SMALL %horiz.model;>
<!ATTLIST SMALL
        %basic;>


<!-- Hypertext anchors.
        CONSTRAINT: A elements are not allowed inside
        other A elements, a fact that XML cannot express. -->
<!ELEMENT A %horiz.model;>
<!ATTLIST A
        %basic;
        href CDATA #IMPLIED
        name CDATA #IMPLIED
        rel CDATA #IMPLIED
        title CDATA #IMPLIED>


<!-- Mandatory line breaks -->
<!ELEMENT BR EMPTY>
<!ATTLIST BR
        %all;>


<!-- Spans of text with changes in basic attributes -->
<!ELEMENT SPAN %horiz.model;>
<!ATTLIST SPAN
```

```
        %basic;>


<!-- Arbitrary embedded XML (not HTML-compatible yet) -->
<!ELEMENT XML ANY>
<!ATTLIST XML
        %basic;>



<!-- ========== Headers =========== -->

<!ENTITY % align        "align (left|center|right) #IMPLIED">

<!ELEMENT H1 %horiz.model;>
<!ATTLIST H1
        %align;
        %basic;>


<!ELEMENT H2 %horiz.model;>
<!ATTLIST H2
        %align;
        %basic;>


<!ELEMENT H3 %horiz.model;>
<!ATTLIST H3
        %align;
        %basic;>



<!-- ========== Lists =========== -->

<!ENTITY % compact "compact (compact) #IMPLIED">

<!-- Definition list -->
<!ELEMENT DL (DT|DD)+>
<!ATTLIST DL
        %compact;
        %basic;>
```

```
<!-- Defined term -->
<!ELEMENT DT %horiz.model;>
<!ATTLIST DT
        %basic;>


<!-- Definition -->
<!ELEMENT DD %vert.model;>
<!ATTLIST DD
        %basic;>


<!-- Ordered list -->
<!ELEMENT OL (LI)+>
<!ATTLIST OL
        %compact;
        %basic;
        start NMTOKEN #IMPLIED
        type (l|a|A|i|I) #IMPLIED>


<!-- Unordered list -->
<!ELEMENT UL (LI)+>
<!ATTLIST UL
        %compact;
        %basic;>


<!-- Directory (minimal) list -->
<!ELEMENT DIR (LI)+>
<!ATTLIST DIR
        %basic;>


<!-- List element -->
<!ELEMENT LI %vert.model;>
<!ATTLIST LI
        %basic;>



<!-- =========== Other vertical elements =========== -->


<!-- Address block -->
```

```
<!ELEMENT ADDRESS (%horiz; | P)*>
<!ATTLIST ADDRESS
        %basic;>


<!-- Block quotation -->
<!ELEMENT BLOCKQUOTE %struct.model;>
<!ATTLIST BLOCKQUOTE
        %basic;>


<!-- General text division -->
<!ELEMENT DIV %struct.model;>
<!ATTLIST DIV
        %align;
        %basic;>


<!-- Horizontal rule -->
<!ELEMENT HR EMPTY>
<!ATTLIST HR
        %all;>


<!-- Paragraph -->
<!ELEMENT P %horiz.model;>
<!ATTLIST P
        %basic;>


<!-- Preformatted text -->
<!ELEMENT PRE %horiz.model;>
<!ATTLIST PRE
        %basic;
        width NMTOKEN #IMPLIED>


<!-- ========== Standard XML and HTML entities ========== -->
<!--

<!ENTITY % XMLlat1 PUBLIC
   "-//XML-DEV List//ENTITIES Latin1//EN"
   "XMLlat1.ent">
 %XMLlat1;
```

```
<!ENTITY % XMLsymbol PUBLIC
   "-//XML-DEV List//ENTITIES Symbols//EN"
   "XMLsymbol.ent">
%XMLsymbol;

<!ENTITY % XMLspecial PUBLIC
   "-//XML-DEV List//ENTITIES Special//EN"
   "XMLspecial.ent">
%XMLspecial;
-->


<!-- =========== END OF ibtwsh.dtd =========== -->
```

To see just how an XML parser will process these many parameter entities, we will take an example element, the DIV element. The declaration for DIV reads as follows:

```
<!-- General text division -->
<!ELEMENT DIV %struct.model;>
<!ATTLIST DIV
        %align;
        %basic;>
```

The parser first needs to expand the %struct.model; parameter entitity in the DIV element declaration, yielding:

```
<!ELEMENT DIV  (%struct;)*>
```

The %struct; parameter entity will then be expanded to:

```
<!ELEMENT DIV  (%vert; | %headers; | ADDRESS)*>
```

Then the %vert; and %headers; parameter entities need to be expanded, yielding:

```
<!ELEMENT DIV  (%horiz; | %blocks; | %lists; | H1 | H2 | H3 | ADDRESS)*>
```

Now the %horiz;, %blocks; and %lists; parameter entities need expansion.

```
<!ELEMENT DIV  (#PCDATA | %local; | A | BR | SPAN | %ibtwsh.include; |
BLOCKQUOTE | DIV | HR | P | PRE | DL | UL | OL | DIR | H1 | H2 | H3 |
ADDRESS)*>
```

Finally, to complete the process, the %local; and the %ibtwsh.include parameter entities must be expanded:

```
<!ELEMENT DIV (#PCDATA | CITE | CODE | DFN | EM | BIG | SMALL
| KBD | SAMP | STRONG | VAR | ABBR | ACRONYM | A | BR | SPAN |
XML | BLOCKQUOTE | DIV | HR | P | PRE | DL | UL | OL | DIR | H1 |
H2 | H3 | ADDRESS)*>
```

These multiple layers eventually resolve into a single enormous mixed content declaration, which can be managed easily by modifying the modules that constitute it. The attribute declarations expand similarly. The original declaration read:

```
<!ATTLIST DIV
        %align;
        %basic;>
```

After the first pass of entity expansion, it looks like:

```
<!ATTLIST DIV
        align (left|center|right) #IMPLIED
        %all; %i18n;>
```

The second pass expands the %all; and %i18n; parameter entities to yield the final:

```
<!ATTLIST DIV
        align (left|center|right) #IMPLIED
        id ID #IMPLIED
        class CDATA #IMPLIED
        style CDATA #IMPLIED
        lang CDATA #IMPLIED
        dir (ltr|rtl) 'ltr'>
```

Apart from making most declarations much shorter, these entities make it much simpler to modify the IBTWSH DTD and provide for new functionality. New attributes can be added to every element in an instant, and content models can be controlled for entire classes of elements rather than requiring the DTD author to modify every single element individually. Parsers take care of the expansion, allowing the DTD author to focus on underlying structures and data modeling rather than the care and feeding of an enormous textual representation of a document structure.

Conditional Sections: **INCLUDE** and **IGNORE**

Developers who want to use the same DTD for multiple applications but need to make some changes for particular usages will find the INCLUDE and IGNORE conditional sections very handy. INCLUDE and IGNORE may only be used in DTDs, not inside documents, and are most useful for situations where the default values of a set of attributes needs to change or where one type of document uses a slightly different structure.

The syntax for INCLUDE and IGNORE sections is much like that for CDATA sections:

```
<![INCLUDE[ completeDeclarations ]]>
<![IGNORE[ completeDeclarations ]]>
```

The information contained inside the INCLUDE or IGNORE section must be complete declarations; INCLUDE and IGNORE may not be used in the middle of a declaration. The content of the section may be a single declaration, a list of declarations, or even the inclusion of external resources.

By themselves, INCLUDE and IGNORE are fairly useless tools. INCLUDE is what DTDs will normally do with declarations, while IGNORE just hides declarations from the parser. Combined with parameter entities, however, INCLUDE and IGNORE provide developers with some powerful options for applying the same DTD to multiple situations, allowing the document itself to specify the situation via a parameter entity declaration (or set of declarations) in the internal subset.

INCLUDE and IGNORE can be used to provide information providing additional structure for a document, giving a DTD extra flexibility for situations that need it. For example, an inventory of a set of computer equipment might include a lot of similar information, like manufacturer, serial numbers, primary user, and location. On the other hand, monitors, computers, and network cards all have very different specifics. A computer might hold memory, while a monitor's most important characteristics are its size and whether it supports color. An Ethernet network card needs the MAC address (unique to every Ethernet card) kept on file. A developer might create a separate DTD for each of these items, or could create a monster DTD that left many components optional, but creating a modular DTD and allowing the document to specify which modules it is using seems more appropriate in this case. The documents will then be required to contain the information for their type, without having to worry about the other types, and remaining easily processed as a group rather than diverging.

A very simple DTD for this kind of implementation follows:

```
<!ELEMENT UNIT (MANUFACTURER, SERIAL, LOCATION, PURCHASE,
DEVICE)>
...
<![%MONITOR[
<!ELEMENT DEVICE (SCREENSIZE, COLOR)>
<!ELEMENT SCREENSIZE (#PCDATA)>
<!ELEMENT COLOR (#PCDATA)>
]]>
<![%CPU[
<!ELEMENT DEVICE (PROCESSOR, RAM, HD)>
<!ELEMENT PROCESSOR (#PCDATA)>
<!ELEMENT RAM (#PCDATA)>
<!ELEMENT HD (#PCDATA)>
]]>
<![%NETWORKCARD[
<!ELEMENT DEVICE (MEDIA, MAC)>
<!ELEMENT MEDIA (#PCDATA)>
<!ELEMENT MAC (#PCDATA)>
]]>
```

Documents that use this DTD must specify the entity declaration for their type of device. For instance, a monitor document might begin:

```
<?xml version="1.0"?>
<!DOCTYPE UNIT [
<!ENTITY % MONITOR "INCLUDE">
<!ENTITY % CPU "IGNORE">
<!ENTITY % NETWORKCARD "IGNORE">
<! ENTITY % unit.dtd "unit.dtd">
%unit.dtd
]>
```

The document would then have to include a DEVICE element with SCREENSIZE and COLOR sub-elements.

WARNING

You must declare the parameter entities before including the external DTD document. Otherwise the parser will be unable to validate your document and will come to a grinding halt.

INCLUDE and IGNORE are also typically used for version control. A document that indicates its version may be able to use features that have been discontinued in newer versions. Similarly, a single parameter entity can be used to control whether a document uses the full version of a DTD or just a subset.

EXTERNAL UNPARSED ENTITIES

External unparsed entities are perhaps the clearest evidence that XML's origins lie in the document management world of SGML and not the Web-based world of HTML. Unparsed entities are a tool for including binary data (typically, though not always, multimedia) into XML documents. In some ways, the use of external unparsed entities is much like the use of the IMG tag in HTML, but in other ways it is quite different.

All unparsed entities must be external, and the declaration for an unparsed entity looks very much like that for an external entity. The only difference is the addition of the NDATA keyword and a notation identifier that provides the application with a description of the unparsed entity's file type:

<!ENTITY **entityName** SYSTEM "**entityContentURI**" NDATA **notation**>

or:

<!ENTITY **entityName** PUBLIC "**PublicIdentifier**" "**entityContentURI**" NDATA **notation**>

Note that there are no quotes around the notation identifier.

NOTE Notation declarations are not required in well-formed documents, but must be provided for a document to be validated and may provide useful information to the application even if validation does not take place. For more information about notation declarations, see the previous chapter.

Unlike parsed entities, unparsed entities may not be included in a document using the simple &entityname; syntax. Instead, applications should reference the name of the entity in an attribute, and the parser should notify the application that a reference to an external unparsed entity has been made.

The entity declaration below declares an unparsed entity which happens to be a GIF image:

```
<!ENTITY CaesarPic "http://www.simonstl.com/latin/pics/caesar1.gif" NDATA
    gif>
```

To use that image later, the author would create an element that used the entity name as an attribute:

```
<IMG PIC="CaesarPic"/>
```

The PIC attribute should be declared of type ENTITY or ENTITIES for this to work in a fully-validated document. In a well-formed document, the application will most likely have to watch for the reference itself. Validating processors are required to notify applications when such references occur. Non-validating processors cannot do this. Unless it processes the attribute declaration structure, a parser has no way to tell whether the value of an attribute is an entity reference or an ordinary string of text, and is technically required to report it as CDATA (character data). Because unparsed entities are fairly complex creatures, requiring notation and attribute declarations to work fully, developers should probably avoid using them in documents intended for non-validating processors or if they do not have complete control over the application. Developers who do have complete control can provide the application with the intelligence about attributes that the non-validating parser lacks.

For example, to define the IMG element properly, so that the parser will know to inform the application of the unparsed entity, the following declarations should be used.

```
<!ELEMENT IMG EMPTY>
<!ATTLIST IMG
    PIC ENTITY #REQUIRED >
```

The IMG element's PIC attribute must now correspond to an unparsed entity declared in the DTD, most likely one declared in the internal subset. The notation does not need to be declared again, though it could be provided in a separate attribute, as shown below.

```
<!ATTLIST IMG
    TYPE NOTATION (GIF | JPG) "GIF">
```

This might be useful for processing that needs to take place in both validating and non-validating environments.

NOTE

Unparsed entities may become less of an issue as the XLink standard matures. See Chapter 10 for more details on this friendlier and more powerful tool for dealing with included content.

STYLES: PRESENTING INFORMATION

XML development encourages the use of tags that describe the content of elements rather than instructions for how to present them. This makes it difficult for browsers and applications to guess how best to display them. In HTML, every element had formatting expectations built into it; while browsers sometimes rendered different tags differently, the overall trend has been toward a fairly consistent set of formats. HTML had a reasonably small, mostly fixed vocabulary, while XML opens up a nearly infinite vocabulary. XML documents still need to be displayed in many situations, however, so the formatting information (the style) needs to be provided. XML documents can reference style sheets, documents which provide the formatting information needed to render documents.

XML has access to two main paths of style sheet development. The more stable of the two, Cascading Style Sheets (CSS), was originally developed for HTML documents, while the newer and more powerful Extensible Style Language (XSL) is focused only on XML. (Its roots lie in the SGML world as well.) Style sheets have had a fairly slow adoption on the Web, though more and more sites are using them as a supplement to the HTML's basic formatting. In this scenario, style sheets provide designers with another tool for creating consistent-looking and highly-formatted documents. In an XML scenario, style sheets become the primary tool for crafting document appearance, allowing designers to provide formatting information for all of the elements in their documents, not just supplemental information that rides on top of an HTML vocabulary's formatting. This chapter will explore both CSS and XSL—CSS as a lightweight tool that is stable, though not yet available for XML, and XSL as the power tool of the future.

NOTE

Because no commercial browser is currently capable of displaying XML with style sheets, none of the applications in this book actually uses style sheets. The Implications section at the end of this chapter will, however, explore how style sheets and browsers may fit into XML development strategies in the very near future.

WARNING

The CSS material described in these chapters has made it through the W3C process to W3C Recommendation status, (see **http://www.w3.org/pub/WWW/ TR/REC-CSS1** for CSS1 and **http://www.w3.org/TR/REC-CSS2/** for CSS2) but implementations of CSS in browsers vary widely even for HTML documents, and do not yet work for XML documents. XSL is still very much under development, and the discussion is based on the first working draft of XSL (**http://www.w3.org/TR/1998/WD-xsl-19980818.html**). XSL will undoubtedly change in many aspects before its final version, which may be a long time arriving. The latest version of the XSL draft is available at **http://www.w3.org/TR/WD-xsl**.

BASIC CONCEPTS

Most of the XML development we have looked at so far has been about describing data in terms that allow it to be reused, not in terms that make it look pretty on a screen. Since its earliest days, HTML has been bedeviled by its combination of formatting information (think <B>, or worse, <FONT>) with structural information. HTML began as a simple set of elements for describing document structures (scientific papers being one of the early targets) and evolved into a complex set of tools for creating graphically compelling (sometimes, anyway) Web pages and sites. The TABLE element, for instance, transformed from a tool for displaying rows and columns of data into a nearly indispensable part of the graphic designer's page layout tool kit. As the development of HTML began to grow more and more complex because of the needs of developers interesting primarily in formatting and presentation, the W3C made a strategic move to create an alternative syntax better suited to the needs of presentation that could layer on top of HTML. Style sheets, initially expressed as Cascading Style Sheets Level 1 and then Level 2, allow designers to specify precisely how a group of elements or a single element should be presented. Designers can specify color, position, padding, font, and hundreds of other aspects of presentation in a document that can then be reused with other HTML documents. By separating formatting from document content, designers can focus on presentation templates, rather than having to handcraft content.

The style sheet model has been used in a number of contexts, from What-You-See-Is-What-You-Get (WYSIWYG) word processors to SGML. SGML spawned a large number of tools for converting SGML documents to presentation formats, the most successful of which (at least the most openly standardized) is the Document Style and Semantics Specification Language (DSSSL) and its lighter-weight counterpart, DSSSL-O. Many of the SGML style applications were transformations, converting the SGML document into another format that was then viewed through a different application. Adding this step to HTML might have fragmented the browser model, and certainly would have complicated HTML's simple model of directly viewable files. Cascading Style Sheets were defined more simply, as supplements to the formatting information already contained in HTML documents, rather than a transformation to a different format. XSL, on the other hand, is a descendant of the DSSSL line of style sheets, and focuses on creating "result trees" with particular formatting information included. These two approaches have significantly different powers and learning curves, and will be explored below.

CONNECTING STYLE SHEETS TO DOCUMENTS

Before we explore the two kinds of style sheets, a brief discussion of how style sheets can be connected to documents is worthwhile. Both XSL and CSS support styles internal and external to a document, expressed either as an attribute or set of attributes or in separate files. In general, the preferred practice is to use separate files, because they are more easily managed, modified, and maintained, and changes to the separate style sheet will be reflected in all the documents that use it. A processing instruction is used to connect documents to their style sheets, appearing before the root element of the document (i.e., before rendering has begun). This PI, mentioned briefly in Chapter 5, takes the general format:

```
<?xml-stylesheet href="stylesheetURL" rel="stylesheet"
                 type="stylesheetMIMEtype"?>
```

An XML document that referred to a CSS style sheet might look like:

```
<?xml version="1.0" encoding="UTF-8"?>
<?xml-stylesheet href="mystyle.css" rel="stylesheet" type="text/css"?>
<!DOCTYPE mydoc SYSTEM "mydoc.DTD">
<mydoc>
...content...
</mydoc>
```

The same document, referring to an XSL spreadsheet instead, might look like:

```
<?xml version="1.0" encoding="UTF-8"?>
<?xml-stylesheet href="mystyle.xsl" rel="stylesheet" type="text/xsl"?>
<!DOCTYPE mydoc SYSTEM "mydoc.DTD">
<mydoc>
...content...
</mydoc>
```

Because XML has no fixed vocabulary, the HTML standbys of META, LINK, and STYLE are not available. Processing instructions avoid the need to modify DTDs to access styles.

THE CSS MODEL

The Cascading Style Sheets model is the "light" model, less capable in some ways than XSL but much less difficult to develop and design. For many applications, CSS is appropriate, though browser implementations at this point vary, to say the least. CSS comes in two "levels" so far, CSS Level 1 and CSS Level 2. CSS Level 2 extended the capabilities provided in CSS Level 1, though there were a few semantic changes (described in Appendix B of the CSS Level 2 specification). Both specifications provide a set of tools that allow designers to prescribe the appearance of elements within a viewer, and allow those prescriptions to appear inside a document or externally, as a separate style sheet document.

NOTE Cascading Style Sheets are among the most approachable of all the W3C's specifications. Both the content and the language of the specification are intended to be used and read by designers, developers, and people from other backgrounds. Investigate the specifications themselves (at **http://www.w3.org/TR/REC-CSS2/**) for more detail on the many options available for formatting documents. In this case, the specifications themselves are the best tutorial, though additional books are also available.

Microsoft was first out of the gate with CSS1 support, providing partial support in Internet Explorer 3.0 and much fuller support in Internet Explorer 4.0. Netscape Navigator and Communicator provided CSS support beginning with version 4.0. These implementations are not perfectly compatible, even among browsers with the same version number from the same vendor on different platforms. (Opera, the third browser in the arena, is promising complete CSS support shortly.) CSS1 support has been spotty in all of the browsers, complicating developers' lives and requiring extensive cross-browser testing of HTML documents. CSS2 support is supposed to arrive in the version 5.0 browsers of both Netscape and Microsoft. None of the browsers currently available supports the use of CSS with XML documents, though experimental Mozilla (the organization working on Netscape's open-code next versions of its browser) builds are available from **http://www.mozilla.org**.

NOTE For a clear table detailing which browsers support which aspects of CSS, see **http://webreview.com/wr/pub/guides/style/mastergrid.html**.

The "Cascade" in Cascading Style Sheets deserves some explanation. Documents may refer to multiple style sheets, both those refered to by documents and (ideally, someday) those specified by viewers. In general, the first style sheet referred to can be overridden by later style sheets, with the STYLE attribute of an element (if it has one, typically in HTML) overriding everything else. This means that a designer could build a style sheet for a corporation, different divisions could add to or override portions of the style sheet, departments within the divisions could customize further, and users could customize yet further. (Corporate design policy will need to be enforced; however, CSS is not a tool for such enforcement. Customized browsers and editors could provide such enforcement.)

Cascading Style Sheets describe how an existing document tree is to be presented, without making any changes to the structure or content of that tree. Cascading

Style Sheets are built with selectors and properties. Selectors identify the elements to be styled (and may be omitted if style information is included as an attribute of the element to be styled), while properties describe the formatting that should be done. Selectors describe a portion of the document tree (a single element, a group of elements, or a nested structure). Selectors may be an element name, a list of element names separated by commas (allowing multiple elements to share the same properties), a list of element names separated by white space (describing a nested structure), a reference to an ID attribute, or a reference to another attribute. Table 8.1 illustrates many of the possibilities for XML documents.

Table 8.1 CSS 2 Selectors

Selector	Meaning
* (asterisk)	Matches all elements
elementName	Matches all elements with the name elementName
elementName1 elementName2	Matches all elementName2 elements nested anywhere underneath elementName1 elements.
elementName1, elementName2[, elementName3...]	Matches all elementName1 and elementName2 elements and possibly additional listed elements.
elementName1>elementName2	Matches all elementName2 elements nested directly underneath elementName1 elements.
elementName:first-child	Matches elementName elements when they are the first child of their parent element.
elementName:link	Matches elementName elements when they are links that have not yet been visited.
elementName:visited	Matches elementName elements when they are links that have been visited.
elementName:active elementName:hover elementName:focus	Matches elementName elements when the user is interacting with them in certain ways.
elementName:lang(language)	Matches elementName elements when they are of language language. This may work with the xml:lang attribute.
elementName1+elementName2	Matches elementName2 elements when they directly follow (and are adjacent to in the document tree) elementName1 elements.

Selector	Meaning
elementName[attName]	Matches elementName elements when they have a value for the attribute attName.
elementName[attName="attValue"]	Matches elementName elements when they have the value attValue for the attribute attName.
elementName[attName~="attValue"]	Matches elementName elements when the value attValue is contained in a list (separated by white space) in the attribute attName.
elementName[attName|="attValue"]	Matches elementName elements when their attName attribute begins with attValue followed by a hyphen.
elementName#IDvalue	Matches elementName elements when they contain an ID-type attribute whose value is IDvalue.

Properties describe the formatting that should be done to the portion of the document tree identified by the selector. In CSS2, properties may contain counters, which help number lists and other document components, but for the most part properties are static. Cascading Style Sheets (like HTML and XML, to some extent) are really descriptions, not programs. Properties and their values use a simple syntax:

property:value

Multiple properties for the same selector may be listed sequentially, separated by semicolons. For example:

HEADER {display:block; font-size:18pt; font-weight:bold; color:blue; font-family:sans-serif}

This declaration would tell the browser (or other viewer or editor) to display the contents of the HEADER element as a separate block, in 18-point sans-serif bold type, in blue, something like:

This is the HEADER element content.

All HEADER elements in the document would be rendered like this.

Table 8.2 provides a selected listing of Cascading Style Sheets 2 properties that may be appropriate to XML documents. Because XML by itself carries no formatting information, many more of these properties will need to be set explicitly than were needed in HTML.

Table 8.2   Selected CSS Properties for Screen and Print Presentations and their Meanings

Property:	Notes:
background	sets all the background properties at once
background-attachment	specifies whether the background scrolls or remains fixed (scroll, fixed, inherit)
background-color	background color of an element
background-image	background image URL of an element
background-repeat	whether the background should repeat. (repeat, repeat-x, repeat-y, no-repeat, inherit)
border	sets all border values for an element at once
border-bottom-color	sets color value for bottom border.
border-bottom-style	none by default; may also be dotted, dashed, solid, double, groove, ridge, inset, outset
border-bottom-width	may be thin, medium, thick, or an explicit measurement
border-left-color	takes color value for left border
border-left-style	see borderBottomStyle
border-left-width	see borderBottomWidth
border-right-color	takes color value for right border
border-right-style	see borderBottomStyle
border-right-width	see borderBottomWidth
border-top-color	takes color value for top border
border-top-style	see borderBottomStyle
border-top-width	see borderBottomWidth
clear	specifies if floating images are allowed on the sides of an object; may be none, left, right, both, or inherit.
color	takes color value for foreground of element
direction	identifies the direction text should flow. May be ltr (left-to-right), rtl (right-to-left), or inherit

Property:	Notes:
display	sets the way an object is displayed by the browser. May be block, inline, listItem, none, run-in, compact, marker, table, inline-table, table-row-group, table-header-group, table-footer-group, table-row, table-column-group, table-column, table-cell, table-caption, or inherit. Typically used values include none, which makes objects disappear; block, which makes objects start a new paragraph; inline, which keeps the element in the same flow; and listItem, which makes the element a list item member.
font	sets all font values for an element at once
font-family	sets the font or font family for an element; serif and sans-serif are common
font-size	sets the font size for an element. May use small, medium, or large as well as point sizes.
font-style	sets the font to normal, italic, or oblique
font-variant	sets the font to normal or small-caps
font-weight	sets the font to a weight from 100 to 900 (if supported), or to normal, bold, bolder, or lighter
height	specifies the height of the element in pixels
left	specifies the position of the left edge of the element in pixels from the left edge of the window.
letter-spacing	permits specifying additional spacing between letters and text.
line-height	specifies distance between text baselines; may be normal, number to multiply by point size, absolute measurement, or percentage
list-style-image	takes a URL, none, or inherit. Allows display of an image as bullet.
list-style-position	takes inside, outside, or inherit. Specifies where the bullet should appear in bulleted lists.
list-style-type	identifies the type of list. Typically used with the values disk, circle, square, decimal, or inherit.
margin	sets all margin values for an element at once

continued on next page

Property:	Notes:
margin-bottom	specifies empty space below element's bottom margin
margin-left	specifies empty space next to element's left margin
margin-right	specifies empty space next to element's right margin
margin-top	specifies empty space above element's top margin
overflow	declares what to do if an element's contents are too large for height and width. May be visible, scroll, hidden, goto or inherit.
page	takes an identifier or auto (the default). Used to identify new pages for printing.
page-break-after	allows elements to specify when page breaks (in printouts) should appear before their appearance. Takes the values auto, always, avoid, left, right, and inherit.
page-break-before	allows elements to specify when page breaks (in printouts) should appear after their appearance. Takes the values auto, always, avoid, left, right, and inherit.
page-break-inside	provides a "keep with next" option. Takes the values avoid, auto, and inherit.
text-align	identifies text alignment. may be left, right, center, or justify
text-decoration	may be none, underline, overline, line-through, or blink
text-indent	may be a measurement or percentage; indents the first line
text-transform	none is default; may also be capitalize, uppercase, lowercase, or inherit
top	specifies the position of the top edge in pixels from the top edge of the window. May also be auto or inherit.
vertical-align	may be baseline (default), sub, super, top, text-top, middle, bottom, text-bottom, or a percentage or length above the baseline
visibility	whether or not to render an object transparently. Values are inherit, collapse, visible, and hidden.
width	specifies width of an image in pixels.
word-spacing	allows designers to specify the spacing between words. May be a length, normal, or inherit.
z-index	Integer specifying layer of a positioned graphic; lower values are "behind" hight values.

Cascading Style Sheets level 2 is adequate for describing most of the rendering needed to create HTML documents. As an exercise to demonstrate what a CSS style sheet for XML looks like, Listing 8.1 shows a style sheet to present the IBTWSH DTD (which was presented in Chapter 7) in viewers with no built-in understanding of the HTML DTD.

Listing 8.1   A CSS Style Sheet for IBTWSH

```
*[dir="ltr"] {direction:ltr}
*[dir="rtl"] {direction:ltr }
* {font-size:12pt; font-family:serif}
CITE {display:inline; font-style:italic}
CODE {display:inline; font-family:monospace}
DFN {display:inline; font-style:italic}
EM {display:inline; font-style:italic}
KBD {display:inline; font-family:monospace}
SAMP {display:inline; font-family:monospace}
STRONG {display:inline; font-weight:bold}
VAR {display:inline; font-style:italic}
ABBR {display:inline}
ACRONYM {display:inline}
BIG {display:inline; font-size:16pt}
SMALL {display:inline; font-size:9pt}

A {display:inline}
BR:before {content:"\A"} /*From CSS2 spec*/
SPAN {display:inline}
XML {display:none}

H1 {display:block; font-size:24pt; font-weight:bold}
H2 {display:block; font-size:18pt; font-weight:bold}
H3 {display:block; font-size:16pt; font-weight:bold}

DL {display:block}
DT {display:block}
DD {display:block; margin-left:40px}

OL {display:block; margin-left:40px; list-style-type:decimal; list-style-
```

```
position:outside}
OL[compact] {list-style-position:inside}
OL[type="a"] {list-style-type:lower-alpha}
OL[type="A"] {list-style-type:upper-alpha}
OL[type="i"] {list-style-type:lower-roman}
OL[type="I"] {list-style-type:upper-roman}

UL {display:block; margin-left:40px; list-style-position:outside}
UL[compact] {list-style-position:inside}

LI {display:list-item}

DIR {display:block}

ADDRESS {display:block; font-style:italic}

BLOCKQUOTE {display:block; margin-left:40px; margin-right:40px}

DIV {display:block;}

HR {display:block; border:1px inset}

P {display:block}

PRE {display:block; font-family:monospace; white-space:pre}
```

Most of the formatting above is fairly readable, though some pieces deserve further discussion. The first two elements allow the dir attribute to define whether text is displayed from right to left or left to right, providing some internationalization support. The use of display properties is recommended for every element; viewers have no way of understanding even the most basic information about elements. By default, all elements will be rendered inline. Blocks and lists need special handling. The BR and HR elements are always difficult, especially since BR is really a line break, not a typical element. A CSS pseudo-element (the :before) and the content property allow BR to function in this environment, while HR is simply a block element with an inset border. The OL list element gets special attention to support the different number and lettering schemes that can be specified with the type attribute.

NOTE A complete CSS style sheet for HTML 4.0, written with a different approach, is provided in Appendix A of the CSS specification, available at **http://www.w3.org/TR/REC-CSS2/**.

THE XSL MODEL

XSL is a heavyweight style sheet language under development at the W3C. More a descendant of DSSSL, the heavyweight formatting language of the SGML world, than a cousin of CSS, XSL provides two key services in its package: formatting and transformation. Unlike CSS, which only describes how to format the existing document tree, XSL also allows developers to describe transformations of the document tree. XSL focuses squarely on XML documents; unlike CSS, it provides no support for "legacy" HTML. Also unlike CSS, XSL uses XML document instance syntax to represent its information. An XSL style sheet is actually an XML document, simplifying processing.

NOTE XSL is much less defined at this point than CSS, and has at least three more drafts to go through before approaching the recommendation phase. The first W3C draft is extremely incomplete. This discussion will remain fairly general as a result.

While it may seem like a bit much for the W3C to sponsor two very different style initiatives simultaneously, the initiatives have different objectives. As the XSL page at the W3C (**http://www.w3.org/Style/XSL/**) states:

> XSL is intended for complex formatting where the content of the document might be displayed in multiple places; for example the text of a heading might also appear in a dynamically generated table of contents. CSS is intended for dynamic formatting of online documents for multiple media; its strictly declarative nature limits its capabilities but also makes it efficient and easy to generate and modify in the content-generation workflow. So they are two different tools; for some tasks, CSS is the appropriate choice and for some tasks, XSL. They can also be used together—use XSL on the server to condense or customize some XML data into a simpler XML document, then use CSS to style it on the client.

> XSL uses a XML notation, CSS uses its own. In CSS, the formatting object tree is almost the same as the source tree, and inheritance of formatting properties is on the source tree. In XSL, the formatting object tree can be radically different from the source tree, and inheritance of formatting properties is on the formatting object tree.

XSL performs two different functions in its presentation of a styled XML document. First it performs a transformation of the original XML document (the "source tree"), creating a remodeled result tree. Once the result tree is built, rules for formatting the result tree are applied to create a presentation. An XSL style sheet contains template rules, which are themselves composed of patterns (for matching elements in the document) and which then provide a template to which the pattern can be transformed. (Template rule processing may be supplemented with ECMAScript—JavaScript—as it was in the original NOTE, but whether this will appear in a W3C draft or recommendation is unclear.) The results of template rule processing become the result tree. After the transformation, style rules may be applied. Like template rules, style rules describe structures, but style rules describe the way in which those structures should be presented rather than matching them to templates for transformations. Style rules use objects and properties similar to those in CSS, but there are many differences yet to be worked out. The transformation and formatting stages take place separately, and are both optional. A style sheet may specify a transformation only (to the HTML vocabulary, for example) or only a set of formatting instructions that should be applied to the original document without a transformation (much like CSS).

The transformation features make possible an enormous number of applications that CSS cannot support (though those transformations might also be supported through other processing models, like CGI or scripted manipulation of a document through the Document Object Model). By providing a combination of transformation and formatting, XSL ensures that documents whose requirements demand transformations have those facilities available. Whether these features need to be linked tightly is a matter of debate (see the XSL mailing list archives at **http://www.mulberrytech.com/xsl/xsl-list/archive** for further details), but they do provide a guaranteed level of service to applications that might need these facilities.

Transformations are useful in a number of situations where simple sets of information (like those returned by a database query) need to be formatted in a complex way repeatedly. Rather than feeding the database output through a program that generates a complete document, the database output, noting its need for a style sheet, can be sent to an XSL processor, on either another server or on the client, as appropriate. The XSL processor will produce a full document structure based on the style sheet, and then format it accordingly. Any situation where document structures need to change for presentation, or where document structures and presentation are sharply divorced from each other, can benefit from this approach.

XSL's transformations are capable of providing many of the services that CGI, servlets, Active Server Pages, and other technologies currently provide, and may eventually (with browser support) provide transformation support on the client. Figure 8.1 shows the current state of transformation technology on the Web: data sources which feed into a server based program, which transforms it into formatted information for presentation in a browser.

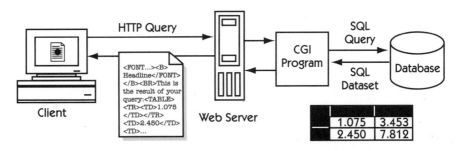

Figure 8.1 Transformations in the HTML Web environment

XSL provides a more generic and more structure way of performing such transformations, as well as a formatting model for the results of that transformation. Figure 8.2 shows what server-side XSL transformations could look like in an HTTP environment, while Figure 8.3 shows an XSL client architecture.

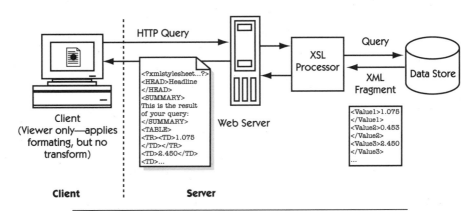

Figure 8.2 Transformations in a server-side XSL Web environment

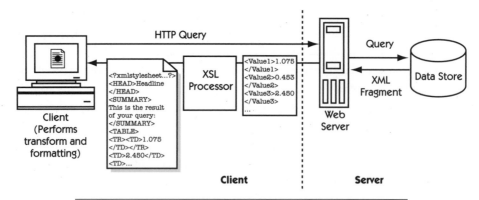

Figure 8.3 Transformations in a client-side XSL Web environment

Ultimately, XSL may make its greatest mark as a tool for enabling client applications to perform transformations, freeing ever more burdened server resources to support more clients and perform new types of processing.

NOTE An enormous amount of XSL information, including tutorials, processors, and products, is available from Robin Cover's SGML and XML site at **http://www.oasis-open.org/cover/xsl.html**. For a listing of XSL software, see **http://www.xmlsoftware.com/xsl/**.

CSS AND XSL?

The potential for conflict between these two presentation standards has a lot of developers pondering their next moves. XSL offers more power, eventually, in the form of a powerful tool for transformations. CSS has the advantage of an installed base. CSS1, however broken, in all of those 4.0 browsers has given it a clear head start, and Netscape, Microsoft, and Opera all promise further CSS support. Microsoft is providing expanded CSS support in FrontPage 2000, and other vendors and developers are getting aboard the bandwagon.

If CSS and XSL are to avoid a duel, some form of coexistence or cooperation will be necessary. XSL already borrows some portions of its vocabulary from CSS, though the XSL working group has not so far been willing to adopt the CSS models for representing documents. Several of the editors of the CSS spec have begun examining what CSS expressed in XML syntax would look like (**http://www.w3.org/ TR/NOTE-XSL-and-CSS.html**), a first step toward combining the existing formatting capabilities of CSS with the transformation tools of XSL.

If CSS and XSL do not come to some form of accommodation, the conse-
quences for XML could be significant. XML is already weighed down by an over-
dose of acronyms, and competing style standards could make this worse. Documents created for one system will not work in tools that require the other, and
building both systems into software could prove prohibitively expensive. XML has
benefited greatly by the availability of free parsers, and XSL or CSS could benefit
similarly from free rendering software. CSS has already has some free rendering
software—in HTML browsers—but until that software base becomes XML-compatible, there is not a large gain. Commercial browsers are great windows, but not
very useful as a development platform on which other programs can build. An
extensible XML/CSS or XML/XSL parser/viewer could change that whole picture, though.

IMPLICATIONS

Styles are a key part of any generic XML application. All the applications in this
book are first-generation applications, custom-building interfaces to display and
process XML documents. Second-generation applications will need to be able to
build on tools with more capacity than parsers, tools which provide support for
interfaces as well as raw data. XML was originally designed to be a part of the Web
infrastructure that has become a key component of thousands of client-server applications around the world, but at present it is limited to relatively bit parts. Making
XML ubiquitous will require a way to display XML information quickly and easily,
without the need to write a separate program for every application. While XML
may survive as an interchange format, operating behind the scenes without every
appearing on users' screens as a styled display, providing formatting services for
XML documents opens up enormous new vistas for development. Client-side formatting tools would allow developers to send XML data to clients with less overhead on the server, while server-side tools will allow them to transmit information
stored in XML to clients without XML display facilities.

Styles can provide XML with a far stronger infrastructure on which developers
can build applications. While "display XML" may not sound enticing to Web developers yet, the potential is enormous. Put simply, the problem with the current system is that XML can provide both interchange and (with the aid of CSS or XSL)
presentation; HTML can only provide presentation. When you send an HTML
document, for the most part, you are sending a pretty picture that is unusable for
anything else. By sending XML, you offer your readers much more than presenta-

tion. HTML is impoverished by comparison. It is a real loss to send presentation-only documents when you could be sending "real" information plus presentation for the same cost. A Web site is an expensive project to support when it provides users only pretty pages to look at. XML, with the aid of style sheets, provides the same pretty pages plus usable (to a computer and a human) information at the same cost, if generic XML support is built into the browsers or other Web-enabled applications.

The key word here, which styles promise more support for, is generic. The cost of developing XML applications now, using the techniques described in this book, remains high. Building projects with XML at present requires significant programming expertise, and would require considerably more expertise if free parsers and APIs were not already available. Building XML applications in an environment where XML viewers use style sheets and XML editors combine document and style creation will not require the same level of programming expertise. Generic tools hold the promise of cost reduction that XML needs to make good on the promises of a "lightweight" SGML. It should not matter to a tool whether the DTD it is processing describes neutrinos or the shipping instructions for a million hamburgers. At present, the tools for parsing can cope with this. The tools for presentation have not yet caught up, and are holding XML back.

The applications at the end of this book provide a variety of custom-built interfaces to XML documents. Most of them present information to humans in some visual form. While some of them would still be necessary in an environment that supported more generic XML, some of the smaller ones could be built at lower cost using simple editors, style sheets, and browser-like interfaces. (In the next edition of this book, we hope to be able to show how to do that, in detail, rather than having to custom-build programs for each application.) A more generic architecture would still rely on some of the components used here—XML document type definitions, XML documents, network transport for XML documents—but the direct contact with parsers would only be needed to custom-build extensions to an existing architecture. Making that architecture extensible, as well as a means to display documents, will take a great deal of development and reconsideration of the entire browser interface, converting a mostly-passive viewing tool into a more directly interactive means of collecting, sorting, storing, and reusing information.

What will these applications look like? For the most part, they combine the current infrastructures of the Web with more powerful clients—extended browsers and, once XML becomes a more common transfer format, improved search engines. The current Web model for information transfer is shown in Figure 8.4.

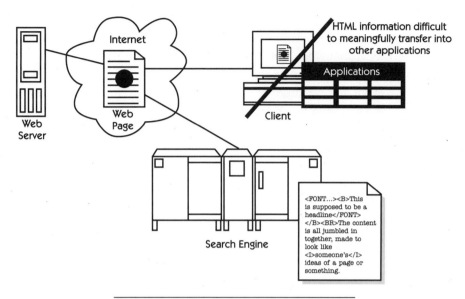

Figure 8.4 HTML transfers on the Web in 1998

Note that the HTML documents have to be treated as large chunks of text, with only a few pointers to provide search engines with clues about the landscape and no easy way (besides cutting and pasting) to move information to other applications.

Figure 8.5 shows a similar model that replaces HTML with XML for everyday document transfer, using CSS or XSL to present that information to the user.

The XML document looks the same on the user's screen, but underneath is a newly rich bed of reusable information that identifies itself and its structure through the use of tags. Search engines can finally get a clear vision of the information they are indexing, and other applications can connect to the browser (or other HTTP interface) to collect and reuse XML information.

An alternative that avoids this support for direct XML display has been put forward by a number of vendors and requested by a number of working groups at the W3C. XML in HTML is not yet a standard, though some implementation like it will be required to incorporate standards like MathML, RDF, and SMIL into the fabric of HTML. The XML in HTML meeting report (**http://www.w3.org/ TR/NOTE-xh**) of the W3C is a good place to start investigating this; Microsoft's "data islands" (**http://www.microsoft.com/xml/authoring/dataIslands/ dataIslandhowto.htm**) are another example of a possible approach. The contrast between the two documents is intriguing: the W3C document refers to "real-world HTML" as "crud", while the Microsoft data island description begins by claiming that "There is an increasing need to be able to embed "islands" of data inside HTML pages." This approach, shown in Figure 8.6, provides a halfway house, avoiding the need to apply styles to XML documents (though why this is any more difficult than providing the existing support for DIV and SPAN element is unclear), while still making it possible for applications and search engines to do something with the information in the "islands".

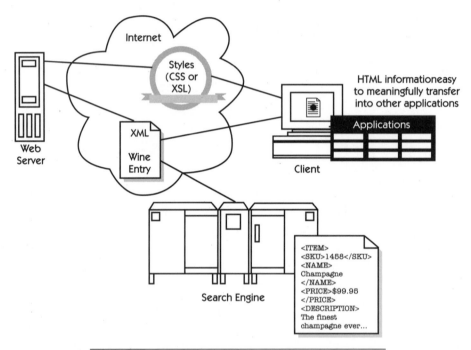

Figure 8.5   XML/style transfers on the Web—coming soon

While this approach is workable for many applications, the great question is why the "crud" is necessary when the style tools needed to replace it are already defined, and simply waiting implementation. Duplication of information between the "islands" and the "crud" is both an efficiency problem and a maintenance problem, especially if the "crud" is effectively custom-built programs used to display the information in the islands.

Styles promise a way out of both the "crud" and the need to develop and maintain custom applications. By making it possible to provide users with material that is both attractive *and* easily reused, they are a key part of the drive to make XML ubiquitous and activate much of its potential. In their current, largely unimplemented state, styles remain a tool of considerable promise but little immediate applicability.

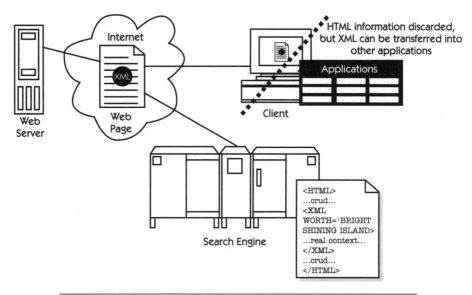

Figure 8.6   XML in HTML transfers—glittering "islands" amid the "crud"

NAMESPACES:
A BRIEF INTRODUCTION

Namespaces are newcomers to the XML scene, a tool with no previous use in the SGML world. They first appear in XML Working Group minutes (see **http://www13.w3.org/ XML/9712-reports.html**) in June 1997, after being proposed by Andrew Layman in March. The Working Group added the colon to the list of characters that may be used in XML element and attribute names, with the provision that it "will be reserved for experimentation with name spaces and schema scoping". When the namespace draft made its first appearance in March 1998, controversies immediately erupted over what namespaces were for, with some people mistakenly thinking they were to be used to achieve goals like inheritance. The Namespaces proposal (which is still very much under development and extremely unstable, as of September 1998) is designed with only one purpose in mind: to provide universal identifiers for XML element and attribute names.

THE PROBLEM OF NAMES

There is no one true DTD that provides a structure encompassing all known needs. The world of documents is fragmented: oil companies do not need elements like SHOESIZE and NUTRITIONINFORMATION, while archivists do not need BARRELS. On the other hand, lots of situations will call for PRICE, and not always in the same context. While industries may standardize DTDs, making these DTDs work together in larger and mixed contexts is difficult. Names may overlap, causing errors as parsers encounter the same element declaration twice and redeclaring attributes for the wrong element. Identifying the DTD that is the "source" of an element is rarely helpful, unless perhaps all the DTDs are declared with public identifiers.(Public identifiers should at least be unique and consistent.) Even if the processor can tell with which DTD a particular element fits, mixing the DTDs will be complicated or disastrous. Most of the time, these problems are purely academic, a crisis yet to happen.

Programmers developing solutions that only require a single namespace, typically only referencing a single DTD, are unlikely to encounter these problems. As standards defining document structures for different areas proliferate, however, more and more applications are likely to reference multiple standards. A books and multimedia site might, for instance, reference an industry-standard DTD for book information and a different one for multimedia. When the user explores the shopping cart, name conflicts could potentially become disastrous. Similarly, electronic ordering tools that process orders for mixed batches of goods could become confused, potentially shipping the wrong goods or charging the wrong amount because of a misunderstanding. If and when XML achieves ubiquity, these problems will creep in on a regular basis.

TRANSFORMATIONS AS SOLUTION

In the past, mostly SGML experience, transformations were a common solution to this problem. Tools known as architectural forms provided information about how to convert an element and its information from one DTD to another. Complex transformations could be driven based on the values of attributes built using a simple vocabulary indicating what should be transformed to what. Architectural forms are quite elegant, providing DTD designers with a powerful set of tools for specifying transformations from one model to another. On the other hand, architectural forms are a fairly heavy-duty tool, useful in situations where two DTDs need to be melded together, but excessive for small situations where elements from multiple vocabularies need to come together.

NOTE

For more information on architectural forms and their intricacies, see David Megginson's book "Structuring XML Documents" or his Web site, **http://www.megginson.com**, which contains a SAX implementation of architectural forms.

Namespaces as Solution

The Namespace proposal takes a different approach, requiring some work that is more bookkeeping than transformation. Globally unique names already exist, in the forms of domain names and URLs. The W3C, for instance, uses **w3.org** to identify itself on the Internet. By prefixing elements and attributes with unique URLs, developers can be assured that their elements and attributes have unique names, avoiding collisions with structures created by other developers. (Similar strategies are used in the naming of Java packages, for instance.) Because adding URLs to the beginning of element and attribute names would be ugly at best (and requires the use of characters which may not appear in legal XML element names), the Namespaces proposal uses prefixes to represent the URL.

NOTE

Remember, unique element names are needed in addition to unique DTDs. The reason that using the URL of the DTD in which the element is defined could not work by itself is that it is not always clear which DTD's description of an element is appropriate when names overlap. It is perfectly acceptable, though not required (at all) for the namespace identifier to point to the DTD, if the developer wants to do it that way. Just remember, not everyone's DTDs will be at the location identified by the namespace, so do not ever rely on this to work.)

The Namespaces proposals have gone through a number of drafts. Until August 1998, the drafts (most recently, **http://www.w3.org/TR/1998/WD-xml-**

names-19980518) recommended using a processing instruction crafted for the purpose of connecting a prefix to a URL, generally in a form like:

```
<?xml:namespace ns="URL" prefix="prefix"?>
```

All elements that used a namespace were then required to use a prefix at the beginning of the element name, separated from the rest of the element name. The following code fragment presents an example:

```
<?xml:namespace ns="http://simonstl.com" prefix="ssl"?>
<ssl:simple>This is an element that uses a namespace referring to
http://simonstl.com.</ssl:simple>
```

Because the prefix is only a marker, a stand-in, for the true identifier behind the namespace, conflicts between namespaces can be avoided by having one or the other sets of elements change its prefix. The "resolved" namespaces will still be correct, uniquely identifying each element with its proper home.

NOTE Remember, the URL used by the namespace does not need to point to anything. There is no requirement that a DTD or even a description of the namespace be at that location. It is used purely as a unique identifier.

This has created significant issue for validation. While changing the prefix might avoid namespace collisions in document instances, it would also explode validation with parsers that were not aware of namespaces, including all the SGML parsers in existence. It also requires that every document instance identify the namespaces to which its prefixes belong (if it used namespaces, of course), which could become a rather significant burden, even if eased through the use of external entities containing the relevant processing instructions.

The latest edition of the Namespaces draft (**http://www.w3.org/TR/1998/ WD-xml-names-19980802.html; August 2, 1998**) takes a different approach to namespace handling, providing an option that does not always require the use of prefixes, but does require that attributes for identifying namespaces (which all begin with xmlns) be built into DTDs for namespaces to be used. Namespaces are declared through attributes, rather than through a processing instruction, as shown below:

```
<elementName xmlns:prefix="identifier">
```

The name of the attribute identifies the prefix used for the namespace, while the value of the attribute contains the unique identifier (a URI typically a URL) used for the namespace. Using the attribute xmlns all by itself, with no trailing colon or prefix, defines the default namespace, which will be used for all elements that don't have a prefix. The namespaces identified by the attributes apply to the element in which they appear and to any subelements, unless new namespace declarations for the same prefixes override them. (This requires namespace-aware parsers to build a stack during the parse to keep track of which namespace prefixes apply to which elements.) The majority of namespace declarations will probably appear in the root element of the document, keeping management simple, but may appear at any time in the document.

The way this works in practice is fairly simple, though it sounds complex. The example below defines and uses three namespaces.

```
<?xml version="1.0"?>
<COMPLEXFRAGMENT xmlns="http://simonstl.com/"
xmlns:ssl="http://simonstl.com/"
xmlns:netscape="http://www.netscape.com/"
xmlns:ms="http://www.microsoft.com">
<MYOWNELEMENT>
<netscape:LAYER>This is a Netscape-specific element</netscape:LAYER>
<ms:CDF>This is a Microsoft-specific element</ms:CDF>
</MYOWNELEMENT>
<ssl:MYSECONDELEMENT/>
</COMPLEXFRAGMENT>
```

The default namespace (used by COMPLEXFRAGMENT and MYOWNELE-MENT) is 'http://simonstl.com/'. The netscape:LAYER element uses the 'http://www.netscape.com' namespace, while the ms:CDF element uses the 'http://www.microsoft.com' namespace. The last element, ssl:MYSECONDELE-MENT, is actually in the same namespace as COMPLEXFRAGMENT and MYOWNELEMENT, because its prefix resolves to the same namespace as the default namespace. (The same namespace may be declared multiple times with different prefixes.)

The main problem with this scheme, though it is perhaps lessened by the addition of a default namespace, is that the XML 1.0 (and SGML) validation process has no understanding of the namespaces underlying the prefix. Changing or adding a prefix to an element name will still break validation, though the newer scheme at least makes conflict resolution somewhat easier. There are a number of other issues to be addressed with regard to validation. Because the attribute name includes the prefix name, the prefix needs to be declared within the DTD. This can be addressed by adding an attribute declaration in the internal subset, but it is still inelegant. Perhaps the most difficult problem with the new specification is that DTDs remain completely unaware of the namespaces they are describing. The new schemas discussed at the end of Chapter 6 are starting to address this, creating namespace-aware tools for defining document structures.

On the bright side, this mechanism makes it very easy for DTDs to define their namespaces with default (or even fixed) values for the namespace attributes, and removes the need for the large scale use of prefixes that was needed with the processing instruction proposal. DTDs can include other DTDs easily, and their namespace information will come along with them, smoothly and transparently. A separate mechanism will still be needed to support namespace resolution, but (provided the prefixes do not need to change) at least the information is centralized instead of being repeated in multiple document instances.

Remember, namespaces are experimental at present and are likely to stay that way for a while. Until the W3C gives its formal blessing to a specification, be ready for (possibly drastic) change. The MSXML parser and the parsers from Sun provide namespace support, but how stable this will prove is unknown at best.

10

XPointers:
Referencing Fragments

The clearly marked structures of XML provide more than easy parsing. They make possible consistent referencing of fragments of documents based on the element structure. Referencing fragments may seem like an odd and unusual task, but it makes an enormous number of things possible, from more sophisticated linking to embedding and annotation of documents. The next chapter will explore some of the tools for using these fragments; this chapter will explain the tools for identifying fragments, and briefly consider what access to fragments may mean for the larger picture of XML processing.

The XPointer standard is not yet a W3C recommendation or even a proposed recommendation. This discussion is based on the 3 March 1998 Working Draft, available at **http://www.w3.org/TR/1998/WD-xptr-19980303**. The latest version will be available at **http://www.w3.org/TR/WD-xptr**. The XPointer spec has been delayed, in large part, by the namespace specifications described in the previous chapter. This chapter's discussion is effectively pre-namespace, and subject to change, but it should provide a basic understanding of a critical component of XML application architectures.

BASIC CONCEPTS

XPointers are intended to be used in concert with Uniform Resource Identifiers (URIs), which are a superset of Uniform Resource Locators (the familiar URLs). While URIs have served the HTML world well, they have very limited tools for making references *inside* a document. XPointers support the current tools for making those references (the HTML #*anchor* mechanism), and go well beyond them, allowing developers and authors to identify any section of a document without having to add explicit markers (like the <A NAME="*anchor*Name"> in HTML) to documents. Using the document structure itself as a reference point, XPointers will make it possible (with the support of the XLink standard, described in the next chapter) for people to add links and references to documents they don't control.

XPointers are descendants of TEI pointers, a set of tools created by the Text Encoding Initiative. For more information on these predecessors to XPointers, visit **http://www.uic.edu/orgs/tei/**.

The HTML mechanism for referencing points inside of a document is simple. Using the A element, authors can place named identifiers in their documents. Links can then reference these named identifiers, and the browser will scroll to the appropriate location in the document. For example, the HTML document below has three anchors in it.

```
<HTML>
<HEAD><TITLE>Sample Document with Anchors</TITLE></HEAD>
<BODY>
<H1>Anchors away!</H1>
```

```
<P><A HREF="#location1">Visit Location No.1</A></P>
<P><A HREF="#location2">Visit Location No.2</A></P>
<P><A HREF="#location3">Visit Location No.3</A></P>
<P>blah...blah...blah...</P>
<P><A NAME="location1">Location 1</A></P>
<P>blah...blah...blah...</P>
<P><A NAME="location2">Location 2</A></P>
<P>blah...blah...blah...</P>
<P><A NAME="location3">Location 3</A></P>
<P>blah...blah...blah...</P>
</BODY>
```

Clicking on the link "Visit Location No.1" should make the browser scroll down to the A element whose NAME attribute is "location1" because of the "#location1" description in the initial A element. Similarly, the Location No.2 link should scroll the browser window down to the A element whose NAME attribute is "location2" and the same goes for Location No.3. These kinds of internal document links have been used to some successful effect in HTML, making it easier for users to reference information in long documents quickly. They require the browser to load the document (if it is not the current document) and parse the document until it finds the NAME attribute matching the fragment identifier. Then the browser should display that element and its surrounding context.

This older model is fully supported by the XPointer proposal, and supplemented, with other tools for marking locations in a document and with ways to reference documents without having to make any modifications to the document itself. This latter task is critical for the XLink standard, which XPointer supports, and allows authors and editors to create sophisticated links quite easily. (Like the fragment identifiers in HTML, XPointers are typically appended to URIs, in the format *URI#XPointer*, where the URI identifies the document and the XPointer the fragment of that document needed). By providing a new and still fairly simple way to identify precisely subsections of a document, XPointers make an entirely new generation of tools possible.

NOTE

XPointers receive most of their use in the XLink standard described in the next chapter. This chapter will only cover the syntax of the XPointers themselves; usage of XPointers will be described in the next chapter.

Most of the XPointer location terms describe elements in terms of their location on the element tree of a document, either in absolute terms, by reference to the position of the element containing the link, by reference to the value of an attribute, or by reference to element content. For convenience, all XPointer examples in this chapter will reference the same document, shown below in Listing 10.1, using all of these different methods to reference different portions of the document.

Listing 10.1   The Sample XPointer Target Document

```
<?xml version="1.0" encoding="UTF-8"?>
<DOCUMENT SECURITY="Why bother?">
<TITLE>XPointer Demonstration Document</TITLE>
<AUTHOR>
<FIRST>Johnny</FIRST>
<LAST>Appleseed</LAST>
</AUTHOR>.
<SUMMARY>This document is just a dart board for XPointers. Different
    XPointers will land different places on it.</SUMMARY>
<PARAGRAPH id="main">Building documents that can be referenced with
    XPointers requires very little effort. There are some picky issues, like the
    need to declare attributes of type ID to use the id() term reliably, but overall
    it's pretty simple. Other document authors can reference the document by its
    structures, but giving them some IDs to hang on would be pretty polite. Other
    authors can use XPointers to reference your document for:</PARAGRAPH>
<LIST id="possibilities" category="links">
<LISTITEM><A NAME="Inclusion">Inclusion in their documents</A>
    </LISTITEM>
<LISTITEM><A NAME="Linking">Links from their documents</A>
    </LISTITEM>
<LISTITEM><A NAME="Annotation">Links from your document to their
    document for annotation</A></LISTITEM>
<LISTITEM><A NAME="FragmentReference">Reference your document as
    fragments, avoiding the need to download the whole thing.</LISTITEM>
</LIST>
<PARAGRAPH id="link">All of these possibilities are described in the <A
    HREF="chap11.xml"next chapter</A> or you can go read <A HREF=
    "#origin().ancestor(1,#element)">this paragraph again.</A></PARAGRAPH>
</DOCUMENT>
```

XPOINTER SYNTAX

XPointers are composed of location terms, which may be strung together and separated by periods. Location terms are separated in to absolute location terms, relative location terms, and other location terms. Absolute location terms may be used only at the beginning of an XPointer, and all other location terms used may not be absolute. By default, if the first term in an XPointer is not absolute, an implicit root( ) location term is used. This means that:

    child(1,#element).(4,#element)

is the equivalent of:

    root().child(1,#element).child(4,#element)

If the location term in an argument is missing (i.e., only the arguments appear), the keyword that was used immediately before it is assumed. For example:

    id(myelement).child(2,#element).(3,#element)

is the equivalent of:

    id(myelement).child(2,#element).child(3,#element)

When you create XPointers, you are navigating among your document structures. Elements are considered nodes in the XPointer vocabulary, used as signposts and guides. XPointers identify a path through the nodes to the desired fragment. There may be multiple paths to the same information. Creating good XPointers is often a matter of choosing the most efficient path through a document.

ABSOLUTE LOCATION TERMS

Absolute locations reference fixed locations in a document and are often used as starting points from which relative locations can build. Remember: absolute locations must be used at the beginning of an XPointer, and may not appear after that. Absolute location terms provide a starting point on which other terms may build, though occasionally they are a clear enough reference to be used by themselves.

root()

The root location term references the root element of the document. It should rarely need to be written out, as it is the default absolute location term used if none is specified. If it is written out, it takes no arguments—the parentheses are required but should remain empty.

The root( ) location for the sample document references the DOCUMENT element and its contents.

origin( )

The origin( ) location term only has meaning in the context of a link. Like root( ), it takes no arguments; the parentheses are required, but blank. origin( ) typically serves as a way for XPointers to reference information in a long document relative to the location of the link.

·   The second A element of the last paragraph contains an XPointer that starts at the origin of the link (the A element) and then uses ancestor, a relative location term described below, to reference the PARAGRAPH element containing the origin A element.

html( )

The html( ) location term is provided for compatibility with existing HTML documents that use the <A NAME="*identifier*"> syntax. The html( ) location term takes as its argument the *identifier*, allowing it to reference elements in existing HTML documents. The id( ) location term, described below, is preferred for use with XML documents (ID attributes follow a stricter set of rules) but html( ) bridges the gap.

html("Annotation") would reference the A element inside the last LISTITEM element.

id( )

The id( ) location term allows XPointers to reference the ID attributes of XML elements to identify a location. The id( ) location has the advantage of being very precise as well as concise, but it requires that the document itself contain attributes of type ID. Documents that don't contain IDs will need to be referenced through the potentially longer relative location terms. The other problem with id( ) location terms is, as the working draft states:

> if an XML document does not declare all attributes whose values are intended to serve as unique IDs, application software cannot reliably distinguish ID attributes from others with the same string value. (3.2.3)

This may have serious repercussions for documents without DTDs, and even for documents that use DTDs but are processed by non-validating parsers. In the absence of explicit attribute declarations, it seems reasonable to rely on a consistent naming convention for attributes of type ID ('id' is a good, common choice), but it remains to be seen how this works out in practice.

Assuming either that the document above has a DTD (the declaration would need to be added, of course) which declares that the id attribute is of type ID, or that naming conventions are followed, the XPointer id(main) would refer to the first PARAGRAPH element, while id(possibilities) would refer to the LIST element, and id(link) would refer to the last PARAGRAPH element.

RELATIVE LOCATION TERMS

Relative location terms allow XPointers to reference elements by their position in the document relative to a starting point. Relative location terms provide considerably more sophisticated power than absolute location terms, and make it possible to link to (and from, as described in the next chapter) documents without the author of that document needing to provide any support for the link.

Relative location terms all take the same set of arguments, of which either two or four arguments may be used. (The last two arguments, which provide attribute constraints, are optional.) The simpler of the two versions, without attribute constraints, provides an instance identifier and a node type:

(instance, nodeType)

The instance argument allows the term to specify whether all instances (identified with all), or a specific instance (identified with a positive or negative number) is referenced. The meaning of the instance argument will vary according the which location term is used, and will be described with each term.

The nodeType argument allows the term to specify what types of nodes will be considered. The nodeType can take two kinds of values: the actual name of an element (PARAGRAPH, for instance), or one of a number of possibilities listed below in Table 10.1.

Table 10.1   XPointer Node Types

nodeType	Meaning
#element	Refers to any XML element; if nodeType is left blank, this is the default.
#pi	Refers to a processing instruction; only the string locator term can follow a locator term using this argument and still be meaningful.
#comment	Refers to a comment; as with #pi, only the string locator term can follow a locator term using this argument and still be meaningful.
#text	Refers to text content inside an element; as with #pi, only the string locator term can follow a locator term using this argument and still be meaningful.
#cdata	Refers to text content inside a CDATA section; as with #pi, only the string locator term can follow a locator term using this argument and still be meaningful.
#all	Allows nodes of all of these types; if attribute constraints (see below) are used, is equivalent to #element.

In addition to these node types, attribute constraints can be used to select nodes based on attribute values and, to a certain extent, attribute types. The syntax for argument sets that use attribute constraints is

(instance, nodeType, attName, attValue)

The attName argument may be either the name of an attribute or the asterisk (*), indicating that any attribute with the specified value will do. The attValue argument may take the values of asterisk (*), for any value; #IMPLIED, meaning that the attribute was declared using #IMPLIED as a default value and no value was provided; or the value of the attributes in quotes. Attribute constraints allow developers to take attribute values into account as well as element types and content.

child()

The child() relative location term references elements which are contained directly by the element referenced in the XPointer location terms to the left of the child() term. (Remember, if there is no prior term used, root() is used by default.) For instance, the child() location term could be used to identify the TITLE element in a number of ways. Because the default is root(), which references the DOCU-MENT element, all references start there. The first possibility references the TITLE element's name:

```
child(1,TITLE)
```

This references the first (because of the 1) element of type TITLE inside of DOC-UMENT. Because TITLE is also the first element of any type, the term below could be used:

```
child(1,#element)
```

This would reference the first child element of the DOCUMENT element.

The LIST element could be referenced several different ways with the child() term. First, it could be the first LIST child element:

```
child(1,LIST)
```

Second, it could be the only element with an attribute named "category":

```
child(1,#element,category,*)
```

Third, it could be the only element with an attribute value of 'links':

```
child(1,#element,*,'links')
```

or

```
child(1,#element,*,links)
```

(The last option is possible because the phrase "links" contains no white space or other characters that could cause problems.) All of these XPointers lead to the same element, demonstrating how easy it is to identify the same element in different ways.

WARNING

Remember that the terms of an XPointer should be chosen carefully to avoid potential conflicts if the document is modified.

descendant()

The descendant() locator term is much like the child() locator term, except that all the elements contained within the starting node may be examined, not just the elements appearing directly underneath the starting node. The descendant() term examines child elements, and their child elements, and so forth. This means that the instance variable takes on new meaning, using positive and negative values to denote different search strategies. If the value is positive, the search begins at the beginning of the element from which the search is starting, and reads down through the entire tree. If the value is negative, the search begins at the end of the element, and reads down through the tree from there.

For example, to reference the first LISTITEM element in the document, this term could be used:

```
descendant(1, LISTITEM)
```

To reference the last LISTITEM element, this term would be used:

```
descendant(-1, LISTITEM)
```

Whichever end of the element is used, this will always find nodes higher in the tree, separated from the root element by fewer levels, first.

ancestor()

The ancestor() term is sort of the reverse of the descendant() term, allowing XPointers to climb the tree from an element further down. The ancestor() term uses the instance term to determine how many matches it must find going up the tree, allowing an XPointer to find its parents, grandparents, and further ancestors. In normal use, the ancestor() term is a good way to determine the context surrounding an element. For this example, we will start with a term that identifies the second LISTITEM element in the document:

```
descendant(2,LISTITEM)
```

Now that we have reached the element, we will climb up from there to discover its context. To reach its parent (LIST) element, the declaration below will work:

```
descendant(2,LISTITEM).ancestor(1,#element)
```

The more specific declaration below could also be used and would only find ancestor elements of type LIST:

```
descendant(2,LISTITEM).ancestor(1,LIST)
```

To reach the element's "grandparent" element, the parent of LIST, the declaration below would be appropriate:

```
descendant(2,LISTITEM).ancestor(2,#element)
```

This would return the DOCUMENT element, which could also be found through:

```
descendant(2,LISTITEM).ancestor(1,DOCUMENT)
```

This declaration completes a full circle, but it might be useful if DOCUMENT were itself a sub-element of another element.

preceding()

The preceding() location term references content that appeared before the current element. (It is not of much use when that element is the root element.) Like descendant, it accepts positive and negative instance values, and uses them to determine which direction the search will proceed. If the instance value given is positive, it will count back from the element. If the instance value is negative, it will count from the root element's beginning toward the element. For example, this XPointer:

```
descendant(2,LISTITEM).preceding(1,#element)
```

references the first LISTITEM element in the document, as it is the first element preceding the second LISTITEM element. On the other hand,

```
descendant(2,LISTITEM).preceding(-1,#element)
```

references the TITLE element, as it is the first element counting in from the DOCUMENT element toward the LISTITEM element.

following()

Following() is very much like preceding(), except that it works with elements appearing after the element instead of before it. A positive instance value begins the search at the end of the element and proceeds through the document, while a negative value begins the search at the end of the document and counts back through the document toward the element. For example,

```
descendant(2,LISTITEM).following(1,#element)
```

references the third LISTITEM element in the document, as it is the first element following the second LISTITEM element. On the other hand,

```
descendant(2,LISTITEM).following(-1,#element)
```

references the last PARAGRAPH element, as it is the first element counting in from the end of the DOCUMENT element toward the LISTITEM element.

psibling()

The psibling() location term (which stands for previous sibling) is much like the preceding() location term, using postive and negative instance values similarly, except that it only searches elements that share a common parent element, not the entire document all the way back to the root. psibling() makes it possible to limit a search much more tightly, keeping it among elements that share a common parent element. For example, this XPointer:

    descendant(2,LISTITEM).psibling(1,#element)

references the first LISTITEM element in the document, as it is the first element preceding the second LISTITEM element, sharing the same parent element. On the other hand,

    descendant(2,LISTITEM).psibling(-1,#element)

references the first LISTITEM element in the document again, because only one element is between the second LISTITEM element and its parent LIST element.

fsibling()

The fsibling() location term (which stands for following sibling) is much like the following() location term, using postive and negative instance values similarly, except that it only searches elements that share a common parent element, not the entire document all the way back to the root. fsibling() also makes it possible to limit a search much more tightly, keeping it among elements that share a common parent element. For example, this XPointer:

    descendant(2,LISTITEM).fsibling(1,#element)

references the third LISTITEM element in the document, as it is the first element following the second LISTITEM element, sharing the same parent element. On the other hand,

    descendant(2,LISTITEM).fsibling(-1,#element)

references the last LISTITEM element in the document, because the XPointer processor will count back from the end of the containing LIST element.

OTHER LOCATIONS

XPointers can perform a few more miraculous feats in addition to climbing the element trees. The "other" location terms can be used to combine information from two locations, return attribute values, and select substrings from text.

span()

The span( ) location term takes two XPointers for its arguments. For example, to reference all three LISTITEM elements without referencing the parent LIST element, the following XPointer would be appropriate:

    span(descendant(1,LISTITEM),descendant(3,LISTITEM))

The span( ) term can be used to reference fragments that may not be well-formed themselves. For instance,

    span(descendant(1,TITLE),descendant(3,LISTITEM))

would be missing a root element, not to mention the closing tag for the LIST element. Applications will need to figure out a way of handling such issues, but for now, because they are only references, XPointers seem to have evaded the normal rules (those for entities) for handling document fragments.

attr()

The attr( ) term references the value of an attribute. The only argument it accepts is the name of the attribute to be referenced.

    attr(SECURITY)

Used by itself, this XPointer would return "Why bother?", the value of the SECURITY attribute for the root DOCUMENT element. This term will more typically be used in conjunction with other terms, as in:

    descendant(2,PARAGRAPH).attr(id)

This would return the id value for the second paragraph in the document, which is 'link'.

string()

The string( ) term uses a different set of four arguments to identify its target:

    string(**instance**, "**string**",**position**,**length**)

The instance argument is the same as it was for relative location terms, including the value all. The string argument is the string to be found. The position argument is an offset from the beginning of the search string to the first character that should be returned. (By default, it is one. The value end may be used as a shortcut for the length of the string argument.) The length specifies the length of the string that should be returned. For example,

```
descendant(1,SUMMARY).string(1,"dart board",end,14)
```

will reference "for XPointers." in the SUMMARY element. Similarly,

```
string(3,doc,1,4)
```

will reference "docu" from the "Other document authors" sentence in the first PARAGRAPH element. It is the third appearance of 'doc', and the term requested that four characters be returned.

IMPLICATIONS

XPointers raise an enormous number of questions for XML at the same time they solve problems for linking. The simplest, though thorniest, issues raised by XPointers are their potential for "grammatical incorrectness" in an environment that rigidly adheres to strict standards for starting and ending every single element properly. XML applications may have to do a lot of extra processing to support fragments, used for whatever purpose, that do not conform to the strict element trees expected by the rest of the XML world.

The more important issues raised by XPointers are the implications of handling fragments on a regular basis. Looking back at the file system and object storage issues raised in Chapter 3, it seems like XPointers will place new strains on old infrastructures. Re-parsing entire documents every time a user needs a fragment is inefficient, a poor use of computing resources. Especially given the potentials for difficulty raised by inherited attributes, XPointers are moving into some stormy seas. How will fragments carry attribute information they previously inherited from ancestor elements? Will processing XPointers require multiple calls to retrieve those attributes? Will XPointer processing take place on the client or on the server? As we shall see in the next chapter, the XLink standard proposes methods for processing documents in both locations.

Fortunately, the XPointer spec is only a working draft, one which appears to have a lot of development yet to come. The ability to work with document fragments will give XML a giant advantage that few of its competitors can claim, but integrating that power with the existing structures may prove difficult. Simple parts of the XPointer spec can probably be used now (the example in Chapter 19, for instance, will use the id( ) location term.) Large-scale planning, however, will be difficult until this specification's details are final.

XLink: Building Connections

Html built a new medium on a very simple foundation of formatting and linking. XML promises to take those simple links and extend them much, much further without creating too much extra complication through the XLink specification. XLink provides HTML-style links as one of its many duties, and then goes on to provide much of the power of the SGML HyTime standard to XML developers. The results are elegant, reasonably easy to use, and potentially revolutionary, dramatically expanding the field of possibilities for an interlinked Web.

WARNING

The XLink standard is not yet a W3C recommendation or even a proposed recommendation. This discussion is based on the 3 March 1998 Working Draft, available at **http://www.w3.org/TR/1998/WD-xlink-19980303**. The latest version will be available at **http://www.w3.org/TR/WD-xlink**. This chapter's contents are subject to change, but it should provide a basic understanding of a critical component of XML application architectures.

BASIC CONCEPTS

The basic HTML link is probably the best place to start. The <A HREF="*targetURI*"> syntax combined power with extreme simplicity. Creating links on the World Wide Web was a task that could be mastered in five minutes, though making sense out of the rest of HTML and the Web's supporting technologies was considerably more difficult, of course. Nonetheless, HTML—and the A tag—were simple enough to allow the World Wide Web to leapfrog a number of other technologies, including a number of SGML initiatives. Simplicity was key to adoption, and the simple linking system the A tag provides has actually held up fairly well.

The HTML links depend greatly on the behavior of the browser, as well as on supplementary navigation tools provided by the browser. When a link is clicked, the browser typically replaces the original page with that of the linked target location, unless the target attribute tells it to put the page somewhere else—a particular frame or a new window. The link appears only on the original page, not the target page, and the original page has no way to make links appear back from the target page. (The browser's "back" button typically provides a simplified form of backward navigation.) The other limitation faced by the current linking mechanism is that links may only point to a single target. The HREF attribute may only take one URI for its value, and there is no way to nest additional HREFs or refer to HREF lists outside of the document (except by redirecting the user to a menu page) without some serious scripting that is both clunky and incompatible across browsers.

Despite all of these flaws, HTML's simple linking has survived, indeed thrived. Its limits are finally coming into view, however, as more sophisticated sites need more advanced navigation and as developers concoct new programs and means of presenting information. Links that can be traversed in multiple directions can tighten the bonds between documents enormously, as well as make possible annotations and other parts of Tim Berners-Lee's original dreams for the Web. Allowing links to reference multiple target locations (accessed, perhaps, through a pop-up menu) makes it possible to give users a far more precise idea of where they're going, without turning every page into a menu. Providing behavior descriptions makes it possible to do different things with links, like embed content in a document or pop up a new window to display information. And finally, allowing links to be specified outside the linking element, indeed outside the document, makes link management much simpler by letting site managers control all of their links in a single location. Instead of having to parse hundreds of files to generate a map of their site, a single file or a small set of files is sufficient.

Making this work requires adding considerably to the vocabulary used for linking. XLink proposes to do this by adding a new set of attributes to elements and by creating a small set of dedicated elements (whose role is actually determine by attributes, allowing the elements to have any name) that can be used to specify link references outside of the resources the user will actually click on. The simple links used in HTML are still available, though they no longer require the creation of extra A elements, but an entirely new set of linking possibilities is specified by this much-expanded vocabulary. Any element can be a link; any link can reference a document or a specified location in a document, using the familiar URI syntax and the XPointers described in Chapter 10.

The URI syntax for XLink is much as it was for HTML links, with the addition of XPointers. To reference a whole document, the locator is just the URI:

```
href="http://www.simonstl.com/articles/index.xml"
```

Relative locations are still permitted, of course:

```
href="articles/index.xml"
```

The syntax for locating points in an HTML document survives to some extent, but with some variation. The separator between the URI and the location inside the document may be either # or |. # specifies that the client should download the entire document and then find the needed piece, while with |, "no intent is signaled as to what processing model is to be used for accessing the designated resource." Further drafts should elaborate on this. For now, we'll use the # separator, followed by a location identifier, as in:

```
href="articles/index.xml#id("naw")
```

A query syntax is also provided to allow processing of the location (especially if it is an XPointer) on the server, instead of requiring the client to download the entire document and then extract the needed piece. The query syntax would look like:

```
href="articles/index.xml?XML-XPTR=id('naw')"
```

The location identifier may be either an XPointer (as above) or the name of an ID value for an element in the document. These two hrefs reference the same resources as the two links above:

```
href="articles/index.xml#naw"
href="articles/index.xml?XML-XPTR=naw"
```

This combination of a URI and an optional locator for a resource inside the document at that URI is called a locator. As we shall see in the examples below, locators are useful for much more than identifying the target of a link. The sections below will examine three scenarios: simple links, which are much like HTML links; extended links, which allow a link to be traversed in multiple directions as well as provide additional behavior information; and extended link groups, which allow specification of links outside of the linked elements.

BUILDING SIMPLE LINKS

Simple links are always contained in the element that acts as the link and are always one-directional. In effect, they allow ordinary XML elements to provide somewhat enhanced linking that behaves like HTML linking, without the need for extra A elements littering the document. Simple links are created by adding attributes to XML documents, and many of those attributes can take advantage of default attribute values *if* the document will be processed in a validating environment.

NOTE

The issues discussed in Chapter 6 with regard to attribute defaults and non-validating parsers are especially important in conjunction with XLink, which relies on attribute values for much of its functionality. Defining default values in the DTD, especially an external DTD, makes using XLink much easier, but also exposes documents to the risk that these default values will not be read into the documents by non-validating parsers. For now, it is safest to use XLink only in an application that always uses a validating parser.

The first attribute that must be added to an element that is providing a simple link is the xml:link attribute. (Remember: you cannot create new attributes that start with XML or xml, but the W3C can. This usage is acceptable because it is W3C-recommended.) For simple links the value of the attribute must be "simple". This is most easily done in the DTD with a #FIXED value:

```
<!ELEMENT EASYLINK ANY>
<!ATTLIST EASYLINK
      xml:link CDATA #FIXED "simple">
```

Linking elements may have any content model. ANY is used here to keep the demonstration simple.

NOTE

The next attribute needed is inline If a link is inline, one of its ends is the element in which it is defined. If it is out-of-line, it describes links between other parts of the document and other documents. Because EASYLINK itself is the link, and it is not describing a link elsewhere in the document, inline will be "true". (True is the default, so if this declaration is missing, the link will still work.)

```
<!ELEMENT EASYLINK ANY>
<!ATTLIST EASYLINK
      xml:link CDATA #FIXED "simple"
      inline (true|false) "true">
```

Now that we have identified the type of link here, it is time to identify a target for the link. The href attribute (XML is case-sensitive, so do not use HREF) holds the locator, as shown above in the previous section. Unlike xml:link or inline, href is unlikely to have a default value, but is needed to make the link work:

```
<!ELEMENT EASYLINK ANY>
<!ATTLIST EASYLINK
      xml:link CDATA #FIXED "simple"
      inline (true|false) "true"
      href CDATA #REQUIRED>
```

At this point, we have all the information that is actually needed to create a simple link. When an XLink-aware document processor, viewer, or browser encounters this element in a document, it will highlight the contents to indicate a link and traverse the link when it is clicked on:

```
<PARAGRAPH>This is my new document. It's got a <EASYLINK
href="nowhere.html">link</EASYLINK> to nowhere in it. Isn't that
grand?</PARAGRAPH>
```

Clicking on the word "link" in this paragraph should bring you to the page 'nowhere.html', as shown below in Figure 11.1.

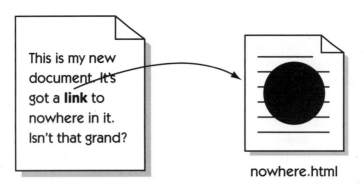

Figure 11.1   Traversing a simple link

So far, all we have really done is re-create the HTML A element with a longer and less-convenient name. XLink provides other features that make these simple links more powerful than their HTML counterparts, however, allowing the link to define semantics for both the target of the link and the origin of the link. The remote resource semantics include information for users about the destination as well as information about suggested processor behavior. The "role" of the target may be described in the role attribute (one of the examples in the spec uses "rebuttal" as a role) and the title of the link may be specified in the title attribute. Processor behavior may be defined with the show, actuate, and behavior attributes. The show attribute accepts the values "embed", "replace", and "new", telling the processor to include the target document in the original document, replace the original document with the target document, or open a new window for the target document, respectively. The actuate attribute allows the creation of links that are traversed automatically, when the document is opened (most useful with the embed value for the show attribute), or only when the user clicks on them, with the values "auto" and "user". The last attribute, "behavior", is much more open to containing any kind of behavior the author wants. As the working draft puts it, "The contents, format, and meaning of this attribute are unconstrained." Of course, this also means that applications may not understand the content of this value if the same document is used in a different environment.

The link may also provide information about the "local resource", the link, though it is less clear how useful this will be. The "content-title" attribute allows the link to provide itself with a title, and the "content-role" attribute allows the link to describe its role.

Applications can do many different things with these attributes. Users could tell the browser to ignore all links with a role other than "annotation", for instance, if they only want links relevant to annotation. Building applications around these linking mechanisms is a significant opportunity for developers who want to create new hypertext interfaces.

The declaration for a simple link with all of these attributes is shown below:

```
<!ELEMENT EASYLINK ANY>
<!ATTLIST EASYLINK
        xml:link CDATA #FIXED "simple"
        inline (true|false) "true"
        href CDATA #REQUIRED
        role CDATA #IMPLIED
        title CDATA #IMPLIED
        show (embed|replace|new) #IMPLIED
        actuate (auto|user) #IMPLIED
        behavior CDATA #IMPLIED
        content-title CDATA #IMPLIED
        content-role CDATA #IMPLIED>
```

Default values could, of course, be provided for any of these attributes, especially the show, actuate, and behavior attributes, which contribute to a consistent interface.

BUILDING EXTENDED LINKS

Extended links build on the set of attributes provided for simple links by using subelements to hold link locator information. Information describing the link as a whole is kept in the parent "extended" element, while information describing link target elements is kept in child "locator" elements. This separation breaks up the "all-in-one" approach used by simple links, creating a more flexible set of tools for linking documents.

The parent "extended" element may be either inline or out-of-line, as we shall see. For starters, we will stick to the simpler inline case. The parent element contains all of the information about this end of the link, reserving information about the target and how to process it to the locator elements. The declaration for the extended element looks like:

```
<!ELEMENT EXTLINK ANY>
<!ATTLIST EXTLINK
        xml:link CDATA #FIXED "extended"
        inline (true|false) "true"
        content-title CDATA #IMPLIED
        content-role CDATA #IMPLIED>
```

NOTE Again, linking elements may have any content model, though extended links must have a place for the locator subelements. ANY is used here to keep the demonstration simple.

The declaration for the child locator elements look like:

```
<!ELEMENT EXTLOCATOR EMPTY>
<!ATTLIST EXTLOCATOR
        xml:link CDATA #FIXED "locator"
        href CDATA #REQUIRED
        role CDATA #IMPLIED
        title CDATA #IMPLIED
        show (embed|replace|new) #IMPLIED
        actuate (auto|user) #IMPLIED
        behavior CDATA #IMPLIED>
```

This model works by nesting the locator (EXTLOCATOR, in this case) elements inside the extended link element.(EXTLINK, in this case). For example:

```
<PARAGRAPH><EXTLINK>Navigation
<EXTLOCATOR href="articles/index.xml" title="article contents" show="new"
actuate="user"/>
<EXTLOCATOR href="projects/index.xml" title="project contents"
show="new" actuate="user"/>
<EXTLOCATOR href="news/index.xml" title="news contents" show="new"
actuate="user"/>
</EXTLINK> is available</PARAGRAPH>
```

This would create an extended link between the word "Navigation" and the three pages listed. When users click the link, a little menu could pop up, asking them which of these fine pages they would like to visit. The link could be multidirectional; after users traverse this link, the Navigation button would be an option on any link menus at the targeted location. Figure 11.2 shows what might happen.

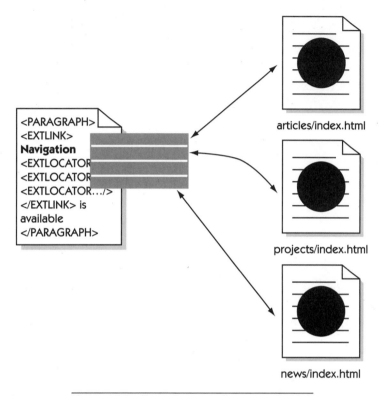

Figure 11.2   Traversing an in-line extended link

While these extended links are useful, they can rapidly become a management headache as their numbers grow. Hundreds or thousands of these links can create a maze no mapping program can display on a two-dimensional (or even three-dimensional) screen. Finding all the links in all the pages, especially when links can appear from multiple directions, becomes a powerful nightmare. To help ease this burden by allowing developers to centralize their linking information, the XLink standard includes extended out-of-line links and extended link groups. Out-of-line links allow developers to put all the links in a document in a single location (the top of the document would be convenient for rendering), while extended link groups, covered in the next section, allow documents to share these links and even put all of their links into a central document. References to linking locations must then be made with URIs and XPointers, so that the processing application can figure out where to highlight links.

The EXTLINK element above can be used to create an out-of-line extended link, because the inline attribute was defined with a non-fixed default value of true. Overriding that with "false" makes it possible to create an out-of-line link. For example, this out-of-line link would generate the same links as the inline link above:

```
<EXTLINK inline="false">
<EXTLOCATOR href="#descendant(1,PARAGRAPH).string
   (1,"Navigation",1,10)" title="Navigation link">
<EXTLOCATOR href="articles/index.xml" title="article contents" show="new"
   actuate="user"/>
<EXTLOCATOR href="projects/index.xml" title="project contents"
   show="new" actuate="user"/>
<EXTLOCATOR href="news/index.xml" title="news contents" show="new"
   actuate="user"/>
</EXTLINK>
<PARAGRAPH>Navigation is available</PARAGRAPH>
```

Although the link looks the same to the user, the mechanism involved are a little more complex, as shown in Figure 11.3.

BUILDING EXTENDED LINK GROUPS

Allowing links to work in multiple directions requires applications to remember links and causes some strange navigational difficulties. The first time you open a page, you see the set of links that are built into that page. After visiting another page, you come back to the original page. The links that were there originally are still present, but more links have appeared. After following several other links, you return to the original page and it has developed into a forest of links, often overlapping. Keeping this forest under control is a task for the site managers, but XLink provides tools that can make this pruning easier. By providing lists of the documents that should be inspected for links when a document is initially loaded, extended link groups make it possible for browsers and other applications to provide a consistent experience.

NOTE   Link groups are not always appropriate. There may well be times you want to surprise the reader with links, especially if you are writing hypertext fiction or doing something else unusual. Outside of those situations, however, extended link groups can make your life and those of your users much easier.

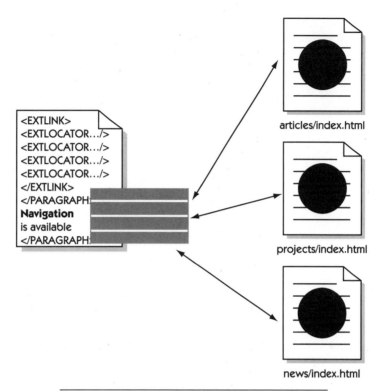

Figure 11.3   Extended out-of-line linking in practice

Extended link groups provide the application with a list of documents that should be visited to find any links (only extended links, which can be traversed in multiple directions, not simple links) that need to be marked in this document. Two elements need to be created for this functionality: a "group" element, and a "document" element. As before, these elements can be named anything; the key is that they must have a "group" or "document" value for their xml:link attribute. The group element also needs to have an attribute named steps, while the document element needs an href attribute. The steps attribute tells the application how far it should go tracking links from multiple documents. A value of 1 means that it should only check each document; a value of two means that it should check each document and any documents linked to it; a value of 3 tells it go yet another round of links, and so forth. The declarations below create a group and a document element:

```
<!ELEMENT LINKGROUP (LINKDOCUMENT+)>
<!ATTLIST LINKGROUP
        xml:link CDATA #FIXED "group"
```

```
        steps CDATA "2">
<!ELEMENT LINKDOCUMENT EMPTY>
<!ATTLIST LINKDOCUMENT
        xml:link CDATA #FIXED "document"
        href CDATA #REQUIRED>
```

NOTE   The XLink specification declares the steps attribute as #IMPLIED. It is unclear how a processor should behave if no steps value is declared, so it makes sense to provide a fairly reasonable default value that can be overridden if necessary.

These elements can now be used to create extended link groups, which tell the processor where to look for additional document links:

```
<LINKGROUP steps="2">
<!--Note that steps was optional because of the default declaration; it's still a
good idea-->
<LINKDOCUMENT href="articles/index.xml"/>
<LINKDOCUMENT href="projects/index.xml"/>
<LINKDOCUMENT href="news/index.xml"/>
</LINKGROUP>
```

This works reasonably well, telling the processor to visit these documents, but becomes annoying when a large site requires creating a large group of these for all of the documents. Creating a "hub" document can reduce this load, making it easy to add a single line to all of these documents that references the entire set:

```
<LINKGROUP steps="2"><LINKDOCUMENT href="hub.xml"/></LINKGROUP>
```

The hub document could then contain:

```
<LINKGROUP>
<LINKDOCUMENT href="articles/index.xml"/>
<LINKDOCUMENT href="projects/index.xml"/>
<LINKDOCUMENT href="news/index.xml"/>
</LINKGROUP>
```

Because the original group specified two steps, the processor would then load all of the documents listed in the hub document to extract their links. An alternate approach, which would reduce the load on the processor needing to parse all of these documents, would put all the link information (expressed as external out-of-line links) in the hub document itself. This would require some work with XPointers (id attributes might make it a bit easier) to make sure that the links all started from and pointed to the right places. The hub document might then contain all of the links directly:

```
<!--other links would precede this-->
<EXTLINK inline="false">
<EXTLOCATOR href="main.xml#descendant(1,PARAGRAPH).string
   (1,"Navigation",1,10)" title="Navigation link">
<EXTLOCATOR href="articles/index.xml" title="article contents" show="new"
   actuate="user"/>
<EXTLOCATOR href="projects/index.xml" title="project contents"
   show="new" actuate="user"/>
<EXTLOCATOR href="news/index.xml" title="news contents" show="new"
   actuate="user"/>
</EXTLINK>
<!--more links would follow this-->
```

All the documents would read all of the links for the entire set, but that might still be a lot easier than requiring to processor to parse entire documents before being able to render the first one correctly with all of its links. The Web site's structure would become much simpler, as documents came to share link documents and DTDs, as shown in Figure 11.4.

IMPLICATIONS

XLink can sound complicated, with all its features for identifying link roles and titles, multidirectional links, out-of-line links, and link groups. Programmers who lack interest in documents may have tuned out by now, wondering when the discussion will return to data-relevant information. Actually, it has not left the world of data-centric XML, though most of the examples so far have been document-centric because links are better understood in that context. XLink has an enormous amount to offer, and raises a significant number of challenges, to programmers and document authors alike.

For document linking, the advantages of XLink are fairly obvious. Having multiple targets from the same link makes it possible to create sophisticated linking systems that users can still cope with (a popup window is not too complex.) Multidirectional linking, using XPointers to indicate link points, makes it possible for those who do not have control over a document to make comments on it, visible only to those who visit the page that provides the annotation. (If you do not know I have set up links to your document, you will not have referenced my document, and my links will not appear in your document. Only when visitors read my document first will the links appear in your document.) The ability of XPointers to span multiple elements even at different levels of the element tree makes it possible to create links precisely, without fear of upsetting the boundaries demanded by the strict syntax rules of XML. If professors need to annotate the last half of a line in a play and the first half of the next line as a single unit, they can do so, even though the link they need to create begins in the middle of one element and ends in the middle of another.

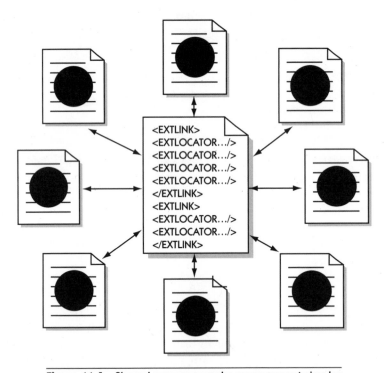

Figure 11.4   Shared resources make management simpler

The "show" and "actuate" attributes make possible some other potentially useful features. By combining the "auto" value for actuate and the "embed" value for show, authors may be able to display documents and document fragments within another document more flexibly than is possible with entities, and without having to worry about the implications for validation. The precise meaning of "embed" is uncertain; the working draft says "the designated resource should be embedded, for purposes of display or processing". It does not sound as though processing is like validation and that links could be used directly in place of entities, but this is certainly a possibility. (Using autoactuation and a replace value for show could work as a redirect, but might be very confusing.) The "new" value for show allows the creation of additional windows, which could be useful with either automatic or user actuation.

The implications of this for developers building browser-type applications are fairly dramatic. (We will see some of this in Chapter 19's sample XLink application.) Browser builders need to keep an ever-growing list of links to pages that may or may not yet have been visited, and manage that list efficiently. The issues surrounding hub documents may create some havoc—how does one render a document without knowing where the links are until an indeterminate number of documents have first been downloaded? When used in relatively simple circumstances, like those in the examples of Chapter 19, this can be handled fairly easily. In more complex scenarios, where a browser could conceivably have to download ten or more times the amount of data that would have been required for the single document, this can be ugly. Undoubtedly, caching tools (for both documents and link listings) will be important in keeping this under control, but the bandwidth and processing hits could be dramatic.

For developers building other applications that use XML, the implications may be less dramatic, but still extremely fruitful. XLink offers a powerful set of tools for describing relationships, one that fits well with data-oriented XML documents as well as more traditional documents. Using the role and content-role attributes to describe relationships, and the behavior attribute (which can, after all, be used for almost anything) developers can create a useful vocabulary for linking persistent (and even live) data between multiple data documents or objects. The Coins project (mentioned in Chapter 3, and on the Web at **http://www.jxml.com/coins**) is working in this direction, using multiple documents for different objects and connecting them with the XLink vocabulary. Once again, a document-focused XML tool has plenty of usage in more generic data-processing applications.

BUILDING XML APPLICATIONS

Now that you have a thorough grounding in XML, you are ready to start creating your own XML applications. Part III of this book provides all the essentials for building Java XML applications, including: choosing an XML parser, working with XML trees, and working with the Simple API for XML (SAX.)

Chapter 12: "Overview of Java XML Parsers" introduces you to the basic principles of XML parsers. Specifically, we will examine the major types of parsers, and examine criteria for choosing a parser. We will also briefly examine each of the major Java XML parsers, including the Ælfred XML Parser, DataChannel XML Parser (DXP), IBM's XML for Java, and Microsoft's XML Parser (MS-XML.)

In Chapter 13: "The Ælfred XML Parser", we begin in-depth survey of XML parser APIs. Ælfred has one of the simplest APIs, and is an ideal candidate for applet development. We examine the entire API, and create a half dozen example applications. Specifically, we will examine the mechanics of searching an XML document, and create an applet to display baseball player statistics and photographs.

In Chapter 14: "The Microsoft XML Parser (MS-XML)", we continue our in-depth survey of XML parser APIs. We compare and contrast the Ælfred API, and recreate many of the same applications. We also examine many of the features that are unique to MS-XML, including the ability to add, edit and delete elements from an XML document. We also examine the mechanics of remapping the internal MS-XML tree structure to your own objects and data structures.

We conclude with Chapter 15: "The Simple API for XML (SAX)". SAX represents a common interface to work with any XML parser. We therefore examine the many benefits of SAX, and provide lots of example code. Specifically, we create a sample application for reading financial stock data, and create a very simple (but extremely useful) XML browser.

By the end of the section, you will have all the basic tools to create your own XML applications. You will also have all the basic tools for following the example applets and applications outlined in Part IV.

12

OVERVIEW OF JAVA XML PARSERS

INTRODUCTION

At the heart of every XML application lies an XML parser. The parser is responsible for two very important tasks. First, it is responsible for checking the general syntax of the XML document, and alerting users to any errors. As we will soon see, some parsers are very strict, and others are more forgiving. Second, the parser is responsible for transforming a stream of XML text into manageable packets of data. The packets can then be transferred to your application, where they can be analyzed and manipulated (see Figure 12.1). As we will soon see, some parsers package data into parse trees whereas others create sequences of distinct parsing events.

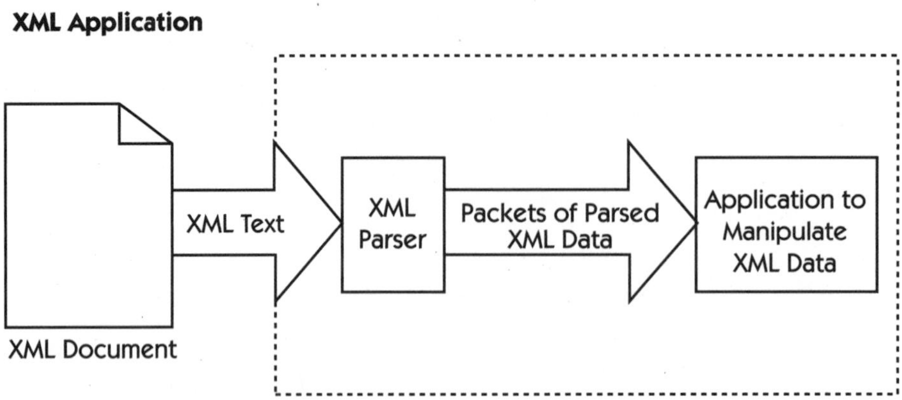

XML Application

Figure 12.1　Every XML application includes at least two pieces: an XML parser and an application to manipulate the parsed XML data. This book focuses on the right hand side of the diagram, and the tube that connects the parser to your application.

You can certainly create your own XML parser from scratch. In fact, XML was specifically designed for parsing simplicity—one of its primary design goals was to enable a reasonably competent programmer to create an XML parser in about one week. The focus of this book, however, is not building parsers, but on building XML applications. The easiest way to build an XML application is to use one of the pre-built XML parsers available on the market today.

During the past year, XML parsers have sprung up at many companies, and have proliferated over the Web. Parsers are now available in C, Tcl, Python, Perl and Java. Fortunately, most of these parsers include very liberal licensing agreements that enable users to package and redistribute the parser free. XML is, however still a relative youngster, and most parsers are only available in version 1.0.

This chapter focuses exclusively on XML parsers written in Java. This includes the Ælfred XML Parser from Microstar Software Ltd., the DataChannel XML Parser (DXP), IBM's XML for Java, and Microsoft's XML Parser (MS-XML.) It also includes parsers written by individuals, including XP, created by James Clark, the guru of SGML parsing, and Lark, created by Tim Bray, co-editor of the XML specification.

Each of these parsers claims a particular niche. The Ælfred XML Parser, for example, was designed for applet development, whereas the DataChannel DXP Parser was optimized for server-side Java. IBM's XML for Java is very strict in checking XML syntax, whereas XP is more lenient.

Different projects demand different parsers. The primary aim of this chapter therefore is to help users evaluate each of the major parsers and determine the right one for a project. To aid in the selection process, the chapter is broken into two parts. The first explains the different types of parsers. We begin by examining the difference between validating and non-validating parsers. We then explore the two primary interfaces for accessing packets of parsed data: tree-based v. event-driven interfaces. We also describe the DOM and the Simple API for XML (SAX)—two of the most important standards for XML parsing and browsing. The second part of the chapter includes individual profiles for each of the major Java XML parsers. For each parser, we examine its major characteristics and provide a short description of its major design goals.

Types of Parsers

Validating v. Non-Validating Parsers

When evaluating an XML parser, the first criterion to consider is validating v. non-validating parsers. Most beginners in XML tend to get very confused by the distinction, but it is actually very simple. A validating parser checks a document against a declared DTD. For example, it checks that the document includes all the right XML elements and that all the elements are in the right place. It also checks that the document includes all the required attributes. If the document fully follows the DTD, the document is valid. Otherwise, the parser will throw an exception, and alert you to the error. Validating parsers are required to follow the latest XML 1.0 specification.

A non-validating parser does *not* match a document against a DTD. In most cases, however, a non-validating parser will check that a document is well-formed. For example, it will check that every start tag has a corresponding end tag, and guard against any egregious nesting errors. In general, non-validating parsers tend to be smaller and simpler than validating parsers, because they do not require the overhead of error handling.

Additional information regarding the differences between validating and non-validating parsers is available in Chapters 4–7.

Tree-Based v. Event-Driven Interfaces

Tree-Based Interfaces

The second major property to consider when evaluating a parser is the interface for accessing parsed data. Currently, there are two types of interfaces on the market.

The first type is a tree-based interface. In this model, the XML parser reads in the entire XML document, and creates an internal tree representation of the data (see Figure 12.2). Your application can then traverse the tree and extract the data.

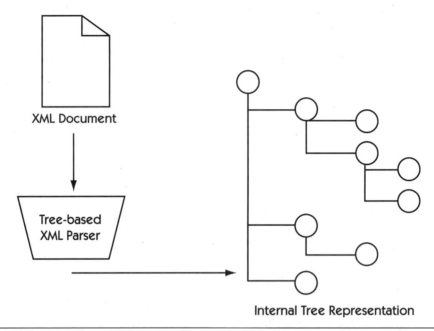

XML Document

Tree-based
XML Parser

Internal Tree Representation

Figure 12.2   A tree-based XML parser will parse the XML document and create an internal tree representation. Your application accesses the parsed XML data by traversing the tree.

To better illustrate the tree-based interface, we will look at a sample XML document. Listing 12.1 provides a sample XML document describing the structure of this chapter (for simplicity, we have not created a DTD.) Here we have defined a CHAPTER element, and within CHAPTER, we have SECTION and SUBSECTION elements. For example, within the CHAPTER element, we have three SECTION elements: Introduction, Types of Parsers, and Parser Profiles. Within the Parser Profilers section we have six SUBSECTION elements, one for each parser.

LISTING 12.1 CHAPTER.XML: SAMPLE XML DOCUMENT

This XML document describes the structure of the chapter.

```
<?xml version="1.0" encoding="UTF-8"?>
<CHAPTER>Overview of Java XML Parsers
```

```
<SECTION>Introduction</SECTION>
<SECTION>Types of Parsers
     <SUBSECTION>Validating v. Non-Validating Parsers</SUBSECTION>
     <SUBSECTION>Tree Based v. Event Driven Interfaces</SUBSECTION>
     <SUBSECTION>About the Simple API for XML (SAX)</SUBSECTION>
</SECTION>
<SECTION>Parser Profiles
     <SUBSECTION>The Ælfred XML Parser</SUBSECTION>
     <SUBSECTION>The DataChannel XML Parser (DXP)</SUBSECTION>
     <SUBSECTION>IBM XML for Java</SUBSECTION>
     <SUBSECTION>Lark</SUBSECTION>
     <SUBSECTION>The Microsoft XML Parser (MS-XML)</SUBSECTION>
     <SUBSECTION>XML Parser in Java (XP)</SUBSECTION>
</SECTION>
</CHAPTER>
```

A tree-based XML parser will read the Chapter.xml file and create an internal tree representation like that depicted in Figure 12.3. Unlike real trees, most trees in computer science grow downward. At the very top of the tree, we therefore have a root node. Descending from root, we can grow branches of nodes and data. For example, the root CHAPTER node in Figure 12.3 includes four branches of data. The first descendant is an element of type PCDATA, and includes the actual text associated with the chapter element. In computer science parlance, this node is referred to as a "leaf" node, as it has no children. The next three descendants are SECTION elements, and refer to the major sections of the chapter. In turn, each of these SECTION nodes includes its own SUBSECTION children nodes.

The tree-based interface is a very convenient structure for representing XML data. First, it contains all the data of the document, including all the tag names and attributes. Second, it directly mirrors the hierarchical structure of the document. For example, SUBSECTION nodes are nicely embedded within SECTION nodes. Third, and most important, the tree interface is conceptually easy to grasp—it just makes sense. Many people learn with visual representations, and the tree is very simple to represent. It is therefore possible to draw an XML tree, populate it with sample data, and create a program to traverse the tree and extract the most important data.

Many programmers also like the tree-based interface because they can utilize much prior computer experience. Trees are fundamental to computer science and many programmers are already quite familiar with techniques for traversing a tree. For example, you may already have experience in creating recursive functions to perform Depth First Search (DFS) or Breadth First Search (BFS.) If not, do not worry. In Chapter 7: "The Microsoft XML Parser (MS-XML)", we cover all the fundamental techniques.

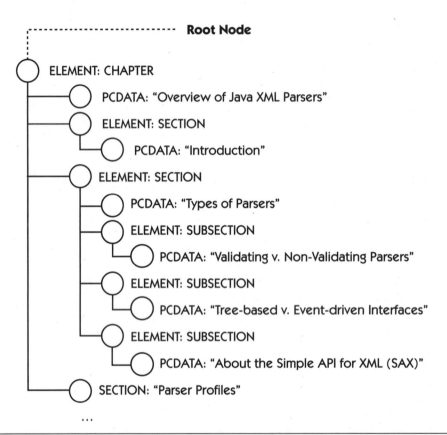

Figure 12.3 The internal tree representation of the Chapter.xml document. Technically, the XML 1.0 specification requires that the tree include a separate node for each string of white space characters. For simplicity, we have chosen to omit the white space nodes here.

ABOUT THE DOCUMENT OBJECT MODEL (DOM)

To help standardize the tree interface across different parsers and web browsers, the W3C is currently developing the DOM, which represents a platform- and language-independent interface for accessing all the elements within an HTML or XML document.

Many people have been introduced to the DOM through the use of dynamic HTML. For example, the DOM makes it possible to specify an HTML layer and dynamically modify its text or update its absolute position. Unfortunately, Microsoft and Netscape have implemented very different DOMs (thereby confusing many developers, and hindering the widespread adoption of dynamic HTML.) It therefore falls to the W3C to hammer out a middle ground between the two companies and create a document model that will work in any browser.

Currently, the W3C has created a working daft of the DOM, which includes specific interfaces for accessing and traversing the XML tree structure. At, present, however, only two parsers, IBM XML for Java, and DataChannel's DXP include support for the DOM. Neither of these parsers, however is fully compliant with the latest DOM working draft. As the DOM matures, it should provide a single standard interface for browsing an XML tree, regardless of the parser.

EVENT-DRIVEN INTERFACES

The second model for accessing parsed XML data is the event-driven interface. This model is quite different from the tree-based approach, but create a tree-based parser can be created from an event-driven interface, and vice versa.

In the event-driven model, the XML parser reads in an XML document and fires off an event for each significant parsing event (see Figure 12.4.) For example, the following XML text: <SECTION>Introduction</SECTION> generates three parsing events:

- The <SECTION> tag generates a "Start Element" event;
- The string "Introduction" generates a "Character Data" event; and
- The </SECTION> tag generates an "End Element" event.

Each piece of XML markup will generate its own events. For example, we may have a "Start of Document" event, a white space event, or a processing instruction event. The exact nature of these events vary among different parsers, but Figure 12.5 illustrates the type of events that might be generated for our Chapter.xml file.

Event-driven parsers usually require that the application developer implement an event interface. The interface includes call-back methods that are called by the parser, and enable the developer to catch the events as they occur. For example, in order to utilize the Ælfred XML parser, you must implement the XmlHandler interface. This interface includes methods, such as startDocument() and startElement() for capturing parse events.

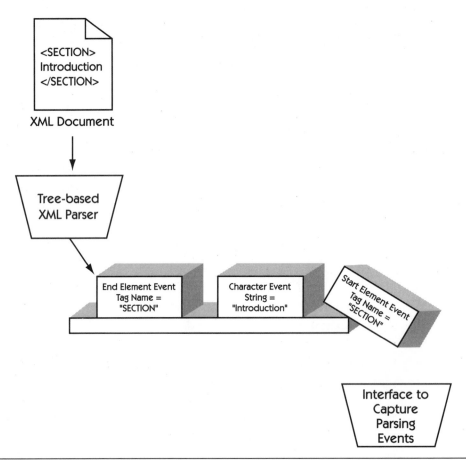

Figure 12.4   An event driver parser generates a sequence of specific parsing events. For example, <SECTION>Introduction</SECTION> generates three separate events, as depicted in the diagram. To access the parsing events, you must "catch" them as they occur.

In general, event-driven parsers tend to be faster, smaller and simpler than tree-based parsers. This is primarily due to the fact that event-driven parsers do not require the large memory and programming overhead required for the internal-tree representation. Event-driven parsers are not, however, as convenient as tree-based parsers. It is relatively easy to traverse a prebuilt tree, whereas an event-driven interface requires that you filter for every parsing event. Frequently, you are also required to capture all the parsing events, and build your own tree structure. These topics and more will be examined in the next chapter, on the Ælfred XML Parser.

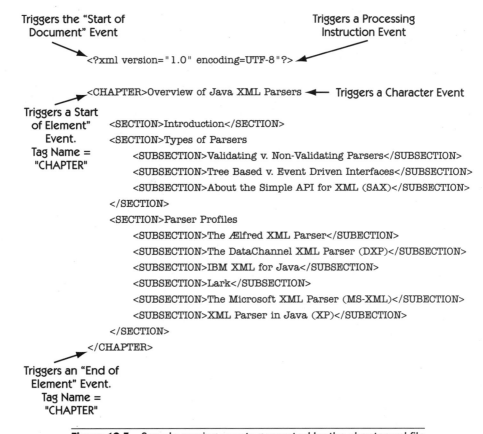

Triggers the "Start of
Document" Event

Triggers a Processing
Instruction Event

`<?xml version="1.0" encoding=UTF-8"?>`

`<CHAPTER>Overview of Java XML Parsers` ◄— Triggers a Character Event

Triggers a Start
of Element"
Event.
Tag Name =
"CHAPTER"

`<SECTION>Introduction</SECTION>`

`<SECTION>Types of Parsers`

   `<SUBSECTION>Validating v. Non-Validating Parsers</SUBSECTION>`

   `<SUBSECTION>Tree Based v. Event Driven Interfaces</SUBSECTION>`

   `<SUBSECTION>About the Simple API for XML (SAX)</SUBSECTION>`

`</SECTION>`

`<SECTION>Parser Profiles`

   `<SUBSECTION>The Ælfred XML Parser</SUBECTION>`

   `<SUBSECTION>The DataChannel XML Parser (DXP)</SUBSECTION>`

   `<SUBSECTION>IBM XML for Java</SUBSECTION>`

   `<SUBSECTION>Lark</SUBSECTION>`

   `<SUBSECTION>The Microsoft XML Parser (MS-XML)</SUBSECTION>`

   `<SUBSECTION>XML Parser in Java (XP)</SUBECTION>`

`</SECTION>`

`</CHAPTER>`

Triggers an "End of
Element" Event.
Tag Name =
"CHAPTER"

Figure 12.5 Sample parsing events generated by the chapter.xml file

ABOUT THE SIMPLE API FOR XML (SAX)

So far, we have seen tree-based and event-driven parsers. Within each of these models, however, we may also have vastly different implementations. MS-XML and IBM for Java, for example are both tree based, but each has its own interface for accessing and traversing the tree. We therefore have many XML parsers and many proprietary APIs.

Amid this din of confusion, we have the Simple API for XML (SAX). The goal of SAX is to provide one single interface that will work with all XML parsers. The easiest way to understand SAX is by way of comparison to another Java standard—Java Database Connectivity (JDBC.) JDBC enables users to connect to any SQL database and create an application which utilizes an Access database. When the user is ready to upgrade to an Oracle database, he plugs in a new driver and the application is ready to go. In much the same vein SAX enables "plug-and-play" compatibility to work with any XML parser. As we will see in Chapter 15, SAX provides this plug-and-play functionality by creating a single event driven interface that works with any parser. A user can therefore create an application to run on the Ælfred XML Parser (an event-driven parser) and substitute in MS-XML (a tree-based parser) without modifying a single line of source code.

SAX was originally developed as a collaborative enterprise of the XML-DEV mailing list community. It is therefore not an official standard of the W3C. Nonetheless, SAX has received wide industry support, and most of the major XML parsers include SAX support, or have plans to do so in the very near future.

SAX is very important because it makes programming life much simpler. You do not need to clutter your mind with all the details of a proprietary API. Rather, you can focus on a single simple API, and create most of applications in SAX. In Chapter 15, we offer a glimpse of the types of applications possible with SAX, including an XML browser written in less than 100 lines of code. Most of the example applications in Part IV are also created in SAX. Of course, there may be times when SAX is not adequate, and you may need to resort to a proprietary API. We therefore offer detailed chapters on the Ælfred XML Parser and MS-XML. If, however, you are aiming to get the most out of this book, in the shortest period of time, we suggest you jump directly to Chapter 15 to examine SAX.

PARSER PROFILES

This section includes profiles of each of the major Java XML parsers. Each profile includes the following information:

- Company Name and Web site
- Type—Indicates whether the parser is validating or non-validating
- Interfaces—Indicates the primary interface for extracting data from the parser; the interface may be specific to the product (in which case it is denoted as "proprietary"), and/or may include support for SAX or DOM.
- Java Version Compatibility—Indicates the version of Java required to use the parser; possible versions are 1.0, 1.1 and 1.2.
- Licensing agreement—A brief summary of the licensing agreement for reusing and redistributing the parser in your own commercial products
- Description—A brief description of the parser, including an overview of its major design goals.

ÆLFRED XML PARSER

Company:	Microstar Software Ltd.
Web Site:	http://www.microstar.com/XML/Aelfred/aelfred.html
Current Version:	Version 1.2a (Released May 1998)
Type:	Non-Validating
Interfaces:	Proprietary event-driven API
	Full Support for SAX 1.0
	No support for DOM
Java Version Compatibility:	Java 1.1 and higher[1]
Licensing Information:	Ælfred is free for both commercial and non-commercial use. See the Web site for the full licensing agreement.
Description:	Ælfred is a fast, compact and non-validating parser. The core Ælfred package consists of just two classes, with a total size of 26K. It is therefore the only parser specifically optimized for applet development. Ælfred was one of the first parsers to include SAX support and now includes full support for SAX 1.0.

DATACHANNEL XML PARSER (DXP)

Company:	DataChannel, Inc.
Web Site:	http://www.datachannel.com/products/ XDK/DXP/index.html
Current Version:	Version 1.0 (Released June 1998)
Type:	Validating
Interfaces:	Proprietary API
	Full Support for SAX 1.0
	Limited Support for the December 9, 1997 working draft of the DOM. Full DOM support is planned for future releases.
Java Version Compatibility:	Java 1.1 and higher

---

1 Prior to version 1.2A, Ælfred was compatible with Java 1.0 and higher. As this book goes to press, Microstar is considering an upgrade to reestablish Java 1.0 compatibility. Check the web site for details.

Licensing
Information: DXP is free for both commercial and non-commercial use. See
                    the Web site for the full licensing agreement.

Description: The DataChannel XML Parser (DXP) is a validating parser
                    based on NXP (Norbert's XML Parser.) NXP was one of the
                    first XML parsers and originally developed at the University of
                    Klagenfurt, in Austria. DXP has been designed for server side
                    Java applications, including Java servlets. Due to its complex
                    error handling capabilities and large class files, it is not a candi-
                    date for applet development. DXP provides full support for
                    SAX 1.0, and plans full DOM support in future releases.

IBM XML for Java

Company: IBM
Web Site: http://www.alphaworks.ibm.com/formula/xml
Current Version: Version 1.0 (Released June 23, 1998)
Type: Validating
Interfaces: Proprietary tree-based API
                    Full Support for SAX 1.0
                    Limited Support for the April 16, 1998 working draft of the
                    DOM. Full DOM support is planned for future releases.

Java Version
Compatibility: Java 1.1 and higher
Licensing
Information: In July, 1998, IBM updated the licensing agreement for XML
                    for Java. It is now free for both commercial and non-commer-
                    cial use. See the Web site for the full licensing agreement.

Description: IBM XML for Java is a validating parser created at IBM Tokyo,
                    and released to the public via the IBM Alphaworks web site.
                    XML for Java is an ideal candidate for standalone Java applica-
                    tions and Java servlets. Originally, IBM had a more restrictive
                    licensing agreement concerning the reuse of the parser, but has
                    since liberalized the agreement in response to developer
                    demands. The parser also provides full support for SAX 1.0,
                    and has plans for full DOM support in future releases.

LARK

Company:	Textuality Services
Web Site:	http://www.textuality.com/Lark/
Current Version:	Version 1.0
Type:	Non-validating
Interfaces:	Proprietary API
	Currently, Lark does not include native support for SAX. A third-party driver is available from the SAX home page at http://www.megginson.com/SAX/.
	No support for DOM.
Licensing Information:	Lark is free for both commercial and non-commercial use.
Description:	Lark was created by Tim Bray, co-editor of the XML Specification. According to Bray, "Lark attempts to achieve good trade-offs among compactness, completeness, and performance."

MICROSOFT XML PARSER (MS-XML)

Company:	Microsoft Corp.
Web Site:	http://www.microsoft.com/xml/
Current Version:	Version 1.8 (Released: January 16, 1998)
Type:	Validating
Interfaces:	Proprietary tree-based interface
	Currently, MS-XML does not include native support for SAX. A third-party driver is available from the SAX home page at **http://www.megginson.com/SAX/**.
	No support for DOM.
Java Version Compatibility:	Java 1.1 and higher
Licensing Information:	MS-XML is free for both commercial and non-commercial use. See the Web site for the full licensing agreement.
Description:	MS-XML is a validating parser that comes bundled with Internet Explorer 4.0. MS-XML is an ideal candidate for standalone Java applications and Java servlets. When used in conjunction with JScript in IE 4.0, it is also a viable candidate for client-side

parsing and HTML rendering. So far, it is the only major XML parser that does not include native support for SAX. A third-party driver is available from the SAX home page.

XML Parser in Java (XP)

Company:	James Clark
Web Site:	http://www.jclark.com/xml/xp/index.html
Current Version:	Version 0.3
Type:	Non-validating
Interfaces:	Proprietary API
	Full Support for SAX 1.0
	No support for DOM
Java Version Compatibility:	Java 1.1 and higher
Licensing Information:	XP is free for both commercial and non-commercial use. See the Web site for the full licensing agreement.
Description:	XP is a non-validating parser created by James Clark. Clark is also the author of EXPAT (EXtensible markup language PArser Toolkit), a high-performance, non-validating parser toolkit written in C. EXPAT is currently being used to add XML support to Netscape Navigator 5 and Perl. XP provides full support for SAX.

13

THE ÆLFRED XML PARSER

Ælfred is a small, fast, non-validating XML parser available from Microstar Software, Ltd. Unlike other parsers on the market today, Ælfred is optimized to work with Java applets. If you want to get your feet wet in XML or want to incorporate XML functionality into existing applets, Ælfred is the ideal choice. Standing in at a total size of just 26K, and capable of parsing up to 1 MB/sec, it is perhaps the most nimble of XML parsers. Best of all, Ælfred is also very simple to use, and therefore the ideal candidate to begin our in depth-survey of XML parsers.

NOTE

INSIDER'S VIEW: ABOUT MICROSTAR SOFTWARE LTD. Microstar Software Ltd. (**http://www.microstar.com**) is a Canadian-based software company which focuses on developing knowledge management software. In particular, it has a long history of providing SGML consulting to a wide range of government and financial institutions, including state governments, banks, and even the U.S. Navy. Microstar is hoping to capitalize on its expertise in SGML to become a leader in XML development. It is therefore working to create a suite of professional XML development tools. The first of these is the Near and Far Designer®, a visual tool for building SGML/XML DTDs. The second is SG/XML®, a tool for embedding XML into Active X controls.

ASSESSING ÆLFRED

According to its creator, David Megginson, Ælfred was named after Alfred the Great, King of England from 871 to 899 A.D.—hardly a reference that most American programmers are likely to understand. According to Winston Churchill, however, King Alfred was arguably the "the greatest Englishman that ever lived." His accomplishments were quite impressive: he successfully warded off invading raids by the Vikings, reformed the entire English judicial system, and presided over a flourishing of scholarly research. According to Megginson, however, his greatest accomplishment was a far-ranging and successful English literacy program. Originally, King Alfred wanted everyone to learn Latin, but was willing to settle for English. Similarly, the folks at Microstar would like everyone to learn SGML, but they are also quite willing to spread the gospel of XML. Hence, the spirit of King Alfred lives on in 26K of Java byte code.

In keeping with the aim of spreading XML literacy far and wide, Ælfred was originally designed to be small, fast, and simple to use. Its strengths are therefore quite impressive:

- **Small Class Files:** Ælfred is one of the smallest XML parsers, with a total size of 26K. As a package, Ælfred consists of only two required class files and three optional class files; it therefore requires few HTTP connections and is an ideal candidate for applet development. When packaged as a compressed Java Archive (JAR) file, the entire Ælfred package takes up a total of 15K.
- **High Performance:** There are currently no industry-wide benchmarks for measuring XML parser performance, but Ælfred can certainly hold its own

against other parsers. According to Microstar, Ælfred can parse about 1 MB/second on a Pentium 166 MHz Windows NT workstation.

■ **Free Distribution:** Ælfred is free for commercial and non-commercial use and distribution. Microstar's only stipulation is that their copyright and disclaimer remain intact.

■ **Effective Memory Management:** Ælfred provides an event-driven interface for accessing parsed data. It therefore does not have the memory overhead required for building an internal-tree representation.

■ **Support for Simple API for XML (SAX):** David Megginson is one of the original creators of SAX. Ælfred was therefore one of the first XML parsers to include full SAX support.

■ **Support for Internationalization:** Ælfred provides complete support for Unicode, and can therefore parse XML documents in most of the world's major languages. According to David Megginson, the Æ in Ælfred is actually a direct reminder of XML's support for Unicode (and, perhaps a reminder that not everyone in the world uses ASCII.)

Though it has all these attributes, Ælfred is a non-validating parser. Furthermore, Ælfred does not check that documents are well formed[1]. Hence, Ælfred works correctly on XML documents that are certifiably valid and well formed, but all bets are off on invalid or ill-formed documents. According to Megginson, adding the additional code to validate a document would have required too much code, and would have rendered Ælfred unusable in applets.

TIP

Because Ælfred is a non-validating parser, it is recommended that you use Ælfred in conjunction with a validating parser. For example, to create an applet, first ensure that the XML document is both valid and well formed:

■ First, run the XML document through the command line tool of a validating parser, such as Microsoft's MS-XML or IBM's XML for Java. Check for any errors in validity and, if necessary, modify the XML document.

■ Once the document has been approved for validity and well-formedness, it is safe for use within Ælfred.

---

1 Actually, Ælfred does perform some well-formedness checking, just not the complete suite. For the finer details, we recommend that you consult the Ælfred README documentation.

OVERVIEW OF API

THE XMLHANDLER INTERFACE

Ælfred consists of a very simple event-driven API. As we now know, an event-driven parser takes an XML document and breaks it into a series of parsing events. Each event signifies some important new piece of data, such as the start or end of the document, the start or end of an element, character data, or attribute data. The job of a developer is to create a Java class that catches these events as they occur (for a general overview of event-driven parsers, see Chapter 12: "Overview of Java XML Parsers").

To catch a parsing event, you must implement the **XmlHandler** interface provided by the Ælfred API. This interface defines a set of 13 call-back methods that indicate specific XML events. At the beginning of the last chapter, we indicated that every XML application consists of at least two pieces: an XML parser, and an application to read and manipulate parsed XML data. In every Ælfred application, you need the same two pieces: an Ælfred **XmlParser** object, and an implementation of the **XmlHandler** interface to catch the parsed XML data (see Figure 13.1).

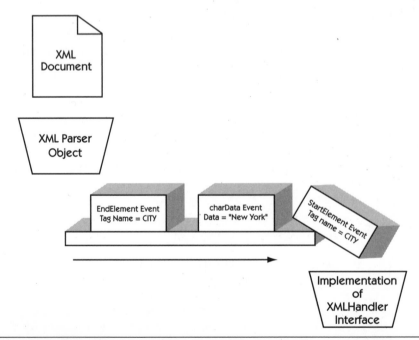

Figure 13.1   Basic Ælfred Application: Every Ælfred application consists of two parts:
an Ælfred XmlParser object, and an implementation of the XmlHandler
interface to catch the parsed XML data.

The most important methods of the XmlHandler interface are summarized in Table 13.1. In order to make sense of the interface as a whole, however, we need to examine a sample Ælfred parsing session.

Table 13.1 The XmlHandler Interface: Main Methods

Method Name	Description
startDocument ()	Indicates the start of a new XML document. This is always the first method called.
endDocument ()	Indicates that Ælfred has completed the parsing of the document. This is always the last method called.
startElement (String elname)	Indicates the start of a new XML element. The name of the element is specified by the elname String.
endElement (String elname)	Indicates the end of an XML element. The name of the element is specified by the elname String.
attribute (String aname, String value, boolean isSpecified)	Indicates an XML attribute. It is important to note that this method is called **prior** to any startElement events. The name of the attribute is specified by the aname String. The value of the attribute is specified by the value String. If the isSpecified boolean flag is true, the attribute has been explicitly defined within the XML document. If the isSpecified flag is false, this is the default attribute value defined within the DTD.
charData (char ch[], int start, int length)	Indicates character data. For example, when parsing <TITLE>Basic Poem</TITLE>, Ælfred will fire off a startElement event, followed by a charData event with the string, "Basic Poem." To retrieve the string, extract it from the ch character array. The string is located at the start index and is length characters long.
error (String message, String systemId, int line, int column)	Indicates a fatal error in parsing. Because Ælfred is a non-validating parser, do not expect this method to alert you to errors in validity. You can extract the error message and the exact location of the error.
ignorableWhitespace (char ch[], int start, int length)	Indicates white-space characters, such as newline or tab character data. Most of the time, white space is ignorable. To retrieve the string, extract it from the ch character array. The string is located at the start index and is length characters long.

Now we will create a sample XML document for major league baseball players. Listing 13.1 shows the Document Type Definition (DTD), and Listing 13.2 shows a sample XML document which conforms to the baseball DTD. We will use Listings 13.1 and 13.2 throughout the remainder of this chapter, as well as in the next chapter.

Listing 13.1 Baseball.dtd: The Baseball Document Type Definition (DTD)

```
<!ELEMENT BASEBALL (TEAM)+>
<!ELEMENT TEAM (CITY, PLAYER*)>
<!ELEMENT CITY (#PCDATA)>
<!ELEMENT PLAYER (LASTNAME, FIRSTNAME, AVG)>
<!ELEMENT FIRSTNAME (#PCDATA)>
<!ELEMENT LASTNAME (#PCDATA)>
<!ELEMENT AVG (#PCDATA)>
```

Listing 13.2 Baseball.xml Sample Baseball XML Document

```
<?xml version="1.0" encoding="UTF-8"?>
<!-- XML Document for American League Teams -->
<!DOCTYPE BASEBALL SYSTEM "Baseball.dtd">
<BASEBALL>
    <TEAM>
        <CITY>New York</CITY>
        <PLAYER>
            <LASTNAME>Jeter</LASTNAME>
            <FIRSTNAME>Derek</FIRSTNAME>
            <AVG>.314</AVG>
        </PLAYER>
        <PLAYER>
            <LASTNAME>Strawberry</LASTNAME>
            <FIRSTNAME>Daryl</FIRSTNAME>
            <AVG>.286</AVG>
        </PLAYER>
    </TEAM>
    <TEAM>
        <CITY>Baltimore</CITY>
        <PLAYER>
            <LASTNAME>Ripkin</LASTNAME>
```

```
                  <FIRSTNAME>Cal</FIRSTNAME>
                  <AVG>.258</AVG>
            </PLAYER>
            <PLAYER>
                  <LASTNAME>Alomar</LASTNAME>
                  <FIRSTNAME>Roberto</FIRSTNAME>
                  <AVG>.287</AVG>
            </PLAYER>
      </TEAM>
</BASEBALL>
```

The baseball DTD in Listing 13.1 is fairly simple. First, note that the BASEBALL element consists of at least one TEAM element. In turn, the TEAM element must include a CITY element, and zero or more PLAYER elements. Each player is required to have a last name, first name and batting average. Remember, however that Ælfred is non-validating, and is unable to check the baseball.xml file against the baseball DTD. The DTD is therefore mainly a reference for you. When we return to the baseball.xml file in the next chapter, the DTD will be very important.

Listing 13.2 contains sample XML data for two American League Teams: the New York Yankees and the Baltimore Orioles. To keep things simple, each team only has two players: the Yankees have Derek Jeter and Daryl Strawberry; the Orioles have Cal Ripkin and Roberto Alomar.

Now take Listing 13.2 and run it through the Ælfred parse engine. As soon as parsing begins, the **XmlHandler** will immediately receive a series of XML parsing events. First, Ælfred will call the **startDocument()** method. **startDocument()** is always the first method called, and indicates that processing is about to begin. Ælfred will then call a series of entity and instruction processing methods. (These methods are not as crucial for building applications, and we therefore describe them in the Advanced API insert below.)

Ælfred will proceed to read in one XML element at a time. Each XML element consists of three events. First, the **startElement()** method is called with the indicated element name. Second, the **charData()** method is called with the actual data. Lastly, the **endElement()** method is called, also with the indicated element name.

For example, you can see in Figure 13.2, that the CITY element: <CITY>New York</CITY> triggers three events:

- **startElement()**: element name set to "CITY";
- **charData()**: string parameter set to "New York"; and

- **endElement()**: element name again set to "CITY".

Each XML element may also have a series of associated attributes. For each attribute, Ælfred will call the **attribute()** method and pass the attribute name and value. It is important to note, however, that the attribute method is called *prior* to the **startElement()** method. For example, the line: <CITY Region="Northeast">New York</CITY> would trigger four events in this order:

- **attribute()**: attribute name set to "Region"; value set to "Northeast"
- **startElement()**: string parameter set to "CITY";
- **charData()**: string parameter set to "New York"; and
- **endElement()**: string parameter again set to "CITY".

In the event of a fatal parsing error, Ælfred will call the **error()** method, and report the specific line and column number of the offending syntax.

Lastly, Ælfred will call the **endDocument()** method. This is an indication that parsing is complete. Your **XmlHandler** is now free to make use of its newly acquired data.

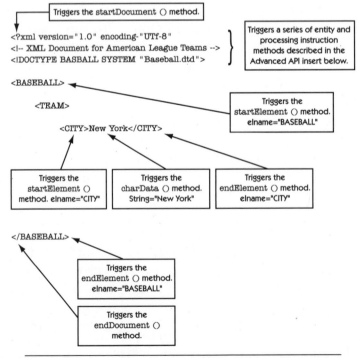

Figure 13.2   Anatomy of a sample Ælfred XML parsing session

As noted above, Ælfred always begins a parse session with the **start-Document()** method. It then proceeds to call a series of entity resolution and processing instructions (see Table 13.2.) These extra methods are rarely, if ever, used in most XML applications. However, there are two cases when an understanding of these additional methods may be helpful.

First, in certain rare cases, you may want to exercise some control over the resolution of external DTD files. For example, your program could look up an external DTD in a public or company-wide database and return a pointer to an updated or revised DTD. To enable this functionality, Ælfred calls a **resolve-Entity()** method each time it encounters a new XML file or external DTD. The **resolveEntity()** method is the only **XmlHandler** method which expects a return value. If you are planning to provide dynamic DTD lookup, you can return a new URL string here. Otherwise, you should return the **systemID** parameter. The **systemID** parameter is the default system name or URL string to your external document.

In other rare cases, you may wish to create your own XML processing instructions. XML instructions begin with the <? characters and can be embedded directly inside your XML documents. Each time Ælfred encounters a processing instruction, it will call the **processingInstruction()** method and pass the instruction along.

Table 13.2   The XmlHandler Interface: Continued

Method Name	Description
public abstract Object resolveEntity (String publicId, String systemId) throws Exception	Indicates that an entity is about to be loaded and processed. This external entity could be the top-level document (the .xml file) or the external DTD (the .dtd file.) In rare cases, you may want to exercise some control over the resolution of external DTD files. For example, your program could look up an external DTD in a public or company wide database and return a pointer to an updated or revised DTD. Most of the time, however, your event handler should just return the systemID string.
startExternalEntity (String systemId)	Indicates the start of an external entity. This could indicate the start of the top-level document entity (.xml) or the external DTD (if any). systemID indicates the URL of the file.

continued on next page

Method Name	Description
endExternalEntity (String systemId)	Indicates the end of an external entity. This could indicate the end of the top-level document entity (.xml) or the external DTD (if any). systemID indicates the URL of the file.
processingInstruction (String target, String data)	Indicates an XML processing instruction. XML Instructions begin with the <? character sequence. If desired, you can also create you own custom processing instructions, and capture them with this method.
doctypeDecl (String name, String publicId, String systemId)	Indicates the start of the Document Type Definition (DTD.) name indicates the name of the DTD. publicID is the public name; systemID is the system name.

THE XMLPARSER CLASS

Now that you have a clear understanding of the **XmlHandler** interface, we need to return to the first half of the Ælfred API: the **XmlParser** class.

The **XmlParser** class is responsible for parsing XML documents and triggering the call-back methods of the **XmlHandler** interface. You may want to refer back to Figure 13.1 to see how these two parts of the API are closely connected.

To utilize the XmlParser class, follow three steps:

■   **Step 1: Create an XmlParser Object:**

```
XmlParser parser = new XmlParser();
```

■   **Step 2: Call the parser's setHandler() method.**

This method registers your chosen event handler and accepts any object which implements the **XmlHandler** interface. For example, you could create an applet which implements the **XmlHandler** interface, and subsequently register it with your **XmlParser**:

```
public class XMLEventApplet extends Applet

    implements XmlHandler {

    .

    public void init () {
```

```
// Create XML Parser Object and set Handler
    parser = new XmlParser();
    parser.setHandler(this);
}


// Implementation of XmlHandler Interface
    .
    .
    .
}
```

■   **Step 3: Call the parser's parse() method.**

The parse() method directs Ælfred to start parsing a document located on the web or on the local hard drive. There are in fact three variations to parse(): you can load a character stream (Reader Object), a byte stream (InputStream Object) or a URL (see Table 13.3.) Note, however that the last two variations of parse() require a suggested Unicode encoding (e.g. "UTF-8", "UTF-16", "ISO-10646-UCS-2" etc.) If you do not know the encoding, you can pass a (String) null variable (the String casting is actually required, otherwise the compiler will be unable to determine which version of parse() you are calling.) Note also that the parse() methods may throw an Exception, and you should enclose each within a try/catch clause. For example, the following code uses the third variation of parse() to load a sample XML document located on the Microstar Web site:

```
try {
    parser.parse ("http://www.microstar.com/xml/Aelfred/
        donne.xml", "-//Megginson//DTD Simple Poem//EN",
            (String) null);
} catch (Exception e) {
    e.printStackTrace();
}
```

Here, the first parameter to parse() represents the System ID or URI; the second parameter represents the Public Name; and the third parameter indicates an unknown text encoding.

The most important methods of the XmlParser class are summarized in Table 13.3. There are, however, over a dozen other methods associated with the XmlParser class. Most of these methods are reserved for querying the DTD associated with a given XML document, and are not needed for most XML applications. If, however, you are planning to create some type of XML text editor, these methods may be of value. (See Chapter 22: "The Ælfred API Quick Reference Guide" for additional details.)

Table 13.3   The XmlParser Class: Main Methods

Method Name	Description
setHandler (XmlHandler handler)	Sets the event handler for the XmlParser object. The event handler receives all the events generated by the parser, and must implement the XmlHandler interface.
public void parse(String systemId, String publicId, Reader reader) throws Exception	Directs Ælfred to start parsing the XML document represented by the Reader object. The systemID (or URI) will become the base URI for resolving relative links, but Ælfred will actually read the document from the supplied Reader object.
public void parse(String systemId, String publicId,InputStream stream, String encoding) throws Exception	Directs Ælfred to start parsing the XML document represented by the InputStream object. The systemID (or URI) will become the base URI for resolving relative links, but Ælfred will actually read the document from the supplied InputStream object. The encoding parameter represents a suggested Unicode encoding (e.g. "UTF-8", "UTF-16", "ISO-10646-UCS-2" etc) or (String) null if encoding is unknown.
public void parse(String systemId, String poblicId, String encoding) throws Exception	Directs Ælfred to start parsing the XML document located at systemID. systemID represents the URI of your document. publicID represents the public name of the document (if any.) The encoding parameter represents a suggested Unicode encoding (e.g. "UTF-8", "UTF-16", "ISO-10646-UCS-2" etc) or (String) null if encoding is unknown.

BASIC EXAMPLES

"The just man builds on a modest foundation and gradually proceeds to greater things".

—King Alfred the Great

Time for some examples. Each of the examples in this section will utilize the Baseball.xml document defined previously in Listing 13.2. First, we will create a simple applet that parses Baseball.xml and displays each XML parsing event as it occurs.

Then, we will explore the mechanics of summarizing and searching an XML document.

INSTALLING ÆLFRED

A copy of Ælfred is available on the CD that accompanies this book. Ælfred is also freely available from the Microstar web site at **http://www.microstar.com/ XML/Aelfred**. To install Ælfred, just extract the files contained in the Ælfred zip archive, and copy them to your hard drive. Once Ælfred is installed, you must also add the Ælfred directory to your Java CLASSPATH environment variable.

TIP

SETTING THE JAVA CLASSPATH VARIABLE: In order to access the Ælfred API, you must explicitly set your CLASSPATH environment variable. The CLASSPATH variable indicates the location of various Java class libraries necessary for the compilation of your program. If CLASSPATH is not defined, the Java compiler will, by default, search the current directory plus the classes.zip file located in the java/classes directory. To set your CLASSPATH variable, follow the instructions below:

Windows 95:
For Windows 95, set the CLASSPATH variable within the autoexec.bat file:
- Launch Notepad and open C:\autoexec.bat.
- Use the SET command to create environment variables. For example, assuming the Ælfred directory is located in c:\xml, write:

    SET CLASSPATH=c:\xml\;

Add additional directories by separating each with a semicolon.

Windows NT:
For Windows NT, set the CLASSPATH variable through the Control Panel:
- Double click the System icon inside the Control Panel.
- Within the System Properties dialog box, click on the lower list box, labeled User Variables.
- Add the CLASSPATH variable here. For example, assuming the Ælfred directory is located in c:\xml, set CLASSPATH to c:\xml\;
Add additional directories by separating each with a semicolon.

Example: Basic Event Handling

Our first example will parse the Baseball.xml document, and display all parsing events as they occur. See Listing 13.3 for the complete code, and Figure 13.3 for sample output.

Listing 13.3   Example #1: Basic Event Handling

```
// AElfred Example Applet #1:
// Demonstrates basic event handling
// for AElfred Parser

import com.microstar.xml.XmlHandler;
import com.microstar.xml.XmlParser;
import java.applet.*;
import java.awt.*;
import java.net.*;

//    XMLEventApplet extends Applet and must
//    implement the AElfred XMLHandler Interface
public class XMLEventApplet extends Applet
   implements XmlHandler {

    private TextArea textArea;
    private XmlParser parser;
    private URL xmlURL;

    // Initialize the applet GUI and XML Parser
    public void init ()
    {
        // Create GUI Layout
        setLayout (new BorderLayout());
        textArea = new TextArea();
        add("Center", textArea);

        // Create XML Parser Object
        parser = new XmlParser();
```

```
        parser.setHandler(this);

        //  Create URL to XML Document
        String xmldoc = getParameter ("url");
        try {
            xmlURL = new URL(getDocumentBase(), xmldoc);
        } catch (MalformedURLException e) {
            e.printStackTrace();
        }
    }

// Start Parsing
public void start () {
    try {
        parser.parse(xmlURL.toString(), null, (String) null);
    } catch (Exception e) {
        e.printStackTrace();
    }
}

//  Method for displaying to Text Area
void displayText (String text) {
    textArea.appendText(text + "\n");
}

/**********************************************************/
/*  Implementation of XMLHandler Interface Methods  */
/**********************************************************/

// Document Events
public void startDocument () {
    displayText("Start document");
}
public void endDocument () {
    displayText("End document");
}

// Start/End Element Events
```

```java
public void startElement (String name) {
    displayText("Start element: name=" + name);
}


public void endElement (String name) {
    displayText("End element:  " + name);
}


// Character Data Event
public void charData (char ch[], int start, int length) {
    String text = new String (ch, start, length);
    displayText("Character data:  "+text);
}


//  Attribute Event
public void attribute (String name, String value,
    boolean isSpecified) {
        String s;
        if (isSpecified) s = new String (" (specified)");
        else s = new String (" (defaulted)");
        displayText("Attribute: name=" + name +
            ", value=" + value + s);
}


//  White Space Event
public void ignorableWhitespace (char ch[], int
    start, int length)
{
        // Since this is ignorable whitespace
        // do not display anything
}


// Entity Events
public Object resolveEntity (String publicId, String systemId) {
    displayText("Resolving entity:  " +
        "pubid=" +publicId + ", sysid=" + systemId);
    return systemId;
}
```

```
public void startExternalEntity (String systemId) {
    displayText("Starting external entity:  " + systemId);
}


public void endExternalEntity (String systemId) {
    displayText("Ending external entity:  " + systemId);
}


// DocTypeDecl Event
public void doctypeDecl (String name,
    String pubid, String sysid) {
        displayText("Doctype declaration:  " +
            name + ", pubid=" + pubid + ", sysid=" + sysid);
}


// Processing Instruction Event
public void processingInstruction (String target,
    String data) {
        displayText("Processing Instruction:  " +
            target + " " + data);
}


// Parsing Error Event
public void error (String message, String url,
    int line, int column) {
        displayText("Parsing Error: " + message);
        displayText("  at " + url.toString() + ": line "
            + line + " column " + column);
}
}
```

There are a number of important items to note regarding Listing 13.3. First, note the series of import statements at the beginning of the program:

```
import com.microstar.xml.XmlHandler;
import com.microstar.xml.XmlParser;
```

In order to access the Ælfred API, remember explicitly to import both the **XmlHandler** interface and the **XmlParser** class. If the compiler is unable to find these files, recheck that the CLASSPATH variable is set correctly.

Second, note that we are passing the URL of the XML document as an applet parameter. This is much more flexible than hard-coding the URL.

Third, and most important, we are creating a new class which extends Applet and implements the **XmlHandler** interface:

```
public class XMLEventApplet extends Applet
implements XmlHandler {
```

The bulk of Listing 13.3 therefore consists of a simple implementation of the **XmlHandler** interface. For each **XmlHandler** method, we display the event name along with any parameter information. For, example, the startDocument() method has no parameters, so we just display the event name:

```
public void startDocument () {
        displayText("Start document");
}
```

For the startElement() method, we display the event name, along with the element's name:

```
public void startElement (String name) {
        displayText("Start element:  name=" + name);
}
```

EXAMPLE: THE HANDLERBASE CONVENIENCE CLASS

Most of the time, you do not need to receive call-backs for all thirteen of the events specified by the **XmlHandler** interface. Ælfred therefore comes with a built-in HandlerBase convenience class that provides a default implementation of the XmlHandler Interface. For most of the methods in HandlerBase, the default action is to do nothing. You can therefore extend the HandlerBase class and override only those methods that you really want. Listing 13.4 provides an example.

Figure 13.3   Output from Example #1. The applet displays a complete list of every XML parsing event associated with Baseball.xml.

Listing 13.4   Example #2: Using the HandlerBase Convenience Class.

```
// AElfred Example Applet #2:
// Demonstrates the Handler Base
// convenience class

import com.microstar.xml.XmlHandler;
import com.microstar.xml.XmlParser;
import com.microstar.xml.HandlerBase;
import java.applet.*;
import java.awt.*;
import java.net.*;

// XMLEventHandler extends Applet
public class XMLEventHandler extends Applet {

     private TextArea textArea;
```

```
private XmlParser parser;
private URL xmlURL;

// Initialize the applet GUI and XML Parser
public void init ()
{
    // Create GUI Layout
    setLayout (new BorderLayout());
    textArea = new TextArea();
    add("Center", textArea);

    // Create XML Event Handler and
    // XML Parser Object
    EventHandler handler = new EventHandler(textArea);
    parser = new XmlParser();
    parser.setHandler(handler);

    // Create URL to XML Document
    String xmldoc = getParameter ("url");
    try {
        xmlURL = new URL (getDocumentBase(), xmldoc);
    } catch (MalformedURLException e) {
        e.printStackTrace();
    }
}

// Start Parsing
public void start () {
    try {
        parser.parse(xmlURL.toString(), null, (String) null);
    } catch (Exception e) {
        e.printStackTrace();
    }
}
}


// EventHandler extends the XML HandlerBase
// Convenience Class
```

```
class EventHandler extends HandlerBase {
    private TextArea textArea;

    public EventHandler (TextArea text) {
        this.textArea = text;
    }

    // Method for displaying to Text Area
    void displayText (String text) {
        textArea.appendText(text + "\n");
    }

    /*************************************/
    /* Override HandlerBase Methods    */
    /* Here, we will only override the    */
    /* Start/End Element events and the */
    /* charData event                  */
    /*************************************/

    public void startElement (String name) {
        displayText("Start element: name=" + name);
    }

    public void endElement (String name) {
        displayText("End element:  " + name);
    }

    public void charData (char ch[], int start,
      int length) {
        String text = new String (ch, start, length);
        displayText("Character data:  "+text);
    }
}
```

Here we have created a new EventHandler class which extends the HandlerBase convenience class. Within EventHandler, we can override any of the default methods provided by HandlerBase but, we have only done so for three methods: startElement(), charData(), and endElement(). For each of these events, we display the parameter information. The net effect is a complete record of every XML element and its embedded data. See Figure 13.4 for sample output.

Since it is much easier to extend the `HandlerBase` class than to provide a full implementation of the `XmlHandler` interface, we will continue to use this method in all the remaining examples in the chapter.

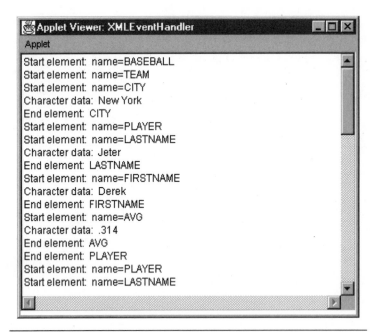

Figure 13.4   Output from Example #2. The applet displays a complete record of every XML element within Baseball.xml.

EXAMPLE: CREATING AN XML SUMMARY DOCUMENT

Using the previous example as a base, we will create two more basic examples. First, we will create an applet that parses the Baseball.xml document and creates a summary report. For example, the applet should read in Baseball.xml and display each player's name and batting average in column format. Doing so is actually much easier than it sounds: override a few of the default `HandlerBase` methods and insert the text formatting within these methods. Listing 13.5 shows how this is done.

Listing 13.5   Example #3: Creating an XML Summary Document.

```
// XML Summary Demo
// Extracts Player Data from XML Document
// and displays in Summary Form

import com.microstar.xml.XmlHandler;
import com.microstar.xml.XmlParser;
import com.microstar.xml.HandlerBase;
import java.applet.*;
import java.awt.*;
import java.net.*;

//  XMLSummary extends Applet
public class XMLSummary extends Applet {

        private TextArea textArea;
        private XmlParser parser;
        private URL xmlURL;

        // Initialize the applet GUI and XML Parser
        public void init ()
        {
            // Create GUI Layout
            setLayout (new BorderLayout());
            textArea = new TextArea();
            add("Center", textArea);

            //  Create XML Event Handler and
            //  XML Parser Object
            EventHandler handler = new EventHandler(textArea);
            parser = new XmlParser();
            parser.setHandler(handler);

            //  Create URL to XML Document
            String xmldoc = getParameter ("url");
```

```
            try {
                    xmlURL = new URL (getDocumentBase(), xmldoc);
            } catch (MalformedURLException e) {
                    e.printStackTrace();
            }
    }


    // Start Parsing
    public void start () {
            try {
                    parser.parse(xmlURL.toString(), null, (String) null);
            } catch (Exception e) {
                    e.printStackTrace();
            }
    }
}


// EventHandler extends the XML HandlerBase
// Convenience Class
class EventHandler extends HandlerBase {
    private TextArea textArea;

    public EventHandler (TextArea text) {
        this.textArea = text;
    }

    // Method for displaying to Text Area
    void displayText (String text) {
        textArea.appendText(text);
    }

    /**********************************************/
    /* Override HandlerBase Methods Here          */
    /* Note:  We only need to override the        */
    /* End Element      and the charData event */
    /**********************************************/

    public void endElement (String name) {
```

```
    // If this is the end of a CITY Element,
    // create a line break and start a new line.
        if (name.equals ("CITY"))
        displayText("\n===========================\n");

    // If this is the end of a PLAYER element,
    // then insert a new line
    else if (name.equals ("PLAYER"))
        displayText ("\n");

    // If this is the end of a LASTNAME element,
    // then insert a comma
    else if (name.equals ("LASTNAME"))
        displayText (",");

    // If this is the end of a FIRSTNAME element,
    // then insert a tab
    else if (name.equals ("FIRSTNAME"))
        displayText ("\t");

    // If this is the end of a TEAM Element,
    // then insert two new lines
    else if (name.equals ("TEAM")) displayText("\n\n");
  }

  public void charData (char ch[], int start, int length) {
      String text = new String (ch, start, length);
      displayText(" "+text);
  }
}
```

As you can see, most of Listing 13.5 is nearly identical to the previous example. The only major difference is the inclusion of additional code within the endElement() method. We use the endElement() method to trigger the proper formatting of the applet's text box and we determine what type of formatting is necessary by checking the element name. For example, when we receive the endElement event for the CITY element, we insert a line of dashes and a newline character (see Figure 13.5 for sample output). When we receive the endElement event for the FIRSTNAME element, we know that the AVG element is about to occur. We therefore insert a tab character so that the batting averages are all lined up in a column form.

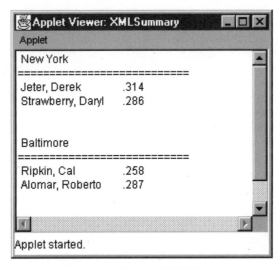

Figure 13.5   Output from Example #3.
The applet displays a summary of baseball player statistics.

NOTE

According to the official Microstar documentation, Ælfred may break large sequences of character data into smaller chunks, and call **charData()** for each chunk. For example, given the text: "New York", Ælfred may generate the following:

- charData() : "New"
- charData() : "York"

In Ælfred Version 1.2, however, we did not encounter any chunking of data, even when we tried a character sequence of 25K. This may change in future versions.

EXAMPLE: SEARCHING AN XML DOCUMENT

For a last basic example, we will consider the mechanics of searching an XML document. We will enable the user to search for a particular baseball player by last name, and display the player's batting average. The complete code is available in Listing 13.6, and sample output is provided in Figure 13.6.

Listing 13.6   Example #4: Searching an XML Document.

```
// XML Search Demo
// Searches XML Document by Last Name
// and displays information in Summary Form

import com.microstar.xml.XmlHandler;
import com.microstar.xml.XmlParser;
import com.microstar.xml.HandlerBase;
import java.applet.*;
import java.awt.*;
import java.net.*;

// XMLSummary extends Applet
public class XMLSearch extends Applet {

        private TextArea textArea;
        private XmlParser parser;
        private URL xmlURL;
        private Button search;
        private TextField target;
        private EventHandler handler;

        // Initialize the applet GUI and XML Parser
        public void init ()
        {
            // Create Panel with Text Field
            // and Search Button
            Panel p = new Panel ();
            target = new TextField(20);
            search = new Button("Search");
            p.add (target);
            p.add (search);
```

```
        // Create Border Layout
        setLayout (new BorderLayout());
        textArea = new TextArea();
        add("Center", textArea);
        add ("North", p);

        // Create XML Event Handler
        // and XML Parser Object
        handler = new EventHandler(textArea);
        parser = new XmlParser();
        parser.setHandler(handler);

        // Create URL to XML Document
        String xmldoc = getParameter ("url");
        try {
            xmlURL = new URL (getDocumentBase(), xmldoc);
        } catch (MalformedURLException e) {
            e.printStackTrace();
        }
    }


// Java 1.0 Event Handler
public boolean action (Event e, Object o) {
    // If the search button is clicked,
    // set string target and start parsing
    if (e.target == search) {
        handler.setTarget (target.getText());
        startParse();
        return true;
    }
    else return false;
}


// Start Parsing
private void startParse () {
    try {
        parser.parse(xmlURL.toString(), null, (String) null);
    } catch (Exception e) {
```

```
                    e.printStackTrace();
            }
    }
}


//  EventHandler extends the XML
//  HandlerBase Convenience Class
class EventHandler extends HandlerBase {
    private TextArea textArea;
    private String target;
    private boolean istarget, lastname;
    private int recordsfound;

    //  Constructor
    public EventHandler (TextArea text) {
        this.textArea = text;
        istarget = lastname = false;
        recordsfound = 0;
    }

    //  Method for displaying to Text Area
    private void displayText (String text) {
        textArea.appendText(text);
    }

    //  Set String Target
    public void setTarget (String target) {
        this.target = target.toUpperCase();
    }

    /******************************************/
    /*  Override HandlerBase Methods Here   */
    /******************************************/

    //  When a LASTNAME element is encountered,
    //  then set lastname flag
    public void startElement (String name) {
        if (name.equals ("LASTNAME")) lastname=true;
```

```
    }

    //  At end of PLAYER and LASTNAME elements,
    //  then set appropriate flags
    public void endElement (String name) {
        if (name.equals ("PLAYER")) istarget = false;
        else if (name.equals ("LASTNAME")) lastname=false;
    }

    public void charData (char ch[], int start, int length) {
        String text = new String (ch, start, length);
        String upper = text.toUpperCase();

        //  Only test LASTNAME Elements against target values
        if (lastname  && upper.indexOf (target) >= 0) {
            istarget = true;
            recordsfound++;
        }

        //  If this is still the target node, keep displaying data
        if (istarget) displayText (text+"\t");
    }

    //  Display Search Results Summary
    public void endDocument () {
        displayText ("\n--------------------");
        displayText ("\nRecords Found:  "+recordsfound+"\n\n");
        recordsfound = 0;
    }
}
```

There are several challenges in searching an XML document. First, we only want to search certain XML elements, in this case LASTNAME elements. Second, once we have identified a match, we only want to store data for that individual player. In both of these cases, we utilize a series of boolean flags to record our current state between call-back methods.

To search LASTNAME elements, remember that each XML element has three events: startElement(), charData(), and endElement(). When charData() is called, Ælfred just passes the character data, and retains no memory of the element name. The developer's job is to make up for these memory lapses.

To do so, we first override the startElement() method. If this is a LASTNAME element, we set the boolean class variable, lastname to true (and, when endElement() is called for LASTNAME, we reset the boolean flag to false.) That way, when charData() is called, we can check the flag to determine a valid string match.

In the event of a match, we set another boolean flag which is responsible for printing the last name, first name, and batting average for our target player. Note, however that this flag is reset when we receive the endElement() method for the PLAYER element.

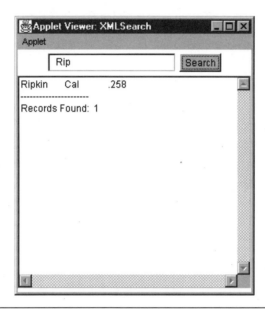

Figure 13.6 Output from Example #4. The applet enables the user to search the Baseball.xml document by last name.

TIP

MAKING ÆLFRED APPLETS AVAILABLE ON THE WEB: When a web browser loads a new applet, it will search the current directory as well as any subdirectories for necessary class files. In order to make any Ælfred applets available on the Web, you therefore must include the Ælfred class files in the same directory as the applet. The easiest way to do this is to copy the com directory file from the Ælfred directory and place it in the same directory as the applet.

EVENT TO OBJECT MAPPING

The previous search example has one glaring inefficiency: the program must reparse the entire XML document each time the user wants to search for a new player. To attack this inefficiency, parse the document only once, and store the embedded data in some easily searchable data structure. Then search this data structure directly, thereby dramatically improving the performance of any XML application.

To understand the significance and challenge of event-to-object mapping, take a step back and consider the following. You want to store all data for one baseball player within a self-contained class. The class, which we will call **Player**, contains encapsulated data for the player's last name, first name, city name and batting average. It also includes a set of accessor methods for extracting this data. The challenge is to create a mechanism whereby we can efficiently map Ælfred XML events directly to a **Player** object. Put another way, we want to collect a series of events for LASTNAME, FIRSTNAME, CITY, and AVG, and place the associated data directly into a **Player** object.

Now, take another step back and consider that we create a vector of **Player** objects (if you are not familiar with vectors, just think of an array). This vector will contain a complete list of every baseball player mentioned in the Baseball.xml document. Again, the goal is to provide a direct mapping between events and objects (see Figure 13.7.)

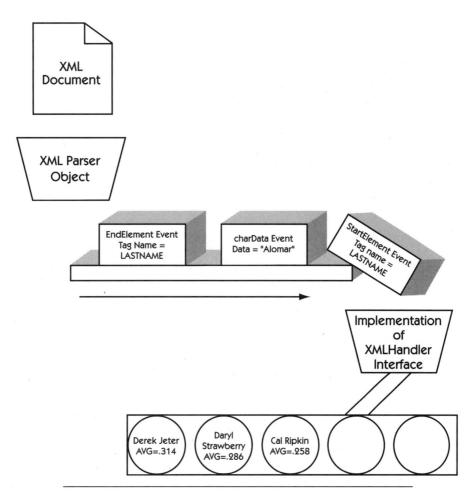

Figure 13.7   To create powerful XML applications, you need to map
XML events to objects. Here, the XML events are collected by the
XmlHandler interface and fed into a vector of Player objects.

EXAMPLE: MAPPING EVENTS TO OBJECTS

With this background in mind, we should redo the search example and make it more efficient. First, we need to create a Player class that will contain data for each individual player. The Player class is defined as follows:

```
// Class for holding Player Information
class Player {
    private String lastName, firstName, cityName;
    private float avg;

    // Constructor
    public Player (String lastName, String firstName,
        String cityName, float avg) {
            this.lastName = lastName;
            this.firstName = firstName;
            this.cityName = cityName;
            this.avg = avg;
    }

    // Accessor Methods
    public String getlastName () {
        return lastName;
    }
    public String getfirstName () {
        return firstName;
    }
    public String getcityName () {
        return cityName;
    }
    public float getAvg () {
        return avg;
    }
}
```

Note that we are storing last name, first name, city name, and batting average, along with a set of accessor methods for retrieving the data.

Next, we must implement the appropriate XmlHandler methods to capture individual XML elements. See Listing 13.7 for the complete code.

The first item to note regarding Listing 13.7 is that we again create an EventHandler class that extends the HandlerBase class. But, we only call parse once, within the applet's init () method. Within EventHandler, we also declare a vector called players, which will contain a full list of Player objects.

In order to capture the actual XML data, we need to implement the charData() method. However, as noted in the previous example, each time charData() is called, it is called with string data only, and retains no memory of the element name. For example, charData() might be called with the string data set to "New York", but there is no reference to the CITY element tag. A developer therefore needs to provide a mechanism to save state regarding the current element tag.

In Listing 13.7, we have done this by creating four boolean flags, one for each XML tag. When startElement() is called, the code checks the tag name and sets the appropriate boolean flag. For example, if startElement() is called with the CITY tag name, the code sets the cityname_elem variable to true. When the endElement() method is called, the code again checks the tag name and resets the appropriate boolean flag. Within charData(), the code checks the entire list of boolean flags to determine where to temporarily store the data.

The only action left is to create a Player object with new data. This is performed in the endElement() method. If endElement() is called for the PLAYER tag, we know that data regarding the player are complete. We can therefore create a new Player object and store that object in the players vector:

```
players.addElement (new Player (templastName,
     empfirstName, tempcityName, tempavg));
```

Once stored within the player vector, we can easily perform a linear search by last name, and display the results directly. This functionality is implemented in the searchTarget() method of the EventHandler class.

Listing 13.7 Mapping XML Events to Objects

```
// XML Event to Object Mapping
// Using XML Parser, map Parser Events
// to a Vector of Player Classes

import com.microstar.xml.XmlHandler;
import com.microstar.xml.XmlParser;
import com.microstar.xml.HandlerBase;
```

```java
import java.applet.*;
import java.awt.*;
import java.net.*;
import java.util.*;

//  XMLEventMap extends Applet
public class XMLEventMap extends Applet {

        private TextArea textArea;
        private XmlParser parser;
        private URL xmlURL;
        private Button search;
        private TextField target;
        private EventHandler handler;

        // Initialize the applet GUI and XML Parser
        public void init ()
        {
            // Create Panel with Text Field
            // and Search Button
            Panel p = new Panel ();
            target = new TextField(20);
            search = new Button("Search");
            p.add (target);
            p.add (search);

            //  Create Border Layout
            setLayout (new BorderLayout());
            textArea = new TextArea();
            add("Center", textArea);
            add ("North", p);

            //  Create XML Event Handler
            //  and XML Parser Object
            handler = new EventHandler(textArea);
            parser = new XmlParser();
            parser.setHandler(handler);
```

```
        // Create URL to XML Document and Start Parsing
        String xmldoc = getParameter ("url");
        try {
            xmlURL = new URL (getDocumentBase(), xmldoc);
            parser.parse(xmlURL.toString(), null, (String) null);
        } catch (Exception e) {
            e.printStackTrace();
        }
    }


    // Java 1.0 Event Handler

    public boolean action (Event e, Object o) {
        // If the search button is clicked, search
        if (e.target == search) {
            handler.searchTarget (target.getText());
            return true;
        }
        else return false;
    }

}


// EventHandler extends the XML HandlerBase Convenience Class
class EventHandler extends HandlerBase {
    private TextArea textArea;        // textArea in applet
    private boolean cityname_elem;    // Indicates CITY element
    private boolean lastname_elem;    // Inidicates LASTNAME element
    private boolean firstname_elem;   // Indicates FIRSTNAME element
    private boolean avg_elem;         // Indicates AVG element
    private Vector players;           // Vector of Players
    private String templastName;      // Temp strings:
    private String tempfirstName;     //    used across invocations
    private String tempcityName;      //    of parser event methods
    private float tempavg;            // Temp batting average

    // Constructor
    public EventHandler (TextArea text) {
```

```java
        this.textArea = text;
        cityname_elem = lastname_elem = false;
        firstname_elem = avg_elem = false;

        // Create vector of Player classes
        players = new Vector();
    }

    // Method for displaying to Text Area
    void displayText (String text) {
        textArea.appendText(text);
    }

    // Set String Target
    void searchTarget (String target) {
        int recordsfound=0;
        Player current;

        // Searching is case insensitive
        target = target.toUpperCase();

        // Linear Search through all Player elements
        for (int i=0; i< players.size(); i++) {
            current = (Player) players.elementAt(i);
            templastName = current.getlastName();
            templastName = templastName.toUpperCase();
            if (templastName.indexOf(target) >= 0) {
                displayText ("\n"+current.getfirstName()+
                    "\t" + current.getlastName());
                displayText ("\t"+current.getAvg()+"\n");
                recordsfound++;
            }
        }
        displayText ("\n==================");
        displayText ("\nRecords found:  "+
            recordsfound+"\n");

    }
```

```
/*********************************************/
/* Override HandlerBase Methods Here   */
/*********************************************/


// When a CITY, LASTNAME, FIRSTNAME or AVG
// element starts, mark the appropriate
// element flag as true
public void startElement (String name) {
     if (name.equals ("CITY"))
          cityname_elem=true;
     else if (name.equals ("LASTNAME"))
          lastname_elem=true;
     else if (name.equals ("FIRSTNAME"))
          firstname_elem=true;
     else if (name.equals ("AVG"))
          avg_elem=true;

}


// When a CITY, LASTNAME, FIRSTNAME or AVG
// element ends, mark the appropriate element
// flag as false.
// When we reach the end of a PLAYER tag,
// create new Player object and insert into
// player vector
public void endElement (String name) {
     if (name.equals ("CITY"))
          cityname_elem=false;
     else if (name.equals ("LASTNAME"))
          lastname_elem=false;
     else if (name.equals ("FIRSTNAME"))
          firstname_elem=false;
     else if (name.equals ("AVG"))
          avg_elem=false;

     // We now have all the info. to create
     // a new player object
     else if (name.equals ("PLAYER")) {
          players.addElement (new Player
```

```
                    (templastName, tempfirstName,
                    tempcityName, tempavg));
        }
    }


    //  Depending on element flag, place character
    //  data in temporary variables for later use
    public void charData (char ch[], int start,
        int length) {
            String text = new String (ch, start, length);
            if (cityname_elem) tempcityName = text;
            else if (lastname_elem) templastName = text;
            else if (firstname_elem) tempfirstName = text;
            else if (avg_elem) {
                Float tempFloat = Float.valueOf (text);
                tempavg = tempFloat.floatValue();
            }
    }


    //  Display Summary of Document
    //  Display all elements in players vector
    public void endDocument () {
            Player current;
            for (int i=0; i< players.size(); i++) {
                current = (Player) players.elementAt(i);
                displayText ("Element #"+i+": --> "+
                    current.getfirstName()+" " +
                    current.getlastName());
                displayText ("\n");
            }
    }
}

//  Class for holding Player Information
class Player {
        private String lastName, firstName, cityName;
        private float avg;
```

```
// Constructor
public Player (String lastName, String firstName,
   String cityName, float avg) {
      this.lastName = lastName;
      this.firstName = firstName;
      this.cityName = cityName;
      this.avg = avg;
   }

// Accessor Methods
public String getlastName () { return lastName; }
   public String getfirstName () { return firstName; }
   public String getcityName () { return cityName; }
   public float getAvg () { return avg; }
}
```

EXAMPLE: WORKING WITH ATTRIBUTES

For the final example, we will put everything all together and create a more compelling interface for our users. First, we will modify the baseball DTD slightly, so
that it now includes an IMG tag, along with a SRC attribute. The SRC attribute will
indicate the URL of a photograph. The revised DTD is available in Listing 8 and the
revised baseball.xml document is available in Listing 13.9. (Again, Ælfred will not be
checking the DTD, so Listing 13.8 is provided mainly for your reference.)

Listing 13.8   Revised Baseball.dtd with new IMG Tag

```
<!ELEMENT BASEBALL (TEAM)+>
<!ELEMENT TEAM (CITY, PLAYER*)>
<!ELEMENT CITY (#PCDATA)>
<!ELEMENT PLAYER (LASTNAME, FIRSTNAME, AVG, IMG)>
<!ELEMENT FIRSTNAME (#PCDATA)>
<!ELEMENT LASTNAME (#PCDATA)>
<!ELEMENT AVG (#PCDATA)>
<!ELEMENT IMG EMPTY>
<!ATTLIST IMG SRC CDATA #REQUIRED>
```

Listing 13.9 Revised Baseball.xml Document with Image Data

```
<?xml version="1.0" encoding="UTF-8"?>
<!-- XML Document for American League Teams -->
<!DOCTYPE BASEBALL SYSTEM "Baseball.dtd">
<BASEBALL>
    <TEAM>
        <CITY>New York</CITY>
        <PLAYER>
            <LASTNAME>Jeter</LASTNAME>
            <FIRSTNAME>Derek</FIRSTNAME>
            <AVG>.314</AVG>
            <IMG SRC="images/newyork1.jpg"/>
        </PLAYER>
        <PLAYER>
            <LASTNAME>Strawberry</LASTNAME>
            <FIRSTNAME>Daryl</FIRSTNAME>
            <AVG>.286</AVG>
            <IMG SRC="images/newyork2.jpg"/>
        </PLAYER>
    </TEAM>
    <TEAM>
        <CITY>Baltimore</CITY>
        <PLAYER>
            <LASTNAME>Ripkin</LASTNAME>
            <FIRSTNAME>Cal</FIRSTNAME>
            <AVG>.258</AVG>
            <IMG SRC="images/baltimore1.jpg"/>
        </PLAYER>
        <PLAYER>
            <LASTNAME>Alomar</LASTNAME>
            <FIRSTNAME>Roberto</FIRSTNAME>
            <AVG>.287</AVG>
            <IMG SRC="images/baltimore2.jpg"/>
        </PLAYER>
    </TEAM>
</BASEBALL>
```

We will use the revised baseball.xml document so that our last example will read in all data regarding individual players, and again place them in a vector of Player objects. Once parsed, the code will display a pull-down menu of all individual players. Users can then pick a player, and the code will immediately download the player's photograph and display it alongside his batting average (see Figure 13.8.)

The code for the final example is available in Listing 13.10. Note that the most significant addition to Listing 13.10 is the implementation of the attribute method. Remember that the **attribute()** method is called prior to any **startElement()** methods. Save any attribute data to a temporary variable.

Listing 13.10   Working with Attributes

```
// XML Event to Object Mapping #2
// Using XML Parser, map Parser Events
// to Player Object
// Illustrates use of Attributes

import com.microstar.xml.XmlHandler;
import com.microstar.xml.XmlParser;
import com.microstar.xml.HandlerBase;
import java.applet.*;
import java.awt.*;
import java.net.*;
import java.util.*;

// XMLEventMap2 extends Applet
public class XMLEventMap2 extends Applet {

    private XmlParser parser;
    private URL xmlURL;
    private EventHandler handler;
    private Choice select;
    private Player current;
    private Dimension dim;

    // Initialize the applet GUI
    // and XML Parser
```

```java
public void init ()
{
    // Create Panel with Pull down menu
    Panel p = new Panel ();
    select = new Choice();
    p.add (select);
    select.addItem ("-- Select a Player --");

    // Create Border Layout
    setLayout (new BorderLayout());
    add ("North", p);
    dim = this.size();

    // Create XML Event Handler and
    // XML Parser Object
    handler = new EventHandler(select);
    parser = new XmlParser();
    parser.setHandler(handler);

    // Create URL to XML Document and
    // Start Parsing
    String xmldoc = getParameter ("url");
    try {
        xmlURL = new URL (getDocumentBase(), xmldoc);
        parser.parse(xmlURL.toString(), null, (String) null);
    } catch (Exception e) {
        e.printStackTrace();
    }
}

// Java 1.0 Event Handler

public boolean action (Event e, Object o) {
    // If the search button is clicked, search
    if (e.target == select) {
        current = handler.getPlayer
            (select.getSelectedIndex()-1);
        repaint();
```

```
            return true;
        }
        else return false;
    }


    // To make for smoother graphics transition,
    // add double buffering technique
    public void paint (Graphics g) {
        if (current!=null) {
            g.setFont (new Font ("TimesRoman", Font.BOLD, 16));
            g.drawString (current.getfirstName(),150,70);
            g.drawString (current.getlastName(),150,90);
            g.setFont (new Font ("TimeRoman", Font.PLAIN, 14));
            g.drawString ("Avg:  "+current.getAvg(), 150, 110);
            Image photo = getImage (getDocumentBase(),
                current.getimgSrc());
            g.drawImage (photo, 75,50,this);
        }
    }


}


// EventHandler extends the XML HandlerBase Convenience Class
class EventHandler extends HandlerBase {
    private Choice select;                // Applet Select Box
    private boolean cityname_elem;        // Indicates CITY element
    private boolean lastname_elem;        // Inidicates LASTNAME element
    private boolean firstname_elem;       // Indicates FIRSTNAME element
    private boolean avg_elem;             // Indicates AVG element
    private Vector players;               // Vector of Players
    private String templastName;          // Temp strings:
    private String tempfirstName;         //    used across invocations
    private String tempcityName;          //    of parser event methods
    private float tempavg;                // Temp batting average
    private String tempimgSrc;            // Temp Image Source


    // Constructor
    public EventHandler (Choice select) {
```

```
        this.select = select;

        //  Set all element flags to False
        cityname_elem = lastname_elem = false;
        firstname_elem = avg_elem = false;

        //  Create vector of Player classes
        players = new Vector();
    }


// Get Player at Specified Index
public Player getPlayer (int index) {
    if (index>=0)
        return (Player) players.elementAt(index);
    else return null;
}


/*******************************************/
/*  Override HandlerBase Methods Here   */
/*******************************************/

// When a CITY, LASTNAME, FIRSTNAME or AVG
// element starts, mark the appropriate
// element flag as true
public void startElement (String name) {
    if (name.equals ("CITY"))
        cityname_elem=true;
    else if (name.equals ("LASTNAME"))
        lastname_elem=true;
    else if (name.equals ("FIRSTNAME"))
        firstname_elem=true;
    else if (name.equals ("AVG"))
        avg_elem=true;
}


// When a CITY, LASTNAME, FIRSTNAME or AVG
// element ends, mark the appropriate
// element flag as false.
```

```
// When we reach the end of a PLAYER tag,
// create new Player object and add to
// player vector
public void endElement (String name) {
if (name.equals ("CITY")) cityname_elem=false;
    else if (name.equals ("LASTNAME"))
        lastname_elem=false;
    else if (name.equals ("FIRSTNAME"))
        firstname_elem=false;
    else if (name.equals ("AVG"))
        avg_elem=false;


    // We now have all the info. to create
    // a new player object
    else if (name.equals ("PLAYER")) {
        players.addElement (new Player
            (templastName, tempfirstName,
            tempcityName, tempavg, tempimgSrc));
    }
}


// Attribute Event
// Note that Attribute event is called *before* the
// startElement event
// We only have one IMG SRC attribute to store here
public void attribute(String aname, String value,
    boolean isSpecified) {
        tempimgSrc = value;
}


// Depending on element flag, place character
// data in temporary variables for later use
public void charData (char ch[], int start, int length) {
    String text = new String (ch, start, length);
    if (cityname_elem) tempcityName = text;
    else if (lastname_elem) templastName = text;
    else if (firstname_elem) tempfirstName = text;
```

```
        else if (avg_elem) {
                Float tempFloat = Float.valueOf (text);
                tempavg = tempFloat.floatValue();
        }
    }


    //  At end of Document, add all players to
    //  Applet selection menu
    public void endDocument () {
        Player current;
        for (int i=0; i< players.size(); i++) {
                current = (Player) players.elementAt(i);
                select.addItem (current.getfirstName()+
                    " " + current.getlastName());
        }
    }
}


//  Class for holding Player Information
class Player {
    private String lastName, firstName, cityName, imgSrc;
    private float avg;

    // Constructor
    public Player (String lastName, String firstName,
      String cityName,
        float avg, String imgSrc) {
        this.lastName = lastName;
        this.firstName = firstName;
        this.cityName = cityName;
        this.avg = avg;
        this.imgSrc = imgSrc;
    }


    //  Accessor Methods
    public String getlastName () { return lastName; }
    public String getfirstName () { return firstName; }
    public String getcityName () { return cityName; }
```

```
public String getimgSrc () { return imgSrc; }
public float getAvg () { return avg; }
}
```

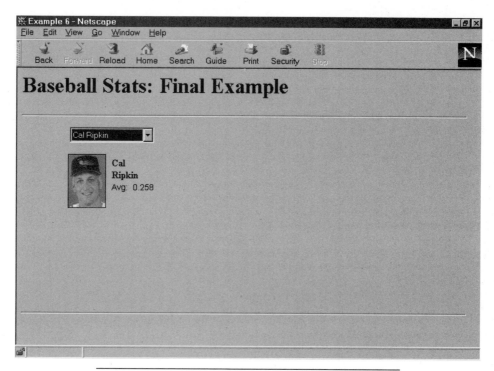

Figure 13.8 The final example running under Netscape 4.0

We hope that this chapter has provided a taste of XML parsing and XML applications. Ælfred is one of the simplest parsers to use. You now have the basic tools to create XML applets, and add XML functionality to your existing applets.

THE MICROSOFT XML PARSER

INTRODUCTION TO MS-XML

Microsoft Corp. is quite serious about XML. It currently has plans to include full XML support in Internet Explorer 5.0, and limited XML support in the next upgrade to Microsoft Office. With the release of Internet Explorer 4.0, Microsoft has also developed its own Java XML parser. The Microsoft XML Parser (MS-XML) was first released in Summer 1997, and has since undergone several upgrades. It is currently available in version 1.8.

MS-XML is a tree-based, validating parser—as it parses an XML document, it automatically checks for validity and creates its own internal tree representation of the data. An application can then traverse this tree and extract the data that it deems significant.

The main challenge to understanding MS-XML is understanding the MS-XML tree structure. This chapter therefore includes several examples that gradually introduce the most important concepts and techniques. We will begin with the MS-XML Object Model itself, and then explore filtering and searching techniques. We will then explore the dynamics of remapping the MS-XML tree structure to your own data structures. Finally, we will conclude with an examination of XML databases, and explore ways to modify the MS-XML tree.

When Microsoft originally released Internet Explorer 4.0, it shipped with two embedded versions of MS-XML: one written in C++ and one written in Java. The Java version of MS-XML is included in the CLASSPATH of the IE 4.0 Java Virtual Machine. It is therefore possible to create applets that access the MS-XML API directly (without requiring end-users to repeatedly download the MS-XML class files.) It is also possible to create JScript applications that interface with MS-XML. To enable this functionality, Microsoft has created the XML Data Source Object (DSO), an applet that enables JScript applications to load, render, and bind XML data.

In intranet environments where IE 4.0 is the standard browser, MS-XML is therefore a viable alternative for applets and scripting (note, however that the current version of MS-XML supersedes the version that originally shipped with IE 4.0). Where IE 4.0 is not the standard, however, MS-XML is rather large (total class files can reach 182 K) for applet development, and we recommend using Ælfred instead.

While MS-XML is not ideal for all applet development, it is however a perfect candidate for standalone applications and server-side Java applications, including servlets. As an extra bonus, MS-XML also includes a command line utility for testing the validity of documents and displaying the document structure. We begin the chapter by examining the command line tool.

TIP   You are free to redistribute MS-XML for non-commercial or commercial applications. Microsoft's only stipulation is that you not use Microsoft's name, logo or trademarks to market your product. For additional details regarding Microsoft's licensing agreement, see the Microsoft XML Web site at **http://www.microsoft.com/xml**.

INSTALLING MS-XML

Version 1.8 of MS-XML is available on the CD that accompanies this book. It is also available from the Microsoft web site at **http://www.microsoft.com/xml**. The version on the CD is a self-extracting executable that will install MS-XML to the c:\msxml directory. To compile MS-XML programs, you will also need to add the c:\msxml\classes directory to your CLASSPATH environment variable (for information on setting your CLASSPATH, see Chapter 13: "The Ælfred XML Parser").

USING THE MS-XML COMMAND LINE PROGRAM

Before we delve into the details of the MS-XML API, we should examine the command line version of MS-XML. The command line tool is easy to use and is very useful for testing the validity of XML documents. It is therefore a handy tool to keep around, even if you decide to use a different XML parser.

As an example, we will try parsing the Baseball.xml document from the last chapter. The Baseball.xml document and its associated DTD are reprinted in Listings 14.1 and 14.2.

Listing 14.1 Baseball.dtd: The Baseball Document Type Definition (DTD.)

```
<!ELEMENT BASEBALL (TEAM)+>
<!ELEMENT TEAM (CITY, PLAYER*)>
<!ELEMENT CITY (#PCDATA)>
<!ELEMENT PLAYER (LASTNAME, FIRSTNAME, AVG)>
<!ELEMENT FIRSTNAME (#PCDATA)>
<!ELEMENT LASTNAME (#PCDATA)>
<!ELEMENT AVG (#PCDATA)>
```

Listing 14.2 Baseball.xml: Sample Baseball XML Document

```
<?xml version="1.0" encoding="UTF-8"?>
<!-- XML Document for American League Teams -->
<!DOCTYPE BASEBALL SYSTEM "Baseball.dtd">
<BASEBALL>
    <TEAM>
        <CITY>New York</CITY>
        <PLAYER>
```

```
            <LASTNAME>Jeter</LASTNAME>
            <FIRSTNAME>Derek</FIRSTNAME>
            <AVG>.314</AVG>
        </PLAYER>
        <PLAYER>
            <LASTNAME>Strawberry</LASTNAME>
            <FIRSTNAME>Daryl</FIRSTNAME>
            <AVG>.286</AVG>
        </PLAYER>
    </TEAM>
    <TEAM>
        <CITY>Baltimore</CITY>
        <PLAYER>
            <LASTNAME>Ripkin</LASTNAME>
            <FIRSTNAME>Cal</FIRSTNAME>
            <AVG>.258</AVG>
        </PLAYER>
        <PLAYER>
            <LASTNAME>Alomar</LASTNAME>
            <FIRSTNAME>Roberto</FIRSTNAME>
            <AVG>.287</AVG>
        </PLAYER>
    </TEAM>
</BASEBALL>
```

Assuming you are using the Java Development Kit (JDK), the command to run MS-XML on Baseball.xml is:

C:\msxml>**java msxml Baseball.xml**

If you receive no messages, your XML document has been certified as valid. But, we should try a few invalid documents so that we can see what types of errors are reported.

First, we will add a new XML element that is not defined within the Baseball DTD file. For example, we will add a new TEAMNAME element under the TEAM element. Here is how the new Baseball.xml document might look:

```
<?xml version="1.0" encoding="UTF-8"?>
<!DOCTYPE BASEBALL SYSTEM "Baseball.dtd">
```

```
<BASEBALL>
    <TEAM>
        <CITY>New York</CITY>
        <TEAMNAME>Yankees</TEAMNAME>
        <PLAYER>
            <LASTNAME>Jeter</LASTNAME>
            <FIRSTNAME>Derek</FIRSTNAME>
            <AVG>.314</AVG>
        </PLAYER>
```
...

If we run MS-XML, we now get the following:

C:\msxml>**java msxml Baseball.xml**
Invalid element 'TEAMNAME' in content of 'TEAM'. Expected [PLAYER]
Location: file:/C:/msxml/Baseball.xml(6,4)
Context: <BASEBALL><TEAM>

MS-XML is comparing Baseball.xml against the Baseball.dtd file, and has identified our invalid TEAMNAME element. It also reports that the PLAYER element was expected instead, and identifies the location of the offending error: line 6, column 4.

Next, we will try a nesting problem and modify Baseball.xml as follows:

```
<?xml version="1.0" encoding="UTF-8"?>
<!DOCTYPE BASEBALL SYSTEM "Baseball.dtd">
<BASEBALL>
    <TEAM>
        <CITY>New York
        <PLAYER></CITY>
            <LASTNAME>Jeter</LASTNAME>
            <FIRSTNAME>Derek</FIRSTNAME>
            <AVG>.314</AVG>
        </PLAYER>
```
...

Can you see the error? Try running MS-XML:

C:\msxml>java msxml Baseball.xml
Invalid element 'PLAYER' in content of 'CITY'. Expected [PCDATA]

Location: file:/C:/msxml/Baseball.xml(6,4)

Context: <BASEBALL><TEAM><CITY>

The close tag for CITY has been mistakenly placed within the PLAYER tag. The DTD specifies that PCDATA is expected here, and MS-XML again reports on the location of the error.

The command line version of MS-XML also hosts a large number of command line options (each of which is summarized in Table 14.1). The most useful of these options is the –d1 option for printing the XML tree representation. For example, we can display the tree representation of Baseball.xml:

```
C:\msxml>java msxml -d1 Baseball.xml
DOCUMENT
|---PI xml " "
|---WHITESPACE 0xa
|---DOCTYPE  NAME="BASEBALL" URL="Baseball.dtd"
|---WHITESPACE 0xa
+---ELEMENT BASEBALL
    |---WHITESPACE 0xa 0x9
    |---ELEMENT TEAM
    |    |---WHITESPACE 0xa 0x9 0x9
    |    |---ELEMENT CITY
    |    |    +---PCDATA "New York"
    |    |---WHITESPACE 0xa 0x9 0x9
    |    |---ELEMENT PLAYER
    |    |    |---WHITESPACE 0xa 0x9 0x9 0x9
    |    |    |---ELEMENT LASTNAME
    |    |    |    +---PCDATA "Jeter"
    ...
```

Note that we have a DOCUMENT element, which serves as the root node. Under the root node, we have a BASEBALL element, and within BASEBALL, we have CITY and PLAYER elements. Note also that white space is accounted for as separate, identifiable nodes. White-space nodes turn out to be very important and we will explore their user later in the chapter.

As you might have guessed, the –d1 tree view option represents the same tree that you access when using the MS-XML API. We now turn to the API.

Table 14.1   Command Line Options to MS-XML

Option	Description
–d	Write parsed XML in original XML format
–dl	Write parsed XML in a tree format.
–f	Fast parsing that bypasses tree building
–t	Specifies how many iterations to time the parser
–o	Provides a filename for dumping output; this is needed if data is in Unicode
–e	Character encoding for output other than that of the input
–c	Output in compact mode (no newlines or tabs).
–p	Output in pretty mode (inserts newlines & tabs)
–i	Switch to case insensitive
–m	Perform object model test
–s	Standalone—do not load external DTD's or entities.

Working with MS-XML

The Document Class

The main class in the MS-XML API is the Document class. The Document class encapsulates all information regarding a particular XML document, and can be used to load an XML document, whether it is located on the local hard drive or on the web. The main methods of the Document class are summarized in Table 14.2 (there are actually a dozen other methods associated with the Document class, but Table 14.2 summarizes the most important ones). For a complete list of methods, see Chapter 23: "The MS-XML API Quick Reference Guide".

Table 14.2 The Document Class: Main Methods

Method Name	Description
public Document()	Constructor
public Element getRoot()	Retrieves the root element of the XML document. This is guaranteed to be of type Element.ELEMENT.
public load (String urlstr) throws ParseException	Loads the XML document located at the indicated urlstr String.
public load (URL url) throws ParseException	Loads the XML document specified by the URL object.
public load (InputStream in) throws ParseException	Loads the XML documented specified by the InputStream object.
public void reportError (ParseException e, OutputStream out)	Displays the MS-XML ParseException error message to the indicated OutputStream.
public void save (XMLOutputStream o) throws IOException;	Saves the document to the specified XMLOutputStream object.

Loading XML Documents

To load and parse a new XML document, first create a new Document object:

```
Document doc = new Document();
```

Then call one of its three load() methods. As you can see from Table 14.2, you can load an XML document via a URL String, via a URL object or via an InputStream. By calling load(), you direct MS-XML to load the indicated XML document and to start parsing. If MS-XML stumbles across any errors (such as ill-formed or invalid XML documents), it will throw a ParseException.

For example, to load a sample XML document located on the Web, we would write:

```
try {
    doc.load ("http://www.acme.com/parts.xml");
} catch (ParseException e) {
    doc.reportError (e, System.out);
}
```

Here, we are catching the MS-XML ParseException and using the Document class reportError() method to display the error message.

Getting the Root Element

MS-XML loads the document, parses it, and creates an internal tree representation of the document structure. This tree structure is built with a series of Element objects. At the root of the MS-XML tree, we have a Document element object. Within this node, we may have Element objects for processing instructions, whitespace characters, document type declarations or individual XML elements. For example, we may have the following tree:

```
DOCUMENT
|---PI xml ""
|---WHITESPACE 0xa
|---DOCTYPE  NAME="BASEBALL" URL="Baseball.dtd"
|---WHITESPACE 0xa
+---ELEMENT BASEBALL
    |---WHITESPACE 0xa 0x9
    |---ELEMENT TEAM
    |   |---WHITESPACE 0xa 0x9 0x9
    |   |---ELEMENT CITY
    |   |   +---PCDATA "New York"
    |   |---WHITESPACE 0xa 0x9 0x9
    |   |---ELEMENT PLAYER
    |   |   |---WHITESPACE 0xa 0x9 0x9 0x9
    |   |   |---ELEMENT LASTNAME
    |   |   |   +---PCDATA "Jeter"
    ...
```

Most applications will not need to handle the first processing instruction or DocType declaration. Rather, most applications will want to skip directly to the XML data itself. To speed this process, you can use the **getRoot()** method:

```
Element root = doc.getRoot();
```

This method will extract the root element defined by the DTD. In the case of the above tree, getRoot() will extract the <BASEBALL> node.

Once you have the root node, you are ready to start traversing the tree and gathering your data. Before we start traversing the tree, we need a better understanding of the Element interface.

Table 14.3   Summary of Steps for Using MS-XML

Step #1	Create a new XML Document Object: Document doc = new Document();

Step #2	Load an XML Document and Start Parsing:
	
	try {
	    doc.load ("http://www.acme.com/parts.xml");
	} catch (ParseException e) {
	    doc.reportError (e, System.out);
	}
	
	You also have the option of loading an XML document via a URL object or via an InputStream object.

Step #3	Obtain the root of the XML document: Element root = doc.getRoot();
Step #4	Starting at the root node, traverse the XML Tree as needed.

WARNING

WORKING WITH LOCAL FILES: Unfortunately, MS-XML is full of bugs when handling local XML files on the hard drive. To illustrate the problem, consider that you want to load the Baseball.xml file from your local hard drive. You first need to create a FileStream object, and then load it using the Document load() method. For example:

```
Document doc = new Document();
fin = new FileInputStream ("Baseball.xml");
```

doc.load(fin);

If Baseball.xml is a standalone document, and does not reference any external DTDs, this code will work just fine. But, if Baseball.xml does include a reference to an external file (as it does), MS-XML is unable to locate the DTD file! Specifically, you get the following error:

```
Couldn't find external DTD 'Baseball.dtd'
Location: null(3,-1)
Context: <null>
```

This is a rather unfortunate error, and Microsoft will hopefully fix the bug for their next release. In the meantime, there is really only one work-around: you need to translate your local file name into an absolute URL, and then load the document using the load (URL url) method. The only problem is that Windows uses the "\" character as the file separator, and UNIX and URLs use the "/" separator. You therefore need to remap the file separator in Windows format to the URL standard. To help you along, you can use the following **createURL()** method:

```java
// Method to create an absolute URL
// from a filename. Note:
// On Windows Platforms, the file separator is \
// On UNIX and for URLs, the file separator is /
public URL createURL(String fileName) {
URL url=null;
File f = new File(fileName);
String path = f.getAbsolutePath();
String fs = System.getProperty("file.separator");
if (fs.length() == 1) {
    char sep = fs.charAt(0);
    if (sep != '/')
        path = path.replace(sep, '/');
    if (path.charAt(0) != '/')
        path = '/' + path;
}
path = "file://" + path;
try {
    url = new URL(path);
} catch (MalformedURLException e) {
```

```
            System.out.println("Cannot create url for: " +
                fileName);
            System.exit(O);
    }
    return url;
}
```

Use the **createURL()** method to translate your file name into an absolute URL:

```
URL url = createURL ("Baseball.xml");
try {
    doc.load (url);
} catch (ParseException e) {
    doc.reportError (e, System.out);
}
```

THE ELEMENT INTERFACE

Every node within the MS-XML tree structure is defined as an **Element** object. Each **Element** object can come in one of eight different flavors. The two most important flavors are of type ELEMENT and PCDATA. ELEMENT nodes refer to XML elements, and PCDATA nodes refer to text embedded within an XML element. For example, the following XML text:

```
<CITY>New York</CITY>
```

creates the following MS-XML tree (Figure A):

First, we have an ELEMENT node with a tag name set to "CITY". Within the CITY Node, we have one PCDATA child, which contains the string "New York."

Next to ELEMENT and PCDATA, the third most important type of element is WHITESPACE. Most application developers would rather ignore white space entirely, but MS-XML creates a node for each string of white space. For example, suppose we have the following snippet of XML text:

```
<TEAM>
<CITY>New York</CITY>
```

At first glance, you might think that MS-XML creates the following tree (Figure B):

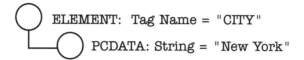

Figure A

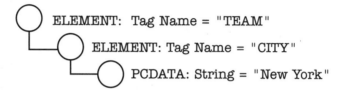

Figure B

Actually, MS-XML creates this tree (Figure C):

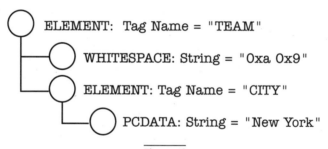

Figure C

First, we have an ELEMENT node for TEAM. But, within the TEAM node, we have two children: one node for white space, and one node for the CITY element. The white-space node contains the string "0xa 0x9", meaning one new line character (ASCII value=10), followed by a single tab character (ASCII value=9.)

It is very important to remember that MS-XML includes white spaces as full-fledged nodes. For example, you cannot assume that the first child of the TEAM node is always a CITY node, and you must always remember to filter out white space nodes (a topic we will return to shortly).

The main methods of the **Element** interface are presented in Table 14.4 (for the complete Element API, see Chapter 23: "The MS-XML API Quick Reference Guide"). We will discuss each of these methods in detail in the next two sections.

Table 14.4 The Element Interface: Main Methods

Method Name	Description
public Object getAttribute (String name);	Returns the value of the specified attribute.
public Enumeration getAttributes();	Returns an enumeration of all attributes associated with the Element.
public Enumeration getElements();	Returns an enumeration of all children elements.
public Name getTagName();	Returns the Tag Name.
public String getText();	Returns the text contained within the Element. For leaf elements, such as PCDATA, CDATA or COMMENT, this is raw text data. For elements with children, getText() traverses the entire subtree, strips out all XML markup, and displays all the text.
public int getType();	Returns the type of Element. There are eight possible return values: DOCUMENT, DTD, ELEMENT, PCDATA, PI, WHITESPACE, COMMENT, or CDATA.
public int numAttributes();	Returns the number of attributes.
public int numElements();	Returns the number of children.

TRAVERSING THE MS-XML TREE STRUCTURE

Now we will try our first example. Listing 14.3 presents an applet which traverses and displays the MS-XML tree structure. Sample output for Baseball.xml is presented in Figure 14.1.

Listing 14.3 First Example: Traversing the MS-XML Tree

```
// MS-XML Example #1
// Displays the Tree Structure
// for the specified XML Document
// Example usage:
```

```
//  <APPLET CODE=BasicApp WIDTH=300 HEIGHT=300>
//  <PARAM NAME="URL" VALUE="Baseball.xml"></APPLET>

import com.ms.xml.om.*;         // Load Object Model Library
import com.ms.xml.parser.*;          // Load Parser Library
import java.applet.*;
import java.awt.*;
import java.net.*;
import java.util.*;

public class BasicApp extends Applet {
    private Document doc;
    private URL xmlURL;
    private TextArea textArea;

    //  Intialize Applet
    public void init () {
        // Create GUI Layout
        setLayout (new BorderLayout());
        textArea = new TextArea();
        add("Center", textArea);

        //  Create Absolute URL to XML Document
        String xmldoc = getParameter ("url");
        try {
            xmlURL = new URL (getDocumentBase(), xmldoc);
        } catch (MalformedURLException e) {
            e.printStackTrace();
        }

        //  Create XML Document Object
        doc = new Document();

        //  Load Document
        try {
            doc.load (xmlURL);
        } catch (ParseException e) {
            doc.reportError (e, System.out);
```

```
            }
    }

    //  Display Tree Structure
    public void start() {
        printNode (doc.getRoot(), 0);
    }

    //  Method for displaying to Text Area
    private void displayText (String text) {
        textArea.append(text);
    }

    //  Recursive printNode Function
    private void printNode (Element node, int level) {

        //  Get Element Type
        int type = node.getType();

        //  Indent
        for (int i=0; i<level; i++) {
            displayText ("        ");
        }
        displayText ("|----");

        //  Print Data for ELEMENTs and PCDATA
        if (type==Element.ELEMENT)
            displayText ("+ ELEMENT:  "+node.getTagName()+"\n");
                else if (type==Element.PCDATA)
                    displayText ("+ PCDATA:  \""+node.getText()+"\"\n");
                else if (type==Element.WHITESPACE)
                    displayText ("+  WHITESPACE\n");

                //  Retrieve and print all children
                Enumeration children = node.getElements();
                while (children.hasMoreElements()) {
                    printNode ((Element)children.nextElement(),
                    level+1);
```

```
            }
        }
    }
```

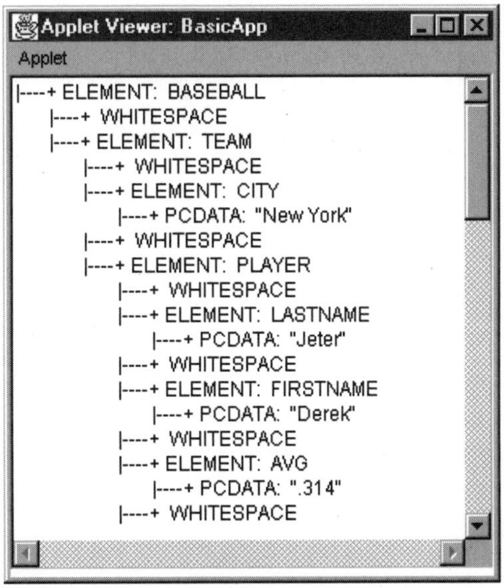

```
Applet Viewer: BasicApp
Applet

|----+ ELEMENT: BASEBALL
    |----+ WHITESPACE
    |----+ ELEMENT: TEAM
        |----+ WHITESPACE
        |----+ ELEMENT: CITY
            |----+ PCDATA: "New York"
        |----+ WHITESPACE
        |----+ ELEMENT: PLAYER
            |----+ WHITESPACE
            |----+ ELEMENT: LASTNAME
                |----+ PCDATA: "Jeter"
            |----+ WHITESPACE
            |----+ ELEMENT: FIRSTNAME
                |----+ PCDATA: "Derek"
            |----+ WHITESPACE
            |----+ ELEMENT: AVG
                |----+ PCDATA: ".314"
            |----+ WHITESPACE
```

Figure 14.1   Output from the first example: Displaying the MS-XML tree structure

Here is how the code works:

1. Import MS-XML Packages:
First, we import two packages from MS-XML:

```
import com.ms.xml.om.*;
import com.ms.xml.parser.*;
```

In the first line, we import the XML Object Model (Package com.ms.xml.om.) This package contains the main classes and interfaces required for application developers, including the **Document** class and **Element** interface. Next, we import the XML Parser (Package com.ms.xml.parser.) This package contains the actual MS-XML parser and is not utilized directly by application developers. Nonetheless, the MS-XML **ParseException** is defined within the parser package, and we are therefore required to import it.

2. **Create the Document Object and Load the XML Document:**
Within init(), we initialize the graphical user interface, and extract the URL applet parameter. We then use the applet's getDocumentBase() to create an absolute URL:

```
// Create Absolute URL to XML Document
String xmldoc = getParameter ("url");
try {
        xmlURL = new URL (getDocumentBase(), xmldoc);
} catch (MalformedURLException e) {
        e.printStackTrace();
}
```

We then create a new XML Document object and load the specified URL object:

```
// Create XML Document Object
doc = new Document();

// Load Document
try {
        doc.load (xmlURL);
} catch (ParseException e) {
        doc.reportError (e, System.out);
}
```

It is recommended that you explicitly catch the ParseException and use the reportError() method to display the error message.

3. **Retrieve the Document Root Element:**
Within the start() method, we extract the root Element of the document, and

```
pass it to our printNode() method:
public void start() {
        printNode (doc.getRoot(), 0);
}
```

The getRoot() method extracts the first node within the MS-XML tree structure that is of type ELEMENT. In our case, this is the BASEBALL element.

4.   Print Each Node within the Tree:

The printNode() method is responsible for printing one node in the tree at a time. It is here that we return to a discussion of the Element interface and its methods.

For each node, we first extract its Element type:

```
int type = node.getType();
```

Understanding the type of element is crucial, because only certain element methods are valid for certain types of elements (for a summary of the main element types as they relate to the Element interface, see Table 14.5.) Additionally, some methods behave differently for different types of elements. For example, the getText() method retrieves the text of a node. For nodes of type PCDATA or WHITESPACE (otherwise known as "Leaf" nodes, because they have no children), getText() retrieves the single string of text embedded inside the node. For nodes of type ELEMENT, getText() traverses the entire subtree and returns all text embedded inside all children elements (this is actually a very effective method of stripping out all XML markup.)

Depending on the type of element, our example takes different courses of action. If this is a node of type ELEMENT, we display its tag name, using the getTagName() method:

```
if (type==Element.ELEMENT)
displayText ("+ ELEMENT: "+node.getTagName()+"\n");
```

On the other hand, if this is PCDATA, we display the embedded text, using the getText() method:

```
else if (type==Element.PCDATA)
     displayText ("+ PCDATA: \""+ node.getText()+"\"\n");
```

Finally, if this is WHITESPACE, we just display the word WHITESPACE, while ignoring the actual white-space characters:

```
else if (type==Element.WHITESPACE)
displayText ("+  WHITESPACE\n");
```

5. Print the Child Nodes:

The last step is to extract the children of each node, and pass each of these children to the recursive printNode() method. The simplest method of retrieving the children is to call the getElements() method. This method returns an enumeration of all child nodes.

You can then iterate through the enumeration and pass each child to the printNode() method:

```
Enumeration children = node.getElements();
while (children.hasMoreElements()) {
    printNode ((Element)children.nextElement(),
    level+1);
}
```

Table 14.5   Main Element Types

Element Type	Description	Useful Methods to Extract Data

ELEMENT	Represents an XML Element.	**Basic Information:**
		public Name getTagName();
		
		Text Information:
		public String getText();
		(**Note:** this method traverses the entire subtree and extracts all text in all descendent nodes.)
		
		Attribute Information:
		public int numAttributes();
		public Object getAttribute(String name);
		public Enumeration getAttributes();
		
		Children Information:
		public int numElements();
		public Enumeration getElements();

PCDATA	Represents Parsed Character Data (PCDATA)	**Text Information:** public String getText(); Elements of PCDATA do not have any attributes, nor do they have any children.
WHITESPACE	Represents a single string of white space characters.	**Text Information:** public String getText(); Elements of WHITESPACE do not have any attributes, nor do they have any children.

CREATING AN XML SUMMARY DOCUMENT

One of the goals of this entire section on parsing is to illustrate the same examples and features using different XML parsers. This better enables you to compare and contrast different XML APIs, and choose the one that best fits the needs of your application. Along these lines, our next two examples are repeats from Chapter 13: "The Ælfred XML Parser". Specifically, we will look at 1) creating an XML summary document and 2) the mechanics of searching an XML document.

To refresh your memory, the XML summary applet reads in the Baseball.xml file, and prints a customized summary report (see Figure 14.2.) With Ælfred, we created this summary by capturing and filtering parse events as they occurred. With MS-XML, we take a very different approach, and create the summary document by selectively traversing the MS-XML tree structure.

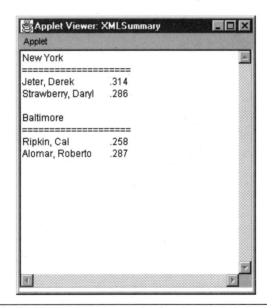

Figure 14.2   Output from second example: Creating an XML summary document

The source code for our second example appears in Listing 14.4. Look briefly at the code now, but to understand this example, we must first revisit the MS-XML API.

Listing 14.4   Creating an XML Summary Document

```
// MS-XML Example
// Creating an XML Summary Document
```

```java
// Example usage:
// <APPLET CODE=XMLSummary WIDTH=300 HEIGHT=300>
// <PARAM NAME="url" VALUE="Baseball.xml"></APPLET>

import com.ms.xml.om.*;        // Load Object Model Library
import com.ms.xml.parser.*;    // Load Parser Library
import com.ms.xml.util.*;      // Load Utility Library
import java.applet.*;
import java.awt.*;
import java.net.*;
import java.util.*;

public class XMLSummary extends Applet {
    private Document doc;
    private URL xmlURL;
    private TextArea textArea;

    // Intialize Applet
    public void init () {

        // Create GUI Layout
        setLayout (new BorderLayout());
        textArea = new TextArea();
        add("Center", textArea);

        // Create XML Document Object
        doc = new Document();

        // Create Absolute URL to XML Document
        String xmldoc = getParameter ("url");
        try {
            xmlURL = new URL (getDocumentBase(), xmldoc);
        } catch (MalformedURLException e) {
            e.printStackTrace();
        }

        // Load Document
        try {
```

```java
            doc.load (xmlURL);
        } catch (ParseException e) {
            doc.reportError (e, System.out);
        }
    }


    //  Start Method
    public void start() {
        printSummary.(doc.getRoot());
    }


    //  Method for displaying to Text Area
    private void displayText (String text) {
        textArea.append(text);
    }


    //  Display Summary
    private void printSummary (Element root) {
        Element child;

        //  Filter out WHITESPACE Elements
        //  The resulting enumeration consists only
        //  of TEAM Elements
        ElementEnumeration enum = new ElementEnumeration
            (root, null, Element.ELEMENT);

        //  Iterate through each TEAM Element
        while (enum.hasMoreElements()) {
            child = (Element) enum.nextElement();
            printTeam (child);
            displayText("\n");
        }
    }


    //  Display TEAM Elements and PLAYER Data
    private void printTeam (Element team) {
        Element child;
        String lastname, firstname, avg;
```

```
        String cityname = extractText (team, "CITY");
        displayText (cityname+"\n");
        displayText ("===================\n");


        // Filter for PLAYER Elements
        ElementEnumeration enum = new ElementEnumeration
            (team, Name.create("PLAYER"), Element.ELEMENT);


        // Iterate through each PLAYER Element
        while (enum.hasMoreElements()) {
            child = (Element) enum.nextElement();
            lastname = extractText(child,"LASTNAME");
            firstname = extractText(child,"FIRSTNAME");
            avg = extractText(child,"AVG");
            displayText (lastname+", "+firstname+"\t"+avg+"\n");
        }
    }


    // Extract Text for Target Element
    private String extractText (Element parent,
        String tagname) {


        // Retrieve Element Specified by tagname
        ElementEnumeration enum = new ElementEnumeration
            (parent, Name.create(tagname),Element.ELEMENT);
        Element target = (Element) enum.nextElement();
        return target.getText();
    }
}
```

In our first example, we retrieved the children of a node using the getElements()
method. This method returns all the children of any given node, and permits iteration through these children one at a time. The MS-XML API also includes an
ElementEnumeration class for retrieving specific children of a node (see Table
14.6.) For example, use an ElementEnumeration object to retrieve only children
of type ELEMENT or to retrieve children with a specified tag name. The

ElementEnumeration class is therefore a very powerful tool for selectively traversing the tree and searching for particular elements.

To utilize an ElementEnumeration object, utilize the Name utility class (see Table 14.7) that appears in the MS-XML Utilities package (Package com.ms.xml.util.) The Name utility is utilized by the MS-XML parser as a means of storing duplicate names within a global hash table, thereby providing more effective memory management. Fortunately, you do not need to know anything about hash tables. You just need to know that to search for a particular tag name, you cannot just search by the String tag. You need to search by the Name object. You can easily create a new Name object by using the static create (String name) method. For example, to find all children nodes of root that are of type ELEMENT and have a tag name of "TEAM", the code would look like this:

```
ElementEnumeration enum = new ElementEnumeration
  (root, Name.create("TEAM"), Element.ELEMENT);
```

This first parameter is the parent Element object. The second parameter is the tag name we are searching (or null if the name is not important.) The third parameter is the Element type (or null if type is not important.) In most cases, type is set to Element.ELEMENT.

Now that we know how to search for certain elements, we should turn our attention to our second example in Listing 14.4. The init() method is identical to the last example: we create the GUI, and load the XML document. The start() method, however calls the private printSummary() method and passes the root element of the document:

```
public void start() {
    printSummary (doc.getRoot());
}
```

The printSummary() method begins a systematic search for the data. During the first phase, we search the root node for all children of type ELEMENT:

```
ElementEnumeration enum = new ElementEnumeration
  (root, null, Element.ELEMENT);
```

The main objective here is to filter out any WHITESPACE elements that may exist under root, and hone in only on the TEAM elements (to help visualize the filtering necessary, see the sample MS-XML tree in Figure 14.3).

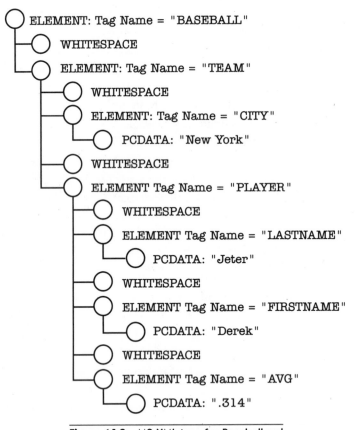

Figure 14.3   MS-XML tree for Baseball.xml

The ElementEnumeration class implements the Enumeration interface, and we are therefore able to iterate through each of the children:

```
while (enum.hasMoreElements()) {
    child = (Element) enum.nextElement();
    printTeam (child);
    displayText("\n");
}
```

Within the printTeam() method we first extract the text of the CITY element using the extractText() method:

```
String cityname = extractText (team, "CITY");
```

The extractText() method is perhaps the most useful part of Listing 14.4, since it is easily reusable in any MS-XML application. The method takes a parent element, and a tag name, and returns the text of the target element. It performs this task by applying yet another filter via the ElementEnumeration object:

```
private String extractText (Element parent,
  String tagname) {


    // Retrieve Element Specified by tagname
    ElementEnumeration enum = new ElementEnumeration
        (parent, Name.create(tagname),Element.ELEMENT);
    Element target = (Element) enum.nextElement();
    return target.getText();
}
```

As this is such a common task when traversing an MS-XML tree, feel free to adopt this method for your own use.

The remainder of the code in Listing 14.4 applies similar filtering techniques for finding PLAYER elements and extracting player data. The output of Listing 14.4 is identical to the Ælfred example, but as you can see, MS-XML demands an altogether different approach.

Table 14.6   The ElementEnumeration Class: Constructors

public
  Element
  Enumeration
  (Element root);
	Creates a new enumerator for retrieving **all** the children of the given root node.

public
  Element
  Enumeration
  (Element root,
  Name tag, int type);
	Creates a new enumerator for retrieving all children of the specified node with matching tag names and/or types.
	Parameters:
	■ Element root: the parent Element object.
	■ Name tag: the name of the tag; this can be null if the name is not important.
	■ int type: the element type; this can be –1 if type is not important.

Table 14.7   The Name Utility Class: Main Methods

Method Name	Description
public static Name create (String name);	Static method for creating a Name object.
public boolean equals (Object that);	Tests for equality. Note that the equals method is not really needed, as you can use the == and != operators directly. For example:
	static Name myName = Name.create("PLAYER");
	whie (e.getTagName() != myName)...
public String toString();	Displays the String name.

TIP

MS-XML API: In addition to the **ElementCollection** class, the MS-XML API includes an **ElementCollection** class. The class provides identical functionality to **ElementCollection**, but provides an array interface rather than an enumeration interface. You can therefore request children nodes at specified index values. For details, see Chapter 23: "The MS-XML API Quick Reference Guide".

SEARCHING AN XML DOCUMENT

Once you have learned to create an XML summary document, the mechanics of searching are very straightforward. Listing 14.5 presents our third example. Sample output is presented in Figure 14.4.

Listing 14.5   Searching an XML Document

```
//  MS-XML Example
//  Searching an XML Document

import com.ms.xml.om.*;       //  Load Object Model Library
import com.ms.xml.parser.*;   //  Load Parser Library
import com.ms.xml.util.*;     //  Load Utility Library
```

```java
import java.applet.*;
import java.awt.*;
import java.awt.event.*;
import java.net.*;
import java.util.*;

public class XMLSearch extends Applet
  implements ActionListener {
      private Document doc;
      private URL xmlURL;
      private TextArea textArea;
      private TextField target;
      private Button search;
      private int numtargets;

      // Intialize Applet
      public void init () {

              // Create Panel with Text Field
              // and Search Button
              Panel p = new Panel ();
              target = new TextField(20);
              search = new Button("Search");
              search.addActionListener (this);
              p.add (target);
              p.add (search);

              // Create Border Layout
              setLayout (new BorderLayout());
              textArea = new TextArea();
              add("Center", textArea);
              add ("North", p);

              // Create XML Document Object
              doc = new Document();

              // Create Absolute URL to XML Document
```

```java
String xmldoc = getParameter ("url");
try {
    xmlURL = new URL (getDocumentBase(), xmldoc);
} catch (MalformedURLException e) {
    e.printStackTrace();
}

// Load Document
try {
    doc.load (xmlURL);
} catch (ParseException e) {
    doc.reportError (e, System.out);
}
}


// Button Event Handler
public void actionPerformed (ActionEvent e) {
    numtargets =0;
    searchDoc (target.getText().toUpperCase());
}


// Method for displaying to Text Area
private void displayText (String text) {
    textArea.append(text);
}


// Search Document
private void searchDoc (String targettext) {
    Element child;
    Element root = doc.getRoot();

    // Filter out WHITESPACE Elements
    // The resulting enumeration consists only
    // of TEAM Elements
    ElementEnumeration enum = new ElementEnumeration
        (root, null, Element.ELEMENT);
```

```
        // Iterate through each TEAM Element
        while (enum.hasMoreElements()) {
            child = (Element) enum.nextElement();
            searchTeam (child, targettext);
        }
        displayText ("\n------------------\n");
        displayText ("Records found:  "+numtargets+"\n");


}


// Search TEAM Elements
private void searchTeam (Element team, String targettext) {
    Element child;

        // Retrieve all PLAYER Elements
        ElementEnumeration enum = new ElementEnumeration
            (team, Name.create("PLAYER"),Element.ELEMENT);

        // Iterate through each PLAYER Element
        while (enum.hasMoreElements()) {
            child = (Element) enum.nextElement();
            searchPlayer (child, targettext);
        }
}


// Search PLAYER Elements
private void searchPlayer (Element player,
  String targettext) {
        String lastname = extractText(player,"LASTNAME");
        String upperlastname = lastname.toUpperCase();
        if (upperlastname.indexOf(targettext)>-1) {
            numtargets++;
            String firstname = extractText(player,"FIRSTNAME");
            String avg = extractText(player,"AVG");
            displayText ("\n"+lastname+", "+firstname+"\t"+avg+"\n");
        }
}
```

```
//  Extract Text for Target Element
private String extractText (Element parent,
   String tagname) {

      //  Retrieve Element Specified by tagname
      ElementEnumeration enum = new ElementEnumeration
         (parent, Name.create(tagname),Element.ELEMENT);
      Element target = (Element) enum.nextElement();
      return target.getText();

   }

}
```

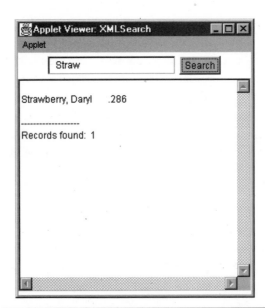

Figure 14.4　Output from third example searching an XML document

Again, the approach is very different from that of the Ælfred example discussed in the last chapter. Rather than filter events generated by the parser, we traverse the tree created by the parser, and systematically search for our target string. In this case, we are searching the last names of all baseball players.

The systematic search employed in Listing 14.5 is nearly identical to the last example. First, we obtain the document root, and filter out all WHITESPACE elements (see Figure 14.5, Phase 1):

```
Element root = doc.getRoot();
ElementEnumeration enum = new ElementEnumeration
  (root, null, Element.ELEMENT);
```

The resulting enumeration now contains only TEAM elements. We then filter each of these elements for PLAYER elements (see Figure 14.5, Phase 2):

```
ElementEnumeration enum = new ElementEnumeration
    (team, Name.create("PLAYER"),Element.ELEMENT);
```

Finally we filter these elements for the LASTNAME elements, using our **extract-Text()** method (see Figure 14.5, Phase 3):

```
String lastname = extractText(player,"LASTNAME");
```

If this string matches the user provided target string, we proceed to extract the remaining elements and display them within the applet's text area.

REMAPPING MS-XML TREE DATA

The MS-XML tree structure is a very convenient data structure for storing XML data. It is easy to traverse the tree, extract nodes, filter for specific nodes, and extract embedded text. As we will see in the next section, it is also easy to modify the tree by adding, editing, and deleting nodes. For many applications, accessing the tree directly is simple and efficient. Nonetheless, there are times when you want to store your XML data within your own data structures, and the MS-XML tree simply will not do.

In these cases, you must develop an efficient mechanism for mapping the MS-XML tree structure to your own data structures. For example, you may want to read in a financial XML document, and map each STOCK element to a Stock object. You can then work with these objects directly. For example, you can pass the stock object to a Java Bean responsible for graphing financial data, or compare the stock object to data obtained from a database.

To illustrate the key concepts, our next example will remap the MS-XML tree structure of Baseball.xml to a vector of **Player** objects. The **Player** class contains all data regarding one Baseball player, including name, team and batting average. It also includes a set of accessor methods for retrieving the data. Here is the code for the **Player** class:

```
class Player {
        private String lastName, firstName
        private String cityName, imgSrc;
```

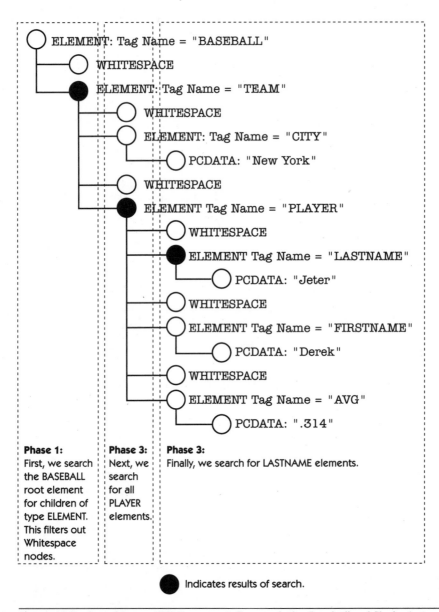

ELEMENT: Tag Name = "BASEBALL"
 WHITESPACE
 ELEMENT: Tag Name = "TEAM"
  WHITESPACE
  ELEMENT: Tag Name = "CITY"
   PCDATA: "New York"
  WHITESPACE
  ELEMENT Tag Name = "PLAYER"
   WHITESPACE
   ELEMENT Tag Name = "LASTNAME"
    PCDATA: "Jeter"
   WHITESPACE
   ELEMENT Tag Name = "FIRSTNAME"
    PCDATA: "Derek"
   WHITESPACE
   ELEMENT Tag Name = "AVG"
    PCDATA: ".314"

Phase 1:
First, we search the BASEBALL root element for children of type ELEMENT. This filters out Whitespace nodes.

Phase 3:
Next, we search for all PLAYER elements.

Phase 3:
Finally, we search for LASTNAME elements.

● Indicates results of search.

Figure 14.5 Searching an XML Document. To search the Baseball.xml file for last names, we must employ a three phase search of the MS-XML tree.

```
        private float avg;

        // Constructor
        public Player (String lastName, String firstName,
          String cityName, float avg, String imgSrc) {
              this.lastName = lastName;
              this.firstName = firstName;
              this.cityName = cityName;
              this.avg = avg;
              this.imgSrc = imgSrc;
        }


        //  Accessor Methods
        public String getlastName () { return lastName; }
        public String getfirstName () { return firstName;}
        public String getcityName () { return cityName; }
        public String getimgSrc () { return imgSrc; }
        public float getAvg () { return avg; }
    }
```

Our goal is to extract each PLAYER element within the document and map the data to a Player object. We then enable users to select an individual player and display the player's photograph (see Figure 14.6 for sample output).

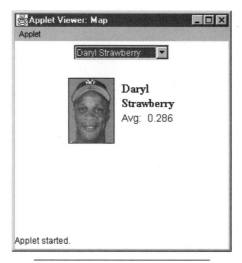

Figure 14.6 Sample output result

Users can select a Baseball player and view the player's stats and photograph.

The code for our example is in Listing 14.6. Listings 14.7 and 14.8 show the revised Baseball.dtd and Baseball.xml files required for the example. These two files are reprinted from the last chapter, and include the IMG tag for a GIF or JPEG photograph.

Listing 14.6 Mapping MS-XML Tree Data

```
//  MS-XML Example
//  Demonstrates Remapping of MS-XML
//  Tree structure to user-defined Data
//  Structure;  also demonstrates use
//  of Attributes

import com.ms.xml.om.*;       //  Load Object Model Library
import com.ms.xml.parser.*;   //  Load Parser Library
import com.ms.xml.util.*;     //  Load Utility Library
import java.applet.*;
import java.awt.*;
import java.awt.event.*;
import java.net.*;
import java.util.*;
import java.awt.Choice;


public class Map extends Applet
      implements ItemListener {
      private Document doc;
      private URL xmlURL;
      private Choice select;
      private Player current;
      private Vector players;

      //  Intialize Applet
      public void init () {

            // Create Panel with Pull down menu
            Panel p = new Panel ();
            select = new Choice();
```

```
select.addItemListener (this);
p.add (select);
select.addItem ("-- Select a Player --");

// Create Border Layout
setLayout (new BorderLayout());
add ("North", p);

// Create vector of Player objects
players = new Vector();

// Create XML Document Object
doc = new Document();

// Create Absolute URL to XML Document
String xmldoc = getParameter ("url");
try {
    xmlURL = new URL (getDocumentBase(), xmldoc);
} catch (MalformedURLException e) {
    e.printStackTrace();
}

// Load Document
try {
    doc.load (xmlURL);
} catch (ParseException e) {
    doc.reportError (e, System.out);
}

// Map to Vector of Player Objects
mapDocument (doc.getRoot());

// Add all players to Applet selection menu
for (int i=0; i< players.size(); i++) {
    current = (Player) players.elementAt(i);
    select.addItem (current.getfirstName()+" " +
        current.getlastName());
```

```java
        }
        current=null;
    }


    //  Event Handler for Choice Selection
    public void itemStateChanged (ItemEvent e) {
        current = (Player) players.elementAt
            (select.getSelectedIndex()-1);
        repaint();
    }


    //  Paint Method
    public void paint (Graphics g) {
        if (current!=null) {
            g.setFont (new Font ("TimesRoman", Font.BOLD, 16));
            g.drawString (current.getfirstName(),150,70);
            g.drawString (current.getlastName(),150,90);
            g.setFont (new Font ("TimeRoman", Font.PLAIN, 14));
            g.drawString ("Avg:  "+current.getAvg(), 150, 110);
            Image photo = getImage (getDocumentBase(),
                current.getimgSrc());
            g.drawImage (photo, 75,50,this);
        }
    }


    //  Map Internal Tree structure to
    //  Vector of Player Objects
    private void mapDocument (Element root) {
        Element child;

        //  Filter out WHITESPACE Elements
        //  The resulting enumeration consists only
        //  of TEAM Elements
        ElementEnumeration enum = new ElementEnumeration
            (root, null, Element.ELEMENT);
```

```
    // Iterate through each TEAM Element
    while (enum.hasMoreElements()) {
        child = (Element) enum.nextElement();
        mapTeam (child);
    }
}


// Map TEAM Elements
private void mapTeam (Element team) {
    Element child;

    // Extract City Name
    String cityname = extractText (team, "CITY");

    // Retrieve all PLAYER Elements
    ElementEnumeration enum = new ElementEnumeration
        (team, Name.create("PLAYER"),Element.ELEMENT);

    // Iterate through each PLAYER Element
    while (enum.hasMoreElements()) {
        child = (Element) enum.nextElement();
        mapPlayer (child, cityname);
    }
}


// Map PLAYER Elements
private void mapPlayer (Element player, String cityname)
{
    // First Extract IMG Element and SRC Attribute
    ElementEnumeration enum = new ElementEnumeration
        (player, Name.create("IMG"),Element.ELEMENT);
    Element image = (Element) enum.nextElement();
    String imgsrc = (String) image.getAttribute ("SRC");

    // Then Extract Player Data
    String lastname = extractText(player,"LASTNAME");
    String firstname = extractText(player,"FIRSTNAME");
```

```java
        String avgtxt = extractText(player,"AVG");
        Float tempFloat = Float.valueOf (avgtxt);
        float avg = tempFloat.floatValue();

        // Create new Player Object and add to vector
        Player newplayer = new Player
           (lastname, firstname, cityname, avg, imgsrc);
        players.addElement(newplayer);
    }


    // Extract Text for Target Element
    private String extractText (Element parent,
        String tagname) {

        // Retrieve Element Specified by tagname
        ElementEnumeration enum = new ElementEnumeration
            (parent, Name.create(tagname),Element.ELEMENT);
        Element target = (Element) enum.nextElement();
        return target.getText();
    }
}


// Class for holding Player Information
class Player {
    private String lastName, firstName
    private String cityName, imgSrc;
    private float avg;

    // Constructor
    public Player (String lastName, String firstName,
       String cityName, float avg, String imgSrc) {
        this.lastName = lastName;
        this.firstName = firstName;
        this.cityName = cityName;
        this.avg = avg;
        this.imgSrc = imgSrc;
```

```
    }

    //  Accessor Methods
    public String getlastName () { return lastName; }
    public String getfirstName () { return firstName; }
    public String getcityName () { return cityName; }
    public String getimgSrc () { return imgSrc; }
    public float getAvg () { return avg; }
}
```

Listing 14.7 Revised Baseball.dtd

The DTD now includes an IMG Element with a SRC Attribute.

```
<!ELEMENT BASEBALL (TEAM)+>
<!ELEMENT TEAM (CITY, PLAYER*)>
<!ELEMENT CITY (#PCDATA)>
<!ELEMENT PLAYER (LASTNAME, FIRSTNAME, AVG, IMG)>
<!ELEMENT FIRSTNAME (#PCDATA)>
<!ELEMENT LASTNAME (#PCDATA)>
<!ELEMENT AVG (#PCDATA)>
<!ELEMENT IMG EMPTY>
<!ATTLIST IMG SRC CDATA #REQUIRED>
```

Listing 14.8 Revised Baseball.xml

Each player now has a photograph.

```
<?xml version="1.0" encoding="UTF-8"?>
<!-- XML Document for American League Teams -->
<!DOCTYPE BASEBALL SYSTEM "Baseball.dtd">
<BASEBALL>
    <TEAM>
        <CITY>New York</CITY>
        <PLAYER>
            <LASTNAME>Jeter</LASTNAME>
            <FIRSTNAME>Derek</FIRSTNAME>
            <AVG>.314</AVG>
```

```
            <IMG SRC="images/newyork1.jpg"/>
        </PLAYER>
        <PLAYER>
            <LASTNAME>Strawberry</LASTNAME>
            <FIRSTNAME>Daryl</FIRSTNAME>
            <AVG>.286</AVG>
            <IMG SRC="images/newyork2.jpg"/>
        </PLAYER>
    </TEAM>
    <TEAM>
        <CITY>Baltimore</CITY>
        <PLAYER>
            <LASTNAME>Ripkin</LASTNAME>
            <FIRSTNAME>Cal</FIRSTNAME>
            <AVG>.258</AVG>
            <IMG SRC="images/baltimore1.jpg"/>
        </PLAYER>
        <PLAYER>
            <LASTNAME>Alomar</LASTNAME>
            <FIRSTNAME>Roberto</FIRSTNAME>
            <AVG>.287</AVG>
            <IMG SRC="images/baltimore2.jpg"/>
        </PLAYER>
    </TEAM>
</BASEBALL>
```

As you examine the code, draw your attention to the **mapDocument()** method. This method initiates the mapping between the MS-XML tree structure and the Player objects. As in the previous examples, the code drills down from the BASEBALL root element to each individual PLAYER element. It does this by first filtering out WHITESPACE nodes, and then searching for all PLAYER elements. Once we have a PLAYER element, the real work takes place in the **mapPlayer()** method. Here, we begin by searching for the IMG element:

```
ElementEnumeration enum = new ElementEnumeration
    (player, Name.create("IMG"),Element.ELEMENT);
Element image = (Element) enum.nextElement();
```

We then use the getAttribute(`String name`) method to extract the SRC attribute:

```
String imgsrc = (String) image.getAttribute ("SRC");
```

As you can see, extracting attributes is very easy!

The remainder of the `mapPlayer()` method extracts the data for first name, last name, and batting average:

```
String lastname = extractText(player,"LASTNAME");
String firstname = extractText(player,"FIRSTNAME");
String avgtxt = extractText(player,"AVG");
```

and, places this data in a new `Player` object:

```
Player newplayer = new Player
        (lastname, firstname, cityname, avg, imgsrc);
```

And, finally, the new player object is added to the vector of **Player** objects:

```
players.addElement(newplayer);
```

We have therefore succeeded in mapping from MS-XML to our own data structure.

MODIFYING XML DOCUMENTS

So far, we have only traversed the MS-XML tree structure, but it is also possible to modify it, for example by adding new nodes, modifying existing nodes, or delete entire subtrees. The newly modified tree can be saved back as an XML text file. By permittig the modification of the tree structure, MS-XML enables you to create a whole host of XML applications, including, XML editors and databases.

CREATING NEW ELEMENTS

The `ElementFactory` interface, and its default implementation, `ElementFactoryImpl` enable you to create new nodes. To create a new node, use the `createNode()` method. This method requires specifying the parent element, the type of element (e.g. ELEMENT, PCDATA, etc.), the tag name (or null if there is no tag name), and the string text (or null if there is no text.) For example, this codes adds a new TEAM element to the root node:

```
ElementFactoryImpl factory = new ElementFactoryImpl();
Element element = factory.createElement (root,
    Element.ELEMENT,Name.create("TEAM"), null);
```

createNode() creates a new TEAM element, and adds it directly to root. The TEAM element is therefore a full-fledged element on par with all other existing elements within the MS-XML tree.

createNode() also returns an **Element** object, which you can use as the parent for other new elements. This is important because there are often at least two steps to creating a new node. In the first step, you create the new element with the specified tag name. In the second step, you add a PCDATA node in order to embed the text. For example, to create a LASTNAME element such as: <LASTNAME>Orsenigo</LASTNAME>, first create a LASTNAME element:

```
Element lastname = factory.createElement (root,
    Element.ELEMENT,Name.create("LASTNAME"), null);
```

and then create a PCDATA element:

```
Element pcdata = factory.createElement (lastname,
    Element.PCDATA, null, "Orsenigo");
```

Note that the pcdata element object is now a child of the lastname object. The newly modified MS-XML tree will therefore look like this (Figure D):

Figure D

Table 14.8   ElementFactoryImpl Class

Method	Description
public ElementFactoryImpl();	Constructor
public Element createElement(Element parent, int type, Name tag, String text);.	Creates a new Element object and adds it to the MS-XML tree ■ parent represents the parent of the newly created element. ■ type represents the type of the newly created element (e.g. ELEMENT, PCDATA, etc.) ■ tag represents a Name object (or null if there is no tag name), and; ■ text string is primarily used for PCDATA or WHITEPSPACE elements (or null if there is no text.)

EDITING/DELETING ELEMENTS

MS-XML also makes it possible to edit or delete any existing nodes within the tree structure. The main methods for editing and deleting are found in the Element interface, and are summarized in Table 14.9.

To edit an element, reset its text string, using the **setText()** method, or reset or remove attributes. You can even move the element by resetting its parent node.

To delete a node, use the **removeChild()** method. Note, however, that this will remove the child and its entire subtree (if any).

Table 14.9   Element Interface: Methods for Editing/Deleting Elements

Method Name	Description
public void setText(String text);	Resets the Element's text string.
public void setParent(Element parent);	Moves the Element to a new Parent.
public void setAttribute(String name, Object value);	Resets the value of the specified attribute.

continued on next page

Method Name	Description
public void setAttribute(Name name, Object value);	Resets the value of the specified attribute. Identical to method above, except the Attribute is specified by a Name object.
public void removeChild (Element elem)	Removes the specified child element.
public void removeAttribute(String name);	Removes the specified attribute from the Element.
public void removeAttribute(Name name);	Removes the specified attribute from the Element. Identical to the method above, except the Attribute is specified by a Name object.

SAVING MODIFIED XML DOCUMENTS

Once you have modified the MS-XML tree structure, you can save it back to disk using the Document save() method. This method requires the use of an XMLOutputStream object. The XMLOutputStream class is a file writer included with MS-XML, and is specifically designed for XML markup, including white space handling.

To create an XMLOutputStream object, you must pass an OutputStream object, such as FileOutputStream to the XMLOutputStream constructor. For example:

```
FileOutputStream out = new FileOutputStream (filename);
XMLOutputStream xout = new XMLOutputStream (out);
```

You can then call the Document save() method:

```
doc.save(xout);
```

When using the save() method, MS-XML will traverse the entire tree, including all white space nodes, and print each element. This enables MS-XML to recreate the tabs and spaces present in the original XML document.

Table 14.10   The XMLOutputStream Class: Main Methods

Method Name	Description
public XMLOutputStream(OutputStream out);	Constructor
public void close() throws IOException;	Closes the stream
public void flush() throws IOException;	Flushes the stream
public void setEncoding(String encoding, boolean littleendian, boolean byteOrderMark) throws IOException;	Defines the character encoding of the output stream
public void write(int c) throws IOException;	Writes a character to the stream
public void writeChars(String str) throws IOException;	Writes a string to the stream
public void writeQuotedString(String str) throws IOException;	Writes a string with quotes around it

CREATING AN XML DATABASE

For the final example in this chapter, we will explore the creation of XML databases. With the ability to add, edit, and delete nodes within an XML document, we can treat XML documents as dynamic databases. These are not databases in the modern sense, as they are not relational, and do not support transaction management. Nonetheless, they are quite useful and can be adapted for a number of Internet applications.

Our final example enables users to update a database of baseball players. To keep the example manageable, we have made two simplifying assumptions. First, the application only works with one baseball team at a time. Second, we only enable users to add new nodes to the tree. Editing and deleting nodes is left as an exercise for the reader.

The database application begins by loading the XML document specified on the command line. We will be using a revised Baseball.xml file which contains data on one team (see Listing 14.9.) The application parses the document and places each player in an AWT list (see Figure 14.7). To add a new player, users press the add button and enter the data (see Figure 14.8). By pressing Apply, the data are added to the tree and the AWT List (see Figure 14.9). Users also have the option of saving the newly modified tree to disk. For example, Listing 14.10 shows the modified Baseball.xml file after we have added Joe Girardi to the line up. As you can see, our new player is added as a single line of XML text. This occurs because the code does not explicitly add any white space elements for formatting.

Figure 14.7 Output from the final example: Creating an XML database

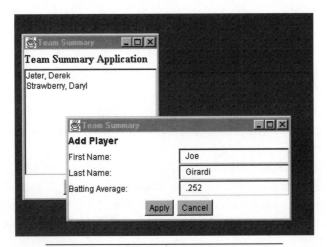

Figure 14.8 Adding Joe Girardi to the line up

Figure 14.9   Modification of MS-XML tree is successful

Listing 14.9   Baseball.xml File for Final Example

The final example only works with one baseball team at a time.

```
<?xml version="1.0" encoding="UTF-8"?>
<!-- XML Document for American League Teams -->
<!DOCTYPE BASEBALL SYSTEM "Baseball.dtd">
<BASEBALL>
    <TEAM>
        <CITY>New York</CITY>
        <PLAYER>
            <LASTNAME>Jeter</LASTNAME>
            <FIRSTNAME>Derek</FIRSTNAME>
            <AVG>.314</AVG>
        </PLAYER>
        <PLAYER>
            <LASTNAME>Strawberry</LASTNAME>
            <FIRSTNAME>Daryl</FIRSTNAME>
            <AVG>.286</AVG>
        </PLAYER>
    </TEAM>
</BASEBALL>
```

Listing 14.10 Updated Baseball.xml File

After adding Joe Girardi, our Baseball.xml file now looks like this.

```
<?xml version="1.0" encoding="UTF-8"?>
<!-- XML Document for American League Teams -->
<!DOCTYPE BASEBALL SYSTEM "Baseball.dtd">
<BASEBALL>
    <TEAM>
        <CITY>New York</CITY>
        <PLAYER>
            <LASTNAME>Jeter</LASTNAME>
            <FIRSTNAME>Derek</FIRSTNAME>
            <AVG>.314</AVG>
        </PLAYER>
        <PLAYER>
            <LASTNAME>Strawberry</LASTNAME>
            <FIRSTNAME>Daryl</FIRSTNAME>
            <AVG>.286</AVG>
        </PLAYER>
<PLAYER><LASTNAME>Girardi</LASTNAME><FIRSTNAME>Joe
</FIRSTNAME><AVG>.252</AVG></PLAYER></TEAM></BASEBALL>
```

The code for the final example appears in Listing 14.11. The code is longer than any of the examples we have seen so far, but do not be deterred. Most of the code deals with GUI building and event handling. Additionally, the most important XML code occurs within just three methods: addXML(), createNode(), and save(). We will focus on these two methods.

Listing 14.11 Creating an XML Database

```
//  MS-XML Example
//  Demonstrates the ability to modify
//  the MS-XML Tree structure and save
//  the modified tree back to a file

import com.ms.xml.om.*;      // Load Object Model Library
import com.ms.xml.parser.*;  // Load Parser Library
```

```java
import com.ms.xml.util.*;        // Load Parser Utility Library
import java.awt.*;
import java.awt.event.*;
import java.awt.Choice;
import java.net.*;
import java.util.*;
import java.io.*;

public class BasicApp extends Frame implements ActionListener{
    private Document doc;
    private Element root;
    private URL xmlURL;
    private List list;
    private String filename;

    // Constructor
    public BasicApp (String filename) {
        super ("Team Summary");
        this.filename = filename;

        // Create BorderLayout and Header
        setLayout (new BorderLayout());
        Label header = new Label ("Team Summary Application");
        header.setFont (new Font ("TimesRoman", Font.BOLD, 16));
        add ("North", header);

        // Create List of Players
        list = new List(10);
        add ("Center", list);

        // Create Panel for add/save buttons
        Panel p = new Panel ();
        Button add = new Button ("Add");
        Button save = new Button ("Save");
        add.setActionCommand ("Add");
        save.setActionCommand ("Save");
        add.addActionListener (this);
```

```
        save.addActionListener (this);
        p.add (add);
        p.add (save);
        add ("South", p);

        // Create WindowListener
        this.addWindowListener(new WindowAdapter () {
            public void windowClosing(WindowEvent e) {
                dispose();
            }
        });

        // Create Absolute URL to XML Document
        xmlURL = createURL (filename);

        // Create XML Document Object
        doc = new Document();

        // Load Document
        try {
            doc.load (xmlURL);
        } catch (ParseException e) {
            doc.reportError (e, System.out);
        }

        // Extract Root Element and Players
        root = doc.getRoot();
        extractPlayers();
    }

// Button Event Handler
public void actionPerformed (ActionEvent e) {
    addPlayer add;
    String action = e.getActionCommand();
    if (action.equals ("Add"))
        add = new addPlayer(this, root);
    else if (action.equals ("Save")) save();
```

```
        }

// Save modified XML Document
public void save () {
    try {
        FileOutputStream out = new FileOutputStream (filename);
        XMLOutputStream xout = new XMLOutputStream (out);
        doc.save(xout);
        xout.close();
    } catch (IOException e) {
        e.printStackTrace();
    }
}

// Extract Players and Place in List
public void extractPlayers () {
    Element currentPlayer;
    String last, first;
    list.removeAll();

    // Filter out WHITESPACE Elements
    ElementEnumeration enum = new ElementEnumeration
        (root, null, Element.ELEMENT);
    Element team = (Element) enum.nextElement();

    // Filter out PLAYER Elements
    ElementCollection players = new ElementCollection
        (team, Name.create("PLAYER"), Element.ELEMENT);

    // Put Players into List
    for (int i=0; i<players.getLength(); i++) {
        currentPlayer = players.getChild(i);
        last = extractText (currentPlayer, "LASTNAME");
        first = extractText (currentPlayer, "FIRSTNAME");
        list.add (last+", "+first);
    }
}
```

```
//  Extract Text for Target Element
public String extractText (Element parent,
    String tagname) {

    //  Retrieve Element Specified by tagname
    ElementEnumeration enum = new ElementEnumeration
        (parent, Name.create(tagname),Element.ELEMENT);
    Element target = (Element) enum.nextElement();
    return target.getText();
}


//  Method to create an absolute URL
//  from a filename.  Note:
//  On Windows Platforms, the file separator is \
//  On UNIX and for URLs, the file separator is /
private URL createURL(String fileName) {
    URL url=null;
    File f = new File(fileName);
    String path = f.getAbsolutePath();
        String fs = System.getProperty("file.separator");
            if (fs.length() == 1) {
                char sep = fs.charAt(0);
            if (sep != '/')
                path = path.replace(sep, '/');
            if (path.charAt(0) != '/')
                path = '/' + path;
        }
        path = "file://" + path;

    try {
        url = new URL(path);
    } catch (MalformedURLException e) {
        System.out.println("Cannot create url for: "+fileName);
        System.exit(0);
    }
    return url;
```

```
            }

    public static void main (String[] args) throws Exception {
        BasicApp app = new BasicApp(args[0]);
        app.pack();
        app.show();
    }
}


class addPlayer extends Frame implements ActionListener{
    private TextField lastname, firstname, average;
    private Element root;
    private BasicApp parent;

    public addPlayer (BasicApp parent, Element root) {
        super("Team Summary");
        this.root = root;
        this.parent = parent;


        // Create Border Layout and add Header
        setLayout (new BorderLayout());
        Label header = new Label ("Add Player");
        header.setFont (new Font ("TimesNewRoman",
          Font.BOLD, 14));
        this.add ("North", header);

        //  Create Panel Insert
        Panel p = new Panel ();
        p.setLayout (new GridLayout(3,2));
        Label firstlabel = new Label ("First Name:  ");
        Label lastLabel = new Label ("Last Name:  ");
        Label avgLabel = new Label ("Batting Average:  ");
        firstname = new TextField (20);
        lastname = new TextField (20);
        average = new TextField (20);
```

```
        p.add (firstlabel);
        p.add (firstname);
        p.add (lastLabel);
        p.add (lastname);
        p.add (avgLabel);
        p.add (average);
        this.add ("Center", p);

        // Create Button Panel
        p = new Panel ();
        Button apply = new Button ("Apply");
        Button cancel = new Button ("Cancel");
        apply.setActionCommand ("Apply");
        cancel.setActionCommand ("Cancel");
        apply.addActionListener (this);
        cancel.addActionListener (this);
        p.add (apply);
        p.add (cancel);
        this. add ("South", p);

        // Create WindowListener
        this.addWindowListener(new WindowAdapter () {
            public void windowClosing(WindowEvent e) {
                dispose();
            }
        });

        // Pack and Show
        pack();
        show();

    }

    // Button Event Handler
    public void actionPerformed (ActionEvent e) {
        String action = e.getActionCommand();
        if (action.equals("Cancel")) dispose();
        else if (action.equals ("Apply")) {
```

```
            addXML();
            parent.extractPlayers();
            dispose();
        }
    }

private void addXML () {
    ElementFactoryImpl factory = new ElementFactoryImpl();

    // Filter out WHITESPACE Elements
    ElementEnumeration enum = new ElementEnumeration
      (root, null, Element.ELEMENT);
    Element team = (Element) enum.nextElement();

    // Create new PLAYER Node
    Element player = factory.createElement (team,
      Element.ELEMENT,Name.create("PLAYER"), null);

    // Create Children Nodes with Data
    createNode (player, "LASTNAME", lastname.getText());
    createNode (player, "FIRSTNAME", firstname.getText());
    createNode (player, "AVG", average.getText());
}

private void createNode (Element parent, String tag,
  String text) {
    ElementFactoryImpl factory = new ElementFactoryImpl();

    // First, create ELEMENT Node
    Element element = factory.createElement (parent,
      Element.ELEMENT,Name.create(tag), null);

    // Then, add PCDATA Node
    Element pcdata = factory.createElement (element,
        Element.PCDATA, null, text);
}
}
```

The addXML() method is responsible for retrieving user input regarding the new player and adding these data to the MS-XML tree. To add a new PLAYER element, we first need to isolate the TEAM element. Once we have isolated the team element object, we are ready to start adding nodes. To add a new player, we actually need to add seven new nodes to the tree. Here, for example is the subtree we need to add for Joe Girardi:

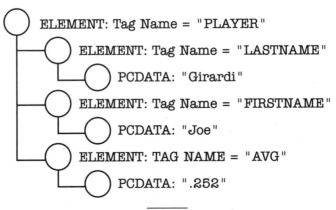

Figure E

First, we must add the PLAYER element:

```
Element player = factory.createElement (team,
     Element.ELEMENT,Name.create("PLAYER"), null);
```

Then, we need to add three elements for LASTNAME, FIRSTNAME, and AVG. Each of these elements, in turn require PCDATA elements to hold the text. To simplify the addition of these elements, we have the createNode() method:

```
private void createNode (Element parent, String tag,
     String text) {
          ElementFactoryImpl factory = new ElementFactoryImpl();

          // First, create ELEMENT Node
          Element element = factory.createElement (parent,
               Element.ELEMENT,Name.create(tag), null);

          // Then, add PCDATA Node
          Element pcdata = factory.createElement (element,
```

```
                Element.PCDATA, null, text);
    }
```

This method first creates the Element node, and then adds a PCDATA child to hold the text.

This completes our tour of MS-XML. We have seen two very different approaches to XML parsing. Ælfred is event based. MS-XML is tree based. Each parser has its own API. It is therefore very difficult to create an application that runs on Ælfred and port it over to MS-XML. Doing so, in fact, requires significant development costs. However, do not lose heart just yet! A simple and elegant solution is just around the corner.

THE SIMPLE API FOR XML (SAX)

SAX DEFINED

The Simple API for XML (SAX) is a standard interface API for XML parsers. Currently, each of the major parsers, including MS-XML, DXP, Ælfred and IBM's XML for Java, has its own proprietary APIs and its own protocols for communication. This makes for difficult coding, because it requires first learning the intricacies of the proprietary API. Furthermore, once the program is working correctly, a new parser can be substituted only at the expense of significant code changes.

SAX solves this problem by creating a standard interface for all XML parsers. Much the way JDBC (Java Database Connectivity) enables any Java application to query any database, SAX enables any application to work with any XML parser. Write a program that adheres to SAX, and get "plug and play" compatibility (see Figure 15.1).

SAX represents a significant development in the continuing evolution of XML. Most importantly, it frees users from implementing proprietary APIs and facilitates concentrating on the real task at hand: building an application. SAX is likely to spur much creativity and enable a new generation of Java XML applications. This flurry of activity is also likely to spill over into other programming languages. Currently, SAX is available for Java and Python, but plans are under way to produce interfaces for C++, Tcl, and Perl.

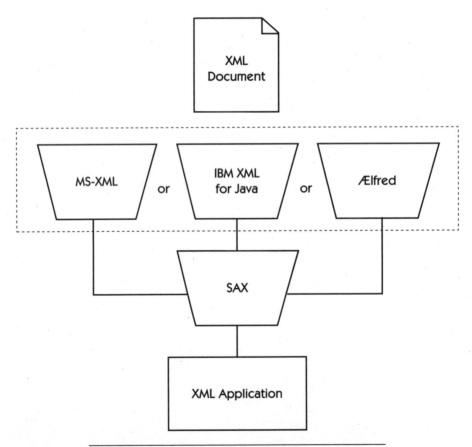

Figure15.1 SAX provides "plug and play" compatibility to work with any SAX-compliant XML parser

ORIGINS OF SAX

SAX was born on (of all places) an Internet mailing list. The XML-DEV mailing list is an open forum for discussing new XML developments (and frequently the site of many heated exchanges). On the night of December 13, 1997, Peter Murray-Rust posted an e-mail to the list, proposing a standard interface for all XML parsers. As the author of the JUMBO XML Browser (which we will visit at the end of the chapter), Murray-Rust was growing weary of rewriting JUMBO to work with three different parsers and three different APIs. His e-mail was greeted with enormous enthusiasm, and sparked the creation of SAX. After close to five months of internal collaboration, SAX 1.0 was released in May 1998.

The origins of SAX are peculiar, and do affect developers. First, SAX is completely free and completely within the public domain. You can therefore use it for non-commercial or commercial applications, redistribute it, or modify the source code. Second, unlike most Internet standards, SAX has no standing or approval by the W3C. There is no formal process for updating or revising SAX. To stay on top of new SAX developments, the best option is to subscribe to the XML-DEV list at **http://www.lists.ic.ac.uk/hypermail/xml-dev/** or visit the SAX web page at **http://www.megginson.com/SAX/**.

SAX-COMPLIANT PARSERS

As this book goes to press, the following XML parsers have built-in SAX support:

- DataChannel's DXP
- IBM's XML for Java
- James Clark's XP
- Microstar's Ælfred.

Separate SAX drivers are also available for: Tim Bray's Lark and Microsoft's MS-XML.

These third-party drivers are considered temporary until native support is available. An updated list of SAX-compliant parsers and third-party SAX drivers is available on the SAX web site.

WORKING WITH SAX

The SAX API consists of nine core classes and interfaces along with several optional helper classes. A subset of this API is reserved for parser writers, and another subset is reserved for application writers. Since this book is primarily focused on building XML applications, as opposed to building XML parsers, we will only be covering the applications API.

As we already know, there are two broad categories of XML parsers: tree-based parsers and event-driven parsers. A tree-based parser reads in an XML document, builds an internal tree representation, and presents the tree to the application. In contrast, an event-driven parser reads in an XML document, fires off specific parsing events, and passes those events to the application. SAX essentially takes any XML parser, even a tree-based one, and transforms it into a standard event-driven interface. We therefore begin our overview of SAX with a discussion of the most important parsing events, along with a sample SAX parsing session.

ANATOMY OF A **SAX** PARSING SESSION

The most important part of the SAX API is the `DocumentHandler` interface. This is responsible for capturing such specific document events, as the start of a document, the start of a new XML element, character data, or the end of a document. For example, the following XML text: `<PRICE>82.58</PRICE>` will generate three document events:

- Start element event: "PRICE"
- Character event: "82.58"; and
- End element event: "PRICE"

All told, there are eight call-back methods defined by the `DocumentHandler` interface (for your reference, the entire interface is summarized in Table 15.1). An application developer needs to implement each of these methods in order to capture the events as they occur. Once the events are captured, you need to make sense of them. To get a better understanding of how this is done, we will examine a sample XML document.

Listing 15.1 presents a DTD for stock portfolios, and Listing 15.2 presents a sample XML document which adheres to the stock portfolio DTD. The stock portfolio DTD is straightforward. An investor, can add as many companies as desired. Each company is required to have a name, a stock ticker symbol, and any number of stock quotes. In turn, each stock quote is required to have a date, and values for the closing, high and low prices. Our sample portfolio includes one day's worth of trading for three companies: Microsoft, Coca-Cola, and Merck. We will be using these two listings throughout the remainder of the chapter.

Table 15.1 The DocumentHandler Interface

Method Name	Description
setDocumentLocator (Locator locator)	At the beginning of a parse session, the XML parser may call this method and pass a Locator object. To determine the location of any subsequent parsing events, save a local copy of the Locator object, and use the Locator accessor methods (See Table 15.2). Note that although SAX-compliant parsers are "strongly encouraged" to call this method, they are **not** required to do so.
startDocument () throws SAXException	Indicates the start of a new XML document.
endDocument () throws SAXException	Indicates the end of an XML document. This is always the last method called.
startElement (String name, AttributeList atts) throws SAXException	Indicates the start of a new XML element. The name of the element is specified by the name String. Attribute data are passed in the atts AttributeList (See Table 15.9 for the AttributeList Interface.)
endElement (String name) throws SAXException	Indicates the end of an XML element. The name of the element is specified by the name String.
characters (char ch[], int start, int length) throws SAXException	Indicates character data. For example, when parsing <TITLE>Basic Poem</TITLE>, SAX will fire off a startElement() method, followed by a characters() method with the string, "Basic Poem." To retrieve the string, extract it from the ch character array. The string is located at the start index and is length characters long.
ignorableWhitespace (char ch[], int start, int length) throws SAXException	Indicates white-space characters, such as newline or tab character data. Most of the time, white-space **is** ignorable. To retrieve the string, extract is from the ch character array. The string is located at the start index and is length characters long.
processingInstruction (String target, String data) throws SAXException	Indicates an XML processing instruction. XML instructions begin with the <? character sequence. It is possible to create custom processing instructions and capture them with this method.

Listing 15.1   Stocks.dtd: The Stock Portfolio Document Type Definition (DTD)

```
<!ELEMENT PORTFOLIO (COMPANY*)>
<!ELEMENT COMPANY (NAME, STOCKSYMBOL, STOCK*)>
<!ELEMENT STOCK (DATE, CLOSE, HIGH, LOW)>
<!ELEMENT NAME (#PCDATA)>
<!ELEMENT STOCKSYMBOL (#PCDATA)>
<!ELEMENT DATE (#PCDATA)>
<!ELEMENT CLOSE (#PCDATA)>
<!ELEMENT HIGH (#PCDATA)>
<!ELEMENT LOW (#PCDATA)>
```

Listing 15.2   Stocks.xml: Sample Stocks XML Document

```
<?xml version="1.0" encoding="UTF-8"?>
<!-- XML Document for Sample Investment Portfolio -->
<!DOCTYPE PORTFOLIO SYSTEM "Stocks.dtd">
<PORTFOLIO>
<COMPANY>
    <NAME>Microsoft Corp.</NAME>
    <STOCKSYMBOL>MSFT</STOCKSYMBOL>
    <STOCK>
        <DATE>May 29, 1998</DATE>
        <CLOSE>84.81</CLOSE>
        <HIGH>85.60</HIGH>
        <LOW>84.75</LOW>
    </STOCK>
</COMPANY>
<COMPANY>
    <NAME>Coca-Cola</NAME>
    <STOCKSYMBOL>KO</STOCKSYMBOL>
    <STOCK>
        <DATE>May 29, 1998</DATE>
        <CLOSE>78.38</CLOSE>
        <HIGH>79.69</HIGH>
        <LOW>78.30</LOW>
```

```
        </STOCK>
    </COMPANY>
    <COMPANY>
        <NAME>Merck</NAME>
        <STOCKSYMBOL>MRK</STOCKSYMBOL>
        <STOCK>
            <DATE>May 29, 1998</DATE>
            <CLOSE>117.00</CLOSE>
            <HIGH>119.94</HIGH>
            <LOW>116.75</LOW>
        </STOCK>
    </COMPANY>
</PORTFOLIO>
```

Using Listing 15.2 as our document source, we will now examine a sample SAX parsing session.

Your XML parser will first call the setDocumentLocator() method[1]. This method enables application writers to determine the exact location of any parsing events. Here's how it works: at the very beginning of parsing, the parser calls the setDocumentLocator() method and passes a Locator object to the document handler. This Locator object can be saved, and then queried it during any subsequent parsing events. For example, it is possible to determine the exact line number and character column for every new event by calling the Locator object's getLineNumber() and getColumnNumber() methods. (See Table 15.2 for the Locator interface). This is only useful if you need to create your own error handlers that are specific to your application, and you want to alert the user to the location of any syntax errors. If you do not need to provide this type of custom error handling, you can safely ignore the Locator object.

---

1 Actually, not all parsers will call the setDocumentLocator() method. SAX, Version 1.0 states that parsers are "strongly encouraged" to call the setDocumentLocator() method, but they are not required to do so.

Table 15.2   The Locator Interface: Main Methods

Method Name	Description
public int getLineNumber()	Returns the line number of the current document event.
public int getColumnNumber()	Returns the column number of the current document event.

After the setDocumentLocator() method, the parser will call the startDocument() method. This tells the application that parsing is about to begin, and is therefore usually a good place to provide for any program initialization.

Subsequently, the parser will call a series of methods for each XML element. For example, the text: <NAME>Microsoft Corp.</NAME> will trigger three call-back methods (See Figure 15.2):

- startElement(): Tag Name = "NAME"
- characters(): String = "Microsoft Corp."; and
- endElement(): Tag Name = "NAME"

The startElement() method includes a complete list of associated attributes. We will return to this topic shortly.

Along the way, the parser may also call the ignorableWhitespace() or processingInstruction() methods. The processingInstruction() method is called any time the parser encounters the <? processing instruction tag. It is possible to create custom processing instructions and capture them with this method.

Finally, the parser will call the endDocument() method. This indicates that parsing is complete and that all XML data has been passed to the application.

NOTE

According to the official SAX documentation, parsers are allowed to break large sequences of character data into smaller chunks, and call characters() for each chunk. For example, given the text: <NAME>Microsoft Corp.</NAME> a parser may generate the following events:

- startElement(): Tag Name = "NAME"
- characters(): "Microsoft "
- characters(): "Corp."
- endElement(): Tag Name = "NAME"

For small sequences of characters, it is generally safe to assume that no chunking will occur. For example, in our experiments with Ælfred and IBM's XML for Java,

we did not record any chunking, even with large sequences of 25K. Note however, that the exact nature of chunking varies from parser to parser.

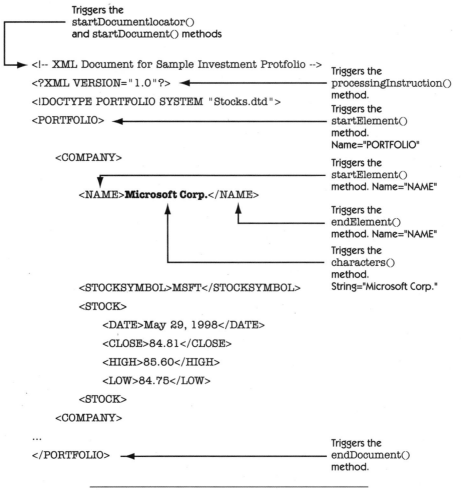

Triggers the
startDocumentlocator()
and startDocument() methods

```
<!-- XML Document for Sample Investment Protfolio -->
<?XML VERSION="1.0"?>
<!DOCTYPE PORTFOLIO SYSTEM "Stocks.dtd">
<PORTFOLIO>

    <COMPANY>

        <NAME>Microsoft Corp.</NAME>

        <STOCKSYMBOL>MSFT</STOCKSYMBOL>
        <STOCK>
            <DATE>May 29, 1998</DATE>
            <CLOSE>84.81</CLOSE>
            <HIGH>85.60</HIGH>
            <LOW>84.75</LOW>
        <STOCK>
    <COMPANY>

    ...
</PORTFOLIO>
```

Triggers the
processingInstruction()
method.

Triggers the
startElement()
method.
Name="PORTFOLIO"

Triggers the
startElement()
method. Name="NAME"

Triggers the
endElement()
method. Name="NAME"

Triggers the
characters()
method.
String="Microsoft Corp."

Triggers the
endDocument()
method.

Figure 15.2 Anatomy of a sample SAX parsing session

INSTALLING SAX

Before we move on to examples, you may want to take the time to install SAX on
your machine. In order to work with SAX, you will need two sets of class files. First,
you need the actual SAX class files, which, along with source code, are available on

the CD that accompanies this book and on the SAX home page at **http://www.megginson.com/SAX/**. Then you will need the class files for a SAX-compliant parser. This chapter uses IBM's XML for Java, but any SAX-compliant parser will do. To use MS-XML or Lark, you will need to install additional third-party SAX drivers (also available from the SAX home page.)

Once you have your SAX class files and your SAX-compliant parser, you need to add both directories to your Java CLASSPATH variable. If you are unsure about setting your CLASSPATH, see Chapter 13: "The Ælfred XML Parser".

HELLO, SAX!

Time for some examples. Most writers introduce readers to a new programming language with the obligatory "Hello, World" application. Our first example is not quite that simple, but it is certainly one of the simplest SAX applications you can create. The application reads in a sample XML document, and displays each parsing event as it occurs. The complete code is available in Listing 15.3 and sample output is provided in Figure 15.3.

Listing 15.3   Basic SAX Example

```
// SAX:  Basic Example
// Basic Implementation of DocumentHandler Interface
// Illustrates Dynamic Parser Loader

import org.xml.sax.Parser;
import org.xml.sax.DocumentHandler;
import org.xml.sax.helpers.ParserFactory;
import org.xml.sax.HandlerBase;
import org.xml.sax.SAXException;
import org.xml.sax.AttributeList;
import org.xml.sax.Locator;
import java.applet.*;
import java.awt.*;
import java.net.*;
import java.io.*;


// Extend Applet, Implement DocumentHandler
public class XMLEvent extends Applet implements DocumentHandler {
```

```java
// Set the Parser:  IBM XML Parser or AElfred
// private String parserClass = "com.microstar.xml.SAXDriver";
private String parserClass = "com.ibm.xml.parser.SAXDriver";

private TextArea textArea;
private URL xmlURL;
private Parser parser;

public void init () {

    // Create GUI Layout
    setLayout (new BorderLayout());
    textArea = new TextArea();
    add("Center", textArea);

    // Create Parser Object using ParserFactory
    // Provide full Exception Handling
    try {
        parser = ParserFactory.makeParser (parserClass);
    } catch (ClassNotFoundException e) {
        System.out.println ("Error:  Parser "+
            "Class Not Found:  "+parserClass);
    } catch (IllegalAccessException e) {
        System.out.println ("Error:  Access "+
            "Violation on Parser Class:  "+ parserClass);
    } catch (InstantiationException e) {
        System.out.println ("Error:  Could not "+
            "instantiate Parser Class:  "+parserClass);
    } catch (ClassCastException e) {
        System.out.println ("Error:  "+parserClass+
            " does not implement the SAX Parser interface.");
    }

    // Create URL to XML Document
    // "URL" is an applet parameter
    String xmldoc = getParameter ("url");
    try {
        xmlURL = new URL (getDocumentBase(), xmldoc);
```

```
        } catch (MalformedURLException e) {
            e.printStackTrace();
        }

        // Set Parser Document Handler
        parser.setDocumentHandler (this);

        // Start Parsing; provide full Exception Handling
        try {
            parser.parse (xmlURL.toString());
        } catch (IOException e) {
            e.printStackTrace();
        } catch (SAXException e) {
            System.out.println ("Error:  "+e.getMessage());
        }
    }


    // Method for displaying to Text Area
    private void displayText (String text) {
        textArea.appendText(text+"\n");
    }


    /*******************************************************/
    //   Implementation of DocumentHandler Interface
    /*******************************************************/

    // Note:  SAX Parsers are not required to call this method
    public void setDocumentLocator(Locator locator) {
        displayText ("Start Document Locator.");
    }

    public void startDocument() {
        displayText ("Start Document.");
    }

    public void endDocument() {
        displayText ("End Document.");
    }
```

```
public void characters
    (char ch[], int start, int length) {
        String text = new String (ch, start, length);
    displayText("Character data:  "+text);
}

public void startElement
    (String name, AttributeList atts) {
        displayText ("Start Element:  "+name);
}

public void endElement (String name) {
    displayText ("End Element:  "+name);
}

public void ignorableWhitespace
    (char ch[], int start, int length) {
        displayText ("Ignorable Whitespace.");
}

public void processingInstruction
    (String target, String data) {
        displayText ("Processing Instruction:  "+target+"  "+data);
}
}
```

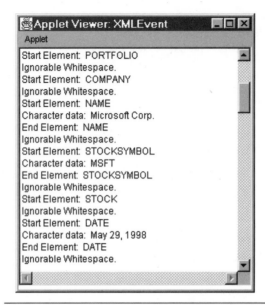

Figure 15.3 Sample output from the first example.
Here, we are parsing the Stocks.xml document from Listing 15.2

Read through the code now, and we will step through it one section at a time.

First, note that we are creating an applet that implements the **Document-Handler** interface:

```
public class XMLEvent extends Applet implements DocumentHandler { ...
```

For each call-back method specified in the **DocumentHandler** interface, we display the event name, along with any parameter information. For example, the startDocument() method simply displays the event name:

```
public void startDocument() {
    displayText ("Start Document.");
}
```

In contrast, the startElement() method displays the event name, along with the XML element name:

```
    public void startElement
(String name, AttributeList atts) {
    displayText ("Start Element:  "+name);
    }
```

The remainder of the code centers on dynamically loading a new XML parser object. For any SAX application, you need to follow three steps:

1. **Create an XML Parser Object:**

   SAX facilitates loading any SAX-compliant XML parser at compile time or even at run-time. Fortunately, this is easy because SAX includes a helpful utility that does all the work for you. This is the **ParserFactory** class. To create a new parser object, just call the **ParserFactory**'s **makeParser()** method. To do so, first determine the location of the SAX driver for your chosen parser. There is no standard name or location for SAX drivers, so you may need to rummage around a bit (just look for a file called SAXDriver.class or Driver.class within your parser directory) Listing 15.3 works with the IBM SAX driver:

   ```
   private String parserClass = "com.ibm.xml.parser.SAXDriver";
   parser = ParserFactory.makeParser (parserClass);
   ```

   You can just as easily substitute in the Ælfred parser:

   ```
   private String parserClass = "com.microstar.xml.SAXDriver";
   parser = ParserFactory.makeParser (parserClass);
   ```

   Note that the **makeParser()** method throws four exceptions. Each of these is summarized in Table 15.4, and it is highly recommended that you explicitly catch each one. If you receive a ClassNotFoundException, you probably need to recheck your CLASSPATH. If you receive a ClassCastException, you probably have an outdated SAX driver.

   TIP

   The **ParserFactory** class is entirely optional. If you know which parser you want to use at compile time, you can use this class directly. For example, here's how to load IBM's XML for Java directly:

   ```
   parser = new com.ibm.xml.parser.SAXDriver();
   ```

2. **Set the Document Handler:**

   Once you have successfully instantiated a **parser** object, you need to register a document handler to receive the XML parsing events. The setDocumentHandler() method takes any object that fully implements the DocumentHandler interface. In our case, we just register the applet:

   ```
   parser.setDocumentHandler (this);
   ```

3. **Start Parsing:**

The final step is to call the parse() method. There are two variations to the parse() method. The first variation parses an XML document located at a specified URI string; the second parses an XML document specified by an InputSource object. We will return to this second variation shortly. To keep things flexible, our example has a "URL" applet parameter. We first extract the URL parameter, and create an absolute URL, relative to the applet's getDocumentBase():

```
String xmldoc = getParameter ("url");
    try {
    xmlURL = new URL (getDocumentBase(), xmldoc);
    } catch (MalformedURLException e) {
    e.printStackTrace();
    }
```

We then call the first variation of parse():

```
    try {
    parser.parse (xmlURL.toString());
    } catch (IOException e) {
    e.printStackTrace();
    } catch (SAXException e) {
    System.out.println ("Error:  "+e.getMessage());
    }
```

As you can see, the parse() method can throw an IOException or a SAXException. Here, we print the SAXException by callings its getMessage() method. For additional information regarding the SAXException, see the section below on Error Handling.

Table 15.3   The ParserFactory Helper Class

Method Name	Description
Parser makeParser (String className) throws ClassNotFoundException, IllegalAccessException, InstantiationException, ClassCastException	Creates a new SAX parser object using the class name provided. Enables application writers to dynamically load any SAX-compliant parser at compile time, or even at run time.

Table 15.4   Exceptions associated with the ParserFactory Helper Class

Exception Name	Description
ClassNotFoundException	The SAX parser class could not be found. Recheck your CLASSPATH variable.
IllegalAccessException	The SAX parser class was found, but you do not have the permissions to load it.
InstantiationException	The SAX parser class was found, but could not be instantiated.
ClassCastException	The SAX parser class was found and instantiated, but it does not implement the org.xml.sax.Parser interface. You probably have an outdated SAX driver.

Table 15.5   The Parser Interface: Main Methods

Method Name	Description
parse (String URI) throws SAXException, IOException	Directs the Parser to begin parsing the XML document located at the indicated URI.
parse (InputSource source) throws SAXException, IOException	Directs the Parser to begin parsing the XML document specified by the InputSource object. Enables applications to read XML documents from a character stream, byte stream or a URI.
setDocumentHandler (DocumentHandler handler)	Registers a document event handler. The handler object must implement the DocumentHandler interface.
setErrorHandler (ErrorHandler handler)	Registers an Error handler. The handler object must implement the ErrorHandler interface.

Table 15.6   The SAXException

Method Name	Description
public String getMessage()	Returns a detail message for this exception.
public Exception getException()	Returns the embedded exception, if any.
public String toString()	Converts this exception to a string.

HELLO, SAX! VERSION 2.0

If you do not want to bother with a full implementation of the DocumentHandler interface, SAX includes a HandlerBase convenience class. This implements the DocumentHandler interface for you. Most of the HandlerBase methods are empty (see Listing 15.4 for an excerpt of source code. You can, therefore extend the HandlerBase class and override only the methods that are relevant to your application.

Listing 15.5 provides an example of extending the HandlerBase class for use within an applet. Here, we have created a new class, myHandler, and overridden three HandlerBase methods: startElement(), characters(), and endElement(). Sample output is provided in Figure 15.4.

Since extending the HandlerBase class is usually much easier than implementing the entire DocumentHandler interface, we will use this method throughout the remainder of the chapter.

Listing 15.4   Excerpt of Source Code to HandlerBase Convenience Class

---

```
// SAX default handler base class.
// No warranty; no copyright -- use this as you will.


package org.xml.sax;


public class HandlerBase implements EntityResolver, DTDHandler,
    DocumentHandler, ErrorHandler {


    ...


    /////////////////////////////////////////////////////////////
    // Default implementation of DocumentHandler interface.
    /////////////////////////////////////////////////////////////


    public void setDocumentLocator (Locator locator) { }
    public void startDocument () throws SAXException { }
    public void endDocument () throws SAXException {}
    public void startElement (String name, AttributeList attributes)
    throws SAXException {}
    public void endElement (String name) throws SAXException {}
    public void characters (char ch[], int start, int length)
```

```
throws SAXException { }
public void ignorableWhitespace (char ch[], int start, int length)
throws SAXException { }
public void processingInstruction (String target, String data)
throws SAXException { }


/////////////////////////////////////////////////////////////////
// Default implementation of the ErrorHandler interface.
/////////////////////////////////////////////////////////////////

public void warning (SAXParseException e) throws SAXException { }
public void error (SAXParseException e) throws SAXException { }
public void fatalError (SAXParseException e) throws SAXException {
    throw e;
}


...

}
```

Listing 15.5   Using the HandlerBase Convenience Class

```
// Example: Working with the HandlerBase Convenience Class

import org.xml.sax.*;
import org.xml.sax.helpers.*;
import java.applet.*;
import java.awt.*;
import java.net.*;
import java.io.*;
import java.util.*;


// Extend Applet
public class Base extends Applet {
    // Set the Parser: IBM XML Parser or AElfred
    // private String parserClass = "com.microstar.xml.SAXDriver";
    private String parserClass = "com.ibm.xml.parser.SAXDriver";
```

```
private TextArea textArea;
private URL xmlURL;
private Parser parser;

public void init () {

    // Create GUI Layout
    setLayout (new BorderLayout());
    textArea = new TextArea();
    add("Center", textArea);

    // Create Parser Object using ParserFactory
    // Provide full Exception Handling
    try {
        parser = ParserFactory.makeParser (parserClass);
    } catch (ClassNotFoundException e) {
        System.out.println ("Error:  Parser "+
            "Class Not Found:  "+parserClass);
    } catch (IllegalAccessException e) {
        System.out.println ("Error:  Access "+
            "Violation on Parser Class:  "+ parserClass);
    } catch (InstantiationException e) {
        System.out.println ("Error:  Could not "+
            "instantiate Parser Class:  "+parserClass);
    } catch (ClassCastException e) {
        System.out.println ("Error:  "+parserClass+
            " does not implement the SAX Parser interface.");
    }

    //  Create URL to XML Document
    String xmldoc = getParameter ("url");
    try {
        xmlURL = new URL (getDocumentBase(), xmldoc);
    } catch (MalformedURLException e) {
        e.printStackTrace();
    }

    //  Set Parser Document Handler
```

```java
        myHandler handler = new myHandler (textArea);
        parser.setDocumentHandler (handler);

        // Start Parsing; provide full Exception Handling
        try {
            parser.parse (xmlURL.toString());
        } catch (IOException e) {
            e.printStackTrace();
        } catch (SAXException e) {
            System.out.println("Error:  "+e.getMessage());
        }
    }
}


// Event Handler
class myHandler extends HandlerBase {
    private TextArea textArea;

    // Constructor
    public myHandler (TextArea textArea) {
        this.textArea=textArea;
    }

    // Method for displaying to Text Area
    public void displayText (String text) {
        textArea.appendText(text+"\n");
    }

    public void characters
        (char ch[], int start, int length) {
            String text = new String (ch, start, length);
        displayText("Character data:  "+text);
    }

    public void startElement
        (String name, AttributeList atts) {
            displayText ("Start Element:  "+name);
    }
```

```
public void endElement (String name) {
    displayText ("End Element:  "+name);
}
}
```

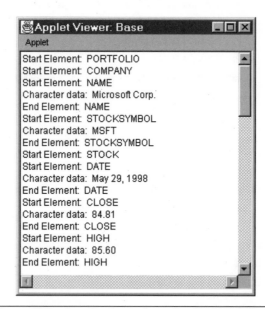

Figure 15.4   Sample output from the second example.

Again, we are parsing the Stocks.xml document from Listing 15.2.

ERROR HANDLING

Error handling is crucial to XML processing. Depending on the parser and the type of application, you may want to implement varying levels of complexity in your error handling. To that end, SAX defines three types of errors:

- **Fatal Errors:** Fatal errors are defined as errors in well-formedness. For example, a <STOCK> tag does not have a corresponding end </STOCK> tag. According to the XML spec, all parsers (validating and non-validating) must report fatal errors to the application.
- **Errors:** Errors represent errors in validity. For example, a stocks.xml file does not adhere to the Stock DTD. Only validating parsers can capture errors in validity.

■   **Warnings:** Warnings represent any other non-fatal errors discovered by the parser.

To receive notification of any of these errors, you must implement the SAX ErrorHandler interface, and register the handler via the setErrorHandler() method. Fortunately, the HandlerBase convenience class provides a default implementation of the ErrorHandler interface. In the event of a fatal error, the HandlerBase will throw a SAXException, causing the immediate cessation of parsing. Note, however that errors and warning are silently ignored (refer to Listing 15.4 for the source code). Therefore, the default implementation of the ErrorHandler will *not* report errors in validity.

Despite the default implementation, you generally want to receive notification of errors in validity. However, discovery of errors in validity does not necessary constitute a reason to stop parsing, and therefore does not warrant the throwing of a SAXException. Therefore, our recommended solution is to reserve the SAXException for fatal errors, and to report errors in validity to the standard output. Listing 15.6 provides such a solution.

Listing 15.6   Error Handling

```
// Example: XML Error Handling

import org.xml.sax.*;
import org.xml.sax.helpers.*;
import java.applet.*;
import java.awt.*;
import java.net.*;
import java.io.*;
import java.util.*;

// Extend Applet
public class Base extends Applet {

        // Set the Parser: IBM XML Parser or AElfred
        // private String parserClass = "com.microstar.xml.SAXDriver";
        private String parserClass = "com.ibm.xml.parser.SAXDriver";

        private TextArea textArea;
        private URL xmlURL;
```

```java
private Parser parser;

public void init () {

    // Create GUI Layout
    setLayout (new BorderLayout());
    textArea = new TextArea();
    add("Center", textArea);

    // Create Parser Object using ParserFactory
    // Provide full Exception Handling
    try {
        parser = ParserFactory.makeParser (parserClass);
    } catch (ClassNotFoundException e) {
        System.out.println ("Error: Parser "+
            "Class Not Found: "+parserClass);
    } catch (IllegalAccessException e) {
        System.out.println ("Error: Access "+
            "Violation on Parser Class: "+ parserClass);
    } catch (InstantiationException e) {
        System.out.println ("Error: Could not "+
            "instantiate Parser Class: "+parserClass);
    } catch (ClassCastException e) {
        System.out.println ("Error: "+parserClass+
            " does not implement the SAX Parser interface.");
    }

    // Create URL to XML Document
    String xmldoc = getParameter ("url");
    try {
        xmlURL = new URL (getDocumentBase(), xmldoc);
    } catch (MalformedURLException e) {
        e.printStackTrace();
    }

    // Set Parser Document and Error Handlers
    myHandler handler = new myHandler (textArea);
    parser.setDocumentHandler (handler);
```

```java
        parser.setErrorHandler (handler);

        // Start Parsing; provide full Exception Handling
        try {
            parser.parse (xmlURL.toString());
        } catch (IOException e) {
            e.printStackTrace();
        } catch (SAXException e) {
            System.out.println ("Error: "+e.getMessage());
        }
    }
}


// Event Handler
class myHandler extends HandlerBase {
    private TextArea textArea;

    // Constructor
    public myHandler (TextArea textArea) {
        this.textArea=textArea;
    }

    // Method for displaying to Text Area
    public void displayText (String text) {
        textArea.appendText(text+"\n");
    }

    public void characters
      (char ch[], int start, int length) {
        String text = new String (ch, start, length);
        displayText("Character data: "+text);
    }

    public void startElement
      (String name, AttributeList atts) {
        displayText ("Start Element: "+name);
    }
```

```
public void endElement (String name) {
    displayText ("End Element: "+name);
}


// For validating parsers, such as IBM XML for Java
// this method will display errors in validity
public void error (SAXParseException e) throws SAXException {
    System.out.println ("Error: "+e.getMessage());
}
}
```

Please note the following regarding Listing 15.6. First, we register the error handler via the setErrorHandler() method:

```
parser.setErrorHandler (handler);
```

Next, we override the HandlerBase error() method to display errors in validity to the standard output:

```
public void error (SAXParseException e) throws SAXException {
System.out.println ("Error: "+e.getMessage());
}
```

If you use a validating parser, such as IBM XML for Java, we recommend that you follow this model for accurate capture of errors in validity. We therefore use the model throughout the remainder of the chapter.

Table 15.7 The ErrorHandler Interface

Method	Description
public abstract void fatalError(SAXParseException exception) throws SAXException	Indicates a fatal error in well-formedness.
public abstract void error(SAXParseException exception) throws SAXException	Indicates an error in validity.
public void n warning(SAXParseException exception) throws SAXException	Indicates any other non-fatal errors discovered by the parser.

Working with InputSources

So far, we have only looked at SAX applets, but creating a SAX application is nearly identical. The only crucial difference is the manner by which you specify an XML source document. In our two previous applet examples, we specified the XML document by its URI. You can do this within applications as well, but you may also want to specify a local file or directory.

To enable this type of flexible access to XML documents, SAX specifies an InputSource class. This class encapsulates all information regarding a single XML document, whether it is located on the web or your local hard drive.

The constructor methods for the InputSource class are summarized in Table 15.8. Note that the first constructor takes any character stream that derives from the new Java 1.1 reader interface; the second constructor takes any byte stream that derives from the InputStream interface; and the third constructor takes a URI string.

Listing 15.7 provides an example of InputSource in action (sample output is provided in Figure 15.5). First, we read in the file specified on the command line, and create a FileReader object (the FileReader class is also new to Java 1.1):

```
FileReader filereader = new FileReader (args[0]);
```

We then pass the FileReader object to a new InputSource object:

```
InputSource insource = new InputSource (filereader);
```

And, finally, we pass the InputSource object to the parse() method:

```
parser.parse (insource);
```

Listing 15.7 Working with InputSources

```
// Example: Working with Applications and Character Streams

import org.xml.sax.*;
import org.xml.sax.helpers.*;
import java.io.*;

public class SAXApp {

    public static void main (String args[]) throws Exception {
```

```
        // Set the Parser:  IBM XML Parser or AElfred
        // String parserClass = "com.microstar.xml.SAXDriver";
        String parserClass = "com.ibm.xml.parser.SAXDriver";

        // Create Parser Object using ParserFactory
        Parser parser = ParserFactory.makeParser (parserClass);

        // Set Parser Document and Error Handlers
        myHandler handler = new myHandler ();
        parser.setDocumentHandler (handler);
        parser.setErrorHandler (handler);

        // Create FileReader, then Input Source
        FileReader filereader = new FileReader (args[0]);
        BufferedReader bufreader = new BufferedReader (filereader);
        InputSource insource = new InputSource (bufreader);
        //InputSource insource = new InputSource (filereader);

        // Start Parsing
        try {
            parser.parse (insource);
        }
        catch (SAXException e) {
            System.out.println ("Error:  "+e.getMessage());
        }
    }
}


// Event Handler
class myHandler extends HandlerBase {

    // Constructor
    public myHandler () {
    }

    public void characters
      (char ch[], int start, int length) {
```

```
        String text = new String (ch, start, length);
        System.out.println("Character data:  "+text);
    }

public void startElement
  (String name, AttributeList atts) {
        System.out.println ("Start Element:  "+name);
    }

public void endElement (String name) {
        System.out.println ("End Element:  "+name);
    }


// For validating parsers, such as IBM XML for Java
// this method will display errors in validity
public void error (SAXParseException e) throws SAXException {
        System.out.println ("Error:  "+e.getMessage());
    }

}
```

TIP

The **Reader** class is new to Java 1.1 and is optimized for Unicode processing (and therefore ideal for XML applications.) By default, however, **Reader** classes are unbuffered. To create a buffered input source, use the **BufferedReader** class. For example:

```
FileReader filereader = new FileReader (args[0]);
    BufferedReader bufreader = new
BufferedReader (filereader);
    InputSource insource = new InputSource (bufreader);
```

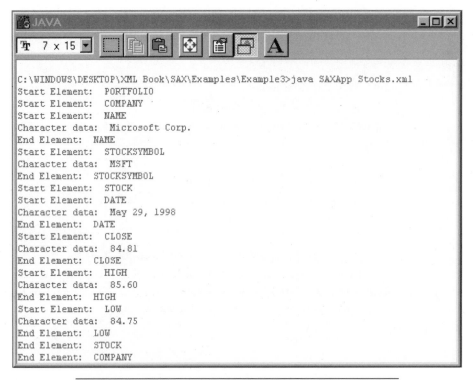

Figure 15.5   Sample output from the SAX application example.
Again, we are parsing the Stocks.xml document from Listing 15.2.

Table 15.8   Main Constructors for the InputSource Class

Constructor	Description
public InputSource(Reader characterStream)	Creates a new input source with the specified character stream.
public InputSource(InputStream Stream)	Creates a new input source with the specified byte stream.
public InputSource(String URI)	Creates a new input source with the specified URI string.

WORKING WITH ATTRIBUTES

If you look back at the stocks.dtd file at the beginning of the chapter, you may notice the marked absence of any attributes. Understanding how to query attributes is, however, an essential part of SAX. We therefore conclude our discussion of basic SAX examples with a revised stocks.dtd file, and a complete overview of SAX's attribute querying capabilities.

Listing 15.8 shows a revised stocks.dtd file, and Listing 15.9 shows a revised stocks.xml document. As you can see, we have added two new attributes to the COMPANY element: INDUSTRY and GROUP. For example, Microsoft's INDUSTRY attribute is set to "Office Equipment and Computers", and its GROUP attribute is set to "Computer Software and Services." Likewise, Coca-Cola's INDUSTRY attribute is set to "Consumer Products", and its GROUP attribute is set to "Beverages."[2]

Listing 15.8 The Revised Stocks.dtd: The Stock Portfolio Document Type Definition (DTD)

```
<!ELEMENT PORTFOLIO (COMPANY*)>
<!ELEMENT COMPANY (NAME, STOCKSYMBOL, STOCK*)>
<!ATTLIST COMPANY INDUSTRY CDATA #REQUIRED>
<!ATTLIST COMPANY GROUP CDATA #REQUIRED>
<!ELEMENT STOCK (DATE, CLOSE, HIGH, LOW)>
<!ELEMENT NAME (#PCDATA)>
<!ELEMENT STOCKSYMBOL (#PCDATA)>
<!ELEMENT DATE (#PCDATA)>
<!ELEMENT CLOSE (#PCDATA)>
<!ELEMENT HIGH (#PCDATA)>
<!ELEMENT LOW (#PCDATA)>
```

Listing 15.9 Revised Stocks.xml: Sample Stocks XML Document

```
<?xml version="1.0" encoding="UTF-8"?>
<!-- XML Document for Sample Investment Portfolio -->
<!DOCTYPE PORTFOLIO SYSTEM "Stocks.dtd">
<PORTFOLIO>
    <COMPANY INDUSTRY="Office Equipment and Computers"
```

---

2 Attribute data was taken from **Business Week**'s most recent industry classification system.

```
        GROUP="Computer Software and Services">
        <NAME>Microsoft Corp.</NAME>
        <STOCKSYMBOL>MSFT</STOCKSYMBOL>
        <STOCK>
              <DATE>May 29, 1998</DATE>
              <CLOSE>84.81</CLOSE>
              <HIGH>85.60</HIGH>
              <LOW>84.75</LOW>
        </STOCK>
        </COMPANY>
    <COMPANY INDUSTRY="Consumer Products"
        GROUP="Beverages">
        <NAME>Coca-Cola</NAME>
        <STOCKSYMBOL>KO</STOCKSYMBOL>
        <STOCK>
              <DATE>May 29, 1998</DATE>
              <CLOSE>78.38</CLOSE>
              <HIGH>79.69</HIGH>
              <LOW>78.30</LOW>
        </STOCK>
    </COMPANY>
    <COMPANY INDUSTRY="Health Care"
        GROUP="Drugs and Research">
        <NAME>Merck</NAME>
        <STOCKSYMBOL>MRK</STOCKSYMBOL>
        <STOCK>
              <DATE>May 29, 1998</DATE>
              <CLOSE>117.00</CLOSE>
              <HIGH>119.94</HIGH>
              <LOW>116.75</LOW>
        </STOCK>
      </COMPANY>
    </PORTFOLIO>
```

When an XML parser triggers a startElement() method, it passes an AttributeList object. You can determine the number of attributes by calling the AttributeList getLength() method. If no attributes are associated with the given XML element, getLength() will return 0. Otherwise, you can query the AttributeList for each name/value pair.

To retrieve the name of any attribute, you can use the **getName(int i)** method. This returns the attribute located at the indicated index position. Note however, that the parser may provide attributes in any arbitrary order, regardless of the order in which they were declared or specified.

To retrieve the value of an attribute, there are two options: you can either retrieve the value by index position, using the **getValue(int i)** method; or you can retrieve the value by attribute name, using the **getValue (String name)** method. The latter is usually more useful, as it allows direct extraction of attribute data for specific XML elements. For example, if you receive a start element event for COMPANY, you can immediately extract the INDUSTRY and GROUP attributes:

```
public void startElement
     (String name, AttributeList atts) {
          if (name.equals("COMPANY")) {
          String industry = atts.getValue ("INDUSTRY");
          String group = atts.getValue ("GROUP");
     }
     //  Processing for other XML Elements...
}
```

Alternatively, you could just as easily iterate through all the attributes for any given XML element:

```
public void startElement
     (String name, AttributeList atts) {
     String aname, avalue;
     System.out.println ("Start Element:  "+name);
     for (int i = 0; i < atts.getLength(); i++) {
          aname = atts.getName(i);
          avalue = atts.getValue(i);
          System.out.println ("\tAttribute -->  "+
               aname+ "= \ " "+avalue);
     }
}
```

Finally, you have the option of querying the attribute type. Again, there are two options. You can either retrieve the type by index position, using the **getType(int i)** method, or you can retrieve the type by attribute name, using the **getType (String name)** method.

Table 15.9   The AttributeList Interface

Method Name	Description
public int getLength()	Returns the number of attributes in this list. The SAX parser may provide attributes in any arbitrary order, regardless of the order in which they were declared or specified. The number of attributes may be zero.
public String getName(int i)	Returns the name of an attribute in this list (by position).
public String getType(int i)	Returns the type of an attribute in the list (by position). The attribute type is one of the strings "CDATA", "ID", "IDREF", "IDREFS", "NMTOKEN", "NMTOKENS", "ENTITY", "ENTITIES", or "NOTATION" (always in upper case).
public String getType(String name)	Returns the type of an attribute in the list (by name). The return value is the same as the return value for getType(int). If the attribute name is not found, the return value is NULL.
public String getValue(int i)	Returns the value of an attribute in the list (by position). If the attribute value is a list of tokens (IDREFS, ENTITIES, or NMTOKENS), the tokens will be concatenated into a single string separated by whitespace.
public String getValue(String name)	Returns the value of an attribute in the list (by name). The return value is the same as the return value for getValue(int). If the attribute name is not found, the return value is NULL.

BUILDING A SAX TREE UTILITY

SAX transforms any XML parser into an event-driven interface. But, it is also fairly straightforward to build an XML tree representation via SAX. This is extremely useful for a whole host of XML applications. Event-driven parsers are essentially stateless. Once a parsing event has been triggered, that event and its data are lost, unless your application explicitly saves it. This is efficient for searching large documents, because you do not have the memory overhead associated with storing the XML data. However, it is not very efficient for other types of applications, such as repeated searches against the same data set, sorting of data, or creating multiple views (such as a table v. a graph view) of the same data set. In each of these cases, you want to read in the XML document only once, and create an internal tree representation of the data. Once in this form, the tree not only has the advantage of containing all your data, it also mirrors the hierarchical nature of that data. You can therefore repeatedly traverse the tree to extract the data and transfer it directly to your application.

The challenge in creating an XML tree representation is taking a series of linear events and transforming those events into a hierarchy of data. As you can see from Figure 15.6, the XML parser breaks an XML document into a series of chronological parsing events, and your application needs to capture those events and rebuild the document structure. The easiest method for performing this type of transformation is via a stack-based algorithm.

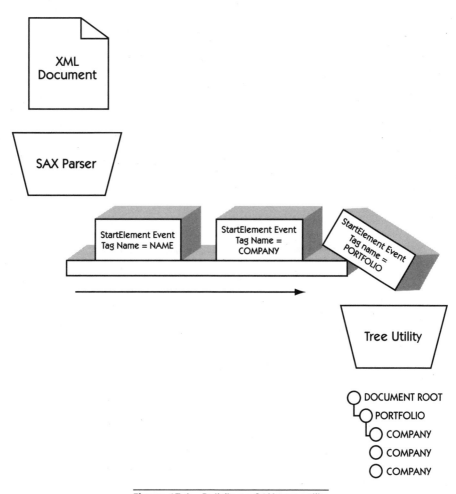

Figure 15.6 Building a SAX tree utility

A stack is perhaps one of the most useful data structures in computer science. It is also one of the most useful data structures for creating parse trees. Rather than jumping directly to the code, we will examine our algorithm for creating a general tree-making utility. The goal of the algorithm is to take any XML document and print its tree structure. For example, if our algorithm were given the Stocks.xml document from Listing 15.2, it would start to print out a tree like this:

```
|----+ DOCUMENT ROOT
    |----+ PORTFOLIO
        |----+ COMPANY
            |----+ NAME:  Microsoft Corp.
            |----+ STOCKSYMBOL:  MSFT
            |----+ STOCK
                |----+ DATE:  May 29, 1998
                |----+ CLOSE:  84.81
                |----+ HIGH:  85.60
                |----+ LOW:  84.75

    ...
```

The first step to creating a generic tree utility is to define a new data structure for each node within the tree. Again, we are not discussing real code yet. You can therefore imagine a node as a generic object which contains data and any number of children nodes. For example, Node A (which we will call the parent node) might contain data, along with two children, A1 and A2. When applied to an XML document, each node will represent a separate XML element, and each child will represent an embedded XML element. For example, Node A might refer to the COMPANY element and include three children: NAME, STOCKSYMBOL and STOCK. The STOCK node will, in turn contain four children nodes: DATE, CLOSE, HIGH and LOW.

The next step is to create a stack. The stack will contain a growing and shrinking list of nodes. Here's how it works:

1. First, we initialize the program by pushing a DOCUMENT ROOT node onto the stack. By definition, the node on top of the stack will be the parent node of all newly created nodes. Therefore, DOCUMENT ROOT will serve as the parent of all new nodes, and by the end of parsing, it will contain the entire XML tree.

2. Each time we receive a start element event, we create a new node. This node is the child of the XML element on top of the stack. We therefore take our

new node and add it to the list of children associated with the top-most XML element. We then take our new node and push it onto the stack. That way, it can act as the parent for any subsequent XML elements.

For example, when we receive a start element event for PORTFOLIO, we check the stack and see that DOCUMENT ROOT is on top of the stack (see Figure 15.7). PORTFOLIO is therefore a child of DOCUMENT ROOT, and we take PORTFOLIO and add it to the list of DOCUMENT ROOT children. We then push PORTFOLIO onto the stack, so that it can act as the parent for any COMPANY elements.

3. Each time we receive an end element event, we pop the stack. By the end of parsing, there should be only one DOCUMENT ROOT node remaining on the stack.[3]

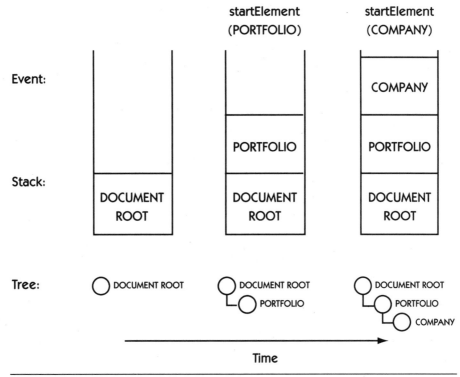

Figure 15.7   A stack-based algorithm for transforming linear events into a tree structure

---

3 This is one of the easiest ways to test if an XML document is well formed. If, at the end of parsing, your stack only includes a DOCUMENT ROOT node, it is verifiably well formed. Otherwise, you probably have a nesting error, in which case your document is not well formed.

Now take a look at the code. First, we need to create a Node class:

```
class Node {
      private String label;
      private Vector children;

      // Constructor
      public Node (String label) {
            children = new Vector ();
            this.label = label;
      }

      // Add Child
      public void addChild (Node child) {
            children.addElement (child);
      }

      // Set Label
      public void setLabel (String label) {
            this.label = label;
      }

      // Access Methods
      public int numChildren () { return children.size(); }
      public String getLabel () { return label; }
      public Vector getChildren () { return children; }


}
```

Each Node object will contain a String label and a vector of children elements. To add a new child, we use the addChild() method. To access the number of children, we use the numChildren () method. And, to retrieve all the children, we use the getChildren() method.

Next, we need to set up our stack. The complete tree making utility is presented in Listing 15.10 (and, sample output is provided in Figure 15.8.) As usual, the main method instantiates a parser object, sets the document handler, extracts the command line file argument, and starts parsing. The myHandler class captures the parsing events and controls the stack. First, the myHandler constructor creates a new stack, and pushes the DOCUMENT ROOT node onto the stack (this is step 1):

```
stack = new Stack ();
root = new Node ("DOCUMENT ROOT");
stack.push (root);
```

We then override the startElement() and endElement() methods. Within startElement() we first create a new node with the designated Tag name (step 2):

```
Node newNode = new Node (name);
```

Remember that the top-most element on the stack is by definition the parent of any new nodes. We therefore take our new node, and add it as a child to this top-most node:

```
Node parentNode = (Node) stack.peek();
parentNode.addChild (newNode);
```

Finally, we take our new node and add it to the stack:

```
stack.push (newNode);
```

The new node can therefore act as the parent of any other new nodes that come along.

Within the endElement() method, we just pop the stack. And, within the characters() method, we add the current string of data to the top-most element on the stack:

```
public void characters
      (char ch[], int start, int length) {
            // Set Label of Node on top of Stack
            String text = new String (ch, start, length);
            Node node = (Node) stack.peek();
            String currentLabel = node.getLabel();
            node.setLabel (currentLabel+":  "+text);
      }
```

Finally we override the endDocument() method. This method triggers the recursive printNode() method responsible for printing the tree hierarchy.

Listing 15.10 Building a SAX Tree Utility

```java
// SAX Tree Making Utility

import org.xml.sax.*;
import org.xml.sax.helpers.*;
import java.net.*;
import java.io.*;
import java.util.*;

// Extend Applet
public class Tree {

    public static void main (String args[]) throws Exception {
        // Set the Parser: IBM XML Parser or AElfred
        // String parserClass = "com.microstar.xml.SAXDriver";
        String parserClass = "com.ibm.xml.parser.SAXDriver";

        // Create Parser Object using ParserFactory
        Parser parser = ParserFactory.makeParser (parserClass);

        // Set Parser Document and Error Handlers
        myHandler handler = new myHandler ();
        parser.setDocumentHandler (handler);
        parser.setErrorHandler (handler);

        // Create FileReader, then Input Source
        FileReader filereader = new FileReader (args[0]);
        InputSource insource = new InputSource (filereader);

        // Start Parsing
        parser.parse (insource);
    }
}


// Event Handler
class myHandler extends HandlerBase {
    private Stack stack;
```

```java
private Node root;

// Constructor
public myHandler () {
    // Create stack, and push root on top
    stack = new Stack ();
    root = new Node ("DOCUMENT ROOT");
    stack.push (root);
}

public void characters
   (char ch[], int start, int length) {
    // Set Label of Node on top of Stack
    String text = new String (ch, start, length);
    Node node = (Node) stack.peek();
    String currentLabel = node.getLabel();
    node.setLabel (currentLabel+":  "+text);
}

public void startElement (String name, AttributeList atts) {
    //  Create new Node
    Node newNode = new Node (name);

    //  Add current Node to Node on top of Stack
    Node parentNode = (Node) stack.peek();
    parentNode.addChild (newNode);

    //  Push current Node on top of Stack
    stack.push (newNode);
}

public void endElement (String name) {
    // Pop Stack
    stack.pop ();
}

// At end of processing, print parse tree
public void endDocument () {
```

```
                    printNode (root, 0);
        }


        //  Recursive Print Method
        private void printNode
          (Node current, int level) {
              for (int i=0; i<level; i++) {
                    for (int j=0; j<5; j++) System.out.print (" ");
              }
              System.out.print (" | ");
              for (int j=0; j<4; j++) System.out.print ("-");
              System.out.print ("+ "+current.getLabel()+"\n");
              Vector children = current.getChildren();
              for (int i=0; i< current.numChildren(); i++)
                    printNode ((Node)children.elementAt(i), level+1);
        }


        //  For validating parsers, such as IBM XML for Java
        //  this method will display errors in validity
        public void error (SAXParseException e) throws SAXException {
              System.out.println ("Error:  "+e.getMessage());
        }
}


//  Node class
class Node {
        private String label;
        private Vector children;

        // Constructor
        public Node (String label) {
              children = new Vector ();
              this.label = label;
        }


        //  Add Child
        public void addChild (Node child) {
```

```
        children.addElement (child);
}


// Set Label
public void setLabel (String label) {
    this.label = label;
}


// Access Methods
public int numChildren () { return children.size(); }
public String getLabel () { return label; }
public Vector getChildren () { return children; }


}
```

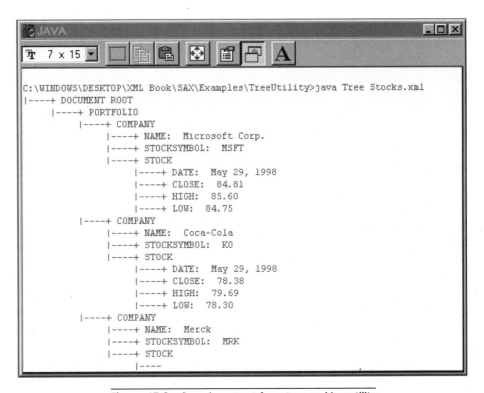

Figure 15.8 Sample output from tree making utility

BUILDING AN XML BROWSER

One of the first XML browsers created was JUMBO (Java Universal Markup Browser for Objects), created by Peter Murray-Rust (Murray-Rust, you may remember, was also one of the main instigators behind the creation of SAX). JUMBO was originally created to handle Chemical Markup Language (CML), an application of XML designed to hold data regarding chemical molecules. Using JUMBO, users can navigate through an XML document, and view the data in a variety of formats. For example, users can browse through molecular spectrum data (see Figure 15.9), and then graph that data within a separate graph applet (see Figure 15.10).

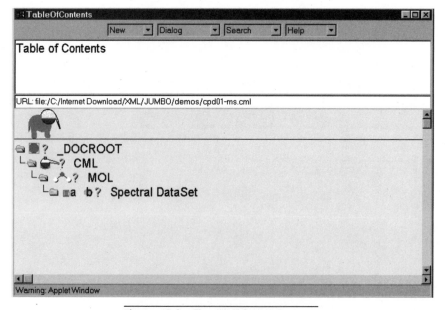

Figure 15.9 The JUMBO XML Browser

It would probably take a while to build a browser with the capabilities and extensibility of JUMBO, but it is actually remarkably easy to build a simple XML browser with Java's new Swing components. In fact, all you need do is take the tree making utility from the last section, and insert your nodes into the new Swing JTree component.

Listing 15.11 creates a simple (but useful) XML Browser written in Swing. If you are not familiar with Swing, see the insert below regarding the Swing JTree class. Otherwise, take a look at the code, and compare it to the tree making utility from the last section.

Listing 15.11   Building an XML Browser

```java
// Simple XML Browser
// Uses SAX and Swing APIs

import org.xml.sax.*;
import org.xml.sax.helpers.*;
import com.sun.java.swing.JTree;
import com.sun.java.swing.tree.DefaultMutableTreeNode;
import com.sun.java.swing.JScrollPane;
import com.sun.java.swing.JPanel;
import com.sun.java.swing.JFrame;
import java.net.URL;
import java.io.*;
import java.util.*;
import java.io.IOException;
import java.awt.*;
import java.awt.event.*;

public class XMLBrowser extends JPanel {
    private String xmlfile;
    private DefaultMutableTreeNode root;

    public XMLBrowser(String file) throws Exception{
        this.xmlfile = file;

        // Create Root Node
        root = new DefaultMutableTreeNode ("DOCUMENT ROOT");

        // Create Tree
        JTree tree = new JTree (root);
        JScrollPane scrollPane = new JScrollPane (tree);
        scrollPane.setPreferredSize(new Dimension(300, 300));

        // Add scroll pane to this panel
        setLayout (new GridLayout (1,0));
        add (scrollPane);
        initParser();
```

```
    }

    // Initialize SAX Parser and start Parsing
    private void initParser () throws Exception {

        // Set the Parser:  IBM XML Parser or AElfred
        // String parserClass = "com.microstar.xml.SAXDriver";
        String parserClass = "com.ibm.xml.parser.SAXDriver";

        // Create Parser Object using ParserFactory
        Parser parser = ParserFactory.makeParser (parserClass);

        // Set Parser Document and Error Handler
        myHandler handler = new myHandler (root);
        parser.setDocumentHandler (handler);
        parser.setErrorHandler (handler);

        // Create FileReader, then Input Source
        FileReader filereader = new FileReader (xmlfile);
        InputSource insource = new InputSource (filereader);

        // Start Parsing
        parser.parse (insource);
    }

    public static void main(String[] args) throws Exception{
        // Create a window.  Use JFrame since this
        // window will include lightweight components.
        JFrame frame = new JFrame("XML Browser");
        WindowListener l = new WindowAdapter() {
            public void windowClosing(WindowEvent e)
                {System.exit(0);}
        };
        frame.addWindowListener(l);
        frame.getContentPane().add
            ("Center", new XMLBrowser(args[0]));
        frame.pack();
        frame.show();
```

```java
        }
}

//  Event Handler
class myHandler extends HandlerBase {
      private Stack stack;
      private DefaultMutableTreeNode root;

      // Constructor
      public myHandler (DefaultMutableTreeNode root) {
            // Create stack, and push root on top
            this.root = root;
            stack = new Stack ();
            stack.push (root);
      }

      public void characters
        (char ch[], int start, int length) {
            // Set Text of Node on top of Stack
            String text = new String (ch, start, length);
            DefaultMutableTreeNode node =
                  (DefaultMutableTreeNode) stack.peek();
            String currentLabel = (String) node.getUserObject();
            node.setUserObject (currentLabel+":  "+text);
      }

      public void startElement (String name, AttributeList atts) {
            //  Create new Node
            DefaultMutableTreeNode newNode =
                  new DefaultMutableTreeNode (name);

            //  Add current Node to Node on top of Stack
            DefaultMutableTreeNode parentNode =
                  (DefaultMutableTreeNode) stack.peek();
            parentNode.add (newNode);

            //  Push current Node on top of Stack
            stack.push (newNode);
```

```
    }

    // Pop Stack
    public void endElement (String name) {
        stack.pop ();
    }

    //  For validating parsers, such as IBM XML for Java
    //  this method will display errors in validity
    public void error (SAXParseException e) throws SAXException {
        System.out.println ("Error:  "+e.getMessage());
    }
}
```

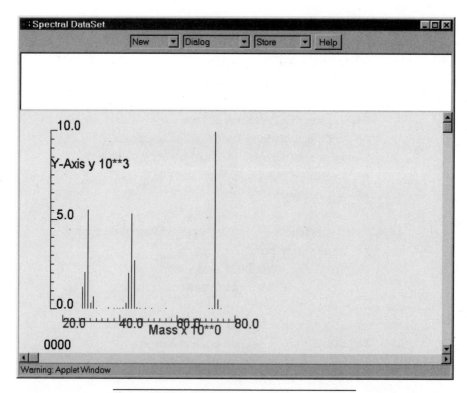

Figure 15.10   Graphing spectral data in JUMBO

The major difference is that the tree making utility maps XML data to our internal Node class structure, whereas the XML browser maps the data to the Swing JTree node. For example, the `startElement()` method creates a new `DefaultMutableTreeNode` with the indicated Tag name:

```
DefaultMutableTreeNode newNode =
new DefaultMutableTreeNode (name);
```

We then add this node to the top element on the stack:

```
DefaultMutableTreeNode parentNode =
(DefaultMutableTreeNode) stack.peek();
parentNode.add (newNode);
```

Finally, we push the new node onto the stack:

```
stack.push (newNode);
```

With only 100 lines of code you can now actually browse any XML document! For example, Figure 15.11 displays data from the stocks.xml document. Figure 15.12 displays an XML-enabled version of Shakespeare's Julius Caesar. Feel free to modify the code for your own use.

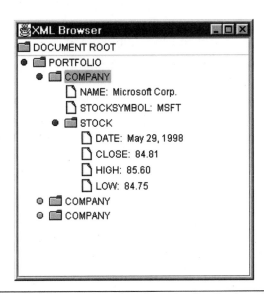

Figure 15.11 XML browser in action: Browsing the Stocks.xml document

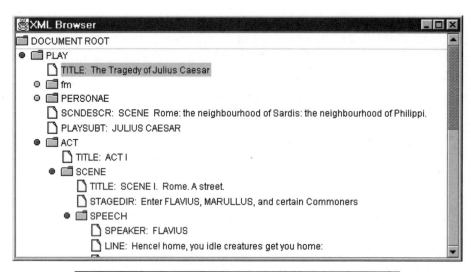

Figure 15.12 The XML browser can display any XML document. Here, we see an XML-enabled version of Shakespeare's Julius Caesar.

The Java Swing set heralds a major upgrade to the Java Abstract Windowing Toolkit (AWT.) Many developers originally complained that the AWT did not provide enough functionality for truly professional GUI applications. Swing therefore aims to provide developers with a very rich array of new windowing components. Components include: new buttons, combo boxes, lists, menus, sliders, tables, progress bars, tool tips, scroll panes, split panes and tabbed panes. All told, the entire Swing tool set includes more than 250 classes and more than 75 interfaces. Among these many new components, however, the JTree component is perhaps the most useful for XML applications. With JTree, you can easily represent hierarchical data with very few lines of code.

In order to create a JTree component, you must first create a tree of node objects. To help developers, Swing provides a default node object, known as the DefaultMutableTreeNode class. To create a node, you simply need to provide a string of text. For example, the following line:

```
DefaultMutableTreeNode root = new DefaultMutableTreeNode ("News");
```

creates a root node for "News" resources.

To add children to the root node, we can use the add() method. For example:

```
    node = new DefaultMutableTreeNode("General News");
root.add(node);
child = new DefaultMutableTreeNode("ABC News");
```

```
node.add (child);
```

Here we add a "General News" node to root. Subsequently, we add "ABC News" to the General News node.

Once we have created our tree of node objects, we pass the root node to the JTree constructor:

```
JTree tree = new JTree (root);
```

That's all there is to it!

Below is an example of a JTree application used to display news resources. It is important to note that Swing applications must derive from JFrame or JApplet (every AWT component has a corresponding Swing component beginning with the letter J.) Note, however that to use JFrame, you cannot add components directly. Rather, you must add components to the JFrame ContentPane. The example below also utilizes the JScrollPane component to enable automatic scrolling functionality.

For additional information regarding the JTree component, see the "How to Use Trees" lesson of the Java Swing Tutorial at: **http://java.sun.com/docs/ books/tutorial/ui/swing/tree.html**.

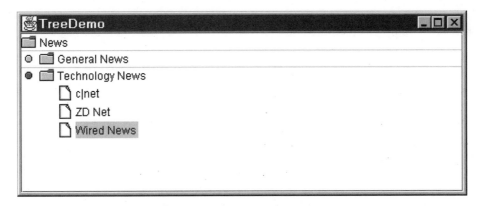

Figure A   Example JTree application

Listing: Example JTree Application

```
// Example JTree Application

import com.sun.java.swing.JTree;
import com.sun.java.swing.tree.DefaultMutableTreeNode;
```

```java
import com.sun.java.swing.JScrollPane;
import com.sun.java.swing.JPanel;
import com.sun.java.swing.JFrame;
import java.awt.*;
import java.awt.event.*;

public class TreeDemo extends JPanel {

    public TreeDemo() {
        //Create the nodes.
        DefaultMutableTreeNode root =
new DefaultMutableTreeNode("News");
        createNodes(root);

        JTree tree = new JTree (root);
        JScrollPane scrollPane = new JScrollPane (tree);
        scrollPane.setPreferredSize(new Dimension(300, 300));

        // Add scroll pane to this panel
        setLayout (new GridLayout (1,0));
        add (scrollPane);
    }

    // Create News Folders
    private void createNodes(DefaultMutableTreeNode root) {
        DefaultMutableTreeNode node;
        DefaultMutableTreeNode child;

        // Create General News Folder
        node = new DefaultMutableTreeNode("General News");
        root.add(node);
        child = new DefaultMutableTreeNode("ABC News");
        node.add (child);
        child = new DefaultMutableTreeNode("CNN");
        node.add (child);
        child = new DefaultMutableTreeNode("MS-NBC");
        node.add (child);
```

```
      // Create Technology News Folder
      node = new DefaultMutableTreeNode("Technology News");
      root.add(node);
      child = new DefaultMutableTreeNode("c|net");
      node.add (child);
      child = new DefaultMutableTreeNode("ZD Net");
      node.add (child);
      child = new DefaultMutableTreeNode("Wired News");
      node.add (child);
   }

   public static void main(String[] args) {
      JFrame frame = new JFrame("TreeDemo");

      WindowListener l = new WindowAdapter() {
         public void windowClosing(WindowEvent e) {
            System.exit(0);
         }
      };
      frame.addWindowListener(l);

      frame.getContentPane().add("Center", new TreeDemo());
      frame.setSize(500,200);
      frame.show();
   }
}
```

4

EXAMPLE XML APPLICATIONS

Most programmers learn best by example. Part IV of this book therefore provides six full-functional, fully-loaded XML applications. With the exception of the first example, all the example programs use the SAX interface. Each example also strives to illustrates a particularly important concept that may be applicable to a wider range of applications.

We begin in Chapter 16 with a very simple applet capable of displaying weather conditions. Chapter 17 illustrates an interactive site map based on the popular Channel Definition Format (CDF). Chapter 18 presents a graphical viewer application capable of rendering vector graphics encoded in the proposed Precision Graphics Markup Language (PGML.) Chapter 19 illustrates the principles of XLinking, from the simplest HTML-like links to the more complex capabilities of extended link groups. Chapter 20 demonstrates a general model for creating XML-encoded preference files. We conclude in Chapter 21 with a discussion of server-side XML and create a flexible model for transforming XML into HTML.

In describing each of the example applications, we include a general description of the program, a technical specification describing the XML parser and interface, and an XML specification with a proposed DTD and sample XML files. We also include a overview of the software architecture and detailed explanations of key sections of code. Source code for all the examples is available on the CD that accompanies this book.

16

THE WEATHER REPORTER APPLET

Our first example XML application is the Weather Reporter applet. Applets are currently the best mechanism for embedding interactive, multimedia programs within Web pages. Many applets can, however, benefit greatly from the extra power of XML. Here we examine a weather applet that could easily have been programmed without the use of XML. By the end of the chapter, however, we hope to convince readers that the additional use of XML makes the applet considerably more robust and flexible.

DESCRIPTION

The Weather Reporter applet is simple. At startup, the applet loads an XML document containing weather data for major cities through out the world. The applet then parses the XML data, and places all the cities within a pull-down menu. When a user selects a city, the applet displays the high and low temperatures, a short description of the current weather conditions and a graphical icon indicating one of six weather conditions: sunny, partly sunny, partly cloudy, cloudy, rain or snow (see Figure 1 for a mock-up of the graphical user interface.)

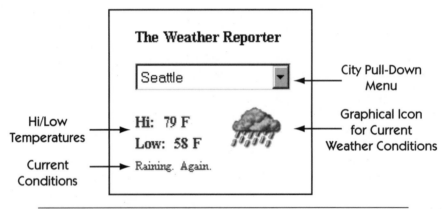

Figure 16.1   Blueprint for Weather Applet Graphical User Interface (GUI)

Ideally, we imagine that the weather applet would be added to an Internet news site. We also imagine that users will be able to select which cities appear in the pull-down menu. We do not, however, include here information on personalization or customization.

IMPORTANT CONCEPTS

In creating the weather applet, we aim to illustrate three very important concepts. First, the use of XML within applets; perhaps, after examining the weather applet, you will dream up your own XML applets. Or perhaps you will conceive of new ways to add XML functionality to your existing applets. In retrospect, many of the applets that we have developed in the past could have benefited greatly from XML support. Our hope is that you begin to view XML as a vital tool in future applet development. Second, we will revisit the Ælfred XML Parser and provide extra practice in its use. Finally, we wish to revisit the issue of event mapping. Event-based parsers, such as Ælfred and the SAX API, do not build internal tree structures, and we therefore need to build our own. In the case of the weather applet, we will map XML parsing events to our own user defined data structures and objects.

TECHNICAL SPECIFICATION

The weather applet uses the native interface of the Ælfred XML parser. In the next chapter, we will utilize Ælfred's SAX interface. The code is written in Java 1.1 and will run in Netscape Navigator 4.0 or Internet Explorer 4.0.

XML SPECIFICATION

Listing 16.1 shows the weather DTD file. The DTD requires a root WEATHER element, which must contain at least one CITY element. The CITY element must have a NAME attribute, and must include sub elements for HI, LOW, DESCRIPTION and ICON. Finally, the ICON element is required to contain a VALUE attribute. The VALUE attribute is restricted to one of six possible values: SUNNY, PARTLYSUNNY, PARTLYCLOUDY, CLOUDY, RAIN or SNOW.

Listing 16.2 shows a sample Weather.xml file which adheres to the Weather DTD. Sample data are available for five cities: Hong Kong, London, New York, San Francisco, and Seattle. Remember, however, that Ælfred is a non-validating parser. Ælfred will therefore not check Weather.xml against the DTD. However, the DTD is still useful to us. It serves as a template for the Weather.xml file, and we have checked the validity of the file by running it through the command line version of MS-XML (see Chapter 14: "The Microsoft XML Parser" for details).

Listing 16.1 Weather.dtd

```
<!-- Weather DTD for Cities-->
<!ELEMENT WEATHER (CITY)+>
<!-- CITY Element has HI, LOW, DESCRIPTION, and ICON Elements-->
<!-- and a required NAME Attribute-->
<!ELEMENT CITY (HI, LOW, DESCRIPTION, ICON)>
<!ATTLIST CITY NAME CDATA #REQUIRED>
<!ELEMENT HI (#PCDATA)>
<!ELEMENT LOW (#PCDATA)>
<!ELEMENT DESCRIPTION (#PCDATA)>
```

```
<!ELEMENT ICON EMPTY>

<!-- The ICON VALUE Attribute is restricted to one of 6 options  -->
<!ATTLIST ICON VALUE
(SUNNY|PARTLYSUNNY|PARTLYCLOUDY|CLOUDY|RAIN|SNOW) #REQUIRED>
```

Listing 16.2   Weather.xml

```xml
<?xml version="1.0" encoding="UTF-8"?>
<!DOCTYPE WEATHER SYSTEM "Weather.dtd">
<WEATHER>
    <CITY NAME="Hong Kong">
        <HI>87</HI>
        <LOW>78</LOW>
        <DESCRIPTION>Partly sunny.</DESCRIPTION>
        <ICON VALUE="PARTLYSUNNY"/>
    </CITY>
    <CITY NAME="London">
        <HI>65</HI>
        <LOW>60</LOW>
        <DESCRIPTION>Showers throughout the day.</DESCRIPTION>
        <ICON VALUE="RAIN"/>
    </CITY>
    <CITY NAME="New York">
        <HI>78</HI>
        <LOW>67</LOW>
        <DESCRIPTION>Sunny, hot and humid.</DESCRIPTION>
        <ICON VALUE="PARTLYSUNNY"/>
    </CITY>
    <CITY NAME="San Fransisco">
        <HI>79</HI>
        <LOW>58</LOW>
        <DESCRIPTION>Partly cloudy.</DESCRIPTION>
        <ICON VALUE="PARTLYCLOUDY"/>
    </CITY>
    <CITY NAME="Seattle">
        <HI>79</HI>
```

```
      <LOW>58</LOW>
      <DESCRIPTION>Raining. Again.</DESCRIPTION>
      <ICON VALUE="RAIN"/>
    </CITY>
  </WEATHER>
```

SOFTWARE ARCHITECTURE

Before we delve into the code, let us take a macro view of the software architecture necessary to build the weather applet. At the core of the applet, we have the Ælfred parser, which is responsible for reading the XML document and generating XML parsing events. Remember, Ælfred requires implementing the XmlHandler interface to catch the events generated by the parser. At a minimum, we therefore need an XmlParser object and an implementation of the XmlHandler interface.

Parsing events are akin to quick flashes in the dark. We may see a flash for a "Start of Element" event or a series of flashes for character data. Taken individually, parsing events do not, however, convey much information. It is only when we capture all the events and start to assemble patterns that the flashes actually amount to meaningful data. The best method of assembling the flashes is to map them to your own objects and data structures.

In the case of our weather applet, we will create a new class called City. The City class will hold encapsulated weather data for an individual city. Our primary goal therefore is to map XML parsing events to a vector of City objects (see Figure 16.2).

The weather applet is broken into three class files. Here is the cast of characters:

- **City.java:** Responsible for encapsulating weather data for an individual city.
- **EventHandler.java:** This class implements the Ælfred XmlHandler interface and maps parsing events to a vector of City objects.
- **Weather.java:** This applet class is responsible for creating the graphical user interface and handling user input.

THE CODE

Enough preliminaries. Let's take a look at the code. First up, the City class. Listing 16.3 shows the code.

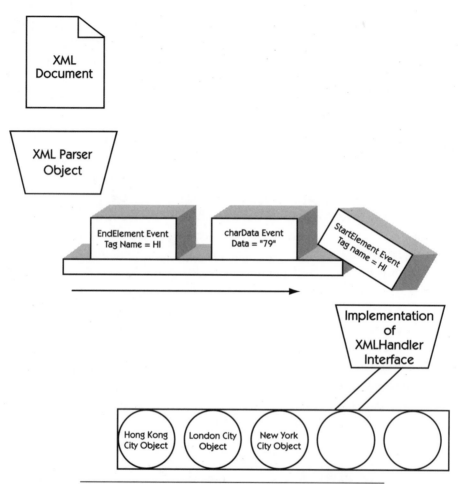

Figure 16.2   The EventHandler class maps sequences of
XML parsing events to a vector of City objects.

As you can see, the City class holds data for the name of the city, the high and low temperatures, a description of the current weather conditions, and a reference to a graphical icon depicting the current conditions. It also includes accessor methods for retrieving the encapsulated data. Simple enough.

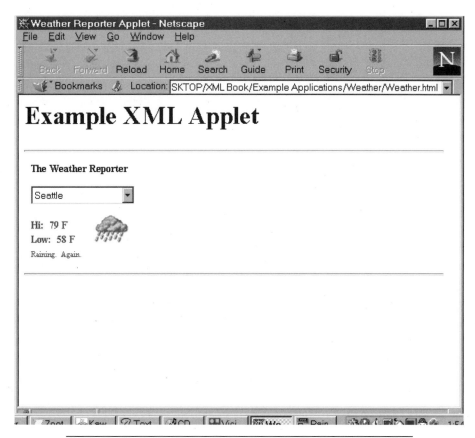

Figure 16.3 The Weather Applet running in Netscape Navigator 4.0

Listing 16.3 The City Class

City.java
import java.util.*;

/**

City Class contains all weather information regarding
an individual City, including Hi/Low Temperatures,
Description of current conditions, and Icon reference

* @author written by Ethan Cerami/Simon St. Laurent
* @version 1.0

```
    */

class City {
    private String name, description, icon;
    private String hi, low;


    /** Constructor
    @param name Name of City
    @param hi Hi Temperature
    @param low Low Temperature
    @param description Description of current conditions
    @param icon Icon Reference,.e.g. "SUNNY", "CLOUDY", etc.
    */
    public City (String name, String hi, String low,
        String description, String icon) {
        this.name = name;
        this.hi = hi;
        this.low = low;
        this.description = description;
        this.icon = icon;
    }


    /** Retrieve City Name */
    public String getName () { return name; }

    /** Retrieve High Temperature */
    public String getHi () { return hi; }

    /** Retrieve Low Temperature */
    public String getLow () { return low; }

    /** Retrieve Description of current conditions */
    public String getDescription () { return description; }

    /** Retrieve Icon Referece */
    public String getIcon () { return icon;        }

}
```

Next up, is the EventHandler class (see Listing 16.2). This is the most important class. Examine the code now, and we will dissect it below.

The EventHandler class extends the Ælfred HandlerBase convenience class:

```
public class EventHandler extends HandlerBase {

...
```

The HandlerBase provides a default implementation of the Ælfred XmlHandler interface. You can therefore override any of the methods directly relevant to your application. For reference, the main methods of the XmHandler interface are reprinted in Table 16.1.

Table 16.1 The XmlHandler Interface: Main Methods

Method Name	Description
startDocument ()	Indicates the start of a new XML document. This is always the first method called.
endDocument ()	Indicates that Ælfred has completed the parsing of the document. This is always the last method called.
startElement (String elname)	Indicates the start of a new XML element. The name of the element is specified by the elname String.
endElement (String elname)	Indicates the end of an XML element. The name of the element is specified by the elname String.
attribute (String aname, String value, boolean isSpecified)	Indicates an XML attribute. It is important to note that this method is called **prior** to any startElement events. The name of the attribute is specified by the aname String. The value of the attribute is specified by the value String. If the isSpecified boolean flag is true, the attribute has been explicitly defined within the XML document. If the isSpecified flag is false, this is the default attribute value defined within the DTD.
charData (char ch[], int start, int length)	Indicates character data. For example, when parsing <TITLE>Basic Poem</TITLE>, Ælfred will fire off a startElement event, followed by a charData event with the string, "Basic Poem." To retrieve the string, extract it from the ch character array. The string is located at the start index and is length characters long.

continued on next page

Method Name	Description
error (String message, String systemId, int line, int column)	Indicates a fatal error in parsing; because Ælfred is a non-validating parser, do not expect this method to alert you to errors in validity. You can extract the error message, and the exact location of the error.
ignorableWhitespace (char ch[], int start, int length)	Indicates white-space characters, such as newline or tab character data. Most of the time, white space is ignorable. To retrieve the string, extract it from the ch character array. The string is located at the start index and is length characters long.

Rather than actually stepping through the rest of the of the code, we will examine a sample parsing session, specifically the parse session for the following XML text:

```
<CITY NAME="Hong Kong">
    <HI>87</HI>
    <LOW>78</LOW>
    <DESCRIPTION>Partly sunny.</DESCRIPTION>
    <ICON VALUE="PARTLYSUNNY"/>
</CITY>
```

This gives us a chance to review the Ælfred event model and the actual code at the same time. We will examine the code in EventHandler.java at specific time slices, starting at Time = 0.

Time 0: In the constructor to **EventHandler**, we create a vector called **cities**:

```
cities = new Vector();
```

Each time we encounter a new CITY element, we create a new **City** object and add it to the **cities** vector. By the end of parsing, the **cities** vector will contain all the data we need.

Time 1: In parsing our snippet of XML text, the parser will first call the **attribute()** method. The **attribute()** method is always called *before* the **startElement()** method. At Time 1, **attribute()** is called with the NAME attribute of our first city, Hong Kong. Event-driven parsers are essentially stateless—once the flash of an event has faded away, the data is lost unless you explicitly save it yourself. We therefore need to save the attribute name and value to temporary variables:

```
public void attribute(String aname, String avalue,
    boolean isSpecified) {
        attrnameTemp = aname;
        attrvalueTemp = avalue;
}
```

We can later use these temporary values to create the City object.

Time 2: The parser will call the startElement() method, indicating the start of the CITY element. In most cases, we need only save the tag name so that we can later associate character data to the correct XML elements. In the case of CITY elements, however, we also have the additional task of saving the attribute value just captured:

```
public void startElement (String name) {
    currentTagName = name;

        // If this is a CITY Element, store
        // City Name Attribute
    if (currentTagName.equals ("CITY"))
            citynameTemp = attrvalueTemp;

        // Else if this is an ICON Element,
        //  store Icon Value Attribute
    else if (currentTagName.equals ("ICON"))
            iconTemp = attrvalueTemp;


}
```

All we have done here is save the Tag name to a private variable called currentTagName. In the case of a CITY element, we know that we just received attribute data. Now that we have the element name, we can associate the attribute data to the CITY element. We therefore save the city name attribute to another private variable, which we will later use when creating the new City object. As you can see, we use a similar technique to save the VALUE attribute associated with the ICON element.

Time 3: The parser calls the startElement() method again, this time for the HI element. There are no attribute values associated with the HI element. We therefore only need to save the tag name.

Time 4: The parser calls the | 10

method with a string set to "87." The challenge with event-driven parsers is that we receive lots of character events, and there is no built in mechanism for identifying which text belongs to which elements. Fortunately, however, we have saved the current tag name, and can therefore associate the text to the appropriate temporary variable:

```
public void charData (char ch[], int start, int length){
String text = new String (ch, start, length);
    if (currentTagName.equals ("HI"))
        hiTemp = text;
    else if (currentTagName.equals ("LOW"))
        lowTemp = text;
    else if (currentTagName.equals ("DESCRIPTION"))
        descriptionTemp = text;
}
```

The first line extracts the text from the character array. We then check the currentTagName variable to determine where to store the data. In the case of the HI element, we save the text "87" to the hiTemp variable. As you can see, we employ a similar technique for saving the LOW and DESCRIPTION text.

Time 5: The parser calls the endElement() method for the HI element. We ignore this event.

Time 6–14: The parser calls a sequence of parsing events for the LOW, DESCRIPTION and ICON elements. We store this data using the same techniques outlined above in Times 1.4.

Time 15: Finally, the parser calls the endElement() method, indicating the end of the CITY tag. This is our cue that we now have all data regarding one individual city. We are therefore ready to create a new City object and add it to our cities vector:

```
public void endElement (String name) {
        // If this is the end of the CITY
```

```
        //  element, create new City Object,
        //  and add to cities Vector
        if (name.equals ("CITY")) {
            City currentCity = new City (citynameTemp,
                hiTemp, lowTemp, descriptionTemp, iconTemp);
            cities.addElement(currentCity);
        }
    }
```

By repeating Times 1–15, we can read in each CITY element and create a City object for each one. By the time we reach the endDocument() method, we have a complete vector that holds all the data we need.

Listing 16.4 EventHandler.java

```java
import com.microstar.xml.XmlHandler;
import com.microstar.xml.XmlParser;
import com.microstar.xml.HandlerBase;
import java.applet.*;
import java.awt.*;
import java.util.*;

/**
    XML EventHandler to catch XML Parsing Events and
    map to vector of City Objects
    <P>Illustrates the use of the Aelfred DocumentHandler
    Interface and the remapping of events to user defined
    data structures
    * @author written by Ethan Cerami/Simon St. Laurent
    * @version 1.0
    */


//  EventHandler extends the AElfred XML HandlerBase
//  Convenience Class
class EventHandler extends HandlerBase {
    private Choice citychoice;      // Applet City Selection List
    private Vector cities;          // Vector of all City Objects
    private String currentTagName;  // Indicates Current Tag Name
```

```java
private String citynameTemp;          // Temporary City Name
private String hiTemp, lowTemp;       // Temporary Temperature
private String descriptionTemp;       // Temporary Description
private String iconTemp;              // Temporary Icon
private String attrnameTemp;          // Temporary Attribute Name
private String attrvalueTemp;         // Temporary Attribute Value

/** Constructor
*@param citychoice Applet City Pull-Down Menu
*/
public EventHandler (Choice citychoice) {
    cities = new Vector();
    this.citychoice = citychoice;
}


/** Retrieve City at Specified Index  */
public City getCity (int index) {
    return (City) cities.elementAt(index);
}


// Override HandlerBase Methods Here

/** startElement:  Store Tag Name and
attribute values (if any) for later use
*/
public void startElement (String name) {
    currentTagName = name;

// If this is a CITY Element, store
//  City Name Attribute
if (currentTagName.equals ("CITY"))
    citynameTemp = attrvalueTemp;

// Else if this is an ICON Element,
//  store Icon Value Attribute
else if (currentTagName.equals ("ICON"))
    iconTemp = attrvalueTemp;
```

```
}


/** endElement: capture City Element only
*/
public void endElement (String name) {

    // If this is the end of the CITY
    // element, create new City Object,
    // and add to cities Vector
    if (name.equals ("CITY")) {
        City currentCity = new City (citynameTemp,
             hiTemp, lowTemp, descriptionTemp, iconTemp);
        cities.addElement(currentCity);
    }

}


/** attribute: Store attribute name and value for later use
Remember that attribute () is called prior to startElement()
*/
public void attribute(String aname, String avalue,
    boolean isSpecified) {
        attrnameTemp = aname;
        attrvalueTemp = avalue;
    }


/** charData: Depending on current Tag Name, place
character data in temporary variables for later use
*/
public void charData (char ch[], int start, int length) {
    String text = new String (ch, start, length);
    if (currentTagName.equals ("HI"))
        hiTemp = text;
    else if (currentTagName.equals ("LOW"))
        lowTemp = text;
    else if (currentTagName.equals ("DESCRIPTION"))
        descriptionTemp = text;
}
```

```
/**
endDocument:  Add Cities to applet pull-down menu
*/
public void endDocument () {
     City city;
     int len = cities.size();
     for (int i=0; i<len; i++) {
          city = (City) cities.elementAt(i);
          citychoice.addItem (city.getName());
     }
}
}
```

The final class file is Weather.java. The code appears in Listing 16.5. This code has three main responsibilities:

■   **Set up the XmlParser Object:** The first responsibility of weather.java is to create an **XmlParser** object, and to load the specified XML document. First, we instantiate a copy of the **EventHandler** class and create a new **XmlParser** object:

```
handler = new EventHandler(citychoice);
parser = new XmlParser();
```

We then set the parser's event handler:

```
parser.setHandler(handler);
```

The XML document is specified as an applet parameter. We therefore need to extract the parameter, and make an absolute URL using the applet's **getDocumentBase()** method. We then call the **parse()** method:

```
String xmldoc = getParameter ("url");
     try {
     xmlURL = new URL (getDocumentBase(), xmldoc);
     parser.parse(xmlURL.toString(), null,
   (String) null);
     } catch (Exception e) {
     e.printStackTrace();
     }
```

■ **Create the GUI:** The second responsibility of weather.java is to create the GUI. The focus of the example is to explore the use of Ælfred, so we will not dwell on the details of creating the GUI. Note, however that we use the **MediaTracker** class to download and wait for all the weather icons. We also use a double buffering graphics technique for smoother graphics transitions.

■ **Responding to User Events:** The final responsibility of weather.java is the handling of user events. When the user selects a city from the pull-down menu, we update the current city object and call the repaint() method.

Listing 16.5   Weather.java

```java
import com.microstar.xml.XmlHandler;
import com.microstar.xml.XmlParser;
import com.microstar.xml.HandlerBase;
import java.applet.*;
import java.net.*;
import java.awt.*;
import java.awt.event.*;
import java.util.*;

/**   Weather Channel Applet
    * @author written by Ethan Cerami/Simon St. Laurent
    * @version 1.0, ©August 1998, All Rights Reserved
*/

public class Weather extends Applet implements ItemListener {
    private XmlParser parser;              // Aelfred XML Parser
    private EventHandler handler;          // Aelfred Event Handler
    private java.awt.Choice citychoice;    // City Pull-Down Menu
    private Label conditions, skies;       // GUI Element Labels
    private Label hi, low;                  // GUI elements Labels
    private Image icons[];                  // Array of Icons
    private MediaTracker tracker;          // Media Tracker for
                                           // tracking images

    private Hashtable hashtable;           // Hashtable for icons
    private Dimension dim;                  // Current Dimensions
    private Graphics offScreenGraphics;    // OffScreen Graphics for
                                           // Double Buffered Imaging
```

```
    private Image offScreen;        //  OffScreen Graphics for
                                    //  Double Buffered Imaging
    private City currentCity;       //  Currently Selected City


/** Initialize the applet GUI and XML Parser */
public void init ()
{
    URL xmlURL;

    initGUI();
    initIcons();

    //  Create XML Event Handler and
    //  XML Parser Object
    handler = new EventHandler(citychoice);
    parser = new XmlParser();
    parser.setHandler(handler);

    //  Create URL to XML Document and
    //  Start Parsing
    String xmldoc = getParameter ("url");
    System.out.println ("URL:  "+xmldoc);
    try {
        xmlURL = new URL (getDocumentBase(), xmldoc);
        parser.parse(xmlURL.toString(), null, (String) null);
    } catch (Exception e) {
        e.printStackTrace();
    }
}


/** Initializes Graphical User Interface */
private void initGUI () {
    this.setLayout (null);
    citychoice = new java.awt.Choice();
    citychoice.addItem ("--  Select a City --");
    this.add (citychoice);
    citychoice.addItemListener (this);
```

```
        citychoice.setBounds (10,40,150,20);
}


/** Download Weather Icons
      Use Media Tracker to wait for all downloads
*/
private void initIcons () {
      String iconstrings []= {"SUNNY", "PARTLYSUNNY",
            "CLOUDY", "PARTLYCLOUDY", "SNOW", "RAIN"};
      tracker = new MediaTracker (this);
      hashtable = new Hashtable();
      icons= new Image[6];

      for (int i=0; i<6; i++){
            icons[i] = getImage (getDocumentBase(),
                  "images/"+iconstrings[i]+".gif");
            hashtable.put (iconstrings[i], new Integer(i));
            tracker.addImage (icons[i], i);
      }
      try {
            tracker.waitForAll();
      } catch (InterruptedException e) {
            e.printStackTrace();
      }
}


/** City Choice Event Handler */
public void itemStateChanged (ItemEvent e) {
      currentCity = (City) handler.getCity (
            citychoice.getSelectedIndex()-1);
      repaint();
}


/** Paint Method */
public void paint (Graphics g) {
      update (g);
}
```

```
/**  Double Buffering Paint Method */
public void update (Graphics g) {

    // Prepare for Double Buffering
    if (dim==null) {
        dim = this.getSize ();
        offScreen = createImage (dim.width, dim.height);
        offScreenGraphics = offScreen.getGraphics();
    }

offScreenGraphics.setColor (Color.white);
offScreenGraphics.fillRect (0,0,dim.width, dim.height);
offScreenGraphics.setColor (Color.black);
offScreenGraphics.setFont (new Font
    ("TimesRoman", Font.BOLD, 14));
offScreenGraphics.drawString ("The Weather Reporter",10,20);
offScreenGraphics.setColor (new Color (139,20,70));

if (currentCity != null) {
    offScreenGraphics.drawString ("Hi:  "+
        currentCity.getHi()+ " F", 10,100);
    offScreenGraphics.setColor (new Color (53,39,150));
    offScreenGraphics.drawString ("Low:  "+
        currentCity.getLow()+ " F", 10, 120);
    Integer iconIndex = (Integer)
        hashtable.get(currentCity.getIcon());
    offScreenGraphics.drawImage
        (icons[iconIndex.intValue()], 100,75, this);
    offScreenGraphics.setFont (new Font
        ("TimesRoman", Font.PLAIN, 11));
    offScreenGraphics.drawString (
        currentCity.getDescription(), 10,140);
    }

    g.drawImage (offScreen, 0,0, null);

    }

}
```

17

THE CDF SITE MAP APPLET

DESCRIPTION

Maintaining clear and consistent navigation is crucial to building user-friendly Web sites. Most sites therefore provide end-users with navigable site maps. The CDF Site Map applet makes it easy to build hierarchical, interactive site maps and embed them within Web pages.

Initially, the CDF applet provides visitors with a list of first-level categories or folders. For example, you may want to display folders for business news, technology news, or sports scores. When a user clicks on a category, the applet displays the category contents. The content may include embedded folders or individual Web pages. When a user selects an individual item, the Web page is displayed, either within the same browser window, or within a designated frame. The user can therefore quickly drill down to the information desired (see Figure 17.1). The CDF applet is capable of representing any arbitrarily large Web site, with multiple levels of content.

The CDF applet works by reading in a XML document which adheres to the Channel Definition Format (CDF). CDF was one of the first (and most widely) used applications of XML. Originally, CDF was proposed for "push" technology applications—applications which automatically deliver content to subscribers. With a few minor modifications, however, CDF is an ideal format for representing Web sites and turns out to be ideal for creating site maps. With the CDF applet, we therefore have the opportunity to explore the use of an already existing XML format and adapt that format for our own use.

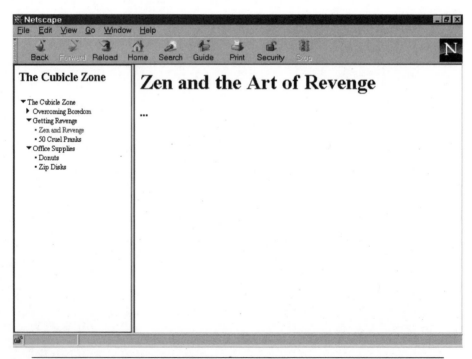

Figure 17.1 The CDF Site Map Applet in action. Clicking on an item in the applet causes the corresponding Web page to appear in the right frame.

TECHNICAL SPECIFICATION

The CDF Site Map applet uses the SAX driver of the Ælfred XML Parser. The code is written in Java 1.1 and will run in Netscape Navigator 4.0 or Internet Explorer 4.0.

XML SPECIFICATION

INTRODUCTION TO THE CHANNEL DEFINITION FORMAT (CDF)

CDF was one of the very first applications of XML. Originally proposed by Microsoft Corp., CDF enables content providers to "push" channels of information to subscribers. Within Internet Explorer 4.0, CDF channels are referred to as *active channels*, and users can now subscribe to over 250 premier channels, including CNN, ESPN, and MS-NBC (see Figure 17.2). IE 4.0 also supports *active desktop components*, small Web pages which are "glued" to the Windows desktop (see Figure 17.3). Much like active channels, desktop components also use CDF and are automatically updated to display breaking news.

Figure 17.2 The MSNBC active channel as seen in Internet Explorer 4.0

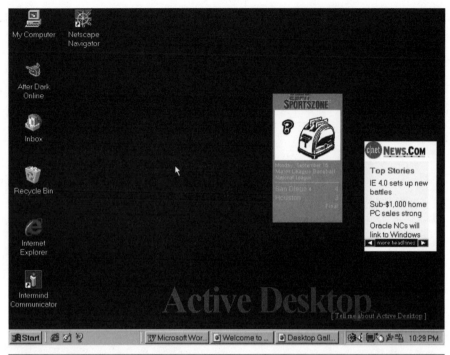

Figure 17.3   The ESPN SportsZone and clnet Technology News desktop components.

CDF works by encapsulating all information regarding a channel in one XML document. This information can include a channel description, an update schedule and a table of contents. Despite the name, most push applications follow a repetitive "client pull" model, rather than a true "server push" (many pundits have therefore labeled push the greatest misnomer in Internet history). At the specified update interval, Internet Explorer scans the CDF table of contents, and downloads each item to the user's desktop. The user is then notified of new content and is free to browse the content offline.

NOTE   Microsoft originally submitted the CDF specification to the World Wide Web Consortium in March 1997. The full proposal is available online at: **http://www.w3.org/TR/NOTE-CDFsubmit.html**.

The best method to learn CDF is to see an example in action. Listing 17.1 provides a CDF representation of a fictional channel, entitled the "Cubicle Zone" (note that the URL http://www.cubiclezone.com is entirely fictional). Having toiled away at far too many office jobs, the publishers of the Cubicle Zone aspire to create a daily on-line magaze devoted to office politics, office supplies (and, what else?) boredom.

NOTE CDF was originally proposed by Microsoft Corp., but has since received widespread industry support from many push companies, including PointCast, BackWeb and Marimba.

Listing 17.1 CubicleZone.cdf: CDF File for Fictional "Cubicle Zone" Web Channel

```xml
<?xml version="1.0" encoding="UTF-8"?>
<!DOCTYPE Channel SYSTEM "http://www.w3c.org/Channel.dtd">
<CHANNEL>
    <TITLE>The Cubicle Zone</TITLE>
    <SCHEDULE>
        <INTERVALTIME DAY="1"/>
    </SCHEDULE>
    <CHANNEL>
        <TITLE>Overcoming Boredom</TITLE>
        <ITEM HREF="http://www.cubiclezone.com/
        boredom/paperclip.htm">
            <TITLE>Paperclip Sculptures</TITLE>
        </ITEM>
        <ITEM HREF="http://www.cubiclezone.com/
        boredom/addicted.htm">
            <TITLE>Internet Addiction</TITLE>
        </ITEM>
    </CHANNEL>
    <CHANNEL>
        <TITLE>Getting Revenge</TITLE>
        <ITEM HREF="http://www.cubiclezone.com/
        revenge/zen.htm">
            <TITLE>Zen and Revenge</TITLE>
        </ITEM>
        <ITEM HREF="http://www.cubiclezone.com/
        revenge/pranks.htm">
        <TITLE>50 Cruel Pranks</TITLE>
    </ITEM>
```

```
</CHANNEL>
<CHANNEL>
     <TITLE>Office Supplies</TITLE>
     <ITEM HREF="http://www.cubiclezone.com/
     supplies/donuts.htm">
          <TITLE>Donuts</TITLE>
     </ITEM>
     <ITEM HREF="http://www.cubiclezone.com/
     supplies/zip.htm">
          <TITLE>Zip Disks</TITLE>
     </ITEM>
</CHANNEL>
</CHANNEL>
```

In examining Listing 17.1, note that we are referencing the Channel DTD on the W3C site:

```
<!DOCTYPE Channel SYSTEM http://www.w3c.org/Channel.dtd">
```

The root CHANNEL element contains all information regarding our channel, including its title, update schedule, and table of contents. The TITLE element, for example, indicates the name of the channel:

```
<TITLE>The Cubicle Zone</TITLE>
```

Likewise, the SCHEDULE element defines a recommended interval for content updates. For example, you can recommend that Internet Explorer check for updates once every 30 minutes, once a day, or once a week. In Listing 17.1, we use the INTERVALTIME tag to recommend updates once every day:

```
<SCHEDULE>
     <INTERVALTIME DAY="1"/>
</SCHEDULE>
```

Following the schedule we have the channel table of contents. This may include individual ITEM elements—in most cases, ITEMs refer to standard Web pages, referenced by the HREF attribute, but they may also identify links to CGI scripts or databases. Additionally, the table of contents may include nested CHANNEL elements. Nested CHANNELs serve as content folders, making it easy to represent hierarchical content. For example, in Listing 17.1, we have created three news sections: Overcoming Boredom, Getting Revenge and Office Supplies.

Most CDF channels are as simple as Listing 17.1. The full CDF specification does, however, include a few more details than represented here. For additional information, we recommend *Delivering Push*, by Ethan Cerami (McGraw-Hill, 1998) or *Implementing CDF Channels*, by Michele Jo Petrovsky (McGraw-Hill, 1998).

Table 17.1 CDF Basic Elements

The <CHANNEL> Tag

Description: Defines a channel

Syntax:

```
<CHANNEL HREF="url">

... Channel Child Elements, including TITLE,

SCHEDULE, CHANNEL and ITEMs...

</CHANNEL>
```

Attributes:
HREF="URL": specifies the cover page URL of the channel; Internet Explorer opens this location when the user first launches the channel. This attribute is optional.

The <ITEM> Tag

Description: Defines an item or article in the channel. Items usually refer to standard HTML pages, but may also identify links to CGI scripts or databases

Syntax:

```
<ITEM HREF="url">

... Item Child Elements, including TITLE

</CHANNEL>
```

Attributes:
HREF="URL": specifies the article's URL.

The <TITLE> Tag

Description: A text string representing the title of the channel or item.

Syntax:

```
<TITLE>Title Text Here</TITLE>
```

continued on next page

The <SCHEDULE> Tag

Description: Defines a recommended channel update schedule; starting at midnight on STARTDATE, channel updating occurs once within each interval specified by the INTERVAL-TIME child element.

Syntax:
```
<SCHEDULE

   STARTDATE="date"

   ENDDATE="date">

 ...

</SCHEDULE>
```

Attributes:

- STARTDATE="date": indicates when the update schedule will begin. The date must be written in ISO-8601 format (YYYY-MM-DD.) If this attribute is omitted, the schedule will start on the current day.

- ENDDATE="date": indicates when the schedule will expire. This date must also be written in ISO 8601 format.

The <INTERVALTIME> Tag

Description: Determines the frequency of channel updates. The days, hours, and minutes are totaled to determine the length of the interval.

Syntax:
```
<INTERVALTIME

   DAY="n"

   HOUR="n"

   MIN="n"

 />
```

Attributes:

- DAY="n": number of days between each scheduled update. For example, DAY="1" updates once a day.

- HOUR="n": number of hours between each scheduled update.

- MIN="n": number of minutes between each scheduled update.

THE CDF SUBSET

CDF is ideal for Web channels, as well as for Web sites. CDF can easily be adapted to represent the entire hierarchy of any arbitrarily large Web site. When combined with our applet, CDF thereby enables users to easily view a site's architecture and navigate through the entire site.

The site map applet does not need all the functionality of CDF (it does not, for example, need scheduling information). To simplify our work, we have therefore created a subset of the original CDF DTD. The new DTD, referred to here as Sub-CDF.DTD, is presented in Listing 17.2. A revised XML file for the Cubicle Zone is presented in Listing 17.3.

Listing 17.2   SubCDF.DTD: Represents a Subset of the Original CDF Specification

```
<!ELEMENT CHANNEL (TITLE, CHANNEL*, ITEM*)>
<!ELEMENT ITEM (TITLE)>
<!ATTLIST ITEM HREF CDATA #REQUIRED>
<!ELEMENT TITLE (#PCDATA)>
```

Listing 17.3   CubicleZone.xml: Revised Version of CubicleZone.cdf

```
(Adheres to the SubCDF Document Type Definition)
<?xml version="1.0" encoding="UTF-8"?>
<!DOCTYPE CHANNEL SYSTEM "SubCDF.dtd">
<CHANNEL>
    <TITLE>The Cubicle Zone</TITLE>
    <CHANNEL>
        <TITLE>Overcoming Boredom</TITLE>
        <ITEM HREF="http://www.cubiclezone.com/
        boredom/paperclip.htm">
            <TITLE>Paperclip Sculptures</TITLE>
        </ITEM>
        <ITEM HREF="http://www.cubiclezone.com/
        boredom/addicted.htm">
            <TITLE>Internet Addiction</TITLE>
        </ITEM>
    </CHANNEL>
    <CHANNEL>
```

```
        <TITLE>Getting Revenge</TITLE>
        <ITEM HREF="http://www.cubiclezone.com/
        revenge/zen.htm">
                <TITLE>Zen and Revenge</TITLE>
        </ITEM>
        <ITEM HREF="http://www.cubiclezone.com/
        revenge/pranks.htm">
                <TITLE>50 Cruel Pranks</TITLE>
        </ITEM>
    </CHANNEL>
    <CHANNEL>
        <TITLE>Office Supplies</TITLE>
        <ITEM HREF="http://www.cubiclezone.com/
        supplies/donuts.htm">
                <TITLE>Donuts</TITLE>
        </ITEM>
        <ITEM HREF="http://www.cubiclezone.com/
        supplies/zip.htm">
                <TITLE>Zip Disks</TITLE>
        </ITEM>
    </CHANNEL>
  </CHANNEL>
```

The SubCDF DTD file is simple. The Root CHANNEL element must have a TITLE, and zero or more embedded CHANNELs and ITEMs. The ITEM element is required to have an embedded TITLE element, and a required HREF attribute. The main difference between Listing 17.1 (CubicleZone.cdf) and Listing 17.3 (CubicleZone.xml) is the omission of scheduling information.

SOFTWARE ARHITECTURE

The CDF Site Map applet works by reading in a site map and creating an internal tree representation of the Web hierarchy. The core of the code is therefore responsible for mapping the SAX parsing events to an internal tree-data structure. To help create modules in the program, the code is also broken into three separate class files:

- **Node.class:** The Node class encapsulates all information regarding an individual CHANNEL or ITEM. The internal tree structure is composed of a series of Node objects.

- **Handler.java:** The `Handler` class is responsible for mapping SAX parse events to the internal tree structure. The class extends the SAX `HandlerBase` convenience class.
- **SiteMap.jav:** The `SiteMap` class handles all graphics rendering and user event handling. It is also responsible for initiating the XML parser object.

THE CODE

NODE.JAVA

The `Node` class (Listing 17.4) encapsulates all information for an individual CHANNEL or ITEM element. This data includes the Title, URL, and a vector of child nodes (CHANNEL nodes will almost always have children, but ITEM nodes will not have any, as they are by definition leaf nodes.) The `Node` class also includes two boolean flags: `isOpen` is reserved for CHANNELs and indicates whether the node is open, and its contents should be displayed to the user. The `isSelected` flag is reserved for ITEMs and indicates that the item was just selected by the user. Selected items will appear in blue, providing users with a visual cue to their whereabouts within the Web site.

The `Node` class also provides a full set of methods for setting and retrieving the `Node` properties. For example, you can retrieve the number of children using the `getNumChildren()` method, or retrieve the entire vector of child Nodes using the `getChildren()` method. You can also query the Node's boolean flags by using the `isOpen()` and `isSelected()` methods.

Listing 17.4 The Node Cass

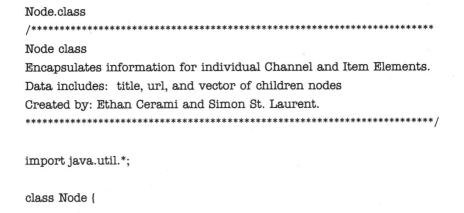

```
Node.class
/*************************************************************************
Node class
Encapsulates information for individual Channel and Item Elements.
Data includes: title, url, and vector of children nodes
Created by: Ethan Cerami and Simon St. Laurent.
*************************************************************************/

import java.util.*;

class Node {
```

```java
    private String title;              //  Node Title
    private String url;                //  Node HREF
    private Vector children;           //  Vector of children nodes
    private boolean isopen;            //  Indicates if this node is
                                       //  currently open or closed
    private boolean isselected;        //  Indicates if this node is
                                       //  currently selected

//  Constructor
public Node () {
    children = new Vector ();
    title = null;
    url = null;
    isopen = true;
    isselected = false;
}

//  Set Methods
public void setTitle (String title) {
    this.title = title;
}

public void setOpen (boolean open) {
    this.isopen = open;
}

public void setSelected (boolean selected) {
    isselected = selected;
}

public void setURL (String url) {
    this.url = url;
}

public void addChild (Node node) {
    children.addElement (node);
}
```

```
// Get Methods
public String getTitle () { return title; }
public boolean isOpen () { return isopen; }
public boolean isSelected() { return isselected; }
public String getURL () { return url; }
public int getNumChildren () { return children.size(); }
public Vector getChildren () { return children; }
}
```

HANDLER.JAVA

The most important code of the CDF applet occurs within the Handler.java class
(see Listing 17.5). This class is responsible for mapping the parse events to a tree of
Node objects. It performs this transformation via a stack algorithm, in much the
same manner as our SAX tree utility from Chapter 15. Rather than walk through
the code line by line, we will examine a sample parse session of **CubicleZone.xml**
and watch how the mapping occurs. We will examine the code at specific time
slices, starting at Time = 0.

Listing 17.5   Handler.java

```
/****************************************************************
Handler Class
Extends org.xml.sax.HandlerBase
Responsible for mapping Parse Events to Tree of Node Objects
Created by: Ethan Cerami and Simon St. Laurent.
****************************************************************/

import org.xml.sax.*;
import java.net.*;
import java.io.*;
import java.applet.*;
import java.util.*;

class Handler extends HandlerBase {
        private Stack stack;              // Stack used to Build Parse Tree
        private Node root;                // Root node
        private Applet applet;            // Parent Applet
```

```
// Constructor
// Create stack and push root on to stack
public Handler (Node node, Applet applet) {
     root = node;
     this.applet = applet;
     root.setTitle ("ROOT");
     root.setOpen (true);
     stack = new Stack ();
     stack.push (root);
}


// Capture startElement Event
public void startElement (String name, AttributeList atts) {
     // If this is a Channel or Item
     // Create Node and push onto stack
     if (name.equals ("CHANNEL") || name.equals("ITEM")) {
          Node newNode = new Node ();

          // Add current Node to Node on top of stack
          Node parentNode = (Node) stack.peek();
          parentNode.addChild (newNode);

          // Extract Item HREF
          if (name.equals ("ITEM"))
               newNode.setURL (atts.getValue ("HREF"));
          stack.push (newNode);
     }
}


// Extract Title Character data
public void characters (char ch[], int start, int length) {
     String text = new String (ch, start, length);
     Node node = (Node) stack.peek();
     node.setTitle(text);
}


// At end of Channel and Item elements, pop stack
```

```
public void endElement (String name) {
    if (name.equals ("CHANNEL") || name.equals("ITEM"))
        stack.pop();
    }


// At end of parsing, call Applet's repaint() method
public void endDocument () {
    applet.repaint();
    }

}
```

Time 0: The Handler constructor method is called. The constructor is first responsible for creating the stack of **Node** objects:

```
stack = new Stack ();
```

The constructor is also responsible for pushing the root node onto the stack:

```
stack.push (root);
```

By definition, the top-most node on the stack is the parent of any subsequent elements. The root node is therefore the parent of all ensuing events. Figure 17.4 (a) displays the initial state of the stack.

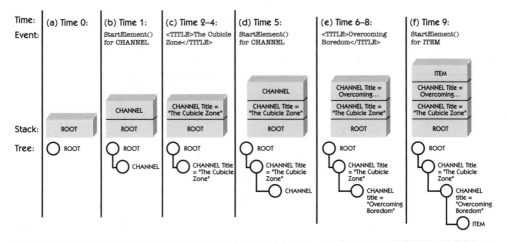

Figure 17.4 Handler.java transforms a sequence of parse events into an internal-tree structure via a stack-based algorithm. Here, we see the creation of the parse tree at specific time slices.

Time 1: The startElement() method is called for the CHANNEL element. The startElement() method first checks the tag name. If this is a CHANNEL or ITEM element, we create a new node:

```
Node newNode = new Node ();
```

By definition, the top-most node on the stack is the parent of newNode. We therefore add newNode to the list of children:

```
Node parentNode = (Node) stack.peek();
parentNode.addChild (newNode);
```

Finally, we push newNode onto the stack.

```
stack.push (newNode);
```

The stack now has two nodes: one root node and one CHANNEL node. See Figure 17.4 (b).

Time 2: The startElement() method is called for the TITLE element. We only want to create new nodes for CHANNEL and ITEM elements. We therefore ignore the start of the TITLE element.

Time 3: The characters() method is called with a string set to: "The Cubicle Zone." Usually, we must check the current tag name to determine where to store the character data. In the case of SubCDF.DTD, TITLE is the only element which includes PCDATA. We can therefore assume that if characters() is called, it refers exclusively to TITLE data of the most recent element. We therefore extract the TITLE text, and use the setTitle() method on the top-most Node:

```
public void characters (char ch[], int start, int length) {
    String text = new String (ch, start, length);
    Node node = (Node) stack.peek();
    node.setTitle(text);
}
```

Time 4: The endElement() method is called for TITLE. Again, we are only really concerned with CHANNEL and ITEM elements. We therefore ignore the end of the TITLE element.

Times 5–8: The startElement() method is called for the TITLE element. This time, it refers to the embedded Folder for "Overcoming Boredom." We therefore repeat steps 1–4: first, we create a new **Node** object for the embedded channel and push it onto the stack. We then capture the TITLE element and place its value in the newly created CHANNEL node.

Time 9: By time interval 9, we finally encounter our first ITEM element. Specifically, the **startElement()** method is called for:

```
<ITEM HREF="http://www.cubiclezone.com/ boredom/paperclip.htm">
```

Again, we create a new **Node** object and push it onto the stack. We also extract the HREF attribute, and set the node's URL property:

```
newNode.setURL (atts.getValue ("HREF"));
```

By now, readers should have a good idea how the tree-making code works. Each time we encounter a new CHANNEL or ITEM element, we create a new node and push it onto the stack. When we finally reach an end tag for CHANNEL or ITEM, we pop the node off the stack:

```
public void endElement (String name) {
    if (name.equals ("CHANNEL") || name.equals("ITEM"))
        stack.pop();
}
```

SiteMap.java

The final class file, SiteMap.java (Listing 17.6) is responsible for all the graphics rendering and handling of user events. First and foremost, however, the **SiteMap class** is responsible for creating the XML **Parser** object and initiating the parsing. Note that the CDF applet requires a URL parameter, identifying the location of the XML site map file.

Most of the SiteMap class is straight Java, and has very little to do with XML. We will not go into too much detail. Note, however, the following important methods:

■ **printNode():** The printNode() method is a recursive function that draws an individual node to the applet's graphic object. If the node is open, the code extracts the child nodes and displays them with recursive calls to the printNode() method:

```
if (node.getNumChildren() > 0 && node.isOpen() == true) {
    Vector children = node.getChildren();
```

```
        for (int i=0; i<children.size(); i++) {
            Node child = (Node) children.elementAt(i);
            y = printNode (x+10, y, child, g);
        }
    }
```

- **checkHotSpots():** The checkHotSpots() method is responsible for mapping a mousedown event to a specific node. It does this mapping by recursively walking the tree in much the same manner as printNode().

Listing 17.6 SiteMap.java

```
/***************************************************
CDF Site Map Applet
Created by: Ethan Cerami and Simon St. Laurent.
***************************************************/

import org.xml.sax.*;
import org.xml.sax.helpers.*;
import java.applet.*;
import java.awt.*;
import java.awt.event.*;
import java.util.*;
import java.net.*;
import java.io.*;

public class SiteMap extends Applet implements MouseListener {
    private Image offScreen;                    // OffScreen Image
                                                // for Double Buffering

    private Graphics offScreenGraphics;         // OffScreen Graphic
                                                // for Double Buffering

    private Dimension d;                        // Current Dimensions
    private int yoffset;                        // Yoffset
    private Node root;                          // Root node for hierarchy
    private int textheight;                     // Height of Text
    private final static int YMARGIN = 15;      // YMargin

    // Applet init() method
    public void init () {
```

```java
        yoffset = YMARGIN;
        startParsing();

        //  Add Mouse Listener
        this.addMouseListener (this);
}


//  Mouse Pressed Event
public void mousePressed (MouseEvent e) {
        checkHotSpots(e.getY(), yoffset,root);
}


//  Unused Methods of Mouse Listener Interface
public void mouseClicked (MouseEvent e) {}
public void mouseEntered (MouseEvent e) {}
public void mouseExited (MouseEvent e) {}
public void mouseReleased (MouseEvent e) {}

//  Create Parser Object and Start Parsing
private void startParsing () {

        //  Create Parser Object
        Parser parser = new com.microstar.xml.SAXDriver();

        //  Set Parser Document Handler
        root = new Node();
        Handler handler = new Handler(root,this);
        parser.setDocumentHandler (handler);
        parser.setErrorHandler (handler);

        //  Create URL to XML Document and start parsing
        URL xmlURL = null;
        String xmldoc = getParameter ("url");
        try {
                xmlURL = new URL (getDocumentBase(), xmldoc);
        } catch (MalformedURLException e) {
                e.printStackTrace();
        }
```

```
System.out.println ("XML SystemID:  "+xmlURL);
try {
      parser.parse(xmlURL.toString());
} catch (SAXException e) {
      System.out.println ("Fatal Error:  "+e.getMessage());
} catch (IOException e) {
      e.printStackTrace();
}

}


// Recursively Checks for Clickable Hot Spots
private int checkHotSpots (int mouseY, int y, Node node) {

      String title = node.getTitle();

      // Check if over current node
      if (mouseY > (y - textheight) && mouseY < y) {

            // Open /Close Channels
            if (node.getNumChildren() > 0) {
                  if (node.isOpen() == true) node.setOpen(false);
                  else node.setOpen (true);
                  root.setOpen (true);
                  repaint();
            }

            // Open Item HREF
            else {
                  AppletContext context = this.getAppletContext();
                  URL base = this.getDocumentBase();
                  URL targetURL= null;
                  try {
                        targetURL = new URL (base, node.getURL());
                  } catch (MalformedURLException e) {
                        e.printStackTrace();
                  }
                  context.showDocument (targetURL, "main");
                  resetSelection (root);
```

```
                node.setSelected (true);
                repaint();
            }
        }

        if (!(title.equals("ROOT"))) y+= textheight;

        // Check Children
        if (node.getNumChildren() > 0 && node.isOpen() == true) {
            Vector children = node.getChildren();
            for (int i=0; i<children.size(); i++) {
                Node child = (Node) children.elementAt(i);
                y = checkHotSpots (mouseY, y, child);
            }
        }
        return y;
    }


// Paint Method
public void paint (Graphics g) { update (g); }

// Double Buffering Graphics Routine
public void update (Graphics g) {
    if (d== null) {
        d = this.getSize();
        offScreen = createImage (d.width, d.height);
        offScreenGraphics = offScreen.getGraphics();
        offScreenGraphics.setFont (new Font
            ("TimesRoman", Font.PLAIN, 12));
        FontMetrics fm = offScreenGraphics.getFontMetrics();
        textheight = fm.getHeight();
    }

    offScreenGraphics.setColor (Color.white);
    offScreenGraphics.fillRect (0,0, d.width, d.height);
    offScreenGraphics.setColor (Color.black);

    // Print all Nodes from Root Node
```

```
        if (root!=null) printNode(5,yoffset,root,offScreenGraphics);
        g.drawImage (offScreen, 0,0, null);
}


// Recursive printNode Method
private int printNode (int x, int y, Node node, Graphics g) {
        // Print Title plus Triangle Navigation
        String title = node.getTitle();
        if (!(title.equals("ROOT"))) {
                if (node.isSelected() == true) g.setColor(Color.blue);
                else g.setColor (Color.black);
                g.drawString (title, x , y);

                if (node.getNumChildren() > 0)
                        drawTriangle (x, y, node.isOpen(), g);
                else g.fillRect (x-7,y-5,3,3);
                y+= textheight;
        }


        // Print Children
        if (node.getNumChildren() > 0 && node.isOpen() == true) {
                Vector children = node.getChildren();
                for (int i=0; i<children.size(); i++) {
                        Node child = (Node) children.elementAt(i);
                        y = printNode (x+10, y, child, g);
                }
        }
        return y;
}


// Draw Open/Closed Triangle Bar
private void drawTriangle (int x, int y, boolean open,Graphics g){
        x -= 12; y -=5;
        g.setColor (new Color (0,0,153));
        if (open == true) {
                y -= 2;
                for (int i = 0; i < 5; i++)
                        g.drawLine (x+i, y+i,x+8-i, y+i);
```

```
        }
        else
            for (int j=0; j<5; j++)
                g.drawLine (x+j, y-4+j, x+j, y+4-j);
        g.setColor (Color.black);
    }


    // Set all nodes to _not_ selected
    private void resetSelection (Node node) {
        node.setSelected (false);
        if (node.getNumChildren() > 0) {
            Vector children = node.getChildren();
            for (int i=0; i<children.size(); i++) {
                Node child = (Node) children.elementAt(i);
                resetSelection (child);
            }
        }
    }
}
```

PGML VIEWER APPLICATION

DESCRIPTION

The Precision Graphics Markup Language (PGML) is an XML format for representing vector-based graphics. Most images on the web, including GIF and JPEG images, are known as *raster images* and include a complete bitmap of pixels. Vector-based images consist of specific mathematical instructions for rendering an image. For example, a vector image may consist of a command to draw a circle at a specific location plus a mathematical formula for drawing a Bezier curve. Because vector-based images consist of commands, they tend to be much more compact than raster images, and are therefore ideal for the Web.

In our third XML application, we create a viewer application capable of rendering PGML graphics. In computer graphic parlance, such an application is known as a *raster image processor*, as it is capable of converting a vector image into a bitmapped (or raster) image. Rather than rendering any PGML image, however, we focus on a specific subset of the PGML specification. The subset represents only a small part of the entire PGML specification, but does enable the rendering of rather sophisticated business presentations, including bar and pie charts.

TECHNICAL SPECIFICATION

The PGML viewer application is written in Java 1.1. It uses the SAX driver of the IBM XML Parser.

INTRODUCTION TO PGML

PGML was originally proposed to the W3C by Adobe Systems in April 1998. Cosponsors of the proposal include IBM, Netscape, and Sun. Around the same time, the W3C also received two very similar proposals for vector-based images. The first, "Schematics for the World Wide Web", was submitted by one of the leading computer science organizations in England. The second, entitle Vector Graphics Format (VML), was submitted by Microsoft, Hewlett-Packard, Macromedia, Autodesk, and Visio Corp.

Each of the three proposed formats is XML based, and it falls to the W3C to hammer out a compromise. Regardless of the exact syntax of the final proposal, however, an XML-based vector graphics format will have several significant advantages over raster images. First, vector images tend to be much smaller than the equivalent raster images. This translates into faster download times for end-users. In conjunction with PGML, Adobe is also proposing an XML compression scheme, which may even further speed up download times. Second, a vector-image format can be manipulated via the Document Object Model (DOM), thereby enabling dynamic scripting and animation. Finally, vector images are resolution independent, thereby enabling the rendering of images on everything from high-end workstations to Personal Digital Assistants (PDAs.)

BASIC PGML

The entire PGML specification is quite lengthy and we will only focus on a small subset. We will examine three topics: predefined shapes, the graphics state and text rendering. For details regarding the entire PGML specification, we suggest you view the original proposal online at: **http://www.w3.org/TR/1998/NOTE-PGML**.

PREDEFINED SHAPES

PGML includes basic support for four predefined shapes: rectangles, circles, ellipses and pie wedges. Each of the shapes is summarized in Table 18.1.

Here, for example, is a very simple PGML document:

```
<pgml>
      <rectangle x="50" y="50" width="100" height="100"/>
</pgml>
```

This document creates a single square object located at location: x=50, y=50.

In contrast, the following XML document creates a single pie wedge object, located at the same position:

```
<pgml>
      <piewedge x="50" y="50" r="100" ang1="0" ang2="90"/>
</pgml>
```

In each of these cases, note that shape properties are set via attributes. Note also that you can create an enormous number of images with just these four predefined shapes.

GRAPHICS STATE ATTRIBUTES

When you draw a PGML object, the exact rendering depends on its current *graphics state*. The graphics state includes a number of important properties, such as the fill color, stroke color, or line thickness. For example, the following text:

```
<rectangle x="50" y="50" width="100" height="100" fillcolor="blue"/>
```

uses the fillcolor attribute to create a solid blue square.

As a second example, this code uses the fillcolor and strokecolor attributes to create a solid blue circle with a red outline:

```
<circle fillcolor="blue" stroke="1" strokecolor="red" x="200" cy="200"
    r="100"/>
```

The PGML specification defines a large number of graphics state properties. The most important are summarized in Table 18.2.

NOTE

The PGML specification enables you to create groups of objects. The members of the group can therefore share the same graphics state. For example, the following code creates two blue rectangles:

```
<group fillcolor="blue">
    <rectangle x="100" y="100" width="100" height="100" />
    <rectangle x="300" y="100" width="100" height="100" />
</group>
```

Table 18.1   Predefined PGML Shapes

Shape	Attributes
rectangle	x: horizontal position
	y: vertical position
	width: width of rectangle
	height: height of rectangle
	rounding: degree of rounding
circle	cx: horizontal position
	cy: horizontal position
	r: radius
ellipse	x: horizontal position
	y: vertical position
	rx: horizontal radius
	ry: vertical radius
piewedge	x: horizontal position
	y: vertical position
	r: radius
	ang1: start angle
	ang2: arc angle

Table 18.2   Main Graphics State Attributes

Attribute	Description	Default Value
fill	The object should be filled with the designated fill color.	1
fillcolor	Paint color to fill object.	black
stroke	The object should be stroked (outlined) with the designated stroke color.	0
strokecolor	Paint color to stroke object.	black
opacity	Specifies the opacity of the object (0-1).	1
antialias	Turns anti-aliasing on and off.	1
linewidth	Specifies the line thickness.	1

TEXT

To render text, PGML includes the <text> tag. For example, the following code:

```
<text x="450" y="170">Hello</text>
```

places the text, "Hello" at the location: x=450, y=170. You can also specify a number of text attributes, including font and size (see Table 18.3.) For example, the following code:

```
<text font="Courier" textsize="20" x="40" y="40">Hello</text>
draws "Hello" in 20 point Courier font.
```

NOTE

The <textspan> tag enables you to format individual words or sentences. For example, this code displays a sentence in two colors:

```
<text x="100" y="150" fillcolor="blue">Please read this <textspan
fillcolor="red">carefully!</textspan></text>
```

Table 18.3 Main Text Attributes

Attribute	Description	Default Value
font	Text font	Unspecified
textsize	Point size	Unspecified
charspacing	Amount of additional space to add between letters.	0
wordspacing	Amount of additional space to add between words.	0

THE PGML SUBSET

Now that we have a basic understanding of PGML, let us define a PGML subset for our viewer application. The goal is to enable the creation of business presentations, including basic business graphs. We therefore need to include support for rectangles, pie wedges, and text. To simplify things further, we will limit the graphics state to a single fillcolor attribute.

The PGML subset is presented in Listing 18.1. Please note the following:

- The root <pgml> element has width and height attributes. This determines the dimensions (in pixels) of the graphic. The default size is 200 x 200 pixels.
- We include support for two predefined shapes: rectangle and pie wedge. Each of these shapes has a number of required attributes. For example, when creating a <rectangle> shape, you must specify its location (x,y) and dimensions (width, height.) Via a parsed entity, each of the shapes also includes the fillcolor attribute. The default fill color is black.
- The <text> tag has only two attributes: font and text size. We set the default font to 12 point Times New Roman.

Listing 18.1 The PGML Subset Document Type Definition (DTD)

```
<!ELEMENT pgml (text | rectangle | piewedge )*>
<!ATTLIST pgml
        width      CDATA "200"
        height     CDATA "200"
>
```

```
<!ENTITY % gs_fillstroke_attributes
        "fillcolor    CDATA 'black'"
>


<!ELEMENT rectangle EMPTY >
<!ATTLIST rectangle %gs_fillstroke_attributes;
            x        CDATA #REQUIRED
            y        CDATA #REQUIRED
            width    CDATA #REQUIRED
            height   CDATA #REQUIRED
>


<!ELEMENT piewedge EMPTY >
<!ATTLIST piewedge  %gs_fillstroke_attributes;
            x        CDATA #REQUIRED
            y        CDATA #REQUIRED
            r        CDATA #REQUIRED
            ang1     CDATA #REQUIRED
            ang2     CDATA #REQUIRED
>


<!ELEMENT text      (#PCDATA) >
<!ATTLIST text      %gs_fillstroke_attributes;
            x        CDATA #REQUIRED
            y        CDATA #REQUIRED
            font     CDATA "TimesNewRoman"
            textsize CDATA "12"
>
```

THE CODE

The code for the PGML viewer application is remarkably simple and illustrates just how powerful XML can be. In a nutshell, here is how it works: we gather all the SAX parse events and map them to a vector of **Shape** objects. The **Shape** class and its various subclasses include all the basic information for drawing predefined PGML shapes, including rectangles, pie wedges and text. For example, given the following XML text:

```
<pgml>
     <rectangle x="430" y="160" fillcolor="cyan" width="10" height="10"/>
     <text x="10" y="50" textsize="24" fillcolor="red">Welcome!</text>
</pgml>
```

we extract information for two shape objects. First, we create a rectangle shape object, then a text shape object, and place both objects into a vector. At the completion of parsing, we iterate through the entire vector of shapes, and draw each one to the screen.

Here then are the details:

The base Shape class (See Listing 18.2) encapsulates the location and fill color property of any predefined PGML Shape. It also includes a single draw() method, which sets the Graphics object to the fillcolor property. To aid in this process, we have a ColorMap class which translates from a color name string to one of thirteen predefined Java Color objects.

Listing 18.2   The Base Shape Class

```java
Shape.java
//  PGML Shape Class
//  Extended by:  Rectangle, Text and PieWedge

import java.awt.*;
import java.util.*;

public class Shape {
     protected int x,y;
     protected String fillcolor;
     private static ColorMap colormap = new ColorMap();

     //  Constructor
     public Shape (int x, int y, String fillcolor) {
          this.x = x;
          this.y = y;
          this.fillcolor = fillcolor;
     }

     //  Draw Method:  Set Fill Color
     public void draw(Graphics g) {
```

```
                g.setColor (colormap.getColor(fillcolor));
        }
}


// Provides a Hashtable mapping between Color names and
// predefined Color Objects
class ColorMap {
        private Hashtable map;

        // Constructor
        public ColorMap () {
                map = new Hashtable();
                map.put ("black", Color.black);
                map.put ("blue", Color.blue);
                map.put ("cyan", Color.cyan);
                map.put ("darkgray", Color.darkGray);
                map.put ("gray", Color.gray);
                map.put ("green", Color.green);
                map.put ("lightgray", Color.lightGray);
                map.put ("magenta", Color.magenta);
                map.put ("orange", Color.orange);
                map.put ("pink", Color.pink);
                map.put ("red", Color.red);
                map.put ("white", Color.white);
                map.put ("yellow", Color.yellow);
        }

        // Returns the Color Object for the indicated Color name
        public Color getColor (String colorname) {
                colorname = colorname.toLowerCase();
                Color color = (Color) map.get (colorname);
                if (color!=null) return color;
                else return Color.black;
        }
}
```

Inherited from **Shape** we have three subclasses: **Rectangle**, **PieWedge** and **Text** (see Listings 18.3, 18.4 and 18.5). Each of these classes encapsulates information specific to the shape, and overrides the draw() method. We are therefore able to take advantage of Java's object oriented features to easily draw any of the three default shapes.

Listing 18.3   Rectangle.java

```
import java.awt.*;

// PGML Rectangle Object
class Rectangle extends Shape {
    private int width, height;

    // Constructor
    public Rectangle (int x, int y, int width,
        int height, String fillcolor) {
        super (x,y,fillcolor);
        this.width = width;
        this.height = height;
    }

    // Draw Method
    public void draw (Graphics g) {
        super.draw(g);
        g.fillRect (x,y,width,height);
    }
}
```

Listing 18.4   PieWedge.java

```
import java.awt.*;

// PGML PieWedge Object
class PieWedge extends Shape {
    private int r, ang1, ang2;

    // Constructor
    public PieWedge (int x, int y, int r, int ang1,
        int ang2, String fillcolor) {
```

```
        super (x, y, fillcolor);
        this.r = r;
        this.ang1 = ang1;
        this.ang2 = ang2;
    }


    // Draw Method
    public void draw (Graphics g) {
        super.draw(g);
        g.fillArc (x, y, r, r, ang1, ang2);
    }
}
```

Listing 18.5 Text.java

```
import java.awt.*;

// PGML Text Object
class Text extends Shape {
    private String text, textfont;
    private int textsize;

    // Constructor
    public Text (int x, int y, int textsize,
        String textfont, String text, String fillcolor) {
        super (x, y, fillcolor);
        this.textsize = textsize;
        this.textfont = textfont;
        this.text = text;
    }

    // Draw Method
    public void draw (Graphics g) {
        super.draw(g);
        g.setFont (new Font(textfont,Font.PLAIN,textsize));
        g.drawString (text, x,y);
    }
}
```

The mapping of parse events to **Shape** objects occurs within the **Handler** class of pgml.java (see Listing 18.6). Most of the processing occurs within the **startElement()** method. Here, we check the element name and continue processing accordingly. In the event of a <pgml> tag, we extract the dimensions of the graphic, and save it for later use. In the event of a <rectangle> tag, we extract all of its attributes including location, dimension and color. For example, we extract the width and height attributes in the following manner:

```
int width = Integer.parseInt(atts.getValue("width"));
int height = Integer.parseInt(atts.getValue("height"));
```

Once we have obtained all the attribute data, we use these data to create a new Rectangle object:

```
Rectangle rect=new Rectangle(x,y,width,height,fillcolor);
```

and, place the object in the shapes vector:

```
shapes.addElement(rect);
```

We take similar actions for <piewedge> and <text> tags. Note, however that we extract the embedded <text> string via the **characters()** method.

Listing 18.6   pgml.java

```
// PGML Viewer Application
// Renders PGML Documents that adhere to the SUBPGML DTD
// Created by Ethan Cerami and Simon St. Laurent

import org.xml.sax.*;
import org.xml.sax.helpers.*;
import java.io.*;
import java.util.*;
import java.awt.*;

public class pgml {
        private String filename;

        public static void main (String args[]) throws Exception {
            // Set the Parser: IBM XML for Java
```

```
        Parser parser = new com.ibm.xml.parser.SAXDriver();

        // Set Parser Document Handler
        Handler handler = new Handler(args[0]);
        parser.setDocumentHandler (handler);
        parser.setErrorHandler (handler);

        // Create FileReader, then Input Source
        FileReader filereader = new FileReader (args[0]);
        InputSource insource = new InputSource (filereader);

        // Start Parsing
        try {
        parser.parse (insource);
        } catch (SAXException e) {
        System.out.println ("Fatal Error: "+e.getMessage());
        }

    }

}


// Document Event Handler
class Handler extends HandlerBase {
        private String filename;        // PGML File Name
        private Vector shapes;          // Vector of PGML Shapes
        private int width, height;      // PGML Dimensions
        private int x, y, textsize;     // Temporary Location
        private String textfont;        // Temporary Text Font
        private String fillcolor;       // Temporary Fill Color

    public Handler (String filename) {
        this.filename = filename;
        shapes = new Vector();
    }

    // Capture <text> Characters
    public void characters
      (char ch[], int start, int length) {
        String textstr = new String (ch, start, length);
```

```
          Text text = new Text (x, y, textsize,
              textfont, textstr, fillcolor);
          shapes.addElement(text);

  }


  //  Capture <pgml> | <rectangle> | <piewedge> | <text>
  public void startElement
    (String name, AttributeList atts) {
        if (name.equals ("pgml")) {
            width = Integer.parseInt(atts.getValue("width"));
            height = Integer.parseInt(atts.getValue("height"));
        }
        else {
            x = Integer.parseInt(atts.getValue("x"));
            y = Integer.parseInt(atts.getValue("y"));
            fillcolor = atts.getValue("fillcolor");

            if (name.equals("rectangle")) {
                int width= Integer.parseInt(atts.getValue("width"));
                int height=Integer.parseInt(atts.getValue("height"));
                Rectangle rect = new Rectangle (x,y,width,height,fillcolor);
                shapes.addElement(rect);
        }
        else if (name.equals("piewedge")) {
            int r = Integer.parseInt(atts.getValue("r"));
            int ang1 = Integer.parseInt(atts.getValue("ang1"));
            int ang2 = Integer.parseInt(atts.getValue("ang2"));
            PieWedge wedge=new PieWedge(x,y,r,ang1,ang2,fillcolor);
            shapes.addElement (wedge);
        }
        else if (name.equals("text")) {
            textfont = atts.getValue("font");
            textsize=Integer.parseInt(atts.getValue("textsize"));
        }
    }
  }
```

```
// Create Framer Viewer
public void endDocument() {
    Frame frame = new viewer("PGML:
        "+filename,width,height,shapes);
    frame.show();
}


// For validating parsers, such as IBM XML for Java
// Report errors in validity
public void error(SAXParseException exception) throws SAXException {
    System.out.println ("XML Error: "+exception.getMessage());
}

}
```

By now, we are able to map all parse events to a vector of **Shape** objects. All that remains is a Frame class to actually display the objects. This rendering occurs within the Viewer class (see Listing 18.7). The main processing occurs within the **paint()** method. Here, we simply iterate through all objects within the shapes vector and draw each one individually:

```
for (int i=0; i<shapes.size(); i++) {
    current = (Shape) shapes.elementAt(i);
    current.draw(g);
}
```

Listing 18.7 viewer.java

```
// PGML Frame Viewer

import java.awt.*;
import java.awt.event.*;
import java.util.*;

public class viewer extends Frame {
    private Vector shapes;

    // Constructor
    // Set Location and windowClosing Handler
    public viewer (String title, int width,
```

```
        int height, Vector shapes) {
            super(title);
            this.shapes = shapes;
            setLocation (200,50);
            setSize (width,height);
            WindowListener l = new WindowAdapter() {
                public void windowClosing (WindowEvent e) {
                    System.exit(0);
                }
            };
            addWindowListener (l);
        }


        // Paint Method
        // Iterate through shapes vector and draw()
        public void paint (Graphics g) {
            Shape current;
            for (int i=0; i<shapes.size(); i++) {
                current = (Shape) shapes.elementAt(i);
                current.draw(g);
            }
        }
    }
```

If you want to try out a few sample PGML files, look at Listings 18.8 and 18.9. Listing 18.8 creates a simple bar chart of projected revenue growth (see Figure 18.1). Listing 18.9 creates a sample pie chart (see Figure 18.2).

Figure 18.1 Graph1.xml represents a 200 x 200 pixel bar chart of projected revenue growth.

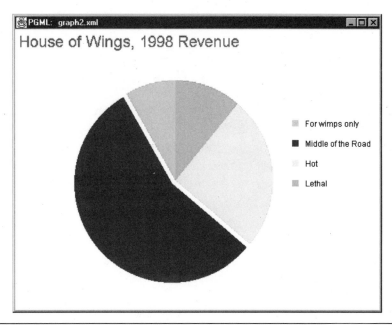

Figure 18.2 Graph2.xml represents a much bigger (570 x 450 pixel large) pie chart

Listing 18.8 Graph1.xml: Sample Bar Chart

```
<?xml version="1.0" encoding="UTF-8"?>
<!DOCTYPE pgml SYSTEM "Subpgml.dtd">
<pgml width="200" height="200">
<rectangle x="30" y="100" width="20" height="40" fillcolor="blue" />
<rectangle x="70" y="80" width="20" height="60" fillcolor="blue" />
<rectangle x="110" y="60" width="20" height="80" fillcolor="blue" />
<rectangle x="150" y="40" width="20" height="100" fillcolor="blue" />

<text x="35" y="150" textsize="10">98</text>
<text x="75" y="150" textsize="10">99</text>
<text x="115" y="150" textsize="10">00</text>
<text x="155" y="150" textsize="10">01</text>
<text x="10" y="50" textsize="14" fillcolor="red">House of Wings</text>

<text x="40" y="170" fillcolor="black">Revenue Projections</text>
</pgml>
```

Listing 18.9   Graph2.xml: Sample Pie Chart

```xml
<?xml version="1.0" encoding="UTF-8"?>
<!DOCTYPE pgml SYSTEM "Subpgml.dtd">
<pgml width="570" height="450">
    <piewedge x="100" y="100" fillcolor="cyan" r="300" ang1="90"
            ang2="30"/>
    <piewedge x="95" y="105" fillcolor="blue" r="300" ang1="120"
            ang2="200"/>
    <piewedge x="100" y="100" fillcolor="yellow" r="300" ang1="320"
            ang2="90"/>
    <piewedge x="100" y="100" fillcolor="green" r="300" ang1="50"
            ang2="40"/>
    <text x="10" y="50" textsize="24" fillcolor="red">House of Wings,
        1998 Revenue</text>

    <rectangle x="430" y="160" fillcolor="cyan" width="10"
            height="10"/>
    <text x="450" y="170" fillcolor="black">For wimps only</text>
    <text x="450" y="200" fillcolor="black">Middle of the Road</text>
    <text x="450" y="230" fillcolor="black">Hot</text>
    <text x="450" y="260" fillcolor="black">Lethal</text>

    <rectangle x="430" y="160" fillcolor="cyan" width="10"
            height="10"/>
    <rectangle x="430" y="190" fillcolor="blue" width="10"
            height="10"/>
    <rectangle x="430" y="220" fillcolor="yellow" width="10"
            height="10"/>
    <rectangle x="430" y="250" fillcolor="green" width="10"
            height="10"/>
</pgml>
```

19

BUILDING AN XLINK APPLET

The XLink spec may look a bit daunting, with its talk of multidirectional links, out-of-line links, and other potential hazards. This chapter will attempt to demystify the standard by explaining some of the larger steps needed to build an XLink-based application. By working with images rather than text, we can avoid the complexity of finding and marking links in text, focusing instead on the components needed to support the different types of linking described in the XLink draft. While some of these sound complicated, implementing them is not particularly difficult, and the potential for user confusion can be warded off with fairly conventional interfaces.

NOTE

The applet built here requires Java 1.1 or later because of its use of popup menus.

WARNING

As Chapter 11 noted, the XLink "standard" is not yet a W3C recommendation or even a proposed recommendation. This discussion is based on the 3 March 1998 Working Draft, available at **http://www.w3.org/TR/1998/WD-xlink-19980303**. The latest version will be available at **http://www.w3.org/TR/WD-xlink**. This chapter's contents are therefore subject to change, but most of the material here should be readily adaptable to cope with changing specs.

NOTE

All photographs in this chapter are Copyright 1998 by Tracey Cranston, and used by her permission.

REBUILDING IMAGE MAPS TO A NEW MODEL

Many HTML developers use image maps on a regular basis to present users with friendly graphics rather than lists of text menus. While the practice has been over-done—visiting a site that uses large graphics for its maps can be an extended exercise in patience, if not downright frustration—image maps are still useful in many contexts. Users are often more comfortable navigating maps and other visually-oriented interfaces through pictures rather than text, and many applications can be more simply created using graphics. While image maps have been used to good effect in sophisticated multimedia applications, most image maps on the Web have been relegated to the status of menu bars. (Of course, many of them are designed to look like menu bars as well.) XLink offers an opportunity to rejuvenate this form and give it new life on the Web. While reviving image maps may be dangerous, encouraging designers to pour on lavish graphics without much content, the examples presented here should show some possible routes for more interesting map applications.

Starting Simple: Creating Maps with Simple Links

As a foundation, the first application will use only simple links to connect its images. These documents contain only image information (for a single image), a caption, and areas that can be clicked to create links. The DTD for these documents is simple, containing a few elements with XLink attributes, as shown in Listing 19.1.

Listing 19.1   The DTD for the Simple Link Documents

```
<!ELEMENT map (image,area*,caption?)>
<!ELEMENT image EMPTY>
<!ATTLIST image
     src   CDATA    #REQUIRED>
<!ELEMENT area EMPTY>
<!ATTLIST area
     xml:link CDATA #FIXED "simple"
     inline (true|false) "true"
     id ID #REQUIRED
     href CDATA #REQUIRED
     shape    (rect | circle)  "rect"
     coords   CDATA    #REQUIRED>
<!ELEMENT caption (#PCDATA)>
```

The documents created using this DTD are quite small and fairly lightweight, as shown in Listing 19.2.

Listing 19.2   A Simple Link Document (map1.xml) Provides Information
about the Image and its Links to the Applet

```
<?xml version="1.0" encoding="UTF-8"?>
<!DOCTYPE map SYSTEM "map.dtd">
<map>
<image src="map1.gif" />
<area id="area1" href="map2.xml" shape="rect"
coords="180,120,195,150"/>
<area id="area2" href="map3.xml" shape="rect"
coords="190,140,215,180"/>
<caption>The Finger Lakes</caption>
</map>
```

A document can contain as many areas as necessary to create its links. The area element includes an ID attribute, used to reference all links, an href identifying the target, and shape and coords attributes that define the shape of the clickable area. (The shape attribute is currently meaningless; as we shall see, all areas are currently rectangular. The coords attribute uses absolute locations: left, top, right, bottom. Either of these may be changed through work with the Area class.)

    The applet that provides XLink services uses four classes: an Area class representing the clickable areas, a Link class that identifies destinations, an EventHandler class that connects the applet to the XML documents, and a LinkMap class that displays the image and presents the user interface. The Area class, shown in Listing 19.3, is extremely small, containing only ID, shape, and dimension information and an isInArea() method that makes it easy to check mouse clicks against areas.

Listing 19.3   The Area Class for Storing Clickable Image Map Areas

```
//** The Area class represents a clickable space*/
public class Area {
        private String id, shape;
        public int left, top, right, bottom;

    public Area(String id, String shape, int left, int top, int right, int bottom) {
            this.id=id;
            this.shape=shape;
            this.left=left;
            this.top=top;
            this.right=right;
            this.bottom=bottom;
    }

    public String getId() {return id;}

    public boolean isInArea(int x, int y){
            boolean result;
            result=(((x>=left) && (x<=right)) && ((y>=top) && (y<=bottom)));
            return result;
    }
}
```

Note that the Area class contains no information about links or link targets. While this might be workable in a pure simple-link image map application, it will not transfer well to more complex situations. Keeping areas and links separate, connected by the ID value, is a more scalable solution. The Link class, shown in Listing 19.4, is similarly simple, and also built to accommodate future demand for more functional links. (The Area and Link classes will both be reused in the next iteration of this application.)

Listing 19.3   The Link Class for Storing Linking Information

```
/** The Link class represents a connection between two locations */
public class Link {
    private String id, url, title, destId, destUrl, destTitle;

public Link(String id, String url, String title, String destId, String destUrl,
String destTitle) {
    this.id=id;
    this.url=url;
    this.title=title;
    this.destId=destId;
    this.destUrl=destUrl;
    this.destTitle=destTitle;
}

public String getId() {return id;}

public String getUrl() {return url;}

public String getTitle() {return title;}

public String getDestId() {return destId;}

public String getDestUrl() {return destUrl;}

public String getDestTitle() {return destTitle;}

}
```

The Link class contains only two pieces of information needed for the simple application: the ID and the destination URL (destUrl). When the user clicks on an area, that ID will be checked against the Link objects available and the user will go to the location specified by the appropriate Link object's destination URL.

The EventHandler class, shown in Listing 19.4, populates Vector objects containing Area and Link objects that the LinkMap applet will then present to the user. Called at the beginning of the LinkMap applet's initialization routine, it uses Ælfred to parse the appropriate map file and creates Area and Link objects based on the attributes of the elements in the file. It also picks out the image file to present and the caption for that image.

Listing 19.4 The Event Handler Class Builds Collections of Links and Areas and
Gets the Key Image and Caption Information from an XML Map File

```
/** The Event Handler class uses the Aelfred parser to extract information
from an imagemap file specified in XML. It returns the information as a set of
areas and a set of links. */

import com.microstar.xml.XmlHandler;
import com.microstar.xml.XmlParser;
import com.microstar.xml.HandlerBase;
import java.net.*;
import java.util.*;

public class EventHandler extends HandlerBase {
    private String image;
    private String caption;
    private Vector links;
    private Vector areas;
    private String currentTagName;
    private String srcTemp;
    private String idTemp;
    private String hrefTemp;
    private String shapeTemp;
    private String coordsTemp;
    private String captionTemp;

    public EventHandler () {
```

```
        //initialize variables
        links=new Vector();
        areas=new Vector();
}

public Link getLink(int index) {
        return (Link) links.elementAt(index);
}

public String getImage() { return image; }
public String getCaption(){ return caption; }
public Vector getLinks() { return links; }
public Vector getAreas() { return areas; }

//Override HandlerBase methods
public void startElement (String Name) {
        //just keep track of the tag name
        currentTagName=Name;
}

public void endElement(String Name){
        int left, right, top, bottom;

        //if image, get file name
        if (Name.equals("image")) image=srcTemp;

        //if area, set up links and areas
        else if (Name.equals("area")) {
                Link currentLink=new Link(idTemp, "", "","", hrefTemp, "");
                links.addElement(currentLink);
                StringTokenizer tokens=new StringTokenizer(coordsTemp, ",");
                //note that areas are specified with absolute coordinates.
                //this wouldn't be hard to change if width and height are
                        preferred.
        left=Integer.parseInt(tokens.nextToken());
                top=Integer.parseInt(tokens.nextToken());
                right=Integer.parseInt(tokens.nextToken());
                bottom=Integer.parseInt(tokens.nextToken());
```

```
            Area currentArea=new Area(idTemp, shapeTemp,
                 left,top,right,bottom);
            areas.addElement(currentArea);
        }

        else if (Name.equals("caption")) {
            //store caption for later display
            caption=captionTemp;
        }

        //clear variables to avoid 'inherited' attributes
        //among sequential elements
        srcTemp= idTemp= hrefTemp= null;
        shapeTemp= coordsTemp= captionTemp= null;
    }

    //capture attributes for later combination
    //into elements
    public void attribute (String aName, String aValue, boolean
         isSpecified) {
        if (aName.equals("src")) srcTemp=aValue;
        else if (aName.equals("id")) idTemp=aValue;
        else if (aName.equals("href")) hrefTemp=aValue;
        else if (aName.equals("shape")) shapeTemp=aValue;
        else if (aName.equals("coords")) coordsTemp=aValue;
    }

    public void charData (char ch[], int start, int length) {
        //gets element content
        //only used for caption
        String text = new String (ch, start, length);
    if (currentTagName.equals("caption"))        captionTemp=text;
    }

}
```

The LinkMap class, shown in Listing 19.5 is the center of activity, calling the EventHandler class and manipulating an applet interface based on the Area and Link objects returned by the handler.

Listing 19.5 The LinkMap Class Presents Image Map Information to Users

```
/** The LinkMap class creates a small imagemap applet that uses XML
files for its source material */

import com.microstar.xml.XmlHandler;
import com.microstar.xml.XmlParser;
import com.microstar.xml.HandlerBase;
import java.applet.*;
import java.awt.*;
import java.awt.event.*;
import java.net.*;
import java.util.*;

public class LinkMap extends Applet {
    protected Image image;
    protected String caption;
    protected Vector links;
    protected Vector areas;
    private XmlParser parser;          /*  Aelfred XML Parser*/
    private EventHandler handler;

    public void init() {
        URL xmlURL;
        String xmlDoc;

        /*open file from src parameter in APPLET element*/
        xmlDoc=getParameter("src");
        load (xmlDoc);

        /*use inner Listener class to pick up mouse events.*/
        this.addMouseListener(new Listener());
    }
```

```java
public void load (String xmlDoc) {
    URL xmlURL;

    /*loads a new map */

    handler=new EventHandler();
    parser=new XmlParser();
    parser.setHandler(handler);

    //minimal error handling
    try {
    xmlURL=new URL (getDocumentBase(), xmlDoc);
    parser.parse(xmlURL.toString(), null, (String) null);
    } catch (Exception e) {
        e.printStackTrace();
    }

//set image, links, areas, caption
image=this.getImage(this.getDocumentBase(), handler.getImage());
links=handler.getLinks();
areas=handler.getAreas();
caption=handler.getCaption();
repaint();
}

public void paint(Graphics g) {
    //display image and caption
    g.drawImage(image, 0, 0, this);
    showStatus(caption);
}

public void destroy() { image.flush();}

public void update(Graphics g) {paint(g);}

//draws box around selected area
//because of XOR, also undraws box
```

```
public void highlight (int i){
Area areaTemp;
areaTemp=(Area)areas.elementAt(i);
Graphics g=getGraphics();
g.setXORMode(Color.gray);
g.drawRect(areaTemp.left,areaTemp.top,(areaTemp.right-areaTemp.left),
     (areaTemp.bottom-areaTemp.top));
}

//inner class provides mouse support
class Listener extends MouseAdapter {
     private int prevArea;

     public void mousePressed(MouseEvent e) {
          Area areaTemp;
          int x=e.getX();
          int y=e.getY();
          prevArea=-1;

          //check to see if clicked in marked area
          for (int i=0; i<areas.size(); i++) {
               areaTemp=(Area)areas.elementAt(i);
               if (areaTemp.isInArea(x,y)) {
               prevArea=i;
               highlight(i);
               break; /*don't need to keep checking; only one hit is
                         enough.*/
          }
     }
}

public void mouseReleased(MouseEvent e) {
     Area areaTemp;
     String idTemp;
     Link linkTemp;
     int x=e.getX();
     int y=e.getY();
```

```
        if (prevArea!=-1) /*clear highlighting*/
              highlight(prevArea);
        for (int i=0; i<areas.size(); i++) {
              areaTemp=(Area)areas.elementAt(i);
              if (areaTemp.isInArea(x,y)) {
                    /*select link based on id*/
                    idTemp=areaTemp.getId();
                    for (int j=0; j<links.size(); j++) {
  linkTemp=(Link)links.elementAt(i);
                        if (idTemp.equals(linkTemp.getId())){
                            /*load the new page!*/
                            load (linkTemp.getDestUrl());
                            break;
                        }
                    }
              }
        }
    }
}
```

At initialization, the LinkMap applet creates an EventHandler object (handler) to parse the map file. (The location of the initial map file is given as a parameter by the APPLET element shown in Listing 19.6 below.) The init() method collects the image and caption information for immediate display and collects the Link and Area objects generated by the parser for linking. Then it sits back and waits for the user to click on an area. If the user clicks the mouse button down in the space indicated by an area element (now an Area object in the areas vector), that area is highlighted by the mousePressed() method of the Listener inner class. When the user releases the mouse button, the mouseReleased() method of the Listener inner class will check to see if the user stayed in that area. The area is un-highlighted and then, if the mouse was still in the area, the mouseReleased() method goes through several additional steps. First, it cross references the ID of the Area to an ID of a Link, and extracts the destination URL from the Link. Then the load () method is passed the URL, and it opens the new file. The load () method takes an argument (the URL), and needs to call repaint() when it is finished.

To put this applet in a document, the APPLET element shown in Listing 19.6 should be used.

Listing 19.6   This APPLET Element Starts the LinkMap Applet

```
<APPLET CODE="LinkMap.class" WIDTH=405 HEIGHT=257>
<PARAM NAME="src" value="map1.xml">
</APPLET>
```

When this is used with the map file shown in Listing 19.2 and appropriate graphic files, the user will be presented with the map (in this case, literally a map) shown in Figure 19.1.

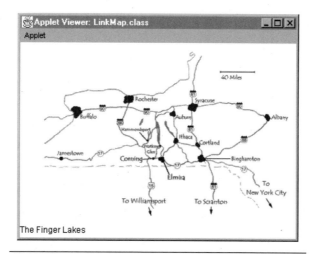

Figure 19.1   The initial appearance of the LinkMap applet

When the user presses the mouse button while the cursor is over an area listed in the map file (here near Hammondsport, to the left of the center of the image), the area will be highlighted as shown in Figure 19.2.

If the user releases the mouse button after moving the cursor outside the indicated area, the highlighting will disappear and the screen will revert to that shown in Figure 19.1. If the user releases the mouse button in the area, however, the sunset on Keuka Lake shown in Figure 19.3 will be visible. The mouseReleased() method will call the loadNew() method with the URL of a map file referencing this image, its caption, and its own set of links.

This applet can be used with any number of similar map files, building a micro-Web of images and links.

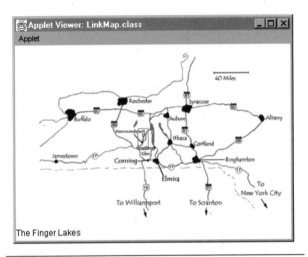

Figure 19.2   The appearance of the LinkMap applet when the user is clicking over a linked area

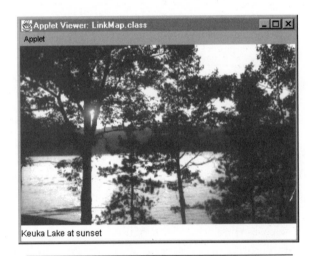

Figure 19.3   The appearance of the LinkMap applet when the user is clicking over a linked area

MOVING UP: CREATING MAPS WITH EXTENDED LINKS

As useful as simple links have been, more complex links can provide a much richer navigational experience for users and a much simpler time for site authors. The implementation in the previous section contained the key parts needed to identify sections of an image and describe the links between images. The Area and Link classes will be used precisely as they were in the previous section. (They were over-built for that purpose anyway). The EventHandler will need a thorough overhaul to be able to cope with the new elements involved and create all their links, and the LinkMap will get a thorough interface overhaul, support for keeping links in memory after the page that created them is gone, and additional support for selecting multiple links from an area and links from multiple overlapping areas.

The map documents themselves will also change, using extended rather than simple links to indicate connections. This DTD, shown in Listing 19.7, requires all links to be extended; a modified DTD, modified Link class, and modified EventHandler class could support simple links as well as extended links, but for this demonstration, extended links will work well by themselves.

Listing 19.7 This DTD Relies on Extended Rather than Simple Links to Connect ImageMaps

```
<!ELEMENT map (image,area*,caption?)>
<!ELEMENT image EMPTY>
<!ATTLIST image
    src    CDATA    #REQUIRED>
<!ELEMENT area (extlocator+)>
<!ATTLIST area
    xml:link CDATA #FIXED "extended"
    inline (true|false) "true"
    id ID #REQUIRED
    shape    (rect | circle)    "rect"
    coords    CDATA    #REQUIRED
    content-title CDATA #IMPLIED>
<!ELEMENT extlocator EMPTY>
<!ATTLIST extlocator
    xml:link CDATA #FIXED "locator"
    href CDATA #REQUIRED
    role CDATA #IMPLIED
    title CDATA #IMPLIED
    show (embed|replace|new) "replace"
    actuate (auto|user) "user"
    behavior CDATA #IMPLIED>
<!ELEMENT caption (#PCDATA)>
```

Documents can now specify groups of links for an area; all the links described in a group can connect to each other, not just to the area element that first described the links. A sample document (which describes family photos rather than the map of the previous example) is shown in Listing 19.8.

Listing 19.8   This document contains three groups of links, two of which include only a pair of endpoints. Note that two areas also overlap.

```xml
<?xml version="1.0" encoding="UTF-8"?>
<!DOCTYPE map SYSTEM "map.dtd">
<map>
<image src="3folks.gif" />
<area id="gavin" content-title="Gavin with his parents" shape="rect"
coords="50,50,150,150">
<extlocator href="gavin.xml" title="Gavin in College" />
</area>
<area id="russ" content-title="Russ with Gavin and Judy" shape="rect"
coords="150,50,300,150">
<extlocator href="russmeet.xml" title="Russ in a Meeting" />
<extlocator href="russ.xml" title="Russ with a patient" />
</area>
<area id="russJudy" content-title="Russ and Judy with Gavin"  shape="rect"
coords="150,50,400,150">
<extlocator href="russjudy.xml" title="Russ and Judy" />
</area>
<caption>Gavin, Russ, and Judy</caption>
</map>
```

Rather than capturing simple ID to URL mappings, the EventHandler class, shown in Listing 19.9, now needs to process groups of links that can be traversed in both directions. (Among other things, it now takes the reference used to open the document as an argument to the constructor so that it can build two-way links.) While some of the information in the DTD above will be ignored (this simple application relies on element names to understand the kind of information it is dealing with, and ignores the xml:link, role, show, actuate, and behavior attributes), the URLs of both the originating and terminating image maps, any appropriate ID information, and the descriptive information needed to build menus are all necessary. The content-title attribute of the areas is used to describe the originating end of the link to users on the terminating end (since they can traverse it in the opposite direction), while the title attribute of the extlocator links provides a description of the link to users still on the originating page. The EventHandler class has to sort through groups of links to make certain they all connect to each other, and not simply back to the area in which the link is declared. As a result, the link processing in the EventHandler class is much more complex, putting links into a holding tank (the linksCombine vector) before letting them into the main localLinks vector. In addition, because IDs in links may not always be specified, a "%none" value is used to identify that no ID was present, making it possible to link entire images rather than just areas. (In a validating environment, %none would not be a legal ID value in a document, making it impossible for an ID with a value of %none to collide with this placeholder.)

Listing 19.9 The EventHandler Class Now Provides Much More Sophisticated Link Determination Tools

---

```
// XML Handler to capture Areas and Links

import com.microstar.xml.XmlHandler;
import com.microstar.xml.XmlParser;
import com.microstar.xml.HandlerBase;
import java.net.*;
import java.util.*;

public class EventHandler extends HandlerBase {
        private Vector localLinks;         /* master list of links*/
        private Vector linksCombine;       /* workspace for links*/
        private Vector areas;              /* list of areas
        private String thisDoc;            /* URL of current document*/
        private String image;              /* Referenced Image
        private String caption;            /* Caption text
        private String currentTagName;     /* Temporary Holding Variables*/
        private String srcTemp, idTemp, hrefTemp;
        private String urlTemp, targetIdTemp, contentTitleTemp;
        private String shapeTemp, coordsTemp, captionTemp;
        private String titleTemp;

        /*  this time we need the url of the originating document  to create
                multi-directional links*/
```

```
public EventHandler (String url) {
    thisDoc=url;
    localLinks=new Vector();
    linksCombine=new Vector();
    areas=new Vector();
}


public Link getLink(int index) {
    return (Link) localLinks.elementAt(index);
}


public String getImage() { return image; }
public String getCaption(){ return caption; }
public Vector getLinks() { return localLinks; }
public Vector getAreas() { return areas; }

//  Override HandlerBase methods
public void startElement (String Name) {
    currentTagName=Name;
}



public void endElement(String Name){
    // working variables
    int left, right, top, bottom;

    /*  image element and caption are simple*/
    if (Name.equals("image")) image=srcTemp;
    else if (Name.equals("caption"))    caption=captionTemp;

    /*  area element combines link info to create genuinely extended
            links, not just two-way links*/

    else if (Name.equals("area")){
        StringTokenizer tokens=new StringTokenizer(coordsTemp, ",");
    left=Integer.parseInt(tokens.nextToken());
        top=Integer.parseInt(tokens.nextToken());
    right=Integer.parseInt(tokens.nextToken());
```

```
bottom=Integer.parseInt(tokens.nextToken());
    Area currentArea=new Area(idTemp, shapeTemp, left,top,right,
        bottom);
    areas.addElement(currentArea);

    // Connect links within area
    connect();

    /* Clear values to avoid 'multiple sequential inheritance'*/
    idTemp="%none";
    shapeTemp= coordsTemp= contentTitleTemp = null;
    linksCombine.removeAllElements();
}

/* Build local links table. Area will combine. */
else if (Name.equals("extlocator")) {
    // check hrefTemp for two strings
    int testId=hrefTemp.indexOf('#');
    if (testId != -1){
        urlTemp=hrefTemp.substring(0,testId-1);
targetIdTemp=hrefTemp.substring(testId+1);
    }
    else{
        urlTemp=hrefTemp;
        targetIdTemp="%none";
    }
    Link currentLink=new Link(idTemp, thisDoc, contentTitleTemp,
        targetIdTemp, urlTemp, titleTemp);
    linksCombine.addElement(currentLink);
    titleTemp=hrefTemp = null;
}
}

/* Capture Attribute Data to temporary variables */
public void attribute (String aName, String aValue, boolean isSpecified) {
    if (aName.equals("src")) srcTemp=aValue;
    else if (aName.equals("id")) idTemp=aValue;
    else if (aName.equals("href")) hrefTemp=aValue;
```

```
            else if (aName.equals("shape")) shapeTemp=aValue;
            else if (aName.equals("title")) titleTemp=aValue;
            else if (aName.equals("coords")) coordsTemp=aValue;
            else if (aName.equals("content-title")) contentTitleTemp=aValue;
    }


    // charData used only for caption
    public void charData (char ch[], int start, int length) {
            String text = new String (ch, start, length);
            if (currentTagName.equals("caption")) captionTemp=text;
    }


    // Connect all the links for this area
    /* Area element combines link info to create genuinely extended links,
            not just two-way links*/
            private void connect () {
                    Link linkTemp, linkNext,linkCombine;
                    int numLinks=linksCombine.size();
                    if (numLinks==1) {
                        linkTemp=(Link)linksCombine.elementAt(0);
                        localLinks.addElement(linkTemp);
                    }
                    else if (numLinks >1) {
                            /* algorithm combines destination links so they connect
                                    to each other. */
                            for (int i=0; i<numLinks; i++) {
    linkTemp=(Link)linksCombine.elementAt(i);
                                localLinks.addElement(linkTemp);
                                for (int j=i+1; j<numLinks; j++){
    linkNext=(Link)linksCombine.elementAt(j);
    linkCombine=new Link(linkTemp.getDestId(),
                    linkTemp.getDestUrl(),
                    linkTemp.getDestTitle(),
                    linkNext.getDestId(),
                    linkNext.getDestUrl(),
                    linkNext.getDestTitle());
    localLinks.addElement(linkCombine);
                    }
```

```
                    }
                }
            }
        }
```

The LinkMap class, shown in Listing 19.10, has undergone an even more significant transformation. Instead of blindly accepting the content the EventHandler
feeds it (and destroying that information every time it changes images), it now filters that information carefully (with the linkAdd() method) to remove duplicate
links while keeping a history of all of the links in all of the documents it has opened.
It then uses that link information in conjunction with the image and area information to present the user with a navigable image. To navigate the image, the user
right-clicks (or, depending on the platform, takes the appropriate action to activate
a JDK 1.1 popup menu) to see a list of the links available from a given location in
the document. Instead of highlighting the areas where the user has clicked, this
applet builds a context-sensitive menu that indicates all the possible links. The user
may then select a link from the menu, or click outside the menu to stay with this
image and lose the menu. Overlapping areas will be reflected in the menu, as will
multiple targets of the same link.

Listing 19.10 The LinkMap Class Now Filters Links for Duplicates, Uses Popup Menus for
Linking, and Presents all Possible Links, Rather than Directing the User to a Single Target

```java
import com.microstar.xml.XmlHandler;
import com.microstar.xml.XmlParser;
import com.microstar.xml.HandlerBase;
import java.applet.*;
import java.awt.*;
import java.awt.event.*;
import java.net.*;
import java.util.*;


/** The LinkMap class creates a small imagemap applet that uses XML files
    for its source material. In this version, it supports extended links in
    multiple directions, building a link list as it goes. */

public class LinkMap extends Applet implements ActionListener {
    protected Image image;
    protected String caption;
```

```
protected String xmlDoc;
protected Vector links;
protected Vector areas;
private XmlParser parser;/*  Aelfred XML Parser*/
private EventHandler handler;
private ContextPopup popup;

//  Initialize and load first page
public void init(){
     URL xmlURL;

          /*links variable must be initialized because it will be added to, not
                    replaced. */
     links=new Vector();
     xmlDoc=getParameter("src");

          // Load and Parse Document
     load (xmlDoc);

          //create new context-sensitive popup menu
     popup=new ContextPopup(this);
     this.add(popup);
     this.enableEvents (AWTEvent.MOUSE_EVENT_MASK);
}

public void load (String xmlLoad) {
     URL xmlURL;
     Link linkTemp;

     xmlDoc=xmlLoad;
     handler=new EventHandler(xmlLoad);
     parser=new XmlParser();
     parser.setHandler(handler);

     try {
          xmlURL=new URL (getDocumentBase(), xmlDoc);
          parser.parse(xmlURL.toString(), null, (String) null);
     } catch (Exception e) {
```

```
                e.printStackTrace();
        }

        //  get image
        image=this.getImage(this.getDocumentBase(), handler.getImage());

        /*  note that links are _added_ on top of each other*/
        linksAdd(handler.getLinks());

        //  areas are replaced
        areas=handler.getAreas();

        //  caption is set
        caption=handler.getCaption();
        repaint();
    }

public void processMouseEvent (MouseEvent e) {
        if (e.isPopupTrigger())
                popup.show(this, e.getX(), e.getY());
        else super.processMouseEvent (e);
    }

public void linksAdd(Vector linksTemp) {
        boolean identical;
        Link linkTemp;
        Link linkComp;

        /*this complicated looking mess simply insures that each link
            appears in the table only once. This will work with small
            implementations larger ones should seek alternatives for higher
            efficiency. */
        for (int j=0; j<linksTemp.size(); j++) {
                identical=false;
                linkTemp=(Link)linksTemp.elementAt(j);

                //compare to existing elements
                for (int k=0;k<links.size();k++) {
```

```
                    linkComp=(Link)links.elementAt(k);
                    identical=(
(linkTemp.getId().equals(linkComp.getId()))) &&
(linkTemp.getUrl().equals(linkComp.getUrl()))) &&
(linkTemp.getTitle().equals(linkComp.getTitle()))) &&
(linkTemp.getDestId().equals(linkComp.getDestId()))) &&
(linkTemp.getDestUrl().equals(linkComp.getDestUrl()))) &&
(linkTemp.getDestTitle().equals(linkComp.getDestTitle())))
                         );
                    if (identical){break;}
            }

            //if we survived comparison, add to list
            if (!identical) {links.addElement(linkTemp);}
            }//end link for
        }

    public void update(Graphics g) { paint(g); }

    public void paint(Graphics g) {
        g.drawImage(image, 0, 0, this);
        showStatus(caption);
    }

    public void actionPerformed(ActionEvent event) {
        /*responds to the menu. URLs are passed as commands*/

        String command = event.getActionCommand();
        if (!command.equals("No Link")) load (command);
    }

}

/* This class does a lot of heavy lifting. It determines what links to what,
   based on the areas and links between them. It also allows for non-id-based
   connections between whole documents. This avoids the need to specify
   areas on _every_ image and makes it easier to go back. */
```

```
class ContextPopup extends PopupMenu {
    private LinkMap parent;

    public ContextPopup(LinkMap parentApplet) {
        super();
        parent=parentApplet; //need this to get links and areas
    }

    public void show(Component pass, int x, int y){
        MenuItem mi;
        Area areaTemp;
        String idTemp;
        String destUrlTemp;
        Link linkTemp;

        //clear menu
        this.removeAll();
        for (int i=0; i<parent.areas.size(); i++) {
            areaTemp=(Area)parent.areas.elementAt(i);
            if (areaTemp.isInArea(x,y)) {
                /*first check for explicit links from this area to others*/
                idTemp=areaTemp.getId();
                for (int j=0; j<parent.links.size(); j++) {
                    linkTemp=(Link)parent.links.elementAt(j);

                    //first forward links
                    if ((idTemp.equals(linkTemp.getId())) &&
(parent.xmlDoc.equals(linkTemp.getUrl()))){
destUrlTemp=linkTemp.getDestUrl();
                            createItem (linkTemp.getDestTitle(),destUrlTemp);
                    }

                    //then backward links
                    if ((idTemp.equals(linkTemp.getDestId())) &&
(parent.xmlDoc.equals(linkTemp.getDestUrl()))){
                        destUrlTemp=linkTemp.getUrl();
                            createItem (linkTemp.getTitle(),destUrlTemp);
                    }
```

```
            }//end link For
        }//end area If
    }//end area For

    /*then check for links that don't spec ID both forward and back-
      ward, again*/
    for (int j=0; j<parent.links.size(); j++) {
        linkTemp=(Link)parent.links.elementAt(j);

        //first forward
        if ((linkTemp.getId().equals("none")) &&
(parent.xmlDoc.equals(linkTemp.getUrl()))){
                destUrlTemp=linkTemp.getDestUrl();
                createItem (linkTemp.getDestTitle(),destUrlTemp);
        }

        //then backward links
        if ((linkTemp.getDestId().equals("none")) &&
(parent.xmlDoc.equals(linkTemp.getDestUrl()))){
            destUrlTemp=linkTemp.getUrl();
            createItem (linkTemp.getTitle(), destUrlTemp);
        }
    }

    //if no links
    if (this.getItemCount()==0)
        createItem ("No Link", "No Link");

    //finally, pass to superclass for display.
    super.show(pass, x, y);
}

// Add Item to Menu
private void createItem (String title, String url) {
    MenuItem mi = new MenuItem(title);
    mi.setActionCommand(url);
    mi.addActionListener(parent);
    this.add(mi);
```

```
    }
  }
```

The user who starts up this applet (using the same APPLET element shown in Listing 19.6) will see the picture of three people shown in Figure 19.4.

Figure 19.4 The initial appearance of the LinkMap applet; no links are visible.

Right-clicking in a part of the image that has no links will bring up a menu that says simply "No Links", as shown in Figure 19.5.

Figure 19.5 Clicking in an area with no links brings up a "No Links" menu.

Clicking on an area of the image that does have links (in this case, two overlapping areas, one of which links to two images and one of which links to one) will bring up a menu of destinations, generated from the title attributes of those links, shown in Figure 19.6.

Figure 19.6 Areas may have multiple links, and areas may overlap, to produce a rich menu of options.

Choosing one of those links (in this case, "Russ in a Meeting") brings up a new image, with its own menu of links. The file used for this particular image is shown in Listing 19.11.

Listing 19.11 This Document Contains No Links, Relying on Other Documents for its Connections

```
<?xml version="1.0" encoding="UTF-8"?>
<!DOCTYPE map SYSTEM "map.dtd">
<map>
<image src="russmeet.gif" />
<caption>Russ in a Meeting</caption>
</map>
```

Note that there are no areas defined here, no links described at all. Because the links are multidirectional (and because this particular link contained multiple destinations), however, the user still has a choice of two options, as shown in Figure 19.7. "Russ with Gavin and Judy" is drawn from the content-title attribute of the area element that created this link; "Russ with a patient" is drawn from the title attribute of another component of that link.

Figure 19.7 Even pages with no built-in links may draw
on multidirectional links from other documents.

Notably, "Russ and Judy", which came from a different but overlapping area on the original page, does not appear in this list. Exploring the original page, as shown in Figure 19.8, demonstrates that that link came from a separate area on the page, accessible from areas without the other menu items.

Figure 19.8 The area for "Russ and Judy" overlapped that
shown in Figure 19.6, but has space of its own as well.

There is still room for considerable improvement in this little applet:

■ Adding out-of-line links (which would require minor modifications and additions to the EventHandler class and the DTD)

■ Hub documents (requiring a massive addition to the EventHandler class, possibly even an intermediary between it and the LinkMap class)

■ Support for larger numbers of links (requiring more efficient processing than the current lists provide)

■ Support for more of the XLink attributes, and reliance on attribute values rather than element names for identifying element function (requiring modifications to EventHandler and the addition of new functionality to the LinkMap class)

■ Support for more of the XPointer specification (requiring more involved parsing of URL fragment identifiers)

■ Support for text documents and real XPointers (requiring a complete rebuilding of the LinkMap and EventHandler classes).

Unfortunately, the XLink and XPointer standards are in specification limbo. As the standards approach stability, it may make more sense to build larger, more powerful XLink processing applications. In the meantime, this applet offers a considerable taste of the power to come.

20

PREFERENCES: STORING AND RETRIEVING

CHANGEABLE INFORMATION

While most of the examples in this book concentrate on presenting information stored in XML, this chapter addresses the somewhat more complex issues involved in using XML as a storage container whose content may change frequently. Preference files are classic examples of documents that need to be read every time a program is opened, and contain information that may be changed at any point during the course of a program. While preference files do not (usually) have the complexity of marked-up documents, they can still require considerable searching, building, and modification. The Document Object Model (DOM), under development at the W3C, provides a set of tools for reading and manipulating tree-based information that will work with a number of parsers. In this preferences example, we will use the DOM in the context of Sun's XML parsers, to navigate the document tree, and add and modify elements.

NOTE   The DOM as discussed here is only a proposed recommendation (dated 18 August 1998) from the W3C. The full text of it, including descriptions of many more interfaces than this chapter could hope to implement, is at **http://www.w3.org/TR/PR-DOM-Level-1/**. Similarly, the Sun parser used here is an early access parser, available from **http://developer.javasoft.com/developer/ earlyAccess/xml/index.html**. The parser itself (and the location for downloading the parser) may change to some extent, but the parts of it used here seem to be simple enough to withstand any minor changes in either the DOM spec or the parser.

Growing and Exploring Trees

The DOM, which was discussed briefly in Chapters 3 and 12, builds a tree from the document. The base ("root") of the tree is the first element in the document, which must contain all the other elements. The first element contains a series of "nodes", which represent attributes of the first element, or elements, text, processing instructions, CDATA sections, comments, notations, or entities within that element. Each of those nodes may in turn contain additional nodes which represent their content, which may contain additional nodes, and so on. A simple XML preferences file is shown in Listing 20.1; the tree that will be constructed from that file is shown immediately afterward, in Figure 20.1.

Listing 20.1   The prefs.xml File

```
<?xml version='1.0' encoding='UTF-8'?>
<DEMO>
<SCREEN>
<HEIGHT>200</HEIGHT>
<WIDTH>300</WIDTH>
<TITLE>Preferences Demo</TITLE>
</SCREEN>
</DEMO>
```

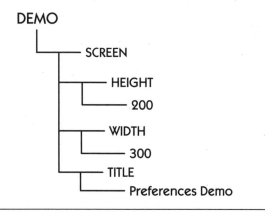

Figure 20.1 The tree representation of the prefs.xml file

Trees lack most of the complication of the XML document; there are no empty tags or end tags in the tree, just nodes with and without children. The same core of functions can be used on any node, making it easy to start at one node and climb up the tree, or down into the tree, or access information within that node. The hardest parts are keeping track of where in the tree structure you have landed, and making certain that you have not skipped over a branch of the tree. For the example, in this chapter, the "tree-walking" is kept simple, walking down explicitly stated paths, rather than searching the entire document for information.

It makes sense to keep the preference application and its corresponding document structure simple. While there may be applications that make better use of attribute values than element content, this preferences file will focus strictly on element content. Apart from "leaf" elements, which contain the information needed, none of the elements in this document has meaningful text—they all contain white space and other elements. (Attributes and mixed content could be added quite easily, requiring only some extra method calls.) This preference file application reads information out of and into an XML preferences document at the request of other objects in the application; it does not attempt to instantiate any objects based on the elements it finds.

NOTE

If you want to use preference files to set up your applications directly, you might want to explore Coins (**http://www.jxml.com/coins**) or explore the XML Beans material provided with the Sun XML parsers. The preference file demonstrated here is merely a repository, not an active tool for setting up objects.

Once your application is well defined, it might make sense to create a DTD for the preference files, and use a validating parser to help detect anomalies in the preferences. This particular demonstration is less concerned with making certain that the preference information follows a strict ordering than with allowing applications to find information and add new entries as needed. As you will see, the setValue() mechanism allows for the creation of additional nodes at any point. (No facility for deleting them completely is provided.) This approach makes it easier to create a preference file as the program develops. Rather than pondering the precise entries needed in a file and building a DTD, you can go ahead and build an application, using the preferences file itself as a readable (if you named the pieces wisely) map to the needs of your program. Naming conventions are a useful part of this process—just remember the limitations XML places on element names, as discussed in Chapter 4.

NOTE

Validation against a schema that could check data types as well as document structure would be an extremely valuable addition to the preference file system. Once schema implementations become standardized and widely available, this change would be extremely worthwhile.

REQUIREMENTS

This preferences file class was built using the Sun XML parser and accesses and modifies most of its information through the interfaces specified in the W3C's Document Object Model Level 1 Core. (Loading the document and writing the document out are both done through the Sun XML parser's interface, since neither of these is specified in the DOM itself.) Using the Sun XML parser requires the Java Development Kit version 1.1.6 or later. The preferences file class expects to be used as part of an application, not in an applet; it requires access to the file system to read and write preference files.

NOTE

An applet version could use HTTP transfers to retrieve its preference file, but would be unable to write the file back. To try this, just modify the constructor method to use an HTTP url instead of a file URL and delete the write() method entirely. The application can still set values, but they will disappear when the applet is closed.

BUILDING AN APPLICATION THAT USES AN XML PREFERENCES FILE

The preferences component performs a small number of key functions. First, it needs to open a file on disk and use the parser to create a document tree. It needs to be able to read items from the document tree and return them to the application. It also needs to allow the application to make changes to the preferences settings when desired. Similarly, it allows the application to add new entries to the preferences files. Finally, it can write the preferences file back out to disk as a regular XML file. Each of these tasks is explored in a section below.

Listing 20.2 shows the opening class declarations and imports.

Listing 20.2   The Foundations of the Prefs class

```
//Preferences file class
//Created for Building XML Applications
//By Ethan Cerami and Simon St.Laurent

import java.io.*;
import java.util.*;
import org.xml.sax.SAXException;
import org.xml.sax.SAXParseException;
import com.sun.xml.tree.*;
import org.w3c.dom.*;

public class prefs {
      private static   String      fileLocation;
      private static   String      uri;
      private static   XmlDocument      doc;


}
```

Most of the imports are for XML-related tools, though the Java I/O libraries and the utility classes are also needed to help glue the preferences application to the local system and to the application. The class' private variables include the tree itself and the tree's location in two different forms, the original file location and the equivalent file:// URI.

Opening the Preferences File

The constructor method for the prefs class relies almost entirely on the Sun XML parser's XmlDocument class, using it to build the tree from the document. File I/O errors and other parsing errors may also be caught at this point in the application. For now, these errors will be reported to the command-line console. If you would rather catch these errors yourself and perform more sophisticated processing (especially in production code), the declarations may be modified to throw the exceptions to a different handler. Listing 20.3 shows the constructor method for the prefs class.

Listing 20.3   The Constructor Method for the Prefs Class

```
public prefs (String fileName){
try {
      //convert filename to URI
      uri='file:'+new File (fileName).getAbsolutePath();
      fileLocation=fileName;

      //load document as parsed XML tree
      doc=XmlDocumentBuilder.createXmlDocument(uri);

/*Note: using try and catch in modules that use this code is recommended. You
may want to turn off the stack tracing for production code. */

//error handling for parse errors - to console.
      } catch (SAXParseException err) {
            System.out.println ('** Parsing error'
                  + ', line ' + err.getLineNumber ()
                  + ', uri ' + err.getSystemId ());
            System.out.println('   ' + err.getMessage ());
            err.printStackTrace ();

      } catch (SAXException e) {
            Exception x = e;
            if (e.getException () != null)
                  x = e.getException ();
            x.printStackTrace ();
```

```
//error handling for file I/O, other errors
    } catch (Throwable t) {
        t.printStackTrace ();
    }
}
```

Once the tree is in memory, we can commence navigation.

READING A PREFERENCE ITEM

Information from any element on the XML document tree is made available to other objects through the getValue() method of the prefs class. getValue() takes a single argument, a string indicating where on the tree to find the preference item. That string, the path, should be specified in a format much like those used to identify objects, as a list of containing elements separated by periods. The root element should not be specified, as the search begins at the root element. In the document listed above, the path to the value for the height of the screen would be:

SCREEN.HEIGHT

The getValue() method uses the java.util.StringTokenizer class to break this path down into its component parts during the search of the document tree, and looks for elements along the way. The full path to each item must be specified. Although it is possible to create a function that searches the entire tree until it finds a similarly-named element (and Sun's TreeWalker class provides that functionality), it can be both inefficient (especially in large documents) and capable of producing false matches when the same element structure appears underneath different elements.

The value of the item specified by the path will be returned as a string, leaving it up to the calling method to convert the string to the needed format. This value is simply the text content of the element. (It would not be too hard to build a method that returned an attribute instead, if desired.) The string will be empty if the element requested does not exist.

All the functionality used to search the tree is derived from the DOM's Node interface, which is used to access the contents of all kinds of nodes. While the only pieces this application actually uses are the element name and its text content, this application will search and skip other kinds of nodes along the way. The Document interface's method for getting the root element of the document (getDocumentElement()), and the Node interface's methods for retrieving child elements (getChildNodes() and getFirstChild()), getting the name of a node (getNodeName()), and retrieving the content of a node (getNodeValue()) are all that is needed to search down the node tree and retrieve the precise item required.

Listing 20.4 shows the getValue method in full:

Listing 20.4   The getValue() Method for the Prefs Class

```
public String getValue(String path){
      Node currentElement;
      Node testNode;
      Node prefNode;
      NodeList childElements;
      int   nodeCounter;
      String tokenName;
      String prefValue;
      StringTokenizer tokens;

  //start by collecting the root element
  currentElement=doc.getDocumentElement();

  /*walk through the document structure to find leaf
  element info. Note that the root element is treated
  as a container and ignored. Do NOT reference the root element in your prefer-
  ence requests*/

  /*duplicate declarations to make sure that variables are properly initialized if
  the path is a total miss.*/

  tokens=new StringTokenizer(path,'.');
  tokenName=tokens.nextToken();
  tokens=new StringTokenizer(path,'.');
  while (tokens.hasMoreTokens())
    {
        tokenName=tokens.nextToken();
        childElements=currentElement.getChildNodes();
        for (nodeCounter=0;
            nodeCounter<childElements.getLength();
            nodeCounter++) {
```

```
/*check through all nodes for one matching the
appropriate element name*/
    testNode=childElements.item(nodeCounter);
    if (tokenName.equals(testNode.getNodeName()))
    {currentElement=testNode;}
  }

  //break to avoid false positives
  if (!tokenName.equals(currentElement.getNodeName()))
    {break;}
}
    //check the results!
    if (tokenName.equals(currentElement.getNodeName())) {
    //extract data value - should only be one child
        prefNode=currentElement.getFirstChild();
        prefValue=prefNode.getNodeValue();
    }else{
    //not found; return empty string
        prefValue='';
    }
return prefValue;
}
```

CHANGING OR CREATING A PREFERENCE ITEM

Changing the value of a preference item is much like getting the value of a preference item, except that once we find the item, we use the **setNodeValue()** method rather than the **getNodeValue()** method. This implementation also performs another service if the path does not work out; it creates the path and sets the value. This requires the use of three additional methods. The first, the Document interface's (in this case, the XmlDocument element's) **createElement()** method, creates a free-floating node with whatever tagName we assign it. Once the element is created, we need to create a text node that can actually store the preference information inside the element, which is done with the Document interface's create-TextNode() method. The third, the Node's **appendChild()** method, is used to glue the element and text nodes into the overall document structure.

The code for the **setValue()** method, which searches the tree and sets (or creates) the values needed, is shown below in Listing 20.5.

Listing 20.5   The setValue() Method for the Prefs Class

```java
public void setValue(String path, String newValue){

Node currentElement;
Node testNode;
Node newElement;
Node prefNode;
NodeList childElements;
int   nodeCounter;
String tokenName;
StringTokenizer tokens;

//start by collecting the root element
currentElement=doc.getDocumentElement();

/*walk through the document structure to find leaf
element info. Note that the root element is treated
as a container and ignored.*/

tokens=new StringTokenizer(path,'.');
tokenName=tokens.nextToken();
tokens=new StringTokenizer(path,'.');
while (tokens.hasMoreTokens())
  {
      tokenName=tokens.nextToken();
      childElements=currentElement.getChildNodes();
      for (nodeCounter=0;
            nodeCounter<childElements.getLength();
            nodeCounter++) {
/*check through all nodes for one matching the
appropriate element name */
      testNode=childElements.item(nodeCounter);
      if (tokenName.equals(testNode.getNodeName())) {
      currentElement=testNode;
      }
    }
  }
//break to avoid false positives
if (!tokenName.equals(currentElement.getNodeName())) {break;}
```

```
        }
            if (tokenName.equals(currentElement.getNodeName())) {
            //extract data value - should only be one child
                prefNode=currentElement.getFirstChild();
            prefNode.setNodeValue(newValue);
            }else {
            //create the value!  Build more tree!
            newElement=doc.createElement(tokenName);
            currentElement.appendChild(newElement);
            currentElement=newElement;
            while (tokens.hasMoreTokens())
              {
                tokenName=tokens.nextToken();
                newElement=doc.createElement(tokenName);
                currentElement.appendChild(newElement);
                currentElement=newElement;
              }
            prefNode=doc.createTextNode(newValue);
            currentElement.appendChild(prefNode);
          }
        }
```

WARNING

Note that the **setValue()** method **only** modifies the document tree in memory. It does not write the value to a permanent file. The **write()** method, described in the next section, does that.

WRITING THE PREFERENCES FILE

The DOM itself does not provide any facilities for saving documents, so once again we turn to Sun's implementation for extra functionality. The XmlDocument class provides a write() method that can be used in conjunction with the Java I/O classes to write the file back out to disk, as shown in Listing 20.6.

Listing 20.6   The write() Method for the Prefs Class

```
public void write() {
//must be called to save values to prefs file.
```

```
        DataOutputStream output;
    try  {
        output=new DataOutputStream(new FileOutputStream(fileLocation));
        /*note that write() is not in the DOM; it is a method of the Sun XmlDocu-
    ment class */
        doc.write(output);
        }
    catch (IOException e)      {
        System.err.println ('File problem\n' + e.toString());
        System.exit(1);
        }
    }
```

TESTING THE PREFERENCES FILE FROM THE COMMAND LINE

The prefs class can be tested fairly easily from the command line. The short **main()**
method listed below relies on the number of arguments to determine what behavior
it should demonstrate. If the Prefs class is run with one argument, the **main()**
method reads the file identified by that argument. (If the file is badly formed, errors
will be reported. Otherwise the user just gets a friendly message.) If the Prefs class
is run with two arguments, the first argument is treated as the file name, and the
second argument is treated as the path to the element that needs to be read. Again,
errors may be reported by the parser, and a blank response means that the file name
could not be found. If the Prefs class is run with three arguments, the first two
arguments remain the file and the path, and the third argument is the value that
needs to be written to that path. The **write()** method will be called, saving the
preferences tree back to the file specified. This makes it easy to find out exactly
what the Prefs class is returning to an application. Listing 20.7 shows the **main()**
method; Listing 20.8 shows a typical command-line session using the **main()**
method to access the Prefs class from the command line.

Listing 20.7 The main() Method for the Prefs Class Provides Command-line Access

```
public static void main (String argv[]) {
        prefsPreferences;
        String Response;
        switch (argv.length){
        case 1:
            Preferences=new prefs(argv[0]);
```

```
        Response='If you get this far, it read the file '+argv[0]+'.';
        break;
    case 2:
        Preferences=new prefs(argv[0]);
        Response='The path ' +argv[1] +' led to ' +
                    Preferences.getValue(argv[1])+'.';
        break;

    case 3:
        Preferences=new prefs(argv[0]);
        Preferences.setValue(argv[1],argv[2]);
        Response='The value '+argv[2]+' was written to '+argv[1]+' and its
                    current value is '+ Preferences.getValue(argv[1])+'. Check
                    the file '+argv[0]+' to see what happened.';
        Preferences.write();
        break;
    default:
        Response='Need the right number (1-3) of arguments!';
    }
    System.out.println(Response);
}
```

Listing 20.8   A Typical Command-line Session with the Prefs Class

D:\jdk1.1.6\prefs>javac prefs.java

D:\jdk1.1.6\prefs>java prefs prefs.xml
If you get this far, it read the file prefs.xml.

D:\jdk1.1.6\prefs>java prefs prefs.xml SCREEN.HEIGHT
The path SCREEN.HEIGHT led to 400.

D:\jdk1.1.6\prefs>java prefs prefs.xml SCREEN.HEIGHT 400
The value 400 was written to SCREEN.HEIGHT and its current value is 400.
Check the file prefs.xml to see what happened.

D:\jdk1.1.6\prefs>java prefs prefs.xml SCREEN.GREEN 500

The value 500 was written to SCREEN.GREEN and its current value is 500. Check the file prefs.xml to see what happened.

Note the last command added to the document tree. The new prefs.xml file is shown in Listing 20.9, complete with its new "GREEN" element.

Listing 20.9 The Modified prefs.xml file after a Command-line Session

```
<?xml version='1.0' encoding='UTF-8'?>

<DEMO>
<SCREEN>
<HEIGHT>400</HEIGHT>
<WIDTH>414</WIDTH>
<TITLE>Preferences Demo</TITLE>
<GREEN>500</GREEN></SCREEN>
</DEMO>
```

USING THE PREFERENCES FILE IN A PROGRAM

Connecting the Prefs class to an application is fairly simple. It can be accessed from most methods, and consistently returns strings to the programs that call its methods. In the sample application below, shown in Listing 20.10, the preference file shown above is used to determine the size of an application's main window, as well as its title. If the user resizes the window, the preference file will be changed to reflect this when the window is closed.

Listing 20.10 The mainWindow Class Demonstrates the Use of Preference Files to Control an Application's Setup

```
import java.awt.*;
import java.awt.event.*;
import prefs;

public class mainWindow {

public static void main (String[] argv) {
    Frame frameWindow;
    prefs preferences;
```

```
    int height,width;
    String title;

    frameWindow=new Frame();
    try {
          preferences=new prefs('prefs.xml');
    height=Integer.parseInt(preferences.getValue('SCREEN.HEIGHT'));
    width=Integer.parseInt(preferences.getValue('SCREEN.WIDTH'));
          title=preferences.getValue('SCREEN.TITLE');
          }
    catch (Exception e){
          //if no prefs, use defaults!
          height=300;
          width=200;
          title='Demo Window';
          }
    frameWindow.setTitle(title);
    frameWindow.setSize(width,height);
    frameWindow.show();
    frameWindow.addWindowListener(new WindowAdapter() {
          public void windowClosing(WindowEvent e) {
          try {
                prefs closePreferences=new prefs('prefs.xml');
                Dimension finalSize=new Dimension();

                finalSize=e.getWindow().getSize();
          closePreferences.setValue('SCREEN.WIDTH',String.valueOf
                          (finalSize.width));
          closePreferences.setValue('SCREEN.HEIGHT',String.valueOf (final-
                          Size.height));
                closePreferences.write();
          }
          finally {System.exit(0);}
          }
    }); //end of inner class
  }
}
```

There are two important things to note about this program. The first is the use of the try and catch clauses at initialization. Preference files have an odd way of getting destroyed, modified, or otherwise misplaced. The XML format encourages users to tinker; it is as readable as the old .ini files of Windows 3.1, but capable of holding many more layers of structure. Having default values available in the catch clause makes sure that the program can run, even if the preferences file is unavailable or modified in an unacceptable way. The second point is the use of the Finally clause in the inner class that supports the frame's closing. Users will not be happy if a problem with a preferences file means that they cannot quit a program except by extraordinary means. The Finally clause ensures that the program will quit, whether or not the preferences file is available.

The first time the user opens the program, the default size of the window (200x300) will be used, as shown in Figure 20.2. If the user resizes the window during the session, the window will reappear in the next session with the resized proportions, as shown in Figure 20.3. The prefs.xml file also changes, as shown in Listing 20.11.

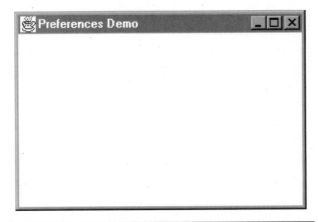

Figure 20.2 The first time the mainWindow program is run,
the window appears at the default size

Figure 20.3   When the mainWindow class is run subsequently, the window will appear at the size it had when the program was exited.

Listing 20.11   The Window Size is Stored in the prefs.xml File When the Program Exits

```
<?xml version='1.0' encoding='UTF-8'?>

<DEMO>
<SCREEN>
<HEIGHT>351</HEIGHT>
<WIDTH>395</WIDTH>
<TITLE>Preferences Demo</TITLE>
</SCREEN>
</DEMO>
```

NOTE

Updates to this code will be available at **http://www.simonstl.com/buildxml** when Sun releases the final version of its parser, now called Java Project X.

E-COMMERCE PRODUCT CATALOG

DESCRIPTION

Our final example creates an e-commerce product catalog, via a server-side XML to HTML transformation. For our product catalog, we present an on-line bookstore (which happens to specialize in XML and Java books). The model presented here is intended to be very flexible, in order that it may be applied to other industries, DTDs or products. The code itself is also quite flexible, as it makes use of the new Java Servlet API.

The Java Servlet API represents a significant new step in the evolution of Java, and represents a viable alternative to traditional CGI programs written in Perl or C/C++. When combined with an XML parser, servlets can perform all XML processing on the server side, and present the results in standard HTML (see Figure 21.1.) This XML-to-HTML transformation is central to many applications and therefore forms for the core of our example.

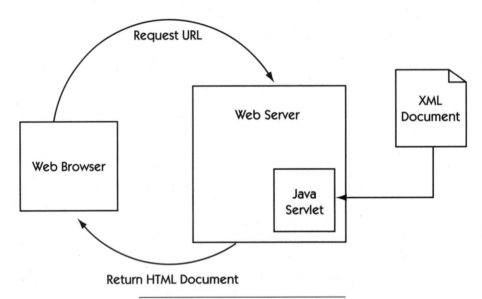

Figure 21.1   Server-side XML processing

By moving XML processing to the server and using HTML for output, you can offer XML functionality to any standard Web browser without requiring the use of Java applets or XML support in the browser. Such functionality is extremely useful for a host of Web-based services, including product catalogs, news aggregation, e-commerce shopping carts, and intelligent agents. At the end of the chapter, we also outline various extensions to our code, including a generic model for aggregating and comparing data from multiple sources.

TECHNICAL SPECIFICATION

The code in this chapter is written in Java 1.1 and utilizes the new Java Servlet API. We aim to keep the servlet coding as simple as possible, so that you can follow the example even if you have no prior servlet programming experience. For additional information regarding servlet programming, we recommend *Java Servlets* by Karl Moss (McGraw-Hill, 1998.)

For XML parsing, we use the SAX interface of the IBM XML Parser. As all the code runs on the server-side, the HTML output can be viewed within any standard Web browser. To run our example, we used LiveSoftware's JRun Servlet Engine (available from **http://www.livesoftware.com/**).

XML SPECIFICATION

By the time you are reading this, understanding DTDs and XML documents should be second nature. We therefore present our Catalog.dtd and sample books.xml file with very little explanation (see Listings 21.1 and 21.2). The DTD itself is straightforward and requires that each BOOK include an author, title, publisher, price and description. The sample books.xml includes information regarding four computer books (and we recommend all of them).

Listing 21.1 Catalog.dtd

```
<!ELEMENT CATALOG (BOOK)+>
<!ELEMENT BOOK (AUTHOR, TITLE, PUBLISHER, PRICE, DESCRIPTION)>
<!ELEMENT AUTHOR (FIRSTNAME, LASTNAME)>
<!ELEMENT FIRSTNAME (#PCDATA)>
<!ELEMENT LASTNAME (#PCDATA)>
<!ELEMENT TITLE (#PCDATA)>
<!ELEMENT PUBLISHER (#PCDATA)>
<!ELEMENT PRICE (#PCDATA)>
<!ELEMENT DESCRIPTION (#PCDATA)>
```

Listing 21.2 Sample books.xml

```
<?xml version="1.0" encoding="UTF-8"?>
<!DOCTYPE CATALOG SYSTEM "Catalog.dtd">
<!-- XML Document for Recommended Computer Books -->

<CATALOG>
    <BOOK>
        <AUTHOR>
            <FIRSTNAME>Karl</FIRSTNAME>
```

```
        <LASTNAME>Moss</LASTNAME>
    </AUTHOR>
    <TITLE>Java Servlets</TITLE>
    <PUBLISHER>McGraw-Hill</PUBLISHER>
    <PRICE>44.95</PRICE>
    <DESCRIPTION>Published July 3rd, 1998, this is the first book to
            focus on the development of Internet-based applications
            using the Java Servlet API. An appendix in the back
            features an alphabetical description of each class in the
            API, along with an illustration of the hierarchy, a method
            summary and a detailed method description for each
            class. The CD-ROM includes the JRun servlet runner from
            Live Software, ServletExec servlet runner from New
            Atlanta, JBuilder IDE from Inprise (formerly Borland)
            and the source code for all the applications in the
            book.</DESCRIPTION>
</BOOK>
<BOOK>
    <AUTHOR>
        <FIRSTNAME>Simon</FIRSTNAME>
        <LASTNAME>St. Laurent</LASTNAME>
    </AUTHOR>
    <TITLE>XML: A Primer</TITLE>
    <PUBLISHER>MIS: Press</PUBLISHER>
    <PRICE>24.99</PRICE>
    <DESCRIPTION>This guide to XML shows developers how XML fits
            into the current landscape of emerging standards. It pre-
            sents a complete guide to the syntax of XML, explaining
            how to create well-formed and valid XML documents.
            Style sheets, including the Cascading Style Sheets stan-
            dard, are applied to XML documents to create documents
            that are attractive to humans as well as to computers.
            Document Type Declarations (DTDs) receive extensive
            coverage, with several chapters exploring their applica-
            tion through well-documented examples. XML: A Primer
            presents DTDs suited to a variety of tasks, including doc-
            ument management, EDI, device control, and traditional
            web page development.</DESCRIPTION>
```

```
    </BOOK>
    <BOOK>
        <AUTHOR>
            <FIRSTNAME>Ethan</FIRSTNAME>
            <LASTNAME>Cerami</LASTNAME>
        </AUTHOR>
        <TITLE>Delivering Push</TITLE>
        <PUBLISHER>McGraw-Hill</PUBLISHER>
        <PRICE>49.95</PRICE>
        <DESCRIPTION>Push technology has come to shove, and this is the
                book/CD-ROM that shows how to implement all of the
                major Push servers and clients on the market. It
                encompasses Push solutions for Microsoft and Netscape
                browsers, and highlights both Microsoft's CDF (Channel
                Definition Format) and Netscape's NetCaster. You'll
                learn how to install and configure BackWeb, Castanet,
                PointCast, and other webcasting tools that allow you to
                deliver scheduled update information across the
                Web.</DESCRIPTION>
    </BOOK>
    <BOOK>
        <AUTHOR>
            <FIRSTNAME>Simon</FIRSTNAME>
            <LASTNAME>St. Laurent</LASTNAME>
        </AUTHOR>
        <TITLE>Cookies</TITLE>
        <PUBLISHER>McGraw-Hill</PUBLISHER>
        <PRICE>34.95</PRICE>
        <DESCRIPTION>Cookies are a mystery of Web programming.
                They're rumored to have been the cause of malevolent
                invasions of privacy, virus mongering, and security
                breaches. In reality, they are a highly efficient program-
                ming tool that helps users keep track of where they are
                in a Web site. These pages show how to make the most of
                cookies.</DESCRIPTION>
    </BOOK>
</CATALOG>
```

THE CODE

Our product catalog is divided into two class files. The first, BookCatalog.java (see Listing 21.3) interfaces with the Java Servlet API. The second, Handler.java (see Listing 21.4) interfaces with the SAX API to perform the XML to HTML transformation.

SERVLET PROGRAMMING

BookCatalog.java extends the Java Servelt **HttpServlet** class. This class makes it possible to receive HTTP requests from clients and return data to the Web browser. Those who have done any CGI programming may remember that the CGI GET method facilitates transfer of parameter data within a URL. Alternatively, the CGI POST method enables transfer of parameter information (usually form data) within the body portion of the HTTP request. For our product catalog, we will use the GET method to pass a URL parameter, indicating the XML file to be processed.

For example, assuming our servlet is running on **localhost**, the following URL will process the books.xml file, located at simonstl.com:

```
http://localhost/servlet/BookCatalog?URL=
    http://www.simonstl.com/xml/books.xml
```

The URL parameter must be absolute, and can process any XML document located on the web.

Upon receiving our request, the Web server will run the BookCatalog servlet, and invoke the **doGet()** method. This method includes two very important parameters: the **HttpServletRequest** includes all information from the client, including any parameter data; in contrast, the **HttpServletReponse** includes all information that will be sent back to the client.

To extract the URL parameter, we use the **HttpServletRequest** **getParameterValues()** method. This method takes a string, in our case, "URL", and returns an array of string values. We then pass the value of the URL parameter to our private **parse()** method:

```
String url[] = req.getParameterValues("URL");
parse(url[0]);
```

Printing data back to the client is just as simple. First we obtain the **ServletOutputStream** via the **HttpServletReponse** **getOutputStream()** method:

```
out = res.getOutputStream();
```

We then set the MIME type via the **setContentType()** method. In our case, we set the MIME type to text/html:

```
res.setContentType("text/html");
```

To write to the client, we use the **ServletOutputStream** just like any other output stream, and encode our output in HTML. For example, we create the page header and title:

```
out.println("<HEAD><TITLE>Book Catalog</TITLE></HEAD><BODY>");
out.println("<CENTER><h1>Books 'r Us</h1></CENTER>");
```

The remainder of BookCatalog.java sets up the SAX parser and initiates the parsing of the URL parameter. We create a new **Parser** class via the SAX **ParserFactory** helper class.

XML to HTML Transformation

Handler.java extends the SAX HandlerBase convenience class to transform incoming XML events into HTML output. Performing this transformation is simple. Via the **characters()** method, the SAX handler copies all incoming data to temporary variables. For example, if we encounter a start FIRSTNAME tag, we save the first name text to the temporary **firstName** variable.

When the Handler encounters the end element event for BOOK, we can be certain that we have all the necessary data stored to temporary variables. We therefore print the data within an HTML ordered list, via the **ServletOutputStream**:

```
public void endElement (String name) {
    try {
    if (name.equals ("BOOK")) {
        out.println ("<P><LI><I>"+title+"</I>");
        out.println (" ("+publisher+")");
        out.println ("<BR>Author:  "+lastName+", "+firstName);
        out.println ("<BR><FONT SIZE=-1><B>Description:</B>  ");
        out.println (description+"</FONT>");
        out.println ("<BR><FONT SIZE=-2 COLOR=RED>Our Price: $");
        out.println (price+"</FONT>");
        out.println ("</LI>");
```

```
        }
    } catch (IOException e) {}
}
```

This creates the HTML output presented in Figure 21.2.

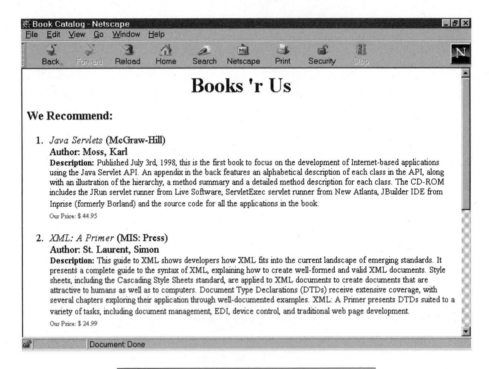

Figure 21.2   HTML output created from books.xml

For debugging purposes, errors in validity are also reported to the **ServletOutput-Stream**, via the error() method:

```
public void error(SAXParseException exception) throws SAXException {
    try {
        String msg = exception.getMessage();
        msg = msg.replace ('<', '[');
        msg = msg.replace ('>', ']');
        out.println ("<BR><FONT COLOR=RED>XML Error:</FONT>"+msg);
    } catch (IOException e) {}
}
```

Note that we replace the "<" and ">" characters with the "[" and "]" characters. This enables us to view XML tag information that would otherwise be hidden within the HTML (see Figure 12.3).

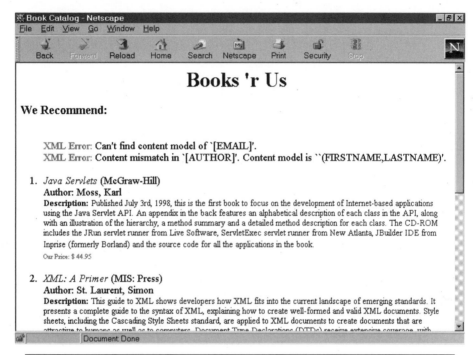

Figure 21.3 For debugging purposes, errors in validity are displayed to the browser

Listing 21.3 BookCatalog.java

```
// E-Commerce Book Catalog
// Performs Server Side XML --> HTML Transformation
// Created by Ethan Cerami / Simon St. Laurent
// Building XML Applications (McGraw-Hill, Inc.)


// Important Notes:
// 1) To compile this program: you must include the following
// packages  within your CLASSPATH:  Java Servlet API, SAX API,
// and a SAX-compliant Parser
// 2) To run this program:
//    a) place class files within the servlet\ directory of
```

```
//    your web server.
//    b) set the CLASSPATH of the Web Server\Servlet Invoker
//    to include:  the SAX API, and a SAX-compliant parser

import java.io.*;
import java.util.*;
import javax.servlet.*;
import javax.servlet.http.*;
import org.xml.sax.*;
import org.xml.sax.helpers.*;

public class BookCatalog extends HttpServlet {
    private ServletOutputStream out;
    private Parser parser;

    public void doGet (HttpServletRequest req, HttpServletResponse res)
      throws IOException, ServletException {

// Get Request OutputStream
        out = res.getOutputStream();

// Set content type
    res.setContentType("text/html");

//  Write response header
    out.println("<HEAD><TITLE>Book Catalog</TITLE></HEAD><BODY>");
    out.println("<CENTER><h1>Books 'r Us</h1></CENTER>");
    out.println("<H3>We Recommend:</H3>");

//  Extract URL Parameter
    String url[] = req.getParameterValues("URL");
    parse(url[0]);

// Print Footer:  Current Date and Requested URL
    Date date = new Date();
    out.println ("<P><P><HR><I>Date:  "+date+"</I>");
    out.println("<h6>File Requested:  "+url[0]+"</h6>");
```

```
// Close output Stream
out.close();
}


// Parse Specified XML File
private void parse (String urlStr)
    throws ServletException, IOException {

// Set SAX Parser
//String parserClass = "com.microstar.xml.SAXDriver";
String parserClass = "com.ibm.xml.parser.SAXDriver";

// Create Parser Object using SAX ParserFactory
// Provide full Exception Handling
try {
    parser = ParserFactory.makeParser (parserClass);
} catch (ClassNotFoundException e) {
    out.println ("Error: Parser "+
        "Class Not Found: "+parserClass);
} catch (IllegalAccessException e) {
    out.println ("Error: Access "+
        "Violation on Parser Class: "+parserClass);
} catch (InstantiationException e) {
    out.println ("Error: Could not "+
        "instantiate Parser Class: "+parserClass);
} catch (ClassCastException e) {
    out.println ("Error: "+parserClass+
        " does not implement the SAX Parser interface.");
}


// Set Parser Document Handler
Handler handler = new Handler (out);
parser.setDocumentHandler (handler);
parser.setErrorHandler (handler);

// Start Parsing
try {
    parser.parse (urlStr);
```

```
        } catch (SAXException e) {
            String msg = e.getMessage();
            msg = msg.replace ('<', '[');
            msg = msg.replace ('>', ']');
            out.println ("<BR><FONT COLOR=RED>XML Error:</FONT>
                    "+msg);
        }
    }
}
```

Listing 21.4   Handler.java

```
// Event Handler to capture and process SAX parse events
// Performs XML to HTML Transformation

import java.io.*;
import java.util.*;
import javax.servlet.*;
import javax.servlet.http.*;
import org.xml.sax.*;
import org.xml.sax.helpers.*;

class Handler extends HandlerBase {
    private ServletOutputStream out;        // Output Stream to print HTML
    private String currentTagName;          // Current Tag Name
    private String firstName, lastName;     // Temp Author Name
    private String title, price;            // Temp Title, Price
    private String publisher, description;  // Temp Publisher, Description

    // Constructor
    public Handler (ServletOutputStream out) {
        this.out = out;
    }

    // Start HTML Ordered List
    public void startDocument () {
        try {  out.println ("<OL>"); } catch (IOException e) {}
    }
```

```java
// Save Character Data to Temporary Variables
public void characters (char ch[], int start, int length) {
    String text = new String (ch, start, length);

if (currentTagName.equals("FIRSTNAME"))
    firstName = text;
else if (currentTagName.equals("LASTNAME"))
    lastName = text;
else if (currentTagName.equals("TITLE"))
    title = text;
else if (currentTagName.equals("PUBLISHER"))
    publisher = text;
else if (currentTagName.equals("PRICE"))
    price = text;
else if (currentTagName.equals("DESCRIPTION"))
    description = text;
}


// Save Tag Name to Local Variable
public void startElement (String name, AttributeList atts) {
    currentTagName = name;
}


// Perform XML to HTML Mapping
public void endElement (String name) {
    try {
        if (name.equals ("BOOK")) {
            out.println ("<P><LI><I>"+title+"</I>");
            out.println (" ("+publisher+")");
            out.println ("<BR>Author:  "+lastName+", "+firstName);
            out.println ("<BR><FONT SIZE=-1><B>Description:</B>
                    ");
            out.println (description+"</FONT>");
            out.println ("<BR><FONT SIZE=-2 COLOR=RED>Our Price:
                    $");
            out.println (price+"</FONT>");
            out.println ("</LI>");
```

```
            }
        } catch (IOException e) {}
    }


    //  Close HTML Ordered List
    public void endDocument () {
        try { out.println ("</OL>"); } catch (IOException e) {}
    }


    //  For validating parsers, such as IBM
    //  Report errors in validity
    public void error(SAXParseException exception) throws SAXException {
        try {
            String msg = exception.getMessage();
            msg = msg.replace ('<', '[');
            msg = msg.replace ('>', ']');
            out.println ("<BR><FONT COLOR=RED>XML Error:</FONT>
                    "+msg);
        } catch (IOException e) {}
    }

}
```

THE FUTURE OF SERVER-SIDE XML

Perhaps you are wondering about the usefulness of transforming an XML document into HTML. Why not just place the book information into a database, query the database, and present these results to the user? The answer: XML makes it possible to aggregate and compare data for multiple data sources. We therefore conclude this chapter with a brief look into the future of server-side XML. The future we envision is not yet possible today, as it requires industry-wide creation and acceptance of DTDs. Such DTD creation is inevitable and we predict that the model presented here will be viable (in fact, we predict that the model will be widespread) within the next 6 months to a year.

DATA AGGREGATION

First, consider data aggregation. As a case study, consider online real estate classifieds, a burgeoning new market in electronic commerce. There are potentially hundreds of real estate Web sites, from realtor.com, apartments.com to local Web sites, such as *The New York Times* or the New York-based *Village Voice*.

Now, make two presumptions (neither of which are too far fetched). First, presume that a core group of real estate sites agree to a Real Estate DTD.[1] Fearful of missing out, most of the other sites agree to follow suit. Second, presume that each real estate site provides an XML-enabled search engine.[2] Sites are likely to have wildly divergent database systems. Regardless of the systems, however, each search engine works the same way: it takes several search patterns, such as location, price range or number of bedrooms, and returns a list of matches, all encoded in the Real Estate Markup Language.

With these two presumptions in pace, we now have the infrastructure for collecting real estate classifieds from multiple data sources and aggregating them in one central location. For example, a new clearinghouse company, called MegaRealtor.com could provide a single HTML form to gather search criteria. Once submitted, a server-side program, much like the one presented in this chapter, would poll the XML search engines of multiple data sites, package the results together, and present one comprehensive list to the end-user (see Figure 21.4.).[3]

The end result is one-stop shopping. The concept could be adopted for a several Web-based services, including job classifieds, personalized aggregation of news, stock analysis, or even search engines.

E-Commerce Shopping Agents

Once there exists the ability to gather data from multiple sources, there is the ability to compare data. One of the most powerful applications of XML may turn out to be electronic commerce and the ability automatically to search the net for the lowest prices.

Consider the book industry and our e-commerce product catalog. Again, we make two assumptions. First, we presume that a core set of companies will establish

---

1 Progress on this front has already begun. OpenMLS Software has already proposed a Real Estate Listing Markup Language (RELML.) The DTD and a related article, "XML Is Helping To Solve Real Estate Problem" are available from **http://www.xml.com/**.

2 Progress on this front has begun as well. Not content to wait for the widespread adoption of DTDs and XML search engines, several companies, including WebMethods and Junglee (recently acquired by Amazon.com) have created search engines that map HTML data to XML data. This enables companies to extract unstructured HTML data and export it to relational databases.

3 OpenMLS Software has created a prototype XML Search engine, called XSearch, based on the RELML. See **http://www.openmls.com/** for a demonstration.

a Book DTD (the one presented in this chapter is certainly not adequate, but does give a glimmer of its most basic elements). Second, we presume that a core of companies provide an XML enabled search engine.

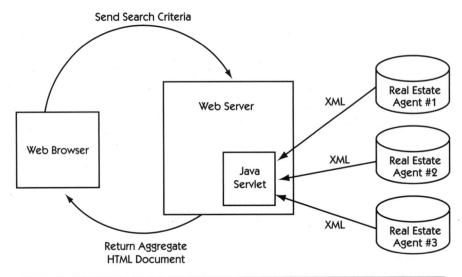

Figuge 21.4 A generic model for aggregating XML data from multiple data sources

In comparing product information, the most crucial element is a single identifier unique to each product. Fortunately, books already have such an identifier, the ISBN created by the ISO. We can therefore compare book prices from multiple sources. Without a unique identifier it is difficult to make accurate comparisons, as we may be comparing apples to oranges.[4]

Once our assumptions are in place, we have the infrastructure for creating intelligent shopping agents. In the case of books, such an agent might work as follows.

First, consumers will visit the site and enter their search criteria, including author, title or keywords. The site will search a local database or another clearinghouse to find any matches and return these matches, indexed by ISBN (see Figure 21.5, Step 1).

Second, the consumer either refines search, or selects one book. With the ISBN in hand, the Web site initiates the aggregation of XML data across multiple sources. In each case, the server passes the ISBN number to the XML search engine, and receives

---

4 Unfortunately, agreeing on a single identifier turns out to be the biggest obstacle. In the case of books, the publishing industry has created a standard. In the case of other products, such as cars, consumer electronics, compact discs, software, and hardware, finding a unique identifier or product number will be difficult, but essential.

book information including cover price, availability, possible discounts, and shipping options (see Figure 21.5, Step 2). These data are processed by the server side application and nicely packaged in HTML. Once all the sites have been polled, the application checks book availability, adds in shipping costs, and finds the vendor with the best price. The best option is highlighted to the consumer (see Figure 21.5, Step 3).

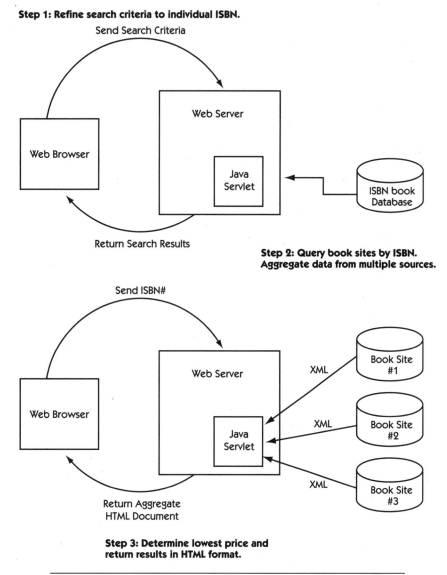

Figure 21.5 A generic model for creating intelligent shopping agents

The greatest strength of XML is the ability to aggregate and compare data from multiple sources. These examples are just two of the short-term applications. Long-term applications may prove to be much more useful and flexible, offering online consumers a vast array of new services.

5

QUICK REFERENCE GUIDES

Part V of this book includes annotated quick reference guides for each of the major APIs discussed throughout this book: the Ælfred XML Parser, the Microsoft XML Parser (MS-XML), and the Simple API for XML (SAX.)

Each quick reference guide includes the following information:

- Description of each API is categorized by package. Each package includes an object diagram detailing its classes, interfaces, and exceptions, and their relation to one another.
- Each package member includes a short description. Where needed, key concepts are illustrated with examples.
- Each package member includes a complete API of methods, organized alphabetically. Method names and class variables are denoted in **bold**.

- Depending on the type of object being described (e.g. class, interface, or exception), we include the following information:
  - Hierarchy: a complete class hierarchy.
  - Implemented by: a complete list of classes that implement the specified interface.
  - Returned by: a complete list of classes and their methods that return the specified class.
  - Extended by: a complete list of classes that extend the specified class.
  - Thrown by: a complete list of methods that throw the specified exception.

THE ÆLFRED API
QUICK REFERENCE GUIDE

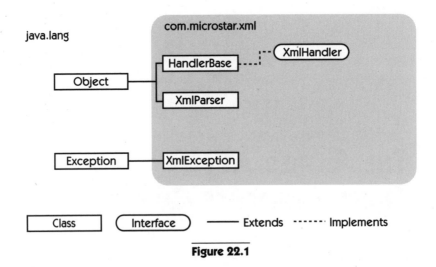

Figure 22.1

XML Package (Package com.microstar.xml)

Class HandlerBase

The HandlerBase convenience class provides a (mostly) empty implementation of the XmlHandler interface. It is usually much easier to extend the HandlerBase class than to implement the entire XmlHandler interface. For example, the following code extends the HandlerBase to capture the startElement, endElement and character events:

```
class Handler extends HandlerBase {

public void startElement (String name) {
System.out.println ("Start element:  name=" + name);
}

public void endElement (String name) {
    System.out.println ("End element:   " + name);
}

public void charData (char ch[], int start,
  int length) {
```

```
        String text = new String (ch, start, length);
        System.out.println ("Character data:  "+text);
    }
}


public class HandlerBase extends Object implements XmlHandler {
    // Constructor
    public HandlerBase();


    // Public Methods
    public void attribute(String aname, String value, boolean isSpecified)
        throws Exception;
    public void charData(char ch[], int start, int length) throws Exception;
    public void doctypeDecl(String name, String publicId, String systemId)
        throws Exception;
    public void endDocument() throws Exception;
    public void endElement(String elname) throws Exception;
    public void endExternalEntity(String systemId) throws Exception;
    public void error(String message, String systemId, int line,
        int column) throws XmlException, Exception;
    public void ignorableWhitespace(char ch[], int start, int length)
        throws Exception;
    public void processingInstruction(String target, String data)
        throws Exception;
    public Object resolveEntity(String publicId, String systemId)
        throws Exception;
    public void startDocument() throws Exception;
    public void startElement(String elname) throws Exception;
    public void startExternalEntity(String systemId) throws Exception;
}
```

Hierarchy: Object → HandlerBase (XmlHandler)

CLASS XMLEXCEPTION

The XmlException class encapsulates all error information for any fatal errors reported by Ælfred. Usually, you can just implement the error() method of the XmlHandler interface to capture errors (the XmlException class is therefore not necessary for routine use of Ælfred). The XmlException class is, however used by the HandlerBase convenience class. Specifically, HandlerBase implements the error() method to throw an XmlException:

```
public void error (String message, String systemId,
int line, int column) throws XmlException, java.lang.Exception {
        throw new XmlException(message, systemId, line, column);
}
```

When using the HandlerBase class, you can therefore either override the error() method, or explicitly catch the XmlException.

```
public class XmlException extends Exception {


        // Constructor
        public XmlException(String message, String systemId,
        int line, int column);


        // Public Methods
        public int getColumn();
public int getLine();
public String getMessage();
        public String getSystemId();
}
```

Hierarchy: Exception → XmlException
Thrown By: HandlerBase.error()

INTERFACE XMLHANDLER

Ælfred is an event-driven parser, and all Ælfred applications must implement the XmlHandler interface in order to capture the parsing events. The startDocument() method is always the first method called, and is therefore a good place for program initialization. The endDocument() method is always the last method called, and is therefore a good place for program clean-up. The following XML text:

```
<SUBJECT STATUS="HIGH">Meeting Today!</SUBJECT>
```

will generate the following parsing events:

- attribute(): Attribute name = "STATUS"; Attribute value = "HIGH"
- startElement(): Tag name = "SUBJECT"
- charData(): String = "Meeting Today!"
- endElement(): Tag name = "SUBJECT"

Note that Ælfred will call attribute() once for each attribute and will call attribute() prior to the startElement() method. Ælfred may also break long lines of text into smaller packets and call charData() for each packet. The resolveEntity() method makes it possible to redirect external entities (such as DTDs) to different URIs.

If you do not want to implement the entire interface, you can extend the HandlerBase convenience class instead (see above).

```
public interface XmlHandler {

    // Public Methods
    public abstract void attribute(String aname, String
        value, boolean isSpecified) throws Exception;
    public abstract void charData(char ch[],int start,
        int length) throws Exception;
    public abstract void doctypeDecl(String name,
        String publicId, String systemId) throws Exception;
    public abstract void endDocument() throws Exception;
    public abstract void endElement(String elname) throws Exception;
    public abstract void endExternalEntity(String systemId)
    throws Exception;
    public abstract void error(String message, String systemId, int line,
        int column) throws Exception;
    public abstract void ignorableWhitespace(char ch[], int start, int length)
        throws Exception;
    public abstract void processingInstruction(String
        target, String data) throws Exception;
    public abstract Object resolveEntity(String publicId,
        String systemId) throws Exception;
    public abstract void startDocument() throws Exception;
    public abstract void startElement(String elname)
        throws Exception;
    public abstract void startExternalEntity(String
        systemId) throws Exception;
```

```
}
```

Implemented by: HandlerBase

CLASS XMLPARSER

The XmlParser class is responsible for parsing XML documents and generating parsing events that are processed by the implementation of the XmlHandler interface. Most developers need only be familiar with four core methods. First, the setHandler() method sets the event handler and receives any object that implements the XmlHandler interface. Second, developers should be familiar with the three variations of the parse() method. The XmlParser can read from a character stream (Reader object), byte stream (InputStream object) or a URI. Note that the last two methods require a Unicode text encoding parameter (e.g. "UTF-8", "UTF-16", "ISO-10646-UCS-2" etc.) If you do not know the encoding, you can pass a (String) null variable (the String casting is required, otherwise the compiler will be unable to determine which version of parse() you are calling.)

The following code creates a new XmlParser object, sets the event handler, and parses the XML document located on the Microstar Web site:

```
Handler handler = new Handler();
parser = new XmlParser();
parser.setHandler(handler);
parser.parse ("http://www.microstar.com/xml/Aelfred/donne.xml",
     "-//Megginson//DTD Simple Poem//EN", (String) null);
```

In addition to the four core methods, the XmlParser class provides methods for querying the DTD (if any.) Ælfred is not a validating parser, but it is "DTD-aware." You can therefore query the DTD for a list of declared elements using the declaredElements() method, or extract a list of declared attributes for a specified element using the declaredAttributes(String elemName) method. For example, the following code extracts element and attribute data from the DTD:

```
String elemName, attributeName;
Enumeration attributes;
// Extract all Elements
Enumeration elements = parser.declaredElements();
while (elements.hasMoreElements()) {
    elemName = (String) elements.nextElement();
    System.out.println ("Element:  "+elemName);
```

```
// Extract all Attributes
attributes = parser.declaredAttributes(elemName);
if (attributes != null) {
    while (attributes.hasMoreElements()) {
    attributeName = (String) attributes.nextElement();
    System.out.println ("-->  Attribute:"+
        attributeName+"  ");
    }
}
}
```

You can also query individual elements, attributes, entities, and notations for a full range of properties. For example, you can retrieve the attribute type (e.g. CDATA, ID, IDREF, etc.) by using the getAttributeType() method, or retrieve the default value of any attribute using the getAttributeDefaultValue() method. Likewise, you can extract information regarding an individual entity, including its value, system URI and Public ID.

```
public class XmlParser extends Object {

    // Constructor
    public XmlParser();

    // Constants
    public static final int ATTRIBUTE_CDATA;
    public static final int ATTRIBUTE_DEFAULT_FIXED;
    public static final int ATTRIBUTE_DEFAULT_IMPLIED;
    public static final int ATTRIBUTE_DEFAULT_REQUIRED;
    public static final int ATTRIBUTE_DEFAULT_SPECIFIED;
    public static final int ATTRIBUTE_DEFAULT_UNDECLARED;
    public static final int ATTRIBUTE_ENTITY;
    public static final int ATTRIBUTE_ENTITIES;
    public static final int ATTRIBUTE_ENUMERATED;
    public static final int ATTRIBUTE_ID;
    public static final int ATTRIBUTE_IDREF;
    public static final int ATTRIBUTE_NMTOKEN;
    public static final int ATTRIBUTE_NMTOKENS;
    public static final int ATTRIBUTE_NOTATION;
```

```
public static final int ATTRIBUTE_UNDECLARED;
public static final int CONTENT_ANY;
public static final int CONTENT_ELEMENTS;
public static final int CONTENT_EMPTY;
public static final int CONTENT_MIXED;
public static final int CONTENT_UNDECLARED;


public static final int ENTITY_INTERNAL;
public static final int ENTITY_NDATA;
public static final int ENTITY_TEXT;
public static final int ENTITY_UNDECLARED;

// Public Methods
public Enumeration declaredElements();
public Enumeration declaredAttributes(String elname);
public Enumeration declaredEntities();
public Enumeration declaredNotations();

public String getAttributeDefaultValue(String name,
     String aname);
public int getAttributeDefaultValueType(String name,
     String aname);
public String getAttributeEnumeration(String name,
     String aname);
public String getAttributeExpandedValue(String name,
     String aname);
public int getAttributeType(String name, String aname);
public int getColumnNumber();
public String getElementContentModel(String name);
public int getElementContentType(String name);
public String getEntityNotationName(String eName);
public String getEntityPublicId(String ename);
public String getEntitySystemId(String ename);
public int getEntityType(String ename);
public String getEntityValue(String ename);
public int getLineNumber();
public String getNotationPublicId(String nname);
```

```
            public String getNotationSystemId(String nname);
            public String intern(String s);
            public String intern(char ch[], int start, int length);
            public void parse(String systemId, String publicId,
                String encoding) throws Exception;
            public void parse(String systemId, String publicId,
                InputStream stream, String encoding)
                throws Exception;
            public void parse(String systemId, String publicId,
                Reader reader) throws Exception;
            public void setHandler(XmlHandler handler);
    }
```

Hierarchy: Object → XmlParser

23

THE MS-XML QUICK REFERENCE GUIDE

ABOUT THIS QUICK REFERENCE GUIDE

The MS-XML (Version 1.8) API is quite large. A good portion of the API pertains to the MS-XML parser itself, and is therefore only of interest to individuals either maintaining or rewriting the parser code. In order to provide you with the most important concepts, this Quick Reference guide focuses solely on those parts of the API relevant to application developers. For a discussion of the complete API, see the online documentation at: **http://www.microsoft.com/xml**.

XML Object Model (Package com.ms.xml.om)

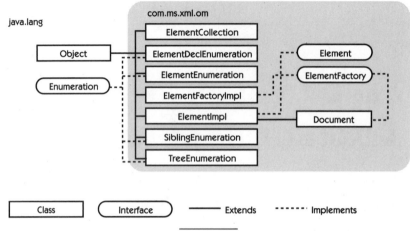

Figure 23.1

Class Document

The Document class is the primary interface to the MS-XML parser. With it, you can perform three main functions:

■ **Load XML documents:** Use the load() method to load and parse a XML document. You can load a document via a URL string, a URL object, or an InputStream object.

■ **Extract the root Element:** Use the getRoot() method to extract the root element of the XML document. This is guaranteed to be of type Element.ELEMENT; and

■ **Report Errors:** In the event of a ParseException, use the reportError() method to extract the error message.

For most applications, there are four standard steps for using MS-XML:

1. Create a new XML document object:

```
Document doc = new Document();
```

2. Load an XML document and start parsing:

```
try {
```

```
            doc.load ("http//www.acme.com/parts.xml");
        } catch (ParseException e) {
            doc.reportError (e, System.out);
        }
```

3. Obtain the root of the XML document:

```
        Element root = doc.getRoot();
```

4. Starting at the root node, traverse the XML tree as needed. For information on traversing the tree, see the Element interface.

Note that the Document class implements the ElementFactory interface, thereby enabling you to create new Element objects. Once you have created new elements or modified existing ones, you can save the modified tree back to disk with the save(XMLOutputStream) method.

```
public class Document extends ElementImpl, implements ElementFactory {
// Fields
protected DTD dtd;
protected ElementFactory factory;


// Constructors
public Document();
public Document(ElementFactory f);


// Methods
public void addChild(Element elem, Element after);
public void clear();
public final Element createElement(Element parent, int type, Name
        tag, String text);
public final Element createElement(int type, String tag);
public final Element createElement(int type);
public XMLOutputStream createOutputStream(
        OutputStream out) throws IOException;
public final Enumeration elementDeclarations();
public Element findEntity(Name name);
public final String getCharset();
public final Name getDocType();
```

```
    public DTD getDTD();
    public final String getDTDURL();
    public Element getElementDecl(Name name);
    public final String getEncoding();
    public long getFileModifiedDate();
    public final String getId();
    public int getOutputStyle();
    public Element getParent();
    public final Element getRoot();
    public final String getStandalone();
    public String getText();
    public int getType();
    public final String getURL();
    public final String getVersion();
    public boolean isCaseInsensitive();
    public void load(String urlstr) throws ParseException;
    public void load(URL url) throws ParseException;
    public void load(InputStream in) throws ParseException;
    public boolean loadExternal();
    public void parsed(Element e);
    public void parsedAttribute(Element e, Name name, Object value);
    public void removeChild(Element elem);
    public void reportError(ParseException e, OutputStream out);
    public void save(XMLOutputStream o) throws IOException;
    public void setCaseInsensitive(boolean yes);
    public final void setCharset(String encoding);
    public final void setEncoding(String encoding);
    public void setLoadExternal(boolean yes);
    public void setOutputStyle(int style);
    public final void setStandalone(String value);
    public void setText(String text);
    public void setURL(String urlstr) throws ParseException;
    public final void setVersion(String version);
}
```

Hierarchy: Object → ElementImpl (Element) → Document (ElementFactory)

INTERFACE ELEMENT

The Element interface represents an individual node in the MS-XML tree. When handling an Element object, it is important to first determine the element type. The getType() method returns one of eight values: DOCUMENT, DTD, ELEMENT, PCDATA, PI, WHITESPACE, COMMENT, or CDATA. Depending on the type of element, you can query the object for additional information.

For nodes of type PCDATA or WHITESPACE, you can extract the embedded text via the getText() method. For nodes of type ELEMENT, you can extract the tag name, attribute information, and child nodes. For nodes with children, the get-Text() method will traverse the entire subtree and return a single concatenated string.

The Element class includes four methods for extracting child nodes. The numElements() method returns the number of children. The getChild(int) method retrieves a child at the specified index. Finally, the getChildren() method returns an ElementCollection of all children, whereas the getElements() method returns the same children encapsulated within an Enumeration object.

To retrieve attribute data, use the getAttribute(String name) or getAttribute(Name n) methods. Alternatively, retrieve an enumeration of all attribute values with the getAttributes() method.

MS-XML enables application writers to modify Element objects directly. You can, for example, add children, delete children, reset parent nodes, and reset attribute values. To store changes back to disk, use the save(XMLOutputStream) method.

```
public interface Element {
  // Fields
  static public final int CDATA;
  static public final int COMMENT;
  static public final int DOCUMENT;
  static public final int DTD;
  static public final int ELEMENT;
  static public final int ELEMENTDECL;
  static public final int ENTITY;
  static public final int ENTITYREF;
  static public final int IGNORESECTION;
  static public final int INCLUDESECTION;
  static public final int NAMESPACE;
```

```
        static public final int NOTATION;
        static public final int PCDATA;
        static public final int PI;
        static public final int WHITESPACE;

        // Methods
        public void addChild(Element elem, Element after);
        public void addChild(Element elem, int pos, int reserved);
        public Object getAttribute(String name);
        public Object getAttribute(Name n);
        public Enumeration getAttributes();
        public Element getChild(int index);
        public ElementCollection getChildren();
        public Enumeration getElements();
        public Element getParent();
        public Name getTagName();
        public String getText();
        public int getType();
        public int numAttributes();
        public int numElements();
        public void removeAttribute(String name);
        public void removeAttribute(Name name);
        public void removeChild(Element elem);
        public void save(XMLOutputStream o) throws IOException;
        public void setAttribute(String name, Object value);
        public void setAttribute(Name name, Object value);
        public void setParent(Element parent);
        public void setText(String text);
        public Element toSchema();
    }
```

Implemented by: ElementImpl

CLASS ELEMENTCOLLECTION

The ElementCollection class makes it possible to retrieve all children of the specified node with matching tag names and/or types. The ElementCollection class provides identical functionality to the ElementEnumeration class. The only difference is that the ElementCollection class provides an array based interface, where-as the ElementEnumeration provides an Enumeration interface. For examples in usage, see the ElementEnumeration class.

```
    public class ElementCollection
{
    // Constructors
    public ElementCollection(Element root);
    public ElementCollection(Element root, Name tag, int type);

    // Methods
    public Element getChild(int index);
    public int getLength();
    public Object item(String name);
    public Element item(String name, int index);
    }
```

Hierarchy: Object →ElementCollection
Returned by: Element.getChildren();

CLASS ELEMENTDECLENUMERATION

A simple Enumeration for iterating over Element Declarations.

```
    public class ElementDeclEnumeration implements Enumeration
    {
    // Constructors
    public ElementDeclEnumeration(Enumeration elemDecls);
    public ElementDeclEnumeration(Element e);

    // Methods
    public boolean hasMoreElements();
    public Object nextElement();
    }
```

Hierarchy: Object → ElementDeclEnumeration

CLASS ELEMENTENUMERATION

The ElementEnumeration class enables you to retrieve all children of the specified node with matching tag names and/or types. The ElementEnumeration constructor requires three parameters:

- Element root: the parent Element object.
- Name tag: the name of the tag; this can be null if the name is not important; and
- int type: the element type; this can be -1 if type is not important.

For example, to find all child nodes of root that are of type ELEMENT (thereby filtering out whitespace elements), we would write:

```
ElementEnumeration enum = new ElementEnumeration
    (root, null, Element.ELEMENT);
```

Alternatively, to find all child nodes of root that are of type ELEMENT and have a tag name of "TEAM", we would write:

```
ElementEnumeration enum = new ElementEnumeration
    (root, Name.create("TEAM"), Element.ELEMENT);
```

```
public class ElementEnumeration implements Enumeration {
  // Constructors
  public ElementEnumeration(Element root);
  public ElementEnumeration(Element root, Name tag, int type);

  // Methods
  public boolean hasMoreElements();
  public Object nextElement();
  public void reset();
}
```

Hierarchy: Object → ElementEnumeration (Enumeration)

INTERFACE ELEMENTFACTORY

The ElementFactory interface enables you (and the MS-XML parser) to create new Element objects. For usage, see the ElementFactoryImpl class.

```
public interface ElementFactory {
  // Methods
  Element createElement(Element parent, int type, Name tag,
      String text);
  void parsed(Element elem);
  void parsedAttribute(Element e, Name name, Object value);
}
```

Implemented by: ElementFactoryImpl

CLASS ELEMENTFACTORYIMPL

The ElementFactoryImpl class is the default implementation of the ElementFactory interface. The createElement() method creates a new Element object. The new object will appear as the child of the specified parent node. The type must be set to one of eight possible values: DOCUMENT, DTD, ELEMENT, PCDATA, PI, WHITE-SPACE, COMMENT, or CDATA.

For example, the following code adds the tag: <LASTNAME>Orsenigo </LASTNAME> to the root node:

```
ElementFactoryImpl factory = new ElementFactoryImpl();
Element lastname = factory.createElement (root,
  Element.ELEMENT,Name.create("LASTNAME"), null);
Element pcdata = factory.createElement (lastname,
  Element.PCDATA, null, "Orsenigo");
```

Note that the Document class implements the ElementFactory interface. You can therefore create new Element objects directly, without the need to instantiate a copy of the ElementFactoryImpl class.

```
public class ElementFactoryImpl implements ElementFactory {
  // Constructors
  public ElementFactoryImpl();

  // Methods
  public Element createElement(Element parent, int type, Name tag,
      String text);
  public void parsed(Element elem);
```

```
    public void parsedAttribute(Element e, Name name, Object value);
}
```

Hierarchy: Object ➔ ElementFactoryImpl (ElementFactory)

CLASS ELEMENTIMPL

The ElementImpl class represents a default implementation of the Element interface. The class is primarily used by the MS-XML parser, and is not critical for application developers.

```
    public class ElementImpl implements Element {
    // Fields
    protected Attributes attrlist;

    // Constructors
    public ElementImpl();
    public ElementImpl(Name tag, int type);

    // Methods
    public void addChild(Element elem, Element after);
    public void addChild(Element elem, int pos, int reserved);
    public Object getAttribute(String name);
    public Object getAttribute(Name attrName);
    public Enumeration getAttributes();
    public Element getChild(int index);
    public ElementCollection getChildren();
    public Enumeration getElements();
    public Element getParent();
    public Name getTagName();
    public String getText();
    public int getType();
    public boolean isAttributeQualified(Name attr, DTD dtd);
    public int numAttributes();
    public int numElements();
    public Name qualifyName(String string);
    public void removeAttribute(String name);
    public void removeAttribute(Name attrName);
```

```
    public void removeChild(Element elem);
    public void save(XMLOutputStream o) throws IOException;
    public void saveAttributes(Atom ns, XMLOutputStream o)
        throws IOException;
    public void setAttribute(String name, Object value);
    public void setAttribute(Name attrName, Object value);
    public void setParent(Element parent);
    public void setText(String text);
    public Element toSchema();
    public String toString();
}
```

Hierarchy: Object ➔ ElementImpl (Element)
Extended by: Document

CLASS SIBLINGENUMERATION

The SiblingEnumeration class enables you to iterate over the sibling nodes of the given Element object. Note, however that the class does not extract all siblings nodes. Rather, you can choose to extract siblings nodes to the left or right of the current node. To extract siblings to the right of the current element, set the boolean enumDir flag to true. To extract siblings to the left of the element, set the boolean enumDir flag to false. The default implementation is to extract siblings to the right.

```
    public class SiblingEnumeration implements Enumeration {
        // Constructors
        public SiblingEnumeration(Element node);
        public SiblingEnumeration(Element node, boolean enumDir);

        // Methods
        public boolean hasMoreElements();
        public Object nextElement();
        public void reset();
    }
```

Hierarchy: Object ➔ SiblingEnumeration (Enumeration)

CLASS TREEENUMERATION

The TreeEnumeration class enables you to iterate over the entire subtree of a given Element object. To perform Depth First Search (DFS), set the boolean **enumDir** flag to true. To perform Breadth First Search (BFS), set the enumDir flag to false. The default implementation is DFS.

```
public class TreeEnumeration implements Enumeration {
    // Constructors
    public TreeEnumeration(Element node);
    public TreeEnumeration(Element node, boolean enumDir );

    // Methods
    public boolean hasMoreElements();
    public Object nextElement();
    public void reset();
}
```

Hierarchy: Object → TreeEnumeration (Enumeration)

XML UTILITIES (PACKAGE COM.MS.XML.UTIL)

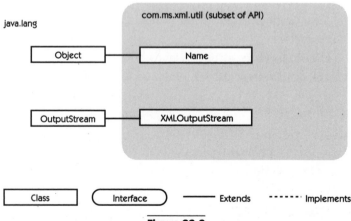

Figure 23.2

NOTE The XML Utilities package includes twelve utility classes and one interface. Of these, only two classes are directly relevant to application developers. For information regarding the remaining classes, see the online API documentation at: **http://www.microsoft.com/xml**.

CLASS NAME

The **Name** utility class is utilized by the MS-XML parser as a means of storing duplicate names within a global hash table, thereby providing more effective memory management.

For most standard applications, you will visually use the **Name** class in conjunction with the **ElemenentEnumeration** class to find specific XML elements. To search for a particular tag name, you cannot search by the String tag. Rather, you need to search by the **Name** object. You can easily create a new **Name** object by using the static create (**String name**) method. For example, to find all children nodes of root that are of type ELEMENT and have a tag name of "TEAM", the code would look like this:

```
ElementEnumeration enum = new ElementEnumeration
    (root, Name.create("TEAM"), Element.ELEMENT);
```

```
public class Name {
  // Constructors
  public String getName();

  // Methods
  public static Name create(String name);
  public static Name create(char val[], int offset, int len);
  public static Name create(String name, String ns);
  public static Name create(String name, Atom nameSpace);
  public boolean equals(Object that);
  public Atom getNameSpace();
  public int hashCode();
  public String toString();
}
```

Hierarchy: Object → Name

Passed to: Document.createElement(), Document.findEntity(),
      Document.getElementDecl(), Document.parsedAttribute(),
      Element.getAttribute(), Element.removeAttribute(),
      Element.setAttribute(), ElementCollection(),
      ElementEnumeration(), ElementFactory.createElement(),
      ElementFactory.parsedAttribute(), ElementImpl.ElementImpl(),
      ElementImpl.isAttributeQualified().
Returned by: Document.getDocType(), Element.getTagName(),
      ElementImpl.qualifyName().

CLASS XMLOUTPUTSTREAM

The XMLOutputStream enables you to save modified XML trees back to disk.
Once you have created a new XMLOutputStream object, use the
Document.save(XMLOutputStream), or Element.save(XMLOutputStream)
methods to store the tree to disk.

    Note that the Document class includes a createOutputStream() method for
easily creating XMLOutputStream objects.

```
public class XMLOutputStream extends OutputStream {
  // Constructors
  public XMLOutputStream (OutputStream out);

  // Methods
  public void close() throws IOException;
  public void flush() throws IOException;
  public void setEncoding(String encoding, boolean littleendian,
     boolean byteOrderMark ) throws IOException;
  public void write(int c) throws IOException;
  public void writeChars(String str) throws IOException;
  public void writeQualifiedName(Name n, Atom ns)
     throws IOException;
  public void writeQuotedString(String str) throws IOException;
}
```

Hierarchy: Object → OutputStream → XMLOutputStream
Passed to: Document.save(), Element.save(), ElementImpl.save(),
      ElementImpl.saveAttributes()
Returned by: Document.createOutputStream()

THE SAX API
QUICK REFERENCE GUIDE

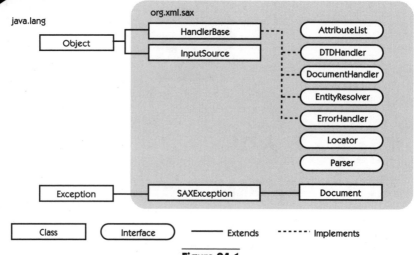

Figure 24.1

SAX (PACKAGE ORG.XML.SAX)

INTERFACE ATTRIBUTELIST

The AttributeList interface encapsulates all attribute information for a single XML Element. The interface is implemented by the parser and is passed as the second parameter to the startElement() method. To access attribute information, the interface supports both array-based and a hash table-based interfaces—it is possible to reference an attribute by index position or by name. For example, you can first retrieve the number of attributes with the getLength() method. You can then retrieve the attribute value by index position with the getValue(int) method. Alternatively, you can retrieve attribute values by name with the getValue(String) method. For example, the following code checks the Element name, and extracts the INDUSTRY and GROUP attribute values:

```
public void startElement  (String name, AttributeList atts) {
    if (name.equals("COMPANY")) {
        String industry = atts.getValue ("INDUSTRY");
        String group = atts.getValue ("GROUP");
    }
    // Processing for other XML Elements...
}
```

The getType() method returns a string indicating the attribute type. Possible values include: "CDATA", "ID", "IDREF", "IDREFS", "NMTOKEN", "NMTOKENS", "ENTITY", "ENTITIES", or "NOTATION" (always in upper case).

```
public interface AttributeList {
        public abstract int getLength ();
        public abstract String getName (int i);
        public abstract String getType (int i);
        public abstract String getValue (int i);
        public abstract String getType (String name);
        public abstract String getValue (String name);
}
```

Passed To: DocumentHandler.startElement()

INTERFACE DTDHANDLER

The DTDHandler Interface provides two call-back methods for capturing notation declarations and external unparsed entities. This is typically useful for including binary data, including multimedia data, within XML documents. To receive DTDHandler events, you must first register your handler using the parser setDTDHandler() method.

The notationDecl() method indicates the presence of a notation declaration. Information includes the notation name, system URI and public name. The unparsedEntityDecl() method indicates the presence of an external unparsed entity. Information includes the entity name, system URI, public name, and associated notation name. Unlike parsed entities, unparsed entities are referenced as attribute values. Application writers will therefore need to store unparsed entities locally (possibly in a hash table) and match them against attribute values.

```
public interface DTDHandler {
public abstract void notationDecl(String name, String publicId,
        String systemId) throws SAXException;
public abstract void unparsedEntityDecl (String name,  String publicId,
        String systemId,  String notationName)  throws SAXException;
}
```

Implemented by: HandlerBase

INTERFACE DOCUMENTHANDLER

SAX applications must implement the DocumentHandler interface in order to capture the most important parsing events, including the start of document, start of elements, and character data. To receive DocumentHandler events, you must first register your handler using the parser setDocumentHandler() method.

The startDocument() method is called first, and is therefore a good place for program initialization. The endDocument() method is always called last, and is therefore a good place for program cleanup. The startElement() method indicates the start of a new XML element, and includes an AttributeList object containing all attribute name/value pairs. For example, the following XML text:

```
<SUBJECT STATUS="HIGH">Meeting Today!</SUBJECT>
```

will generate the following three parsing events:

- startElement(): Tag name = "SUBJECT"; AttributeList object containing Attribute name = "STATUS"; Attribute value = "HIGH"
- chararacters(): String = "Meeting Today!"
- endElement(): Tag name = "SUBJECT"

Note that parsers may break long lines of text into smaller packets and call characters() for each packet. The setDocumentLocator() method passes a Locator object, which can be saved and queried during any subsequent parsing events. This enables you to determine the exact line number and character column of all ensuing parsing events. Note, however that parsers are not required to call the setDocumentLocator() method.

If you do not want to implement the entire interface, you can extend the HandlerBase convenience class instead.

```
public interface DocumentHandler {
        public abstract void setDocumentLocator (Locator locator);
        public abstract void startDocument () throws SAXException;
        public abstract void endDocument () throws SAXException;
        public abstract void startElement (String name, AttributeList atts)
            throws SAXException;
        public abstract void endElement (String name)  throws SAXException;
        public abstract void characters (char ch[], int start, int length)
            throws SAXException;
        public abstract void ignorableWhitespace (char ch[], int start, int length)
```

```
        throws SAXException;
    public abstract void processingInstruction (String target, String data)
        throws SAXException;
}
```

Implemented by: HandlerBase

INTERFACE ENTITYRESOLVER

The EntityResolver interface allows applications to redirect or resolve external entities. To receive the ntityResolver event, you must first register your handler using the parser setEntityResolver() method.

In rare cases, you may want to exercise some control over the resolution of entities, including external DTD files. For example, your program could look up an external DTD in a public or company wide database and return a pointer to an updated or secure DTD. In these cases, you can implement the resolveEntity() method to return an InputSource of your choosing. For example, the following code returns an updated InputSource object for the specified system URI:

```
public InputSource resolveEntity (String publicId, String systemId) {
    FileReader reader = null;
    if (systemId.equals ("Stocks.dtd")) {
        try {
            reader = new FileReader ("Portfolio.dtd");
        } catch (FileNotFoundException e) {
            e.printStackTrace();
        }
        return new InputSource(reader);
    }
    // use the default behavior
    else return null;
}
```

```
public interface EntityResolver {
    public abstract InputSource resolveEntity (String publicId, String systemId)
        throws SAXException, IOException;
}
```

Implemented by: HandlerBase

INTERFACE ERRORHANDLER

The ErrorHandler interface enables developers to intercept warnings, errors and fatal errors discovered by the XML Parser. According to the XML specification, *fatal errors* constitute a breach in well-formedness, whereas *errors* constitute a breach in validity.

To receive notification of any of these errors, you must implement the ErrorHandler interface, and register the handler via the parser setErrorHandler() method.

The HandlerBase convenience class provides a default implementation of the ErrorHandler interface. In the event of a fatal error, the HandlerBase will throw a SAXException, causing the immediate cessation of parsing. Note, however that errors and warning are silently ignored. Therefore, the default implementation of the ErrorHandler will not report errors in validity. To capture errors in validity, you will need to override the error() method.

```
public interface ErrorHandler {
    public abstract void warning (SAXParseException exception)
        throws SAXException;
    public abstract void error (SAXParseException exception)
        throws SAXException;
    public abstract void fatalError (SAXParseException exception)
        throws SAXException;
}
```

Implemented by: HandlerBase

CLASS HANDLERBASE

The HandlerBase convenience class provides a (mostly) empty implementation of four interfaces: EntityResolver, DTDHandler, DocumentHandler, and ErrorHandler. It is usually much easier to extend the HandlerBase class than to implement the entire DocumentHandler interface. For example, the following code extends the HandlerBase to capture the startElement, endElement, and character events:

```
class myHandler extends HandlerBase {
    public void characters
        (char ch[], int start, int length) {
            String text = new String (ch, start, length);
```

```
        System.out.println ("Character data: "+text);
    }

public void startElement
    (String name, AttributeList atts) {
        System.out.println ("Start Element: "+name);
}
public void endElement (String name) {
    System.out.println ("End Element: "+name);
}
}
```

public class **HandlerBase** implements EntityResolver, DTDHandler, DocumentHandler, ErrorHandler {

public InputSource **resolveEntity** (String publicId, String systemId) throws SAXException;

public void **notationDecl** (String name, String publicId, String systemId);

public void **unparsedEntityDecl** (String name, String publicId, String systemId, String notationName);

public void **setDocumentLocator** (Locator locator);

public void **startDocument** () throws SAXException;

public void **endDocument** () throws SAXException;

public void **startElement** (String name, AttributeList attributes) throws SAXException;

public void **endElement** (String name) throws SAXException;

public void **characters** (char ch[], int start, int length) throws SAXException;

public void **ignorableWhitespace** (char ch[], int start, int length) throws SAXException;

public void **processingInstruction** (String target, String data) throws SAXException;

public void **warning** (SAXParseException e) throws SAXException;

public void **error** (SAXParseException e) throws SAXException;

public void **fatalError** (SAXParseException e) throws SAXException;

}

Hierarchy: Object → HandlerBase (EntityResolver, DTDHandler, DocumentHandler, ErrorHandler)

CLASS INPUTSOURCE

The InputSource class encapsulates information regarding a an XML entity.

Application writers can choose from three InputSource constructor methods: read from a byte stream (InputStream object), read from a character stream (Reader object), or read from a URI. Developers can also choose to use the zero-argument InputSource() constructor, and set its properties, using the setByteStream(), setCharacterStream(), or setSystemID() properties. In any of these cases, developers also have the option of setting a public identifier with the setPublicID() method.

InputSource objects are typically used as parameters to Parser.parse(). For example, the following code parses the file specified on the command line:

```
FileReader filereader = new FileReader (args[0]);
InputSource insource = new InputSource (filereader);
parser.parse (insource);
```

setEncoding() enables developers to explicitly set the character encoding of a specific entity. All XML parsers must be able to parse UTF-8 and UTF-16.

```
public class InputSource {
    // Constructors
    public InputSource ();
    public InputSource (String systemId);
    public InputSource (InputStream byteStream);
    public InputSource (Reader characterStream)

    // Public Methods
    public void setPublicId (String publicId);
    public String getPublicId ();
    public void setSystemId (String systemId);
    public String getSystemId ();
    public void setByteStream (InputStream byteStream);
    public InputStream getByteStream ();
    public void setEncoding (String encoding);
    public String getEncoding ();
    public void setCharacterStream (Reader characterStream);
    public Reader getCharacterStream () ;
}
```

Hierarchy: Object ➔ InputSource
Passed To: Parser.parse()
Returned By: EntityResolver.resolveEntity()

INTERFACE LOCATOR

The Locator interface enables developers to associate a specific SAX event with a document location. The Locator object is initially passed to the DocumentHandler via the setDocumentLocator() method. Note, however that parsers are not required to pass a Locator object.

To reference the location of parse events, you must first save a local reference to the Locator object. You can then query this object during subsequent parse events. For example, you can query the object via the getLineNumber() or the getColumnNumber().

The following example code indicates the location of all startElement events:

```
class myHandler extends HandlerBase {
    private Locator locator;

    public void setDocumentLocator (Locator locator) {
        this.locator = locator;
    }

    public void startElement
        (String name, AttributeList atts) {
            System.out.print ("Start Element: "+name);
            System.out.println (" ["+locator.getLineNumber()+", "+
                locator.getColumnNumber()+"]");
    }
}


public interface Locator {
    public abstract String getPublicId ();
    public abstract String getSystemId ();
    public abstract int getLineNumber ();
    public abstract int getColumnNumber ();
}
```

Passed To: Parser.setDocumentLocator()

INTERFACE PARSER

The Parser class enables developers to initiate parsing and to register any number of event handlers.

The parse(InputSource) method initiates parsing of the XML document specified by the InputSource object. Alternatively, you can parse a document specified by its systemID URI.

The Parser class enables you to register four different classes of events: setEntityResolver(), setDTDHandler(), setDocumentHandler(), and setErrorHandler(). The setLocale() method enables you to set a Locale object for errors and warnings. (The java.util.Locale object enables developers to set a recommended geographic locale, and is useful for custom formatting of dates, times and numbers).

```
public interface Parser {
        public abstract void setLocale (Locale locale)  throws SAXException;
        public abstract void setEntityResolver (EntityResolver resolver);
        public abstract void setDTDHandler (DTDHandler handler);
        public abstract void setDocumentHandler (DocumentHandler handler);
        public abstract void setErrorHandler (ErrorHandler handler);
        public abstract void parse (InputSource source)  throws SAXException,
            IOException;
        public abstract void parse (String systemId)  throws SAXException,
            IOException;

}
```

CLASS SAXEXCEPTION

The SAXException encapsulates error information generating by the XML parser. For an overview of SAX error handling, see the ErrorHandler interface.

Application developers can extend the SAXException to provide custom error handling. The SAXException is primarily used to report fatal errors. For example, the following example embeds the call to parse() within a try/catch clause :

```
try {
        parser.parse (xmlURL.toString());
} catch (IOException e) {
        e.printStackTrace();
} catch (SAXException e) {
```

```
        System.out.println ("Error: "+e.getMessage());
    }
```

The getMessage() method returns a detailed message regarding the exception.
The getException() method returns an embedded exception, if any.

```
public class SAXException extends Exception {
    //  Constructors
    public SAXException (String message);
    public SAXException (Exception e);
    public SAXException (String message, Exception e);


    //  Public Methods
    public String getMessage ();
    public Exception getException ();
    public String toString ();
}
```

Hierarchy: Object → Throwable (Serializable) → Exception → SAXException
Thrown by: DTDHandler.notationDecl(), DTDHandler.unparsedEntityDecl(),
DocumentHandler.startDocument(), DocumentHandler.endDocument(),
DocumentHandler.startElement(), DocumentHandler.endElement(),
DocumentHandler.characters(), DocumentHandler.ignorableWhitespace(),
DocumentHandler.processingInstruction(), EntityResolver.resolveEntity(),
ErrorHandler.warning().

CLASS SAXPARSEEXCEPTION

The SAXParseException extends SAXException to provide additional information regarding parsing errors. An instance of SAXParseException is passed to the
warning(), error(), and fatalerror() methods of the ErrorHandler class. Implementing any of these methods, will make it possible to determine the exact location
of any errors via the getLineNumber() and getColumnNumber() methods.

```
public class **SAXParseException** extends SAXException {
    //  Constructors
    public **SAXParseException** (String message, Locator locator) ;
    public **SAXParseException** (String message, Locator locator, Exception e);
    public **SAXParseException** (String message, String publicId,
        String systemId, int lineNumber, int columnNumber)
```

public **SAXParseException** (String message, String publicId, String systemId, int lineNumber, int columnNumber, Exception e)

// Public Methods
public String **getPublicId** ();
public String **getSystemId** ();
public int **getLineNumber** ();
public int **getColumnNumber** ();
}

Hierarchy: Object → Throwable (Serializable) → Exception → SAXException → SAXParseException

Passed to: ErrorHandler.warning(), ErrorHandler.error(), ErrorHandler.fatalerror().

HELPERS (PACKAGE ORG.XML.SAX.HELPERS)

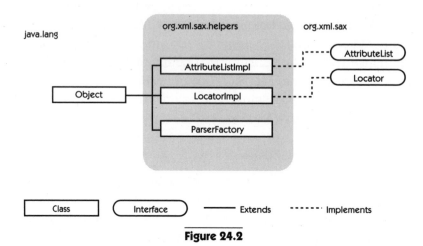

Figure 24.2

CLASS ATTRIBUTELISTIMPL

The AttributeListImpl class provides a convenience implementation of the AttributeList interface. It is primarily useful to parser writers who want to build attribute lists dynamically. It is also useful to application writers who want to store a persistent copy of an element's attributes. For example, the code below copies an element's attributes to a local variable:

```
AttributeList attributes;

public void startElement (String name, AttributeList atts) {
    System.out.println ("Start Element: "+name);
    attributes = new AttributeListImpl (atts);
}


public class AttributeListImpl implements AttributeList {
    // Constructors
    public AttributeListImpl ();
    public AttributeListImpl (AttributeList atts);


    // Public Methods
    public void setAttributeList (AttributeList atts);
    public void addAttribute (String name, String type, String value);
    public void removeAttribute (String name);
    public void clear ();
    public int getLength ();
    public String getName (int i);
    public String getType (int i);
    public String getValue (int i);
    public String getType (String name);
    public String getValue (String name);
}
```

Hierarchy: Object → AttributeListImpl (AttributeList)

CLASS LOCATORIMPL

The LocatorImpl class provides a convenience implementation of the Locator interface.

The class is primarily useful to application writers who want to store a persistent copy of a Locator object. For example, the code below stores the location of the CITY element tag:

```
class myHandler extends HandlerBase {
    Locator locator;
    Locator CityLocator;

public void setDocumentLocator (Locator locator) {
    this.locator = locator;
}

public void startElement (String name, AttributeList atts) {
    if (name.equals ("CITY"))
        CityLocator = new LocatorImpl (locator);
    }
}


public class LocatorImpl implements Locator {
    // Constructors
    public LocatorImpl ();
    public LocatorImpl (Locator locator);

    // Public Methods
    public String getPublicId ();
    public String getSystemId ();
    public int getLineNumber ();
    public int getColumnNumber ();
    public void setPublicId (String publicId);
    public void setSystemId (String systemId);
    public void setLineNumber (int lineNumber);
    public void setColumnNumber (int columnNumber);
}
```

Hierarchy: Object ➔ LocatorImpl (Locator)

CLASS PARSERFACTORY

The ParserFactory class enables developers to dynamically load SAX drivers at run-time. When loading a SAX diver, you have two options:

■ You can load the driver at compile time. For example, the following code loads the IBM XML for Java Parser:

```
Parser parser = new com.ibm.xml.parser.SAXDriver();
```

■ Or, you can load the parser at run time using the **ParserFactory** class. For example, the following code also loads the IBM XML for Java Parser:

```
String parserClass = "com.ibm.xml.parser.SAXDriver";
parser = ParserFactory.makeParser (parserClass);
```

Note that the **makeParser**() method may throw one of four exceptions:

■ **ClassNotFoundException**: The SAX Parser class could not be found. Recheck your CLASSPATH variable.

■ **IllegalAccessException**: The SAX Parser class was found, but you do not have the permissions to load it.

■ **InstantiationException**: The SAX Parser class was found, but could not be instantiated.

■ **ClassCastException**: The SAX Parser class was found and instantiated, but it does not implement the org.xml.sax.Parser interface. You probably have an outdated SAX driver.

```
public class ParserFactory {
      public static Parser makeParser () throws
            ClassNotFoundException, IllegalAccessException,
            InstantiationException, NullPointerException,
            ClassCastException;
      public static Parser makeParser (String className) throws
            ClassNotFoundException, IllegalAccessException,
            InstantiationException, ClassCastException;
            }
```

Hierarchy: Object → ParserFactory

INDEX

ABOUT THE AUTHORS

SIMON ST. LAURENT is an Internet and Web programming consultant. His previous books include *Cookies*, a definitive reference on one of the most controversial Web programming tools around, and *XML: A Primer*.

ETHAN CERAMI is a Senior Software Engineer at methodfive, Inc., and an Adjunct Faculty member at New York University, where he teaches undergraduate courses in computer programming. He is the author of the book *Delivering Push*.

SOFTWARE AND INFORMATION LICENSE

The software and information on this diskette (collectively referred to as the "Product") are the property of The McGraw-Hill Companies, Inc. ("McGraw-Hill") and are protected by both United States copyright law and international copyright treaty provision. You must treat this Product just like a book, except that you may copy it into a computer to be used and you may make archival copies of the Products for the sole purpose of backing up our software and protecting your investment from loss.

By saying "just like a book," McGraw-Hill means, for example, that the Product may be used by any number of people and may be freely moved from one computer location to another, so long as there is no possibility of the Product (or any part of the Product) being used at one location or on one computer while it is being used at another. Just as a book cannot be read by two different people in two different places at the same time, neither can the Product be used by two different people in two different places at the same time (unless, of course, McGraw-Hill's rights are being violated).

McGraw-Hill reserves the right to alter or modify the contents of the Product at any time.

This agreement is effective until terminated. The Agreement will terminate automatically without notice if you fail to comply with any provisions of this Agreement. In the event of termination by reason of your breach, you will destroy or erase all copies of the Product installed on any computer system or made for backup purposes and shall expunge the Product from your data storage facilities.

LIMITED WARRANTY

McGraw-Hill warrants the physical diskette(s) enclosed herein to be free of defects in materials and workmanship for a period of sixty days from the purchase date. If McGraw-Hill receives written notification within the warranty period of defects in material or workmanship, and such notification is determined by McGraw-Hill to be correct, McGraw-Hill will replace the defective diskette(s). Send request to:

Customer Service
McGraw-Hill
Gahanna Industrial Park
860 Taylor Station Road
Blacklick, OH 43004-9615

The entire and exclusive liability and remedy for breach of this Limited Warranty shall be limited to replacement of defective diskette(s) and shall not include or extend to any claim for or right to cover any other damages, including but not limited to, loss of profit, data, or use of the software, or special, incidental, or consequential damages or other similar claims, even if McGraw-Hill has been specifically advised as to the possibility of such damages. In no event will McGraw-Hill's liability for any damages to you or any other person ever exceed the lower of suggested list price or actual price paid for the license to use the Product, regardless of any form of the claim.

THE McGRAW-HILL COMPANIES, INC. SPECIFICALLY DISCLAIMS ALL OTHER WARRANTIES, EXPRESS OR IMPLIED, INCLUDING BUT NOT LIMITED TO, ANY IMPLIED WARRANT OF MERCHANTABILITY OR FITNESS FOR A PARTICULAR PURPOSE. Specifically, McGraw-Hill makes no representation or warranty that the Product is fit for any particular purpose and any implied warranty of merchantability is limited to the sixty day duration of the Limited Warranty covering the physical diskette(s) only (and not the software or information) and is otherwise expressly and specifically disclaimed.

This Limited Warranty gives you specific legal rights, you may have others which may vary from state to state. Some states do not allow the exclusion of incidental or consequential damages, or the limitation on how long an implied warranty lasts, so some of the above may not apply to you.

This Agreement constitutes the entire agreement between the parties relating to use of the Product. The terms of any purchase order shall have no effect on the terms of this Agreement. Failure of McGraw-Hill to insist at any time on strict compliance with this Agreement shall not constitute a waiver of any rights under this Agreement. This Agreement shall be construed and governed in accordance with the laws of New York. If any provision of this Agreement is held to be contrary to law, that provision will be enforced to the maximum extent permissible and the remaining provisions will remain in force and effect.